SAVING
STALIN

SAVING STALIN

Roosevelt, Churchill, Stalin, and the Cost of Allied Victory in Europe

———

JOHN KELLY

hachette BOOKS

New York

Hachette Books
Hachette Book Group
1290 Avenue of the Americas
New York, NY 10104
HachetteBooks.com
Twitter.com/HachetteBooks
Instagram.com/HachetteBooks

First Edition: October 2020

Published by Hachette Books, an imprint of Perseus Books, LLC, a subsidiary of Hachette Book Group, Inc. The Hachette Books name and logo is a trademark of the Hachette Book Group.

The Hachette Speakers Bureau provides a wide range of authors for speaking events. To find out more, go to www.hachettespeakersbureau.com or call (866) 376-6591.

The publisher is not responsible for websites (or their content) that are not owned by the publisher.

Print book interior design by Jeff Williams.

Library of Congress Cataloging-in-Publication Data
Names: Kelly, John, 1945- author.
Title: Saving Stalin : Roosevelt, Churchill, Stalin, and the cost of Allied
    victory in Europe / John Kelly.
Other titles: Roosevelt, Churchill, Stalin, and the cost of Allied victory
    in Europe
Description: First edition. | New York : Hachette Books, 2020. | Includes
    bibliographical references and index.
Identifiers: LCCN 2020025140 | ISBN 9780306902772 (hardcover) | ISBN
    9780306902765 (ebook)
Subjects: LCSH: Lend-lease operations (1941-1945) | United States--Military
    relations--Great Britain. | United States--Military relations--Soviet
    Union. | Great Britain--Military relations--United States. | Great
    Britain--Military relations--Soviet Union. | Soviet Union--Military
    relations--United States. | Soviet Union--Military relations--Great
    Britain. | World War, 1939-1945--Equipment and supplies. | World War,
    1939-1945--Diplomatic history. | International
    cooperation--History--20th century. | Stalin, Joseph, 1878-1953. |
    Roosevelt, Franklin D. (Franklin Delano), 1882-1945. | Churchill,
    Winston, 1874-1965. | Hopkins, Harry L. (Harry Lloyd), 1890-1946.
Classification: LCC D753.2.R9 K45 2020 | DDC 940.53/22--dc23
LC record available at https://lccn.loc.gov/2020025140

ISBNs: 978-0-306-90277-2 (hardcover); 978-0-306-90276-5 (ebook)

Printed in the United States of America

LSC-C

10 9 8 7 6 5 4 3 2 1

CONTENTS

Contents

1

THE DAY BEFORE
THE DAY OF DEAD

IN HIGH SUMMER WESTERN RUSSIA IS A RIOT OF BRILLIANT COLORS: white lights, green willows, mauve lilacs, purple Judas trees. But two or three times a century, the pageant is disrupted by the sound of marching feet approaching from the west. The first contingent of Napoleon's Great Army arrived in Russia on June 24, 1812; the kaiser's Imperial German Army on August 22, 1914—and the armies of Adolf Hitler on June 22, 1941.

To soothe his eve-of-battle nerves, at around 5:00 P.M. on the twenty-first, Hitler summoned his driver and ordered him to drive him out to Potsdam. A few minutes later the Führer's Mercedes-Benz slipped past the two black nude statues guarding the Court of Honor at the entrance to the Reich Chancellery and disappeared into the stream of late-afternoon traffic. Except for a handful of pockmarked streets—a by-product of the Royal Air Force raids—Berlin had survived the first twenty-two months of the war largely unscathed. Most of its buildings remained intact; its stores were full of delicacies from France, Norway, and other parts of the Reich's new empire, and on this warm summer evening the streets and outdoor cafés were crowded with twenty-four- and twenty-five-year-old veterans, each eager to share their adventures in Poland and

France with a pretty young barmaid. Some Berliners found the cruelly, casually lumped-together poster art on the city's streets—an ugly cartoon of a hook-nosed Jew on one street; a photo of a scantily clad young woman advertising sunglasses on the other—distasteful and embarrassing. But a decade of prosperity, two victorious wars, and the return of the German provinces seized at Versailles had washed away the memory of Germany's two million Great War dead and made the average German more tolerant of the Führer's embarrassing idiosyncrasies.

When the Mercedes reached Potsdam, Hitler ordered the driver to turn around and take him back to the chancellery. Tomorrow he would implement a plan he had been preparing for a year and imagining for decades. Three million men and four thousand tanks would cross into Russian-occupied Poland under an umbrella of a thousand fighters and bombers. "We shall populate the Russian desert!" Hitler had vowed to his generals a few days earlier. "We shall take away its character as an Asiatic steppe and Europeanize it. . . . There can be no remorse about this, gentlemen. We are absolutely without obligation as far as these people [the Russians] are concerned. . . . We'll let them know just enough to understand our highway signs so they won't get themselves run over when they cross the road but little else. For them, the word 'Liberty' [will] mean the right to wash on feast days. . . . There is only one duty— to Germanize this country. The natives [will be] looked upon as redskins. In this business, I shall go straight ahead cold-bloodedly. . . . Terror is a salutary thing."

On his return to the chancellery, Hitler busied himself with paperwork for a few hours, then turned to what had become an eve-of-battle ritual: selecting a piece of music to accompany the declaration of war. After consulting Albert Speer, his architect, he chose Franz Liszt's *Les Préludes*. Its somber melodies expressed the gravity of the hour, and the piece was familiar to thousands of German music lovers. The introduction to *Préludes* also had something to say about the adventure that Germany was about to embark upon: "What is our life but a series of preludes to that unknown hymn . . . Death?"

IN THE EARLY HOURS OF June 22, 1941, Ilya Zbarsky awoke to the sound of a ringing telephone. The caller, a coworker at the Lenin Museum, was so agitated he forgot to say hello; he just said, "German forces attacking; hundreds of Soviet aircraft destroyed on ground." Zbarsky was not completely surprised. For the past several months, there had been rumors of a German "invasion," but he thought Germany's dependence on Russian raw material made a war unlikely. He turned on a Moscow radio station expecting to hear patriotic music and reports of the German proletariat rising up to support their Russian brothers the way they did in *If War Comes Tomorrow*, one of the most popular Russian movies of 1938. Instead, there was just the usual dreary Sunday morning fare: an exercise class for early risers and a discussion of Soviet steel production. Earlier in the evening Alfred Liskow, a German deserter and dedicated communist, crossed into the Russian lines to warn that an attack was imminent. The German heavy guns were already in place, he told his Russian interrogators, and the tanks and the infantry units were en route to their starting positions. A few hours later, Wilhelm Korpik, another German communist, entered Soviet lines with a similar story. However, the Kremlin viewed the German incursions as provocations intended to squeeze concessions out of Moscow—not acts of war. After their interrogations, Liskow and Korpik were both executed.

In Sevastopol, a time zone away from the border, couples strolled the broad boulevards; rowdy young sailors from the Black Sea fleet crowded into cabarets and dance halls; fights broke out; patriotic songs were sung; drinking contests were held; couples disappeared into alleys to copulate. It was a typical summer evening—until a raft of planes suddenly appeared out of the night. "Are those ours?" someone asked. "It must be another exercise," someone else said. Then machine-gun fire raked the streets and the question answered itself. In Minsk, General D. G. Pavlov, commander of the western military district, was attending a performance of *Wedding in Malinovka*, one of his favorite plays, when his intelligence chief, Colonel Blokhin, slipped into his theater box to tell him there were reports that a large German force was massing near the border and there were reports of shots being fired. As commander of the western military district, Pavlov was responsible for border security, but relations with Germany were already fragile. *Why provoke them more?* "The rumors can't be true," he told his deputy commander I. V. Boldin—and turned back to the play.

The next morning public speakers across the Reich would transmit the opening bars of *Les Préludes*, which would announce the attack, now code-named Operation Barbarossa. "You will hear it often in the future," Hitler told Speer. Then Hitler made a prediction: "Before three months have passed, we shall witness a collapse in Russia the likes of which has never been seen in history." Another of Hitler's guests that evening, Joseph Goebbels, the minister of propaganda, marveled at Hitler's composure. The Führer "seems to lose his fear" as the decisive moment approaches. "All the exhaustion seems to drop away."

It is impossible to know what the German people were thinking about the war that evening, but if Berlin was any measure of the national mood, young Berlin was doing what young Sevastopol and young Minsk had been doing until a few hours earlier: people were walking hand in hand through the twilight streets. Here and there, in the cafés and drinking establishments, worried voices expressed concern about Germany becoming engulfed in a continental war. But conventional wisdom held that such was the power of the new Germany, Stalin would gift the Ukraine to the Reich rather than face another war.

At the Russian embassy Valentin Berezhkov, the first secretary, was attempting to reach Joachim von Ribbentrop, the German foreign secretary. A few days earlier the embassy had obtained a copy of a new German army handbook. Berezhkov wanted to know why the book contained phrases like "Surrender!" "Hands up!" "Are you a communist?" and "I'll shoot." Berezhkov called Ribbentrop several times on the twenty-first to arrange a meeting, but the twenty-first was a Saturday, and every time he called he was told the foreign secretary was unavailable. Technically, this was true. Ribbentrop spent the day preparing the declaration of war. The man who would present the document to the Soviets—the German ambassador, Count Friedrich-Werner Graf von Schulenburg—spent most of the afternoon burning secret papers. At around 7:00 P.M. he was summoned to the Kremlin by Vyacheslav Mikhailovich Molotov, the Soviet foreign minister. The sixty-five-year-old Schulenburg was not who he seemed. A member of the old Imperial German aristocracy, he abhorred the jumped-up rabble-rousers, the chicken farmers, and the champagne salesmen he served. In early June, at great personal risk, he had told a Russian colleague that a German attack was imminent. When the colleague dismissed the warning, Schulenburg concluded that it was foolish to risk his own safety for such a suspicious and ungrateful people. "When?" Molotov asked. "Why does Germany seem dissatisfied with her Russian ally?" During a talk on the afternoon of the twenty-first Schulenburg said he had no information on that subject. A few floors above Molotov's office General Marshal S. K. Timoshenko, the people's commissioner of defense, and Marshal Georgy Zhukov were meeting with Stalin. In another army Timoshenko would be considered a competent commander of no special merit; but in a nation that had imprisoned a good part of its officer corps a few years earlier, an officer of mediocre talents could rise swiftly if he was seen as trustworthy. Zhukov—younger, bolder, and more gifted militarily—was one of the Red Army's rising stars. Stalin, who looked "plainly worried," had called the meeting to discuss how to respond to the German provocations. His inclination was to ignore them for the time being and wait on events. Timoshenko and Zhukov disagreed, and they urged Stalin to increase the readiness level. The three men were still arguing when the members of the Politburo filed into Stalin's office. After everyone was seated, Stalin scanned the room and again asked, "What are we to do?" No one answered. Finally, Timoshenko spoke, saying, "All troops in frontier districts should be placed on full battle alert." Zhukov said that was insufficient—the entire army should be put on high alert. "Too provocative," Stalin replied. "Perhaps we can still solve the problem by peaceful means."

It was too late for that. It was now after midnight, and German special forces units, some dressed in Russian uniforms, were infiltrating the Russian rear, blowing up power lines and disrupting signals traffic. The 800th Special Purpose Construction Regiment, an elite German special forces unit, had been in place for almost a day. On the night of the twenty-first the regiment slipped across the Russian frontier, hidden under loads of gravel in train trucks. When the Berlin–Moscow Express crossed into German-occupied Poland without incident that night, the German high command was exultant. The Red Army was still confused and uncertain. Timoshenko picked up the phone and began calling his commanders. To each he asked the same question: "How is it where you are?" It was now a little after 1:00 A.M. *Wedding in Malinovka* had been over for two hours, and General Pavlov was examining a situation map in his headquarters and trying to ignore the rumble of the motorcycles passing outside the window. As yet, there had been no reports of large-scale German activity, but if his sector was attacked Pavlov doubted he could hold it. His troops were scattered across the countryside on training exercises, and his stocks of fuel and ammunition were low. "Try to worry less," Timoshenko told him.

An hour later Timoshenko called again. This time he spoke to Pavlov's deputy, General Ivan Boldin. "Will you please tell Pavlov that Comrade Stalin has forbidden the army to open artillery fire against the Germans?" he asked. Boldin was shocked. "Our troops are in full retreat. . . . People are getting killed all over the place."

"There is to be no air recognizance thirty-five miles beyond the frontier," Timoshenko said—and hung up.

The clearest picture we have of Stalin's thinking on the night of the twenty-first is General Order Number 1, the document he approved before leaving for his dacha in suburban Moscow. The order warned that "a surprise attack is possible during June 22–23," and it listed appropriate and inappropriate responses to an attack. Appropriate responses included ordering troops to take up firing position—and camouflaging and dispersing aircraft. Inappropriate responses included firing on German troops before they entered Soviet territory. The cautionary tone of the order may have reflected a fear that haunted many senior Soviet officials that night: Would the Russian peasants fight for a regime that had inflicted so much hardship and suffering on their people? General Nikolay Vonorov, a Soviet artilleryman, breathed a deep sigh of relief when he learned that "Soviet troops were fighting—not everywhere, but in enough places to ease concerns about mass surrenders."

At around 3:00 A.M. a German border unit invited its Russian counterpart to a meeting on the German side of the frontier. When the Russians arrived they were machine-gunned. A few minutes later a cannonade of seven thousand artillery guns lit up the night sky from horizon to horizon. And all along a thousand-mile front, men in coal scuttle helmets emerged from tree lines and trenches and marched eastward into the rising day behind a screen of tanks, the young commanders standing erect in the turrets like masters of the universe. When General Ivan Fedyuninsky's tanks reached the Soviet-German frontier at around 4:00 A.M. that morning the air smelled of cordite and the fighting had become desperate. "Even the wives of the [Russian] frontier guards were in the firing line," Fedyuninsky recalled later. Some of the women were carrying water and ammunition and nursing the wounded; others were firing at the advancing Germans. The ranks of the frontier guards quickly melted away. Homes and barracks were set on fire. The Germans also took heavy casualties, but replacements immediately emerged from tree lines and trenches. "What are we to do?" radioed one stranded Soviet unit. On the morning of June 22, the only man who could answer that question was asleep in his dacha in suburban Moscow.

"Who's calling?" the duty officer at the dacha asked.

Zhukov identified himself and asked to speak to Comrade Stalin. "It is urgent."

"Comrade Stalin is sleeping," the duty officer said.

"Wake him up immediately!" Zhukov ordered. A few minutes later a groggy voice came on the line. "Comrade Stalin," Zhukov said, "the Germans are bombing our cities!" There was no reply—just heavy breathing. "Did you understand me?" Zhukov asked.

The voice said, "Bring Timoshenko to the Kremlin and tell Poskrebyshev [Stalin's chief aide] to summon the Politburo." Stalin was sitting at a table, toying with a pipe, when the members of the Politburo arrived at around 4:30 A.M. Over the past few hours the news had grown progressively worse. Commands that had boasted ten or fifteen thousand men yesterday had few numbers now. In heavily bombed cities, women were tying birth certificates and home addresses around the necks of their children so that their bodies could be identified if they were killed. The Soviet frontier air force lost twelve hundred aircraft in twelve hours. Cut wires left officers unable to reach their commands. In some places whole divisions and regiments were vanishing into the cauldron. Almost everywhere across the front Russian troops were in retreat, and Stalin was still refusing to believe that Russia was under attack. A war has a distinct footprint, he told Timoshenko and Zhukov during the Politburo meeting. It is preceded by negotiations and foreign ministers' meetings, and it includes a formal declaration of hostilities. The current attack displayed none of those characteristics. "Hitler simply does not know about [the attack]. It is the work of a cabal of German generals."

It fell to Count Schulenburg, who arrived in Molotov's office a little before 6:00 A.M. on the morning of the twenty-second, to make Stalin face reality. There are two versions of that meeting. In one, provided by an eyewitness, the count bursts into "angry tears" and denounces Hitler for invading Russia, calling the invasion "madness." In the second version Molotov loses his temper and accuses Germany of fomenting "a breach of faith unprecedented in human history." However, in both versions, the end is the same: Schulenburg presents Molotov with a declaration of war. And Stalin, finally forced to accept the truth, slumps in his chair and falls into heavy thought.

A young aide named Yakov Chadaev was struck by how drawn and haggard Stalin's pockmarked face looked in early-morning light. Then, abruptly, Stalin rallied. "The enemy will be beaten all along the line!"

"No!" said Timoshenko. "Annihilated!"

Stalin slumped back in his chair. The rush of confidence vanished as quickly as it had appeared. The Russian people would not hear from their leader today. Over the objection of his colleagues, Stalin had decided that Molotov, not he, would tell the country that Russia was at war.

Outside the Kremlin the Sunday morning streets were beginning to fill up. A few people were already aware of the fighting along the border, but most Muscovites would not learn of the German invasion until noon, when the city's public speaker system came to life and a flat, toneless voice announced, "Today at four o'clock in the morning, without addressing any grievances to the Soviet Union, without a declaration of war, German forces fell on our country, attacked our frontiers in many places and bombed our cities . . . [fomenting] an act of treachery unprecedented in the history of civilized nations." When Molotov finished, the crowds gathered around the loudspeakers and cheered. But they were resigned cheers, if cheers can be called thus: the cheers of a people made elderly in soul by years of wars and purges going stolidly into battle to kill or be killed.

2

STALIN REGAINS
HIS NERVE

IN 1938, WHEN HITLER INVADED AUSTRIA, WAR WAS ALREADY PEERING over the horizon; and in 1939, when he seized the parts of Czechoslovakia he had left on the table at Munich, it was beginning to seem unavoidable. Stalin tried to buy time to strengthen Russia's defense, but half of the Russian officer corps had been killed or imprisoned during the purges of the early 1930s, and, with some notable exceptions, the men who replaced them were cut from the same cloth as General Pavlov. During the Soviet-German invasion of Poland in September 1939, the Germans found their Soviet ally wanting on almost every important military metric, including speed, quality of equipment, quality of leadership, and training. While the German army leaped across the Polish steppe, sometimes at the rate of fifteen to twenty miles per day, Russian soldiers sat in fields and roads, drinking vodka while they waited for the supply units to bring up fuel and tank parts. In Finland, which the Russians invaded two and a half months later, the Red Army cemented its reputation for incompetence. For the first two months of the campaign, half-trained eighteen- and nineteen-year-old Soviet soldiers charged blindly into Finnish machine guns and were killed and wounded by the thousands. "It was the most horrible sight I have ever seen," James Aldridge, an Australian war correspondent, wrote after visiting a battlefield near the Finnish village of Suomussalmi. "There were two or three thousand Russians and Finns frozen in a fighting attitude: their faces recording something between bewilderment and horror." Eventually, the Red Army overwhelmed the Finns by sheer force of numbers, but it took five months, three-quarters of a million men, and hundreds of tanks and aircraft to defeat a two-hundred-thousand-man Finnish force, armed with skis, rifles, a few dozen planes, tanks, and a few hundred machine guns. Hitler took notice.

The Soviet winter war games of 1940 confirmed that Finland and Poland were not flukes. In the two scenarios tested in the war games—a German attack into central Russia and a breakthrough into southern Russia—the attacking force overwhelmed the Soviet defenders. During the post-games assessment, Marshal G. I. Kulik took to the floor to argue that the way to remedy the army's deficiencies was to abandon the tank and return to horse-drawn transport. When a young tank officer ridiculed the idea, Kulik threatened to "shoot the officers' tanks to pieces with artillery fire." Between 1939 and 1941 the Soviet Union did begin to mobilize. Stalin expanded the Red Army two and a half fold; increased war production; built new fortifications; seized Lithuania, Estonia, and Latvia to provide Russia with a buffer against attack; and signed a nonaggression pact with Hitler. In return for Russian raw materials, the Soviet Union would receive access to German manufactured goods. The agreement also provided Stalin with more time to prepare the Soviet Union for war. "Hitler . . . thinks he's outsmarted me," Stalin boasted shortly after signing the nonaggression pact, "but it is I who outsmarted him. War will pass us by a little longer."

And it might have, had Stalin used the extra time the pact bought to strengthen Russia's defenses, but he did not. In the six months prior to Operation Barbarossa, the training of a Soviet tank gunner consisted of an hour of practice. Seventy-four percent of the Russian tank force needed repairs, and Soviet pilots were training on obsolete aircraft. In the spring of 1941, when German reconnaissance aircraft began making regular appearances in Soviet airspace, Russian flyers were ordered not to engage them. Stalin also ignored the warnings of British and American officials. Given that men like Winston Churchill and Herbert Hoover had spent the 1920s and 1930s demonizing the Soviet Union, Stalin's reluctance to believe information provided by Western sources was understandable. More puzzling was his refusal to credit the intelligence provided by his master spy, Richard Sorge. Sorge was the real-life version of the character Humphrey Bogart played in *Casablanca*: a cynical, hard-drinking rogue with an eye for beautiful women and an idealistic streak. Yet the nearer war came, the more phobic Stalin's reaction to bad news became. When Sorge warned him a German force of 150 divisions would descend on the Soviet Union within a month, Stalin disparaged him—according to firsthand sources, calling him a "little shit."

By the spring of 1941, Stalin's reluctance to hear the truth was so pronounced that General Filipp Golikov, director of Russian army intelligence, reconfigured the intelligence service's risk analysis protocol. Henceforth, Golikov instructed his agents, all documents claiming war to be imminent would have to be regarded as forgeries, while reports rating a German attack unlikely were to be labeled reliable. In May, Stalin finally seemed ready to look reality in the eye. In an address to a class of newly commissioned officers early that month, he said it was no longer a question of *if* war would come but *when*—and his decision to promote himself from general secretary of the Communist Party to head of state a day later suggested that he expected war to come soon. Most members of the diplomatic community in Moscow agreed—though not Count Schulenburg, who had schooled himself on Stalin's idiosyncrasies. In a cable to Berlin, he said Stalin was behaving like a leader desperate to keep his nation out of the war. The theory seemed counterintuitive. But Schulenburg seems to have been right.

Stalin is believed to have been behind the much-talked-about Tass news service article at the time, published on June 14, eight days before the invasion. Tass labeled "absurd" the current rumors of Soviet-German discord and declared that both nations were "fulfilling to the letter" the terms of the Soviet-German nonaggression pact. Tass also dismissed "as completely without foundation" rumors of a German attack and of troop movements adjacent to the Russian border. "The movements," Tass asserted, "must be explained by other motives," though the news service failed to explain what they might be. Four days later, on June 18, what may have been the first German deserter crossed into Soviet lines; the German had struck his officer in a drunken rage and surrendered himself to the Russians to avoid a court-martial and a hanging. Probably to ingratiate himself with his Soviet interrogators, the deserter said the main German assault would begin at 4:00 A.M. on the morning of June 22. He was right almost to the minute.

"We were expecting a war but not this war."
—DAVID SAMOYLOV, *poet and war veteran*

AT 7:00 P.M. GERMAN TIME on the morning of June 22, Joseph Goebbels, the German propaganda minister, stepped in front of a microphone and read Hitler's declaration of war to a waking nation. It began: "Weighed down by heavy cares, condemned to months of silence, I can at last speak freely. German people: At this moment a march is taking place that, for its extent, compares with the greatest the world has ever seen. I have decided again today to place the fate and future of the Reich and our people in the hands of our soldiers. May God aid us especially in this fight."

By the time Goebbels finished, three German armies were already on the march. The twenty-nine divisions of Army Group North, under Field Marshal Wilhelm Ritter von Leeb, were driving northward toward Leningrad and the Baltic states. The forty-one divisions of Army Group South, under Field Marshal Gerd von Rundstedt, were heading to the Ukraine, and the fifty-two divisions of Army Group Center, under Field Marshal Fedor von Bock, were going due east to the prize of prizes: Moscow. On paper, the Red Army matched up to the Germans: 304 divisions, including 61 tank and 31 mechanized divisions, were spread across a thousand-mile front that ran from Leningrad in the north to Odessa in the south. However, with the exceptions of the T-34 (the best tank in its class in 1941), the Katyusha rocket, and a few other weapons, the Red Army's equipment was outdated and its organization and training were substandard. There were a number of talented young officers in the army, but it would require a crisis to bring them to the fore.

That crisis arrived on the morning of the twenty-second. The day began with rumors that a German unit had lured a group of Soviet frontier guards to the German side of the Russo-German border earlier that morning—and had executed them. The rumor was true. By midmorning, the fighting along the frontier had become so ferocious that the wives of the Russian guards were serving as nurses, weapons carriers, and, in a few cases, as fighting soldiers. Stalin put in several calls to Berlin that morning but was unable to get anyone on the line. Frustrated, he gave up and called the Japanese embassy.

Operation Barbarossa was in its tenth hour when a Red Army staff car carrying General Ivan Boldin arrived in the Polish town of Bialystok. Boldin had not had an easy trip. Half the world seemed to be in flight that afternoon, and they all seemed headed in the same direction: east. Just outside of Bialystok, Boldin was cut off by a chauffeured ZIS-101s—the Soviet equivalent of a Rolls-Royce. In the back seat two well-dressed women were chatting, oblivious to the peasant families marching along the roads with a two-day supply of food and no idea where they were going, except that it was away from the sound of the guns. Boldin looked at the women again. He knew their type. They were the wives of Soviet officials, and judging from the cars in which they sat, their husbands were senior officials. Still, had it not been for the aspidistra tree dangling from the back window of their car, Boldin would have suppressed his irritation and gone on his way; but the plant bothered him. It seemed indecently opulent amid the sea of suffering. Just outside Bialystok he lost his temper and shouted at the women, "Surely, at a time like this you might have more important things to transport than your aspidistra!"

The question was never answered. A burst of machine-gun fire killed the women, their two children, and the driver, who was found slumped over the steering wheel in the front seat of the car. Only the aspidistra tree survived the attack unmolested. Boldin spent the rest of the afternoon organizing work parties to bury the dead; then he went in search of the 10th Army, the unit charged with defending Bialystok. He found the commander, General Konstantin Golubev, huddled in a birch tree a few miles from the town. "The men are fighting like heroes," Golubev said. "But the Luftwaffe has destroyed our fuel dumps, aircraft, and anti-aircraft guns."

In the midst of the conversation, General Pavlov came on the line from Minsk and ordered the 10th Army to mount a counterattack. Boldin protested the order. The fighting had reduced the 10th to a ghost army. Pavlov hesitated for a moment, then repeated the order: "Attack!" Shortly thereafter, the Luftwaffe appeared—and Bialystok disappeared into a ball of fire.

Acting on outdated intelligence, at 9:15 that evening Marshal Timoshenko issued Order Number 3: the next morning Soviet forces would throw themselves on the German invaders and drive them back across the frontier. Forty-eight hours later the Red Army was in a shambles. German panzers were pouring through an eighty-mile gap in the Russian line, and General Pavlov was losing control of his command—and of his nerve. Broad-cheeked, heavy-bodied, and hard-eyed, Pavlov had the physical aspect of a fighting soldier, but his talents were more political than military. He moved up the chain of command by knowing whom to cultivate. Many of the Soviet officers who served as advisers during the Spanish Civil War were sent to the gulag upon their return home. Pavlov came home a hero of the Soviet Union. Two years later, when a Finnish army of 32 tanks and 114 aircraft held a Soviet force of 2,514 tanks and 3,880 aircraft at bay for three and a half months, Pavlov, who won a few minor victories at the end of the campaign, was awarded one of the most coveted posts in the Red Army: commander of the western front. It was not a good choice, for despite his medals, Pavlov rattled easily. A few weeks before the German invasion, a colleague had heard him screaming hysterically at an officer who had reported a German border breach: "Those at the top know better!"

Once the fighting began, more disturbing deficiencies began to emerge. Pavlov would promise supplies to a unit, then he would fail to deliver them. Or he would disappear for hours without explanation. Then came Minsk. During the battle for the city, Pavlov summoned his staff and announced that he was moving the western front's command center to Babruysk, a small town 90 miles to the east of Minsk. Twenty-four hours later he a changed his mind and announced he would move his command to Mogilev, 123 miles from Minsk. From there, Pavlov planned to direct the defense of the city by way of small spotter planes and parachutists who would deliver his instructions to the officers defending the city.

As the battle progressed, Pavlov's disappearances became more frequent and lasted longer. "He is at the front," his beleaguered chief of staff would say when an officer asked to speak to him. In late June, when Pavlov disappeared for a six-day stretch, he was summoned to Moscow, put on trial—and executed. Pavlov was not the only general that Stalin was unhappy with. Candor is essential in war, but the purge trials of the 1930s had made many Soviet officers wary of truth telling. No one wanted to end up like Pavlov, yet withholding the truth could have serious military consequences. In the early hours of June 28,

Stalin marched into Marshal Timoshenko's office at the People's Commissariat of Defense and demanded to know why he had not received any updates on the situation in Minsk. Timoshenko's vague reply only made him angrier. "It is your duty to keep the facts before you and keep us up to date," he told Timoshenko. "At present, you are afraid to tell us the truth." After the exchange Zhukov, who was also present, asked, "Comrade Stalin, do we have permission to go on with our work?" The question only annoyed Stalin more. He wondered, "What sort of chief of staff is it who, since the first day of the war, has had no connection with his troops? He represents nobody and commands nobody."

It is not often that a marshal of the Soviet Union bursts into tears and flees the room, but Zhukov did so that night, and this produced an even rarer scene: Vyacheslav Molotov, a cold-blooded hangman, standing in a hall, consoling a weeping Zhukov. When the two men reappeared Stalin was told the truth: Minsk was gone and, with it, a large chunk of the Soviet frontier army. Earlier in the day two panzer groups had met up east of Minsk, opening the road to Moscow and trapping 290,000 Soviet troops in what became known as the Bialystok-Minsk pocket.

Stalin averred that a big mistake had been made.

It was nearing dawn, and Stalin, Molotov, and Lavrentiy Beria, the head of the Soviet security service, were standing in the driveway of the Commissariat of Defense. Above them the day was gathering itself in the June sky. "Everything is lost," Stalin wailed. "I give up! Lenin founded our state and we've fucked it up." (Yes, according to one who recorded it, Stalin apparently spoke in the modern-day vernacular.) The next day at noon, Stalin's Kremlin office was still empty. Alexander Poskrebyshev, Stalin's chief of staff, told callers that Comrade Stalin was not in, adding, "I don't know when he will be here."

By evening Poskrebyshev had switched to a blunter formulation. "Comrade Stalin is not here and unlikely to be here," the chief of staff said. For the next few days, rumors had Stalin wandering through his dacha in suburban Moscow: depressed, confused, and unable to sleep. However, remembering that Alexander the Great and Ivan the Terrible had withdrawn from power to assess the loyalty of their followers, not everyone was convinced Stalin's breakdown was real. Rumor had it that he was reading books about Ivan the Terrible during his retreat and that he was so impressed by one biography, he had scribbled "We shall prevail!" on its cover. It's also possible that both theories were correct.

The tremendous losses sustained in the first week of war left Stalin politically vulnerable—and uncertain of whom to trust. Anastas Mikoyan, one of the Politburo members who visited him at his dacha on the afternoon of June 30, wrote later, "I have no doubt Stalin decided we had arrived to arrest him." On the drive back to Moscow that evening Beria had a more chilling thought. "We were witness to Stalin's moments of weakness," he told his colleagues, adding that "Josef Vissarionovich"—the ethnic name for Stalin—"will never forgive that."

Upon his return to the Kremlin on July 1 Stalin began to take command of the major organs of state. He appointed himself chairman of the defense committee, chairman of the state defense committee, commissar of defense, and supreme commander. He also ordered Lenin's Mausoleum to be moved to Siberia, out of range of the German bombers. On the night of the transfer Stalin made a personal visit to a blacked-out Red Square to say farewell to the man whose dying wishes included removing Stalin as general secretary of the Russian Communist Party's Central Committee.

The final week of June brought temperatures of a hundred degrees, swirling clouds of dust, and reports of further defeats. Brest-Litovsk, one of the most important Soviet strongpoints on the western front, was on the verge of capitulation. In the north, a German panzer group had smashed though the Russian positions in the Baltics and was driving on Leningrad—Russia's second city and the German Army Group Center—and was hurtling eastward toward Smolensk, just 247 miles west of Moscow. Only in southern Russia was the Red Army enjoying success. A force under General Zhukov had slowed down Army Group South's advance on the Ukraine. In early July, the morale reports from the NKVD, a kind of police force that Stalin used to keep an eye on people, and other government agencies painted a complicated picture: enlistments were up and morale was high among idealistic young communists and blood-and-soil Russian patriots whose complicated relationship with the motherland was given voice in the poem "The Roads Around Smolensk."

> By the graves on the edge of every small village
> Guarding the living with the sign of the cross
> Our forefathers gather together to pray
> For their grandsons who no longer believe in God

In the Ukraine, where a man-made famine had claimed between 3.3 and 7.5 million lives in the early 1930s, there was much less enthusiasm for fighting under the flag of the nation that had perpetrated the massacre. There was also a sizable number of ethnic Russians with defeatist leanings—men like Dr. Grebeshinkov, who was overheard telling a colleague: "With half the country opposed to the government, it would be hard to get people to fight." There was Mr. Kurbanov of the Soviet Tourist Bureau, who saw no honor in dying for a corrupt regime, and there was Dr. Tobias, who predicted a long, bloody war, ending in a Soviet defeat.

On July 3, in his first wartime address to the Soviet people, Stalin attempted to undo the past by painting a reassuring picture of the future around which Soviet citizens of all nationalities and political persuasions could unite.

"Comrades, citizens, brothers and sisters; fighters of our army and navy," he began. "I am speaking to you, my friends. . . . War has been inflicted on us, and our country has entered into a life-and-death struggle with its most wicked and perfidious enemy." Stalin's words had the power of simplicity, but to one listener, Konstantin Simonov, a war correspondent, what made the speech so effective was his delivery. He "spoke in a toneless slow voice with a strong Georgian accent," Simonov noted, observing, later, that you could hear his glass clink when Stalin reached over and took a sip of water from it on the podium. His voice was low and soft and might have seemed perfectly calm but for the heavy, tired breathing and the water he kept drinking. Simonov thought there was a discrepancy "between [Stalin's] even voice and the tragic situation of which he spoke." Yet in that discrepancy Simonov heard strength. "People were not surprised," he said. "Stalin performed the way they expected. There were no tunes of glory, just a leader speaking hard truths that had to be spoken. . . . They loved him in different ways, wholeheartedly or with reservations; admiring him yet fearing him; some of his listeners did not like him at all. Yet nobody doubted his courage or his iron will. And now was a time when these two qualities were needed in the man who stood at the head of the country. . . . The truths Stalin told on that July day were hard and bitter, but in uttering them he won the trust of his people."

Simonov was only half-right about Stalin's truth telling. He kept the most bitter truth—that the Soviet army, navy, and air force no longer existed together as a coherent whole—to himself. By July 10, the Soviet forces on the western front had lost 4,799 tanks, 1,777 fighter aircraft, and 341,000 soldiers. Watching the defeated Red Army retreat eastward after the battle of Minsk, one Soviet officer was reminded of a lava flow "moving slowly toward the sea." "Some of the troops [were] in trucks, outdated rifles hanging loosely from their shoulders. Their uniforms were worn out, covered with dust," and there was "not a smile on their mostly despondent, emaciated faces." Another officer recalled how the Luftwaffe would circle over the retreating Russian columns, waiting for a bottleneck of men and matériel to develop, then sweep down like birds of prey. On their way out of Minsk in early July, a German loudspeaker informed the retreating Russians that their German opponents had decided to present them with a reward for their "valiant" defense of the town: "twenty minutes to finish off the Commissars and the Kikes."

A few days after the Minsk victory General Franz Halder, chief of the German general staff, wrote that it was "no exaggeration to say the Russian war has been won in two weeks." Most British and American military men agreed. The Russians would fight long enough to satisfy military honor; then, like the British and French in 1940, they would surrender or retreat. However, the assessment overlooked history. From the Polish invasion in 1605 to Napoleon's attack in 1812, the Russian soldier had displayed uncommon courage and grit. Frederick the Great, who encountered the Russian soldier in the eighteenth century, wrote of the experience: "In order to defeat [him] you must kill him, then bayonet him and then shoot the bastard." The crushing Soviet defeat on the Polish frontier in June had produced hundreds of instances of extraordinary heroism. In July, a month after the fighting had moved far to the east, a handful of Red Army men continued to hold out in the citadel at Brest-Litovsk on the Soviet-Polish border. Before his death, one of the defenders scribbled on the wall: "I am dying but do not surrender. Farewell, motherland."

IN EARLY JULY THE RESIDENTS of Smolensk, a city of hills and churches just inside the Russian border, awoke to the heavy clank of metal and grinding gears. When the sun burned off the morning haze, the horizon was filled with German tanks. The scale and speed of the German successes at Bialystok and Minsk—twenty Russian divisions destroyed and almost three hundred thousand men captured in a little over a week—had emboldened Berlin and alarmed Moscow. In both capitals, maps were taken out, and the name Smolensk, the last major city before the capital, was circled in red. In early July, the battle for the city began under a sweltering sun. The Germans who arrived in its environs—waving battle flags and singing patriotic songs—were the embodiment of martial glamour; Smolensk defenders were the antithesis of it. The ill-equipped, ill-trained soldiers of the Soviet reserve army knew little about soldiering in the classic sense and were only in Smolensk because no one else was left to defend the city; but folklore and culture had armed the Russian soldier with two classic skills: Firstly, he knew how to kill. German prisoners were shot out of hand—or, if time allowed, they were mutilated. Secondly, the Soviet soldier knew how to die. When bullets rang out, he would fight with knives, and if no artillery was available to offer covering fire, he would charge German tanks with petrol bombs, better known now as Molotov cocktails. Before he was found and executed, one wounded Russian radio operator spent two weeks inside the hulk of a burned-out tank relaying German positions to his comrades. In late July, after weeks of brutal combat, the Russian line began to waver, and the roads around Smolensk swelled with long columns of men, marching eastward, under the last Russian sky they would ever see, to a fate they dare not think about. When the fighting wound down in August, six hundred thousand Russians were either dead, wounded, or in captivity—and Hitler was making plans for the colonization of Russia.

"There is only one duty: to Germanize the country," he told his generals. "With this objective in mind, we have undertaken the construction of roads that will lead to the southernmost part of the Crimea and Caucasus. These roads will be studded along their entire length with German towns and around those towns our colonists will settle. . . . We shan't settle the Russian towns. We'll let them go to pieces without intervening. And, above all, no remorse on this subject. To struggle amongst the hovels, chase away the fleas, provide German teachers, bring out newspapers . . . very little of that for us. We'll confine ourselves, perhaps, to setting up a radio transmitter under our control. For the rest, let them [the Russians] know just enough to understand our highway signs so that they won't get run over by our vehicles."

Viewed through the long lenses of history, the battle of Smolensk emerges as a strategic victory for Russia. It bought the Soviets time to reinforce Moscow's defenses and to make good on the tremendous human and matériel losses incurred in the early weeks of fighting. It was also at Smolensk that the German general staff became aware that the price of victory would be much higher than they had imagined. In 1939 and 1940 Germany had acquired most of western and central Europe for the bargain price of fifty thousand dead. In Smolensk, the price of victory was eighty thousand dead and wounded; and that was before Moscow and before the hundreds of other cities, towns, villages, forests, and steppes that lay beyond Moscow. In early August, with the German casualty rate running at 50 percent, General Halder revised his view of the Red Army. "The Russian colossus has been underestimated by us. . . . Whenever a dozen divisions are destroyed, the Russians replace them with another dozen."

3

SAVING STALIN

H ARRY HOPKINS WAS SUI GENERIS: HALF BROADWAY WISE GUY and half bighearted do-gooder, he spent most of his professional life annoying people, first as a social worker in New York City, then as director of the Works Progress Administration, where his managerial skills brought him to the attention of Franklin Roosevelt.

Some friendships are self-explanatory. The friendship between Roosevelt and Hopkins was not. The president was an American aristocrat with a bloodline that sparkled with famous names; Hopkins was the scion of a hardscrabble midwestern family, with tastes that ran to racetracks, midnight card games, nightclubs, highballs, and pretty women. The link that bound the two men together was the shared experience of living in the shadow of death. Roosevelt was crippled by polio in 1921—and, later in his presidency, by heart disease. Hopkins lost three-quarters of his stomach to cancer in 1937 and thereafter became vulnerable to a severe form of anemia. In wartime photos, Hopkins is always the frailest face in the frame.

A quick wit and an almost feline sensitivity to Roosevelt's moods made Hopkins a presidential favorite in the 1930s, but the deep relationship the two men forged during the war years arose from Roosevelt's position as a wheelchair president. Limited in mobility and frail in health, the president needed a surrogate who could be trusted to speak for him when he was unable to speak for himself, and by the early 1940s no one was more attuned to Roosevelt's thinking or could explain that thinking more clearly than Hopkins. One evening during Hopkins's first visit to Britain in January 1941, Churchill burst into a soliloquy about the Anglo-American relationship. When he finished, Hopkins brought him back down to earth with some American straight talk. "I don't think the president will give a damn about all of that," he said. "You see, we're only interested in seeing that that goddamn son of bitch Hitler gets licked."

On a July morning six months later Hopkins was circling over a Scottish RAF base in the cockpit of a B-24 bomber. Below the plane Prescott, a Glasgow suburb, was beginning to stir. A group of children were playing soccer in a field next to a Presbyterian church, and a gardener was mowing the lawn in front of the town hall. Hopkins's visit arose out of a recent talk with Roosevelt: on the evening of July 11, the president summoned him to the White House for what amounted to a tour d'horizon of the world at war. Nowhere on the globe that evening was the position of the democracies secure. The British were on the back foot from the Middle East to Hong Kong; a large swath of China, Mongolia, and Indonesia were under Japanese control, and the U-boat threat in the Atlantic had become perilous. Russia also figured prominently in Roosevelt's survey. General George Marshall, the US Army's chief of staff, doubted that the Red Army could survive for more than another month or two; Roosevelt was more optimistic. Still, even if Marshall was right, every day that Russia remained in the war relieved pressure on the Western democracies and made Stalin think twice about coming to terms with Germany, which he was likely to do if he thought the Soviet Union could not rely on the United States and Britain for support.

As a nonbelligerent, the United States could not deliver supplies directly to the Soviet Union, but it could facilitate their delivery indirectly. To illustrate to Hopkins how this could be done, Roosevelt tore a small map of the Atlantic Ocean from a *National Geographic* magazine and circled the region that began on the East Coast of the United States, extending eastward deep into the Atlantic and southward through the Azores. Currently the region was jointly patrolled by the US Navy and the Royal Navy. Under Roosevelt's plan, British vessels would be transferred to convoy duty on the Russian route, and America would police the regions that Roosevelt had outlined. When he finished, Roosevelt handed Hopkins the *National Geographic* map and told him to pack his bags—he was going back to England.

Before leaving that evening, Hopkins received two instructions. He was to arrange a meeting between Roosevelt and Churchill, preferably for sometime in August, and he was warned not to let Churchill draw him into discussions about America's entry into the war.

Seventy-two hours later, Hopkins was sitting in a British railway car, trying to ignore the nausea that overcame him on long journeys. Outside the window miles of deep green grass and fields of cowslips and daffodils followed the wind of the train southward toward London. In January, on Hopkins's first visit, the Blitz was at its peak and the city had the sweet smell of doom about it. At dusk the sky would fill with cones of brilliant white light, and the drone of approaching aircraft would echo through the darkness—and streets and office buildings would explode into a bonfire of flame and smoke. By July, nearly two years of war had given London the look of a grande dame caught without her makeup, but with the Luftwaffe focusing its attention on Russia, London was coming alive again. The parks and shops and dance halls were filling up once more; fewer people were carrying gas masks, and the summer weather was so fine that Hopkins and Churchill held their first meeting on July 17 on the terrace behind Downing Street. When the meeting with Roosevelt came up in conversation, Hopkins said the president's preference was for "some lonely bay or other" in the second week of August. Churchill agreed immediately.

For the next several days, Hopkins devoted most of his time to his other brief. Unbeknownst to the American public, which polling showed did not want to become entangled in another European war, the US government was quietly building up a sizable military presence in Britain, and Hopkins was one of the architects of the buildup. In his capacity as director of the lend-lease program, he spent a great deal of time conferring with British and American industrialists and picking the brains of shipping and ordnance experts. In his capacity as presidential adviser, he was also instrumental in finalizing arrangements for the Roosevelt-Churchill meeting in August. More unwisely, during his London visit, Hopkins also involved himself in military strategy.

During a meeting of senior British and American military leaders on July 19, Hopkins gave a provocative speech on a delicate subject: the large British military presence in the Middle East. "I know perfectly well you here in Britain are determined to go on fighting to hold the Middle East," he said, "but you have to remember that we here in the United States just simply do not understand your problems there and . . . your interest in the Muslim world and India." Strategically, Hopkins's critique had merit. At a time when the home island remained under threat of invasion, it was dangerous to station a dozen or more divisions almost four thousand miles away. Nonetheless, coming from a former social worker of a still-neutral country, the advice was unwelcome. The Middle East was Britain's gateway to India and the other parts of its Asian empire; it was a symbol of the country's status as a great power at a time when that status was under threat, and for Britain's professional soldiers, service in the Middle East was often part of a family tradition—it was where fathers and grandfathers had served. After Hopkins finished, Churchill, who was in attendance, wisely changed the subject to Japan.

Initially, Hopkins planned to return to Washington after the London trip, but Russia was impinging on almost every issue he dealt with, especially lend-lease, and his only sources of information on the Soviet Union were the newspapers and Foreign Office and State Department reports. On July 20 Hopkins drove out to Chequers, the Berkshire country house that Arthur Lee, a wealthy industrialist, had gifted to the British State in 1917. Lee had envisioned Chequers as a weekend retreat for overworked prime ministers, but its current occupant, Winston Churchill, had transformed the house into a way station for the good and great of the Western world. On any given day in 1941, a visitor might encounter the celebrity journalist Clare Boothe Luce inspecting one of the house's ancient staircases, Mrs. Churchill presiding over lunch for an exiled monarch in the cavernous main dining room, or Averell Harriman, the American industrialist, flirting with Pamela Churchill, the wife of the prime minister's son, Randolph. Hopkins did not get much time with Churchill during his visit, but he did have a long talk with Ivan Maisky, the Soviet ambassador to Britain. Maisky was an uncommonly clever man with sharp political instincts who numbered among his friends George Bernard Shaw, John Maynard Keynes, H. G. Wells, and Churchill. Not much came of the talk the two men had that afternoon, but Maisky came away impressed by Hopkins. He had the usual quota of American brashness, but he was possessed of an earnestness that, in the ambassador's experience, was uncommon among

Americans. Five days later the two men visited the American embassy in Grosvenor Square to meet with the new American ambassador, John Winant, a New Hampshire man who, upon his arrival in London, had won over the British public with a single sentence: "There is no place I'd rather be at this time than England." The subject at hand that afternoon was the Soviet Union's supply needs, but toward the end of the conversation Hopkins asked Maisky what could be done to bring Roosevelt and Stalin closer.

Stalin was little more than a name to Roosevelt, the abstract head of the Soviet government. Hopkins's request was so unusual that at first Maisky wasn't sure what he was being asked to do. But by the time the two men left the embassy Maisky had agreed to pass on Hopkins's request to meet Stalin.

In the summer of 1941, the war in the east was a black box in Britain and the United States. There were reports that the dogged Soviet defense of Smolensk had slowed the German drive on Moscow, but there were also reports that the German Army Group North had encircled Leningrad and that Army Group South was approaching Kiev, the capital of the Ukraine. The only thing the reports had in common was their questionable reliability. Even if Stalin was not completely frank, which was likely, a trip to Moscow would allow Hopkins to make an informed assessment of the Red Army's staying power and of Stalin the man. On the day of his departure Hopkins spent the morning in the bathroom at Chequers, watching the prime minister of Great Britain prepare his travel schedule from the bathtub. That evening Hopkins would leave Chequers for the RAF base in Inverness, Scotland, where a PBY Catalina would fly him to Archangel in northern Russia. From there he would be put on a flight to Moscow.

Hopkins had no difficulty keeping himself busy until departure time. Chequers had the usual weekend complement of international celebrities. Hopkins lunched with the novelist Sinclair Lewis and his wife, the journalist Dorothy Thompson, whom *Time* magazine had recently named the second-most influential woman in America. He spent the afternoon with Quentin Reynolds, the hard-drinking foreign correspondent and novelist, and at twilight he gave a speech on the BBC. After the talk, he and Churchill walked out onto the lawn at Chequers. It was after 10:00 P.M. but there was still light in the summer sky. Off in the distance there was the faint sound of artillery fire.

The Luftwaffe had not completely abandoned Britain. The two men took in the scene for a few moments, then Hopkins said, "What should I ask Stalin?" The question excited Churchill. "Tell him, tell him, tell him that Britain has but one desire—to crush Hitler," he said. "Tell him he can depend on us—goodbye and God bless, Harry." A moment later he disappeared into the house. And there remained just Hopkins, the night sky, and the prospect of a two-thousand-mile journey across some of the most heavily defended terrain on earth.

FORTY-EIGHT HOURS LATER, HOPKINS WAS gazing out the window of a Soviet transport plane. Below, the Russian forest ran to the horizon in all directions. It was nature on a scale that Hopkins had never encountered before. Over the millennia dozens of invaders had marched into its vastness, singing songs of battle, and few had ever been heard from again.

An hour later a glint of light caught the wing of the plane, and the roofs of Moscow came into view. The city was a strange mixture of war and peace. Marching soldiers, collapsed buildings, the rumble of tanks on the thoroughfares. Alleys, crowded with noisy children playing *koldunchiki*, an ancient Russian version of tag; and in the market stalls by the Moskva River, old peasant women hawking *plyushka*, a bread-and-sugar dish. Aside from the marching men, the most ubiquitous reminders of the war were the propaganda posters. One featured a Russian tank crushing a giant crab with a Hitler mustache; another, a soldier slamming his bayonet down the throat of a giant Hitler rat. The latest issue of *Bezbozhnik*, known unofficially as the "godless paper," heralded another wartime change: a greater tolerance of religion. The paper was sharply critical of Hitler's persecution of Protestant and Catholic clerics in Germany. The war news was carefully censored, but Muscovites had learned to read between the lines. "Fighting in the Smolensk direction" usually meant a battle was about to be lost, and "heavy defensive battles against superior enemy forces" meant the battle had been lost and the Soviet armies were in full and disorderly retreat.

Hopkins arrived in Moscow around noon on July 30 and after a short nap was briefed by Laurence Steinhardt, the American ambassador. Steinhardt described Russia's military position as precarious but said that two things in history gave him a measure of hope: one, the fact that, in 1812, Russia had repelled Napoleon's armies; and, two, the character of the Russian people. Those dead ancestors standing guard in the poem "Smolensk Roads" were not a literary conceit. The young men marching off to war, the members of the Women's Auxiliary Militia, the old peasant women hawking *plyushka* by the river: they were all part of a chain of being that extended deep into Russia's past and which it was the duty of every generation to keep unbroken.

Hopkins arrived in the Kremlin at a little before 6:30 that evening and was taken to Stalin's residence, an unprepossessing three-story building in the middle of the Kremlin complex. He was not sure what to expect, but he did not expect the man who greeted him. His host was shorter than Hopkins had expected, about five feet four inches, and was "built like a football coach's dream of a tackle," Hopkins wrote—"heavily boned" with a "powerful frame, a broad chest . . . and hands as huge and hard as his mind. He assures you that Russia will stand against the German onslaught, and he takes it for granted that you have no doubts about that, either." The study in which the two men conferred was perhaps fifty feet by thirty and sparsely decorated. A death mask of Lenin hung on one wall, a painting of Stalin on the other. After an exchange of pleasantries Stalin launched into an overview of the war. He said "the Germans had underestimated the strength of the Red Army and have not now enough troops on the whole front to carry on a successful offensive war and at the same time guard their extended lines of communication." Stalin said he "did not underrate the German army; their organization was of the very best." Nonetheless, he believed Russia had a great advantage at the moment. "Summer has left the Germans tired," he opined, and "with no stomach for another offensive"; and even if they did attempt to mount a new offensive, the weather was against them. "It would be difficult for the Germans to operate offensively much after the first of September when the heavy rains . . . begin, and after October 1, the ground would be so bad . . . they would have to go on the defensive." When Hopkins asked about the Soviet Union's military needs, Stalin placed antiaircraft guns, aluminum for aircraft, machine guns of .50 caliber, and rifles of .40-caliber variety at the top of the list.

Missing from the interview were probing questions about the huge Soviet losses in men and matériel, and the next morning—July 31—Major Ivan Yates, the military attaché at the American embassy, was so angry about the oversight that he accused Hopkins of being too accommodating. If the Russians wanted US aid, Yates said, they should provide the War Department with detailed information on their munitions plants, troop dispositions, and the other data the War Department needed to make an accurate assessment of Soviet needs and the Soviets' chances of surviving. As Yates listed his complaints tempers flared, fists were banged on tables, breakfast dishes bounced up and down, and other diners turned away in embarrassment. Then, abruptly, Hopkins rose from the table, said, "I don't care to discuss the subject further"—and left.

It is impossible to say whether Yates's complaints had any influence on Hopkins, but later that day when he met Stalin for their second and final talk he noted that as yet the Soviets had not provided any information to the military attachés at the British and American embassies. Despite the sharper tone, Hopkins's admiration for Stalin did not wane. In an article on his Moscow trip for *American Magazine* he wrote: "No man could forget the picture of the dictator of Russia as he stood watching me leave—an austere, rugged, determined figure in boots that shone like mirrors, his voice harsh but ever in control. What he says is all the accent and inflection his words need."

Hopkins's reading of Stalin was half-right.

Even with the benefit of hindsight—in other words, Stalin's crimes—in the main, modern historians continue to rate him highly as a war leader. Among them is Richard Overy, a preeminent historian of World War II, who wrote: "Stalin brought a powerful will to bear on the Soviet war effort that motivated those around him and directed their energies. In the process he expected and got exceptional sacrifices from his besieged people. . . . It is difficult to imagine any other Soviet leader of the time could have wrung such efforts from the population."

However, Overy was writing about the Stalin of 1944 and 1945. The Stalin of 1941 still had much to learn about the conduct of a continental war; in the interim he disguised his failures with falsehoods and exaggerations. Much of what he told Hopkins were falsehoods, exaggerations—or both. German pressure on Russia did not slacken at any point in July, as Stalin claimed; rather, it intensified. Stalin's assertion that Germans had lost the stomach for further offensives was also a falsehood. On September 9 Army Group North completed the encirclement of Leningrad, and on September 26 Army Group South seized Kiev. Stalin also failed to mention the butcher's bill at Bialystok—290,000—and Minsk—almost 758,000 dead or wounded. It is possible that, bewitched by Stalin, Hopkins allowed himself to be seduced, but it is at least as possible that Hopkins knew who he was dealing with. Both the purges of the late

1930s and the man-made famine in the Ukraine in the early 1930s had been widely reported on in the Western press. Hopkins's embrace of Stalin may have been an exercise in realpolitik. Though the Soviet leader was wicked, he was also a fighter, and, as Professor Overy noted, he had a gift for leadership equal to Churchill's and Roosevelt's. Another consideration that may have influenced Hopkins was the casualty rate. The higher the Soviet combat losses, the lower American and British losses were likely to be.

At the end of the second meeting, the *Life* magazine photographer Margaret Bourke-White was ushered into Stalin's office. White took out her camera and got down on her knees in front of Stalin's desk. "As I crawled . . . from one low camera angle to another Stalin thought it was funny," White recalled later. But "when [his] smile ended, it was as though a veil had been drawn over his feature. This was the strongest, most determined face I had ever seen."

ON AUGUST 4 WINSTON CHURCHILL boarded the battleship *Prince of Wales* at Scapa Flow, a naval base of low, forbidding skies and deep drafts at the northern tip of Scotland. In the half-light of morning, the scars on the *Wales*'s hull, the result of a recent encounter with the German battleship *Bismarck*, were barely visible. The other passengers included Sir John Dill, chief of the Imperial General Staff; Dill's naval opposite number, Admiral Dudley Pound; and Harry Hopkins. In a cable to Roosevelt that morning Churchill reported that Hopkins had returned from Russia so physically depleted he required several blood transfusions but that he was now "lively again." The prime minister also reminded the president of the date. "Twenty-seven years ago today the Huns began their last war," he said. "We must make [a] good job of it this time. Twice ought to be enough." The *Wales* was under orders to observe radio silence at sea, and, with no work to take their minds off the "mighty swelling sea" crashing against the ship's hull, the guests were forced to resort to leisure-time activities. Churchill read his first book since the war began, *Horatio Hornblower*. Then he selected a movie for evening viewing by his entourage. "Awful bunk, but the PM loves it," Sir Alexander Cadogan, permanent under secretary for foreign affairs, said of Churchill's choice, *High Sierra*.

Roosevelt's journey to Placentia Bay had the character of a schoolboy's prank. On August 3 he left the capital with a small entourage and traveled north on the presidential train to New London, Connecticut. In New London he transferred to his yacht, the *Potomac*, and then disappeared into the Long Island Sound as evening approached. The next morning he reappeared fishing off Cape Cod in the company of two royals: the exiled Princess Martha of Norway and Prince Carl of Sweden. Then he disappeared again until the following morning, when he was seen sailing through Cape Cod Canal. The cheering tourists on the shore imagined they were paying homage to the president of the United States, but the man seated on the afterdeck of the *Potomac* talking with friends was a Roosevelt double. Earlier in the day the president had transferred to a warship shrouded in the fog off Martha's Vineyard. "Even at my ripe old age," Roosevelt wrote to his cousin and confidant Daisy Suckley, "I feel a thrill making a getaway."

On the morning of August 7, the heavy cruiser *Augusta* arrived off Placentia Bay, a desolate cove rimmed by low hills and scrawny pines near the Newfoundland fishing village of Argentia, accompanied by the *Tuscaloosa*, the *Arkansas* (a World War I battleship), and a destroyer escort. The *Prince of Wales* entered the bay two days later with a panache that bespoke three centuries of empire. At around 10:00 A.M. the *Wales* emerged out of a thin mist, looking like every schoolboy's idea of a battleship: 750 feet long, compared to the *Augusta*'s 600 feet, and displacing thirty-six thousand tons versus the *Augusta*'s nine thousand. As the big ship's destroyer escort sailed through the lane of American vessels in the bay, foghorns honked, whistles blew—and young sailors from Texas and Oklahoma stood on the decks of the *Augusta* and the *Tuscaloosa*, cheering.

At around eleven a barge ferried Churchill to the *Augusta*, where Roosevelt awaited him on the ship's upper deck. Also present was the president's son Elliott, his arm inconspicuously bracing his father—which allowed the president to greet the prime minister standing upright. "At last we meet," Roosevelt said—according to what Elliott later recalled, in a memoir—and extended his hand. "Yes, we have!" a pleased Churchill replied. As the two men talked, the band on the *Prince of Wales* struck up "The Stars and Stripes Forever." Then the band on the *Augusta* reciprocated with a rousing rendition of "God Save the King."

The informal lunch that followed was Hopkins's idea. He thought the two men, who had only met once before—in 1919—would be more at ease in an informal setting, free from distractions of noisy aides and disgruntled generals. Churchill embraced the idea; Roosevelt said yes, but with reservations. "Watch. See if the PM doesn't start off by immediately demanding we declare war against the Nazis," he told Elliott the day before the *Prince of Wales* arrived. Roosevelt was right about Churchill's intentions but wrong about his timing. Churchill had taken Hopkins's advice to keep the conversation light at lunch. Sensitive topics like lend-lease aid and American public opinion—the August polls showed that 74 percent of the country favored neutrality—were touched upon, but, as the atmosphere around the table warmed, the conversation grew more personal and intimate. The two men discussed their correspondence, their transatlantic telephone conversations, their health, and their worries.

The meeting ended as Hopkins had hoped, with the two men on a first-name basis. However, the prime minister did not come three thousand miles to make small talk with the president of the United States. That evening at a dinner party aboard the *Augusta*, "Churchill reared back in his chair, slewed his cigar from cheek to cheek at a jaunty angle," Elliott said, "and hunched his shoulders forward like a bull; his hands slashed the air . . . his eyes flashed. He told of the course of battle, he told of battle after battle lost, [adding] Britain always wins in the end. He told . . . how close to defeat his country had come." And he spoke of the desperate need for American assistance. "You've got to come in beside us," Churchill told his American listeners. "If you don't declare war . . . [and] wait for them to strike first, they'll strike [you] after we've gone under and their first blow will be their last."

"Father . . . usually dominated every gathering, but not that night," Elliott noted, later that evening, adding that "somebody else was holding the audience [and] holding it with grand, rolling [phrases], never quite too florid, always ripe and fruity to the point where it seemed like you'd be able to take [Churchill's] sentences in your hands and squeeze them until the juice ran out." The night ended with the prime minister scoring an odd sort of victory. The American guests left the party as convinced that the United States should stay out of the shooting war as they had been when they arrived; still, they were deeply impressed by what they had heard and by the man from whom they had heard it. Churchill's eloquence left everyone wishing that "both sides could have won the argument," Elliott wrote.

The ceremony aboard the HMS *Prince of Wales* the next morning produced some of the most iconic images of World War II. Festivities began a little before 11:00 A.M., when an American destroyer delivered the president to the deck of the *Wales*. The three hundred sailors and marines standing on the ship's deck snapped to attention. Trumpets blared, sunlight peered through the leaden sky, and, swinging one heavily braced foot in front of the other, the president of the United States propelled himself across the deck of the *Wales* on a pair of crutches. Photographers snapped pictures, off-duty tars and bluejackets scurried up on to the *Wales*'s big guns to get a better view of the generals and admirals gathered on the main deck below, and Roosevelt and Churchill placed themselves on the fantail, facing the warm morning sun, next to a pulpit decorated with the Stars and Stripes and a Union Jack.

Prayer books emerged from pockets, and "Onward Christian Soldiers," "Eternal Father," "O God Our Help in Ages Past," and other beloved hymns of the English-speaking world echoed across the bay. "You would have to be pretty hard-boiled not to be moved by it all," John Martin, a Churchill aide, recalled later—"hundreds of men of both fleets mingled together, one rough British sailor sharing his hymn sheet with one American ditto." Three months later nearly half of the young men standing on the deck that morning would be dead. On December 10, three days after Pearl Harbor, a Japanese air attack would claim between 317 and 327 sailors on the *Wales*, and 513 members of the heavy cruiser *Repulse*, the *Wales*'s sister ship. It would send both vessels to a final resting place far from home—at the bottom of an Asian sea.

During the last days of the meeting, the two sides found themselves disagreeing on several important issues. Churchill wanted Roosevelt to extend the US Navy's policing duties beyond the line he committed to on July 11. But the president refused. Roosevelt wanted to give immediate aid to Russia on a very large scale; Churchill was fearful that more Russian lend-lease aid would mean less aid for Britain, and so he objected. When the subject of Russia came up at the dinner party on the *Augusta*, the prime minister had said, "Of course the Russians are much stronger than we ever dared to hope. But no one can tell for how much longer?"

"Then you don't think they'll be able to hold out?" a guest asked.

Churchill replied to the question in half sentences. "When Moscow falls . . . when the Germans [get] beyond the Caucasus . . . when Russian resistance . . . ceases . . ." Then he stopped and left his listeners to ponder the prospect of a Russian collapse.

Churchill and Roosevelt also disagreed on how to counter Japanese expansion. At first glance, the prime minister's preference for taking a hard line in Asia seemed nonsensical; Britain was already overburdened with commitments. But Churchill thought the strategy could create a win-win opportunity for Britain. If the Japanese bowed to Anglo-American pressure and surrendered their conquests in China and Indochina and foreswore further expansion, Britain would win. If they ignored the Anglo-American warnings and continued to rampage through Asia, Britain would also win. The United States would have to defend its bases in Hawaii and the Philippines, and once the Americans were fighting in the East the logic of war dictated that they soon would be fighting in the West. However, Roosevelt had his own win-win strategy, and it did not look anything like Churchill's: stay out of the shooting war if that were possible, and if it were not, stay out of it until the American army and navy were better trained and equipped and public opinion was more receptive to intervention. In the meantime, "drag things out, parlay, stall," Elliott reported of the strategy.

Several sharp differences also emerged between senior American and British officers. Sir John Dill and Sir Dudley Pound spent hours trying to persuade their American counterparts that if the United States entered the war now, victory would come sooner and at a lower cost in lives. At the same time, the most senior American military men—General George Marshall, the army chief of staff; and Admiral Ernest King, the chief of naval operations—spent hours trying to convince Dill and Pound that the American armed forces were presently too small, too ill trained, and, thanks to the lend-lease aid provided Britain, too ill equipped to enter the war at present. These strategic differences fostered confusion and distrust on both sides, and on the British side the confusion and distrust were accompanied by a measure of contempt. On August 11, after a particularly frustrating meeting with his American colleagues, Ian Jacob, military assistant secretary to Churchill, wrote in his diary: "The American navy seems to think the war can be won by simply not losing it at sea." While "the American army sees no prospect of being able to do anything for a year or two and is . . . completely taken up with equipment problems. Not a single American office has shown the slightest keenness to be in the war on our side. They are a charming lot of individuals but they appeared to be living in a different world than ourselves."

Jacob was right about Britain and America occupying different worlds. In 1941 world leadership was passing from Britain to the United States, and the changing of the guard was evident in another exchange that Churchill and Roosevelt had at Placentia Bay. The exchange was occasioned by Roosevelt's remark that, as Hopkins later wrote, he was "firmly of the belief that if we are to arrive at a stable peace it must involve the development of backward countries. There can be no more eighteenth-century methods." Churchill took umbrage at the reference. "Who's talking about the eighteenth-century methods?" The term applied to nations who take wealth and raw materials out of a country "but . . . return nothing to the people of that country." Roosevelt replied and offered several examples of what he called "Twentieth Century methods . . . increasing the wealth of a people by increasing their standard of living, by educating them, by bringing them sanitation after the war." Later that night, when Elliott asked his father what he thought of Churchill as a leader, Roosevelt grunted and, as Elliott recalled it, he said, "He's a real old Tory . . . [but] I'll be able to work with him. . . . I think we'll even talk some more about India before we're through, and Burma, and Java . . . and Indonesia. And all the African colonies. And Egypt and Palestine. We'll talk about . . . all [the colonies]."

"Don't forget," Roosevelt said, "Winnie has one supreme mission in life but only one. He's a perfect wartime prime minister." Then Roosevelt paused for a moment and added, "But Winston Churchill will not lead England after the war. It'll never work."

On August 11 the president and the prime minister gathered in the admirals' quarters on the *Augusta*. It was a rare warm day, and the president had unbuttoned the collar of his gray suit. The prime minister paid homage to the nautical setting by arriving in a naval uniform. The purpose of the meeting was to formulate a set of shared principles that Britain and America could jointly announce to the world at the end of the conference. The problem was beyond a desire to defeat the Axis powers. The two countries did not share many priorities. Churchill's main goals were to increase American aid and eventually to bring the United States into the war; Roosevelt's goal was to avoid any war commitments other than those Congress had already authorized under the Lend-Lease Act. The Atlantic Charter—the statement of aims that emerged from the conference—sidestepped Anglo-American differences by ignoring them.

The Atlantic Charter was an updated version of the principles Woodrow Wilson had espoused a quarter of a century earlier: democratic elections, free speech, free trade, freedom of the seas, reduced armament, and collective security.

Roosevelt returned from Placentia Bay hoping the extensive press coverage of the meeting would encourage Americans to look past the current crisis to a better, more just, and more equitable world, where nations would live in peace with one another. But, as historian Robert Dallek has noted, Placentia Bay affected Roosevelt more deeply than it did his countrymen. During a press conference on August 19 he tried to excite the press by describing the moving prayer ceremony on the *Prince of Wales* but to no avail. The reporters kept shouting, "Are we any closer to entering the war?"

4

WAR WITHOUT END

———

UNDER A FORBIDDING SKY "FANTASTICALLY SHAPED CLOUDS race from west to east ... blotting out the [light] ... as if ... the world were on the eve of destruction." That was strange language for the urbane Ivan Maisky, Russian ambassador to Britain. But on September 4, 1941, Russian forces in the Ukraine and Leningrad were close to collapse—and, according to the cable on Maisky's desk, Germany was about to send an additional thirty-four divisions to the east in preparation for the assault on Moscow. Including the twenty-six Romanian and the twenty Finnish divisions already in the Soviet Union, on that September afternoon there were almost three hundred Axis divisions in Russia. "If a second front is not established in Europe within three to four weeks," the cable on Maisky's desk warned, "we may lose everything." It was signed "D. I.": Stalin's code name.

A few hours later a porter escorted Maisky through a poorly lit corridor pulsating with clerks and typists and deposited him in front of a conference room. When the door to the room opened, one could see that Churchill was seated at a table halfway down the room. He looked up. "Bearing good news?" he asked.

"I'm afraid not," Maisky replied, and he handed Churchill Stalin's cable, which ran to several pages. Churchill put on his glasses and began to read. After finishing each page, he would pass the page on to Anthony Eden, the foreign secretary. In Maisky's assessment of the British leadership class, Eden was placed somewhere in the middle. He was earnest, handsome, and competent enough, but, in Maisky's view, he was made "of the soft clay which yields easily to the fingers of a skilled artisan." At the bottom of Maisky's list was Neville Chamberlain, Churchill's predecessor. Maisky's pet name for Chamberlain was "the Grave Digger," and it derived from the ambassador's belief that, in the end, Chamberlain's appeasement policy would destroy the British Empire.

Just above Chamberlain on Maisky's list was "the Bishop," Lord Halifax. Six feet four inches tall, with a cultivated voice that bespoke generations of good breeding, Halifax suggested what the British Empire might sound like if it could speak. Maisky found the foreign secretary a bore, what with his sanctimony and his addiction to prayer—both unforgivable flaws, in Maisky's view.

At the top of Maisky's list was Churchill, who compensated for his antediluvian Toryism with great qualities of leadership. Over the years, the ambassador and the prime minister had developed a personal friendship of sorts. Maisky was a frequent visitor at Chequers, but on this late-summer afternoon he was visiting Churchill on official business. The Red Army was under terrific pressure, and Stalin wanted Britain to open a second front in the west. Immediately.

When Churchill placed the final sheaf of paper on the table, Maisky said, "So now, Mr. Churchill, you and the British government know the real state of affairs. We have withstood the terrible assault of the German war machine on our own for eleven weeks." He added that "nobody helps us in this struggle" and averred that "the situation has become difficult and menacing. . . . It is essential to carry out immediately what Stalin writes about. If the right measures are not taken—"

Churchill interrupted at this point. "Remember," he said, "only four months ago we in this island did not know whether you were . . . coming in against us on the German side." Maisky stated that Churchill continued, "Indeed, we thought it quite likely you would. . . . Whatever happens and whatever you do, you of all people have no right to make reproaches to us."

"More calm, please, my dear Mr. Churchill," Maisky said, realizing he had overstepped.

The rest of the meeting proceeded without incident. As the ambassador was leaving, Churchill said, "I don't want to mislead you. We'll not be able to provide you with any essential [military] aid before winter, either by creating a second front or through supplies. All we are capable of sending you at present—are trifles compared to your needs. . . . The future is a different matter." Here Churchill paused and permitted himself a half smile as he said, "For the next six or seven weeks." Then: "Only God, in whom you don't believe, can help you now."

Finding God unwilling to help, on September 13 Stalin made a second appeal to Churchill. "It seems to me that Britain could safely land twenty to twenty-five divisions in Archangel or ship them to southern areas of the USSR to cooperate with Soviet troops on Soviet soil." Smelling a fume of desperation, Churchill declined the offer. Meanwhile, Hitler had begun moving the knights and pawns on his chessboard to new positions. After the heavy German losses at Smolensk, he decided to postpone the march on Moscow, put Army Group Center in reserve to rest and refit, and turn south to the golden fields of the Ukraine. The region was rich in agricultural and industrial resources and sat adjacent to the Caucasus, which possessed a nearly limitless supply of oil. The Germans arrived in the Ukraine in high summer and found themselves in a fairy-tale landscape. "All about us the corn makes a soft rustling sound like the rustle of a silk gown," a German soldier wrote. General Zhukov, who was sent to the Ukraine to assess the situation, concluded that the region could not be held, and he recommended a general withdrawal. Fearful of the effect that withdrawal would have on civilian morale and on the willingness of Britain and the United States to provide aid, Stalin sacked Zhukov and ordered a last-man/last-round defense of the Ukrainian capital.

Even by the standards of the eastern front, the fighting around Kiev was savage. "The behavior of the Russians in action is simply incomprehensible," a German soldier wrote. "They are incredibly stubborn and refuse to budge even when under the most powerful gunfire." Another German spoke of dead Russian bodies "stretching for miles through the cornfields." Daily, the same scene played itself out under the burning steppe sun. Soviet troops would throw themselves heedlessly on the advancing enemy and die in the hundreds or thousands, depending on the scale of the attack. And at battle's end the victorious Germans would wonder where the Russians had found the courage to sustain war on such a horrendous scale.

Neither side offered quarter, and neither gave it. The Russians killed almost every German who fell into their hands and often made them die hard: eyes were plucked out, fingers cut off, genitals severed. The Germans were equally pitiless. Four thousand Russians were executed after a German unit came across the mutilated bodies of more than a hundred of their comrades hanging from trees. Daily, from late July until mid-September, German planes pounded the Soviet positions in Kiev. The streets and alleys filled with panzers, infantry units, human waste, lice, and barefoot men and women surviving on the body parts of feral animals. The official German figures for the battle of Kiev—665,000 Soviet prisoners—are almost certainly an exaggeration. Yet whatever the real figure was, it was large enough to make Stalin confront his limitations as a war leader. He recalled Zhukov and appointed him commander of the Leningrad front.

In August Stalin had assured the visiting Hopkins that the Soviet Union's three major cities—Kiev, Moscow, and Leningrad—would still be in Soviet hands in the spring of 1942. The fall of Kiev on September 26 gave lie to that promise, and the German forces massing in front of Leningrad threatened to give lie to it a second time. But the assault on one of Russia's second cities was complicated. With casualty rates rising, some of the troops assembling for the march on Moscow would have to be redeployed. There was also the logistics problem: Leningrad had nearly three million inhabitants. Who would feed them? In August Hitler provided an answer. He announced that it was his "firm decision to level the town and make it uninhabitable [so as to] relieve us of the necessity of having to feed the population." Once the city was razed, Hitler planned to turn it over to the Finns, who had contributed a significant force to the Leningrad front. Cognizant of the logistical problems the city posed, the Finns refused the gift, leaving Hitler with a public relations challenge. How could Germany starve Leningrad into submission without producing an international uproar? Joseph Goebbels, the Reich minister of propaganda, proposed a simple solution: destroy the city and blame the Russians. Other proposals included mollifying international opinion by allowing children and the elderly to leave Leningrad before razing it—and sealing the city off and surrounding it with electrically charged barbed wire fences and machine-gun installations. But none of the proposed plans addressed the serious risk of epidemic disease, which would ensue if several million malnourished people were forced to live in close quarters. Hitler ended the debate by reverting to a version of his original plan: destroy Leningrad with heavy artillery and aerial bombardment, then starve out the survivors.

On September 4, the first bombs fell on the city, and on the eighth Zhukov arrived in Leningrad to lead the defense. Aware that the city would be a priority German target, the municipal government began preparing for an attack in late summer. By the end of August almost seven hundred thousand people, mostly women and children, had been evacuated—and seventeen miles of barricades and antitank positions were erected. Shops, apartment buildings, and offices were surrounded by sandbags. Almost every street had its own barricade of stone or wood, and a network of fortified rifle and machine-gun positions snaked through the city center. Under Zhukov, the defense grew larger and more sophisticated. Antiaircraft guns were repurposed as antitank guns, and naval guns from the Baltic fleet were repurposed to provide support for infantry attacks and to defend armored trains. The NKVD was a heavy presence in Leningrad that autumn, but anecdotal evidence suggests that the people of Leningrad did not have to be coerced into defending their city. As the German danger grew in early September, a good part of the population made their own private assessment of the danger and decided to remain in the city and fight and die where they lived, surrounded by familiar place and faces. Like Stalin, Zhukov often saw humanity in the mass—as faceless tools to be used in the pursuit of a greater good. But in Leningrad he began to see people in the singular again. "The courage, endurance, and tenacity the ordinary people [of Leningrad] displayed that September impregnated itself on my memory for life," he wrote in his memoirs.

The defense of the city reached a climax in the third week of September. On the morning of the nineteenth Leningrad awoke to a tremendous barrage that roared throughout the day. Later that morning, German forces swept through the suburbs of the city, capturing one township after another. Along the approaches to Leningrad, the fighting disintegrated into a series of individual combats and for both sides every yard won or successfully defended was regarded as worth the sacrifice of a human life. The British historian Richard Overy believes a last concerted effort on the twentieth or twenty-first might have carried the Germans to the gates of Leningrad, but fate intervened in the form of Adolf Hitler. On September 20 the intelligence reports picked up a surprising piece of news: the Germans forces encircling Leningrad were digging in and sending their tanks and armored vehicles south where the forces for Operation Typhoon, the final assault on Moscow, were assembling.

In America that September the war was being fought in the newspapers, over backyard fences, in barrooms, and in barbershops. In a thousand hamlets and a hundred cities, pro- and anti-war forces argued back and forth—and the weapon of choice on both sides was the public opinion poll. In the bleak rudderless spring of 1941 pollster mania was at its peak. One day Gallup would report that 51 percent of the country believed America should enter the war; then, a few days later, Roper, the other major pollster of the era, would report that 56 percent of Americans believed the decision to go to war should be put to a national referendum.

A government report issued that spring found a significant portion of the country dissatisfied with the president's handling of domestic and international affairs. In April a series of brilliant German successes in the Balkans, the Western Desert, and along the Atlantic heightened the sense of national drift. "I feel very keenly something must be done," declared Henry Stimson, who was the secretary of war and one of the leading wise men of the era. "There is no leadership here at the center," he opined, "and I am beginning to feel very troubled at the lack of it." In a letter to the president, Churchill was blunter: "Mr. President, I am sure that you will not misunderstand me if I speak to you exactly what is on my mind," he wrote. "The one decisive counterweight I can see to balance the growing pessimism . . . would be if the United States would immediately range herself with us as a belligerent power."

Roosevelt did not reply to the letter.

That spring he was spending more weekends at his home in Hyde Park, and he seemed increasingly to seek solace in the mundane aspects of life. He rearranged his stamp collection, planned a Key West fishing trip for himself and Hopkins, roughed out a sketch for a hurricane-proof house, spoke to the Roosevelt Home Club in Hyde Park and to a group of Dutchess County schoolteachers. He was also eating and exercising less, and he required more sleep than he was used to. About these changes the president remained remarkably uncurious. When Edwin "Pa" Watson, the White House physician, appeared in the Oval Office to take his blood pressure, Roosevelt would roll up his sleeve and offer up his arm, but he evinced no interest in Watson's findings, which relieved Watson of the burden of telling him he had a life-threatening illness, diastolic hypertension. The other issues the president had to deal with that spring could not be manipulated as easily as Pa Watson's silence. Nonetheless, Roosevelt found a way.

In a fireside talk on May 27, Roosevelt had something to offer everyone. Secretary Stimson, Interior Secretary Harold Ickes, Navy Secretary Frank Knox, and the other hawks in the administration got the tough talk they wanted. They were, Roosevelt said, confronted with "a Nazi-provoked world war for world domination," he told one of the largest radio audiences of the era. "The war is approaching the brink of the western hemisphere itself. It is coming very close to home. . . . Our people and our government will not fail to meet the challenge." Then Roosevelt announced he was declaring an "unlimited state of emergency." It was a shocking announcement, but the doves in the administration—led by Cordell Hull, the soft-spoken, courtly secretary of state—were unworried. The most frightening thing about the president's unlimited state of emergency was its title. Left in place were most of the safeguards Roosevelt had created to keep America out of a shooting war, including the ban on arming American merchantmen—allowing them to carry matériel to belligerent nations (e.g., Britain)—or permitting US Navy vessels to convoy British merchantmen. Hull and the other isolationists wisely muted their criticism. The speech was a tremendous success with the American public. Roosevelt's favorability rating rose to 76 percent from 73 percent—and 95 percent of the thousands of letters that poured into the White House gave the speech a thumbs-up.

"You know I am a juggler," Roosevelt once told a colleague. "I never let my right hand know what my left hand does. I may have one policy for Europe and one diametrically opposed policy for North and South America. I may be entirely inconsistent, and, furthermore, I am perfectly willing to mislead and tell untruths if it will help win the war." In the early autumn of 1941 that kind of wizardry was becoming hard to sustain even for a master like Roosevelt. On the roads to the east of Smolensk, German troops were completing their final preparations for the march on Moscow, and in the Pacific, Japan and the United States were also only a misunderstanding away from a shooting war. A decade of aggressive expansion had made Tokyo the dominant power in the East and had earned it the displeasure of the United States, which increasingly viewed Japan as a threat to its commercial, political, and military interests in the Pacific region—and had telegraphed its displeasure by freezing Japan's assets in the United States and placing an embargo on the sale of oil, airplane parts, iron, and steel to Tokyo.

On August 28, the day that Kichisaburo Nomura, the Japanese ambassador, visited the White House, Japan's geopolitical options had been reduced to two: continue on its present course and risk a war with the United States—or reach an accommodation. If the famously sunny Nomura was sunnier than usual that August morning, there was a reason for that. Inside his briefcase was a proposal from Fumimaro Konoe, the Japanese prime minister. Like Nomura, Konoe was a geopolitical realist. In the note that Nomura presented to Roosevelt, Konoe proposed a détente. Japan would withdraw from Indochina and pledge not to attack Russia—in return for a modus vivendi with the United States.

However, by late August, events—not men—were increasingly in command. From the stormy latitudes of the North Atlantic to the exquisite meeting rooms of the Imperial Palace in Tokyo, to the roads beyond Smolensk, where the stubborn Soviet defense had persuaded the Japanese to abandon plans for a surprise attack and turn south to the thinly defended latitudes of Manila, Pearl Harbor, and Singapore, the prospects of maintaining the peace were growing ever-more challenging. On September 3, at a meeting of Japanese military and political leaders in the Imperial Palace, Admiral Osami Nagano, the naval chief of staff, warned his colleagues that Japan's window of opportunity was closing. "The enemy is growing stronger by the day," he said. "A timetable must be set. Military preparations must get under way." Alarmed by Nagano's bellicosity, the next morning Emperor Hirohito summoned his Lord Keeper of the Privy Seal, Koichi Kido, and instructed him to inform the military men that Hirohito would refuse to sanction a war as long as peace remained possible. A few hours later the conference room in the east wing of the palace again filled with military and civilian officials.

The mood in the room was aggressive. Even Konoe, the prince of peace, rode with the gods of war that morning. The empire would choose war, he declared, "if Japan was unable to achieve its minimum demands through diplomacy. Chief among the demands were: freedom to pursue

Japan's war against China unhindered, no further Anglo-American military buildups in the Asia-Pacific region, and a promise to increase economic cooperation with Japan."* The meeting concluded with near unanimity on one point: if by early October there was still no prospect of attaining Japan's demands by peaceful means, Tokyo would immediately open hostilities against the United States, Britain, and the Netherlands.

The lone dissenter was Hirohito. At the end of the meeting he took a piece of paper from his pocket "and in his high-pitched voice read a poem composed by his grandfather Emperor Meiji":

> *All of the seas in every quarter*
> *are as brothers to one another*
> *Why then do the winds and waves of strife*
> *rage so turbulently through the world*

According to reports, "all present were struck with awe" by the beauty of the poem.

However, it changed no minds.

IN THE ATLANTIC, THE WINDS of war also howled at gale force that October. On the seventeenth a U-boat torpedoed the USS *Kearny* off the coast of Iceland; eleven crew members were killed and twenty were injured in the attack.

TWO MONTHS EARLIER AND HALF a half world away, the war in the east also entered a new phase. It had long been the dream of Walther von Brauchitsch, commander in chief of the German army, and of Heinz Guderian, the "Panzer King" who emerged from the Battle of France a hero to every German schoolboy, and to a dozen other German generals to end the war in Moscow with a triumphant victory parade through Red Square. The generals' desire to seize the capital was not just a fit of vainglory, though that aspect played a part in their thinking. Moscow was the capital of the Soviet Union, a major communications center, and a hub of the Russian armaments industry; for reasons of both prestige and of

---

* Some of Konoe's defenders have argued unconvincingly that the tough stance he took at the war council was a ploy.

military necessity Stalin would be forced to defend the city with every available man, aircraft, and tank, thereby providing an opportunity to destroy what remained of the Red Army in a final decisive battle. Hitler listened to the arguments of his generals. Then he ignored them. "Only ossified brains could think of such an idea," he told Brauchitsch. On June 22 he had gone to war believing the road to victory lay in the destruction of the enemy's strategic assets, his factories and farms and industries—not in prestige targets; by mid-August Hitler felt vindicated. Though the summer fighting had produced more casualties than expected, the Ukraine—the breadbasket of the Soviet Union—was now a German breadbasket. Leningrad, Russia's second city and an important industrial center, was about to be encircled, and the German and Romanian forces on the north shore of the Black Sea were within striking distance of the Crimea and its vital petrochemical plants.

In this context Moscow now looked like a logical next step. "I will raze the damn city and in its place put an artificial lake with central lighting," Hitler declared. "The name Moscow will disappear forever." On September 6, he issued Order 35, authorizing an assault on the capital. Shortly thereafter the operation received a more martial name, Typhoon; a commander, Field Marshal Fedor von Bock; and a force of 1.9 million men, including four infantry armies and three panzer groups, which, combined, fielded over 2,500 tanks. The one serious weak point in the German plan was the Luftwaffe. It had lost over 1,600 aircraft in the summer fighting, and it currently had only 549 serviceable planes on hand.

Typhoon's battle plan was relatively simple. Two German armies would attack the Soviet forces defending the southern flank of Moscow, then drive north to the town of Vyazma, which was roughly parallel to Moscow, and push due east toward the capital.

On September 30, six days before the first winter snow, Guderian opened Operation Typhoon with a ferocious assault on the Bryansk front (a Soviet front was the equivalent of a Western army group), a key defensive point on the Red Army's southern flank. By October 3 the panzers had reached Oryol, another town on the southern flank, and the German descent had been so swift that Oryol's residents mistook the invaders for Russian troops and were waving and smiling when machine-gun fire began to rake the town square. Of the panic that ensued in Oryol and its environs, Vasily Grossman, a Soviet war correspondent, wrote,

I thought I'd seen . . . retreats before, but I'd never seen anything like this. . . . It was like a biblical exodus. Vehicles were traveling in eight lines, engines screaming hysterically. People driving huge flocks of sheep and cows over the fields, and farther [up the road] horse-drawn carts creaked along; thousands of carts covered with colored sackcloth, carrying refugees from the Ukraine. Ahead of the Ukrainians were crowds of pedestrians with sacks, bundles, and suitcases. It was not a stream, not a river; it was the slow movement of the flowing ocean, hundreds of yards wide from side to side. There were the black and white heads of children looking out from covered carts, the biblical beards of Jewish elders, the head scarves of peasant women, older men in Ukrainian caps, black-haired girls. In the evening, the frightened townsfolk took refuge in the fields to the east of Orel [Oryol] and turned their faces to the setting sun . . . Its rays were so broad and immense, it seemed to Grossman that they stretched down from heaven to earth like [a picture] of one of those terrible biblical scenes when the wrath of the heavenly powers comes down upon the earth.

A few days after the exodus, Grossman visited Leo Tolstoy's estate, which lies about 120 miles south of Moscow. Grossman was standing in the front yard, pondering the parallels between the scenes he had witnessed on roads outside Oryol and the scene in *War and Peace* where Princess Maria flees her estate to avoid the invading French, when Tolstoy's granddaughter Sofia Andreyevna appeared on the porch. She told Grossman she had come to the estate to rescue her grandfather's papers. The two talked for a while, then walked through Tolstoy's garden. Overhead a flight of German bombers was passing by. The planes hung in the big Russian sky for a moment, then turned north toward Vyazma.

Two days before the commencement of Operation Typhoon a flight of four DC-3s touched down at the Moscow airport. The fighter escort peeled off, the doors of the planes opened, and the two senior Anglo-American delegates to the Moscow Conference emerged into the afternoon sunlight. Averell Harriman, the leader of the American delegation, was a product of Groton and Yale, a successful banker, and a railroad tycoon. Like many men of his class and time, Harriman had been drawn to public service by a sense of noblesse oblige and a desire to be at the center of things. He had entered politics in the 1930s as a member of the National Recovery Administration, and he was currently a coordinator of the lend-lease program. Colleagues regarded Harriman as levelheaded, a skilled organizer, and politically ambitious.

Lord Beaverbrook, the leader of the British delegation, was born Max Atiken, the tenth son of an impecunious Canadian minister. Except for his title, there was nothing lordly about Beaverbrook. The greatest press baron of his generation had a gnomelike face that bordered on ugly. He dressed like a London bookmaker, had a loose relationship with the truth, and was infatuated by power, especially his own. Beaverbrook used the *Daily Express*, the crown jewel of his newspaper empire, to promote his favorite causes, which were as variable as Beaverbrook's promises. In the 1930s the *Express*, the largest-selling newspaper in the world at the time, was a fervent champion of appeasement. Now the Beaverbrook papers were promoting Russian aid just as fervently. Churchill, who had a transactional view of the Anglo-Soviet relationship, was prepared to abide his old friend's enthusiasm for Stalin, but only up to a point. On the eve of the Moscow Conference he reminded Beaverbrook: "Your function will be not only to aid in the forming of the plan to help Russia but to make sure we are not bled white in the process; and even if you find yourself affected by the Russian atmosphere I shall be quite stiff about it." Beaverbrook's enthusiasm for Russia also troubled Harriman. "B. seems disposed to hand over every conceivable American weapon or material to the Russians without counting the cost to Britain," he wrote in his diary.

The reception at the Moscow airport was somewhat awkward. The senior Soviet officials were unhappy about the slow trickle of Western aid, but, being seasoned diplomats, they knew when to display anger and when to hide it. Several of the younger Soviet diplomats at the reception had yet to master that skill. None of the younger men accused the Western visitors of wanting to fight the war to the last Russian, but the accusatory look in their eyes suggested that that was what they were thinking.

The short, powerfully built figure who greeted Harriman and Beaverbrook in his Kremlin office six hours later was more aloof than the Stalin who greeted Hopkins eight weeks earlier. When asked a question, Stalin would address his answer to the translator, as if trying to avoid eye contact. However, he was forthright about the military situation. Eight weeks earlier he had assured Hopkins that the Red Army would hold the same positions in the spring of 1942 that it had held in the summer of 1941. The two panzer groups lurking on Moscow's southern flank had blown up that prediction. The Soviet Union was fighting for survival now, and Stalin admitted it. "Moscow is the key to everything," he said. It must be held "at all costs. It is the nerve center of all Soviet operations." If worse came to worst, the Red Army would fall back to the Urals and fight from there, but that would mean abandoning Moscow and most of European Russia. Just the thought of that made Stalin almost sigh, "If Hitler had given us one more year, it would have been different."

On the drive back to the embassy that evening Harriman was surprised at how few German planes were in the air. When he mentioned this to a Russian colleague the next day, the colleague said that the Soviet antiaircraft crews had put the fear of God into the German pilots. But Harriman wondered if there might be a different explanation. The Germans expected to be in Moscow in a few weeks and wanted to take the city relatively intact.

The next evening Beaverbrook and Harriman may have been the first Westerners to experience the Dr. Jekyll and Mr. Hyde routine that Stalin would become notorious for later in the war. On the twenty-eighth they had encountered the aloof but polite Mr. Hyde. On the twenty-ninth the angry, menacing Dr. Jekyll was waiting for them in Stalin's office. A few sentences into the conversation, he abruptly accused his guests of "lacking good faith" and of wishing to see "the Soviet regime destroyed by Hitler." As proof, Stalin cited Britain's and America's failure to provide his armies with more tanks and aircraft. "The paucity of your efforts clearly shows you want to see the Soviet Union defeated," he said. In hopes of calming their host Harriman offered five thousand armored cars; Stalin dismissed the offer with the wave of the hand—the cars were "death traps," he sneered. As the minutes passed and the tension deepened, Stalin began pacing nervously up and down the room, smoking cigarette after cigarette. When Beaverbrook handed him a letter from Churchill, he ripped it open with his big peasant hands, briefly glanced at its contents—and then threw it, unread, on a table. When Molotov, who was also present, reminded him of the letter at the end of the meeting, Stalin nodded, put it in an envelope, and handed it unread to a clerk.

In his report on the Moscow Conference, Harriman noted that he and Beaverbrook had concluded that there were three possible explanations for Stalin's behavior at the second meeting.

1. He believed he would get more from the Anglo-Americans if he was tough.
2. He was unhappy with the aid package the Allies were offering. Or
3. He was concerned about the military situation.

Harriman and Beaverbrook guessed number three—and they were correct. The next day—September 30—Operation Typhoon began.

The operation immediately lived up to its name. Eighty thousand Soviet troops were killed in the Oryol, Bryansk region; fifty thousand were taken prisoner; and four thousand were wounded. Other strongpoints on Moscow's southern flank were also being overrun or were about to be. The most pivotal day in the battle was October 5. That morning a Soviet reconnaissance aircraft spotted a German panzer column twelve miles in length approaching the town of Yukhnov, which lay due west of Moscow. The pilot's report was unnerving—Bryansk was almost 240 miles from the capital; Oryol, 200; Yukhnov, barely 100—a quick two-day march. A second Soviet spotter plane was sent up. When its pilot verified the presence of the panzers, Lavrentiy Beria, the NKVD chief, threatened to have the commander of the air unit shot "for panic mongering." The road to Moscow was open.

"Mobilize everything you have," Stalin ordered the Moscow district command that afternoon. Later he chaired an emergency meeting of the State Defense Committee and ordered Zhukov, who was overseeing the defense of Leningrad, to return to Moscow immediately. He also summoned troops from Siberia, the Manchurian frontier, and from other regions of the Soviet Far East. In early September eight hundred thousand troops had been available to defend Moscow. At present there was only a ninety-thousand-man Soviet force to defend Moscow. On October 6, Moscow received its first snow of the season. For half a day the city looked as pristine as a Siberian forest in high winter. Then the sun came out, and the gray, filthy, battle-weary city emerged from the melting snow. "There is a mood of . . . catastrophe," wrote Peter Miller, a well-known Soviet historian.

"The shops are empty," Miller noted. "Even coffee has disappeared. . . . Pressure is increasing to evacuate the children, even though children's ration cards for milk were issued three days ago, which means they were assuming children would remain in the city. . . . Oryol has surrendered, Vyazma has been surrendered. . . . There is feeling of approaching catastrophe in the air. The mood is particularly bad today." On the seventh Zhukov, newly arrived from Leningrad, had a long talk with an ailing Stalin at his dacha. The meeting marked the beginning of a turning point in Stalin's leadership. He would remain in overall command of the war, but after almost six months of withdrawals and defeats, he was now prepared to take the advice of the professional soldiers. Zhukov's plan for the defense of Moscow was accepted almost without modification.

For Hitler, the early autumn of 1941 brought a renewed sense of optimism after a summer of heavy casualties, slackening momentum, and unprecedented logistic and supply difficulties. Unpaved Russian roads clogged German engines, wore out German tires, and destroyed German carburetors. Differences in German and Russian railway gauges slowed the flow of men and matériel to the front; and in the vast expanses of the Russian steppe, every mile conquered put the German infantrymen a mile farther away from the supply chain that provided them with food, medicine, and the other essentials of war. Operation Typhoon was intended to regain the momentum of June and early July, and by early October Hitler was convinced it had. He had seen the face of victory before—in France, in Norway, in Belgium, and in Poland—and this is what it looked like: mass Russian surrenders, unsustainable casualty rates, abandoned weapons, piled roadsides. Moscow would fall by November or early December. But—cautioned by the hard summer fighting and, perhaps, by the ghost of Napoleon—Hitler did not advertise his optimism. Only Joseph Goebbels, the minister of propaganda; Hermann Göring, the Reich marshal; and a few other intimates were privy to his confidence that victory was at hand. In public Hitler said little about the Moscow battle until a speech on October 4. The venue was the Berlin Sportpalast, a somber Teutonic structure that gained notoriety in the 1920s for its six-day indoor bicycle races and was now a favorite venue for the friends of the Reich. The autumn afternoon Hitler spoke, all of the stadium's fourteen thousand seats were filled. Wounded soldiers occupied the first row; Nazi officials, the party faithful, and curiosity seekers, the upper rows. Hitler stood silently on the podium, examining his notes as the guests took their seats. In repose like this, he could be the minor bureaucrat his father had been. Then he put down his notes and began, as he began many of his speeches, with a personal denunciation of his enemies. It was not the Soviet Union and Great Britain that wished to destroy the German people—it was Winston Churchill and Joseph Stalin. The peroration lasted a minute or two and served Hitler the way a warm-up serves an athlete. His eyes grew hypnotic, his clenched fist cut the air, his forelock became unstuck. His fleshy face tightened into an arc of anger. Then the man at the podium disappeared, replaced by a vengeful Germany in all her righteous wrath.

INTOXICATED BY THE SHOUTS OF "Heil Hitler!" he assumed a martial stance, folded his arms across his chest, and announced, "I've just come from the greatest battle in world history. . . . The Soviet enemy has been defeated and will never rise again."

Six days later Otto Dietrich, Hitler's press chief, announced to the world that Germany had won the war in the east. The setting for the announcement was the handsomely decorated theater hall at the Reich Ministry of Public Enlightenment and Propaganda in Berlin. The audience was a mixture of journalists from neutral and Axis countries and German officials in Nazi uniforms. Even officials who had never heard a shot fired in anger were given an Iron Cross to wear for the occasion. According to some accounts Dietrich deliberately delayed his appearance in the hall to heighten the drama. "For all military purposes," he began, "Soviet Russia is done with. The last remnants of the Red Army have been trapped in two steel vises, tightened daily by German forces. Upon the Red Army's fall, there will be nothing left but vastness of the undefended Russian steppe with all its agricultural and material treasure." When Dietrich finished, the German, Italian, and Romanian newspapermen leaped to their feet, arms outstretched in the Nazi salute. The American and Swedish journalists sat in the chairs and stared down at the floor.

CAMPAIGN IN THE EAST DECIDED. THE GREAT HOUR HAS STRUCK, the German papers proclaimed.

For the most part, the Soviet press dealt with the threat to Moscow by lying about it or ignoring it. On October 8, with the shops full of looters and with rumors that a German descent on the city was imminent, the lead article in the mass circulation *Pravda* was THE WORK OF WOMEN IN WARTIME. In this instance, however, reality was too powerful to be spun. The Luftwaffe had reduced a large swath of Moscow's office blocks and apartment buildings to hulks, and the factory district was empty except for a handful of small shops. Spurred by the State Defense Committee, between July and November 1941, 1,523 industrial plants were relocated to Siberia and Central Asia. Relocation of the Soviet government and of the international diplomatic community began on October 15. That morning hundreds of bureaucrats and diplomats arrived at a Moscow train station to await passage to Kuybyshev, a Volga town five hundred miles to the east. Stalin planned to follow the next day.

Late on the sixteenth Nikolay Ponomariev, Stalin's telegraphist, arrived at the designated rail station expecting to see Stalin pacing back and forth in front of his armored train. The train was there, as were Stalin's bodyguards, but not Stalin. His decision to remain in Moscow was last minute and may have arisen from a belief that his presence would strengthen morale—and perhaps also out of a sense of duty. There were already rumors of German penetrations into the suburbs, and, expecting the enemy's arrival to be imminent, shop owners were giving away food and whatever they had on hand. Outside the capital the roads were crowded with leave-takers eager to flee before Armageddon arrived. On the seventeenth, the capital was rife with rumors; some had Stalin arrested in a Kremlin coup, others had German paratroopers dropping into Red Square. In railway stations people fought each other for tickets on eastbound trains, and, as hunger deepened, Muscovites fought each other for pieces of week-old bread.

On the eighteenth the German army breached the Mozhaisk line, a hastily constructed double set of fortifications that the Red Army built in October. The line was the last major Soviet defensive position west of Moscow. On the nineteenth Stalin summoned members of the Politburo and asked if any of them were planning to leave Moscow. No one had the nerve to say yes, including the NKVD chief, Beria, who had been talking about fleeing east for several days. On the nineteenth, Stalin also introduced a new strategy to control civilian panic: "Use fear to crush fear." The NKVD was given license to use all means necessary to enforce the order. "It isn't peacetime," Vladimir Ogryzko, the NKVD commander in Moscow, told his units. "Nor are you going to shoot in the air. Of course not. You shoot them on the spot." Ogryzko warned that any officer who failed to implement the kill order immediately would himself be shot on the spot. On Zhukov's orders, demolition squads mined the city's bridges and railway junctions.

Though careful to hide it, by mid-October, Stalin's confidence was shaken. During a talk with Zhukov, who had been recalled from Leningrad to lead the defense of the capital, Stalin said, "You are convinced we shall be able to hold Moscow. I ask this with pain in my heart. Answer truthfully, as you are a communist."

Zhukov lied and said he was confident that the city could be defended. Stalin did receive one important piece of good news that autumn. From Tokyo Richard Sorge reported that the Japanese forces facing the Soviet frontiers in the Far East would not attack before the spring of 1942. That news allowed Stalin to move eight to ten divisions and a thousand tanks and aircraft west for the purpose of defending Moscow.

Amid the chaos and confusion some people were quietly preparing for the arrival of the new order. "Have you gone off your head?" an artist named Alexander Osmerkin asked a neighbor, who was preparing to flee Moscow. In Kiev, said Osmerkin, the Germans had set up a Social Revolutionary government. They were giving great support to the arts. They were, after all, the most cultured people in Europe. "I'm sure they won't persecute people like you and me," he said. "On the contrary, I am waiting for them impatiently. As you know, my wife is Jewish. Well, I'll tell her, 'You'll have to wear a Star of David on your sleeve for a while. But there will be no Cheka,'" he said, referring to the communist secret police.

In late October the *rasputitsa*—the season of mud and rain—spread across the battlefields to the north and south of the capital, and the miseries of war expanded to include chronically wet clothing, mud so dense it could pull a boot from a foot, frozen tanks and half-track engines, and a raw wind that stung the face and hands and made fingers difficult to move. Both sides experienced the miseries of the heavy weather equally, but the Russian soldier stood up to them more successfully. This was in part because he was acclimated to the harsh Russian winter; the "Siberian boys," as Muscovites called the troops arriving from the east, were beginning to appear in significant numbers; and the Russian soldier had a clearer idea of what he was fighting for. The fighting was not for conquest or glory or power or land. It was to defend a set of values and beliefs that can be best summed up in the term *Mother Russia*. "Even those of us who knew our government was wicked felt we must fight," said one veteran. "We knew that we would die, of course. But our children would inherit . . . a land free of the invader." On the German side the ghost of Napoleon loomed increasingly large as October became November and the season of deep snows and bitter winds swept across the steppe. "Most of the commanders were now asking: when are we going to stop?" General Günther Blumentritt, a veteran of the Moscow battles, wrote in his memoirs. They remembered what had happened to Napoleon's army. Most of them had read Caulaincourt's grim account of 1812. (General Armand de Caulaincourt was a companion of Napoleon's and one of his most influential biographers.) That book had a weighty influence at this time in 1941. "I can still see von Kluge [commander of Army Group Center] now, trudging through the mud from his sleeping quarters to his office and standing before the map with Caulaincourt's book in his hand," the general wrote. Exhausted and awaiting reinforcements, the Germans were regrouping on the evening of November 6 when Stalin addressed a gathering of the party faithful and senior administrators at the cavernous Mayakovskaya subway station in central Moscow. Tomorrow was the twenty-fourth anniversary of the Bolshevik Revolution, and over the years these night-before talks by Stalin had become part of the annual celebration.

Stalin was not a compelling speaker, but that night the setting and the circumstances lit a light within him. After several sharply worded paragraphs, he ended with a fiery sentence that brought the room to its feet: "If they want a war of animation, we shall give them one." The next morning, standing on a Kremlin balcony in a cold wind, he gave a Soviet version of Winston's Churchill's "Never Surrender" speech. "Comrades," he told the crowd assembled in Red Square, "the whole world is looking at you. . . . The enslaved peoples of Europe, who have fallen under the yoke of the German invader, look to you. A great liberation mission has fallen to you. Be worthy of this mission. The war you are waging is a war of liberation, a just war." Then Stalin evoked Alexander Nevsky, Dmitry Donskoy, and Suvorov, the general who drove Napoleon from Moscow—Russian, not communist, heroes. The crowd in the streets understood the message: this was a Russian war—a war to protect the motherland. When Stalin finished, the corps of drums of the Moscow Military Music School struck up a martial tune and for the next several hours cadre after cadre of young men marched out of Red Square and westward toward the sound of the guns.

The final battle for Moscow began eight days later. Field Marshal Bock, commander of Army Group Center, ordered the 3rd and 4th Panzer Armies to attack Moscow from the north; General Heinz Guderian would attack the capital from the south; and then the two forces would link up at Noginsk, a town twenty miles to the east of Moscow—and drive on the capital. However, by mid-November, frostbite cases were already beginning to reduce the German order of battle, and by Christmas they would claim a hundred thousand men—almost equal to the combat casualty rate. The bitter cold also disabled German tanks, trucks, and railway trains—and the unpaved Russian roads further complicated the movement of men and matériel.

Finally there was the German soldier. In Poland, Norway, and France his performance seemed to give truth to the old saw that in the end it is the quality of the soldier that wins battles. But in November 1941, the German soldier on the eastern front had been fighting for nearly six months, and presently he was fighting in temperatures as low as minus-ten and sometimes minus-twenty degrees, often without gloves, mufflers, heavy jackets, or any other form of winter clothing. Hitler had thought the war in the east would be won by the beginning of autumn, and he had failed to prepare for a winter campaign.

Initially, none of these difficulties seemed to matter. The frozen forest trails and ice-covered swamps to the north of the city allowed Bock's army to make steady progress. In the final weeks of November, the German forces slid southward toward Moscow, seizing one strategic town after another along the way: Klin, fifty miles to the north of the capital; Solnechnogorsk, forty-five miles to the north; and the Leningrad Highway, twenty-seven miles to the north. By November 27 German forces had reached the Moscow-Volga Canal, and after several days of brutal, often hand-to-hand fighting, they were forced to retreat. Within days the Soviets retook Krasnaya and Polyana and checked General Guderian's drive from the south—the second prong of the assault that was supposed to strangle Moscow into submission. At the beginning of December Bock consulted his maps and concluded that the opportunity for a strategic success had passed. Moscow would remain Russian until the spring of 1942.

The next few days passed in relative quiet. Then, on the morning of December 5, German soldiers awoke to the *whoosh!* of Katyusha rockets. Zhukov ordered four armies to the attack, and on the morning of December 6 tens of thousands of Siberians, Uzbeks, and Kazakhs came pouring out of the forests around the capital in thickly padded, white camouflage suits, and they fell upon an exhausted, confused enemy. The Russian counterattack, which pushed the Germans back a hundred miles along some parts of the front, would have been the biggest story of 1941 had not the next day been December 7.

5

ONE DAY IN DECEMBER

D ECEMBER 6, 1941, FELL ON A SATURDAY, AND, AS ON MOST
Saturday nights in the 1940s, America was listening to the radio
that evening. *Duffy's Tavern*, a favorite show with male listeners, was
playing on CBS, and Tommy Dorsey's band, which enjoyed a large
female following, was broadcast from the Mutual network. There was
also plenty of war news that evening. The Red Army had launched its
counteroffensive around Moscow hours earlier, and the international
press was abuzz with rumors of a Japanese assault on Thailand.

Still, to most Americans the war felt far away, especially on a Saturday night when, on the radio, you could also hear Frank Sinatra, the
new young heartthrob, sing "Nancy (with the Laughing Face)" on NBC
or Benny Goodman's swing band on the Mutual network. During the
summer of 1940 a visiting French journalist had described America "as
literally drunk with pacifism." A year later not much had changed.

The pacifism of the average American had many sources, but the
most immediate and powerful was the country's experience in the Great
War. For its 116,708 dead, the United States had amassed roughly $10
billion in still-unpaid European debt and precious little else. Beyond
that, millions of Americans had their own personal reasons for favoring
isolationism: Irish and German Americans because of a historic enmity

toward Britain, and isolationists of all nationalities because of a conviction that the only country an American should fight for was his own.

These views were manifest in the polls taken in the late summer and autumn of 1941. At the conclusion of the Atlantic Conference in August Roosevelt's popularity soared to 73 percent, but public support for staying out of the war scored a point higher. Two other polls taken in the late summer and early autumn of 1941 also found little appetite for war. The public said a flat no to a proposal that would permit draftees to serve outside the western hemisphere—and a reluctant yes to a measure that raised the current one-year draft term to eighteen months.

The draft extension act polled at 50 percent, better than the 27 percent rating for the proposal to permit US troops to serve outside the Americas but not well enough to silence the 45 percent of the population who disapproved of extending the draft. This group included isolationists, pacifists, religious leaders, and a significant portion of the political class. The draft extension passed the House of Representatives by a one-vote margin. The soldiers whose lives had been turned upside down by the draft extension expressed their feelings by plastering barracks and latrines with a witty new piece of graffiti, OHIO: Over the Hill in October, signifying the month the one-year draft term ended.

By the beginning of September 1941, Roosevelt, Hopkins, and other leading figures in the administration believed that the navy and army air forces were battle-ready. About public support for sending American forces into action, however, the president and his aides were less sure. Roosevelt was careful not to get too far ahead of public opinion, and in the late summer of 1941 his political instincts told him that only an unprovoked attack would send America into battle unified. On September 4 what might be called the gods of war provided the provocation: that morning the American destroyer USS *Greer* and a German U-boat exchanged shots off the coast of Iceland. The *Greer* provoked the incident. Alerted to the U-boat's presence by a British spotter plane circling overhead, the *Greer* went looking for a fight. A two-hour game of cat and mouse ensued over some the most forbidding seas in the world. Then, having avoided the *Greer*'s depth charges for a final time, the U-boat vanished back into the wild latitudes of the North Atlantic.

The *Greer* figured prominently in Roosevelt's address to the nation on September 11. But in the president's version of events there was no British plane circling overhead and no attempt by the *Greer* to sink the

U-boat with depth charges. "This was piracy—piracy legally and morally," the president told an audience of several million listeners. "We have sought no shooting war with Hitler. We do not seek it now. But . . . when you see a rattlesnake poised to strike, you do not wait from him to strike before you crush him." Though it polled well, the speech did not change many minds. As Roosevelt's biographer James MacGregor Burns noted, the only polling question of the era that almost always received the same answer was: Do you think the United States should go to war? "Then the people shrank from action," Burns said.

In a Navy Day speech on October 27, Roosevelt again attempted to mobilize public opinion, this time in a more unorthodox fashion. His subject that evening was another incident at sea. Eleven days earlier a second American destroyer, the USS *Kearny*, was attacked by a U-boat off the coast of Iceland, and this time there were casualties; eleven sailors were killed. "We have wished to avoid shooting, but the shooting has started," Roosevelt told a radio audience of millions. The next part of his presentation can only be described as surreal. He told his listeners that he had in his possession two secret Nazi documents. One was the blueprint of a German plan that would realign South America and Central America and make them into five vassal states. The other was a Hitler-like plan to abolish all religions. The day after the speech Churchill cabled Roosevelt that he was "deeply moved by your wonderful speech." American reaction to the speech was muted, perhaps because people sensed that there were no secret Nazi documents. Roosevelt wasn't idly boasting when he said he was prepared to do just about anything to defeat Hitler.

Three days later public sentiment about the war was again tested— this time in an unprecedentedly provocative manner. A U-boat torpedoed the USS *Reuben James* in the North Atlantic, killing 115 members of its crew. As news of the attack spread across the country there were expressions of sadness and indignation but only muted cries for revenge. "Even the President, with all his rhetorical gifts, was unable to stir the nation to anger," playwright and Roosevelt aide Robert Sherwood wrote in a postwar memoir. By the middle of November 1941 events had rendered Roosevelt "relatively powerless" to move public opinion. "He had said everything . . . that could be said," Sherwood wrote. "He had no more tricks left. The hat from which he had pulled so many rabbits was empty. The President of the United States was now a creature of circumstance, which [would] be shaped not by his will . . . but by the unpredictable determination of his enemies."

Sherwood was also puzzled by the placidity of the American public. If after a year and a half of strident anti-German propaganda the public remained willing to turn the other cheek on an incident as grave as the *Reuben James*, how would Americans react if Japan, which the American press was treating more gingerly, attacked the big British naval base at Singapore—or invaded Australia? "Would the country be willing to sacrifice American blood to defend parts of the world most Americans had never heard of?" Sherwood wondered. Would Americans be willing to die to defend outposts of the British Empire? In early November, with peace still polling at a healthy 63 percent, the chairman of the isolationist America First Committee challenged Roosevelt to ask Congress for a declination of war. Knowing he would lose, the president declined.

"Good morning, Commander! Honolulu sleeps!"

"How do you know?" Captain Mitsuo Fuchida asked the young officer seated across the table from him. It was a little after 3:00 A.M. on December 7, 1941, and the rising sun was painting the sea with shards of light. Belowdecks on the *Akagi*, which was one of the six strike carriers in the Pearl Harbor task force, a maintenance crew was inspecting a group of fast but accident-prone Zero fighters. The top deck was empty except for the occasional pilot surfacing from a briefing to have a cigarette and for Fuchida, who was pacing back and forth feverously in the morning wind. Fuchida's postwar life as a Christian evangelist would baffle his countrymen. In national memory, he remained the lanky, hard-faced airman who'd led the strike on Pearl Harbor. Fuchida arrived over Pearl Harbor a little after 7:40 that morning. Behind him a 360-plane strike force filled almost two miles of sky. In the soft morning light the harbor and its environs looked serene: neat rows of barracks and aircraft; a white highway winding gently through the hills above the harbor; battleships neatly anchored two by two along the mooring quays; a group of young sailors in T-shirts tossing a baseball back and forth. When one of those sailors looked up and saw a large group of planes circling in the distance he assumed they were on maneuver and he went back to the game.

A few moments later another large group of planes swooped out of the sky. The radio operators on duty assumed the planes were attached to the flight of B-17s that were due to arrive at Hickam Field later in the morning. At 7:49 A.M. Fuchida scanned the harbor a final time, then reached for the microphone in his plane and shouted, "All squadrons, plunge to the attack!" A few moments later Honolulu awoke to the sound of exploding ships.

Just shortly after 9:00 P.M. the previous evening Roosevelt and Hopkins were talking in the president's study when a young naval officer appeared with a deciphered message from Tokyo to the Japanese ambassador, Kichisaburo Nomura. The message was in thirteen parts, with a fourteenth to come. Roosevelt didn't need the fourteenth part. "This means war," he said as he handed the decryption to Hopkins, who scanned it and said he agreed. The president's initial impulse was to summon Admiral Harold Stark, but he changed his mind. Paging the chief of naval operations from a crowded Washington theater on a Saturday night would immediately raise questions and fears. Tonight America would have a final opportunity to listen to Glenn Miller, Tommy Dorsey, and the latest episode of *Fibber McGee and Molly* in peace.

"My God, this can't be true!" Frank Knox declared. It was 1:40 the following afternoon, and a bulletin from Pearl Harbor was clattering across a teletype in the Navy Department. Knox, the navy secretary, was surprised. For the last few months conventional wisdom held that if Japan did attack, the attack would follow the German model: go after soft targets first—these being the Asian equivalents of Austria and Poland—and leave Russia until last. Pearl Harbor was not Russia, but it was home to the United States' formidable Pacific fleet. Forty-five minutes later, the US Army Signal Corps established contact with Honolulu, and the president was able to speak to Joseph Poindexter, the governor of the territory. Midway through the conversation Roosevelt suddenly turned white and shouted to his press secretary, Steve Early, "My God! There's another wave of Jap planes over Hawaii right this minute!"

As the drama in the Pacific unfolded, the president put in a call to Secretary of State Cordell Hull. It was a little after 2:00 P.M., and outside Hull's window the Washington streets were filled with Christmas shoppers. The war would not enter their lives for another hour or two. Roosevelt instructed Hull to read the statement. Nomura and Special Envoy Saburo Kurusu saw them to the door. Hull had his own ideas about how to deal with his visitors. The secretary was as famous for his Christian rectitude as for his sanctimonious speeches, but Nomura and Kurusu had lied to him for weeks, and Hull's Christian charity was exhausted. When the envoys arrived in his office, he made them stand in front of his desk like errant schoolboys while he pretended to read the Japanese statement, a copy of which he had seen earlier in the day. Upon finishing, Hull told his guests that "in all my fifty years of public service I have never seen a document that was more crowded with infamous falsehoods and distortions so huge that I never imagined until today that any government on this planet was capable of them." When Nomura attempted to reply, Hull pointed to the door and nodded.

News of the Pearl Harbor attack arrived at Chequers in the midst of a cheerless Sunday evening dinner party. Mrs. Churchill, feeling unwell, had retreated to her bedroom, and the prime minister's old nemesis—the black dog, depression—had arrived earlier in the day and appeared to be planning to stay for dinner. An interesting new guest might have shaken him out of his depression, but that evening there were only the usual familiar faces: Major General Hastings "Pug" Ismay; Commander Tommy Thompson, Ismay's aide-de-camp; John Winant, the American ambassador; and Averell Harriman and his daughter Kathleen.

Churchill spent most of the evening brooding in his chair. Then, at a little after nine, Sawyer, the prime minister's butler, appeared in the dining room with a small flip-top radio. The BBC presenter led with a report on an Anglo-German tank battle in Libya. From the tone of his voice, Harriman guessed the British were on the losing end of the encounter. Then the presenter circled back and gave a more detailed account of the day's other stories, including a new one that had just come over the wire.

"Japanese aircraft have raided Pearl Harbor, the American naval base in Hawaii," the presenter said. "The announcement of the attack was made by President Roosevelt. The principal Hawaiian Island of Oahu has also been attacked. No further details are yet available."

Churchill immediately put in a call to Washington. "What's this I hear about Japan?" he asked.

"They have attacked us at Pearl Harbor," Roosevelt replied. "We're all in the same boat now."

Before ringing off, Roosevelt said he planned to ask Congress for a declaration of war the next morning. Churchill said Britain would follow suit immediately thereafter. When Knox, Hopkins, Secretary of War Henry Stimson, Army Chief of Staff General George Marshall, and the other members of the president's ad hoc war council gathered in the

White House at around 3:00 that afternoon the mood in the capital was somber but not defeatist. The casualties had yet to be counted, that fact allowing the White House to blame the attack solely on the Japanese. However, as the days passed and the number of military deaths rose, the president and his aides began to fear that the White House would come in for sharp criticism. And the president was vulnerable on several accounts, noted historian Nigel Hamilton, the author of a generally sympathetic account of Roosevelt's presidency. "Against the advice of his war council, [Roosevelt] persisted in perusing a meandering course of initial appeasement . . . followed by belated military posturing—all carried out in spite of . . . ominous signs of imminent Japanese hostilities," Hamilton wrote. He "refused to order a preemptive attack on Japanese forces [that were] . . . clearly massing for a new invasion of Southeast Asia. And he discouraged the British from launching a preemptive strike against a Japanese force approaching their base at Singapore."

Labor Secretary Frances Perkins, who was at the White House on the evening of the seventh, said Roosevelt was having "a dreadful time . . . knowing that the navy was caught unawares, that bombs dropped on ships that were not in fighting shape and not prepared to move." The casualty figures released to the press after the attack put the dead at 2,403 and put the number of ships sunk or badly damaged at 19, including 8 battleships, 4 of which were destroyed beyond repair. But the losses in the secret report that Winston Churchill was given privy to during his visit to the United States "were considerably higher than [those] given to the press." Despite the scale of the Pearl Harbor disaster, the congressional inquiry that followed, and the taunts from the isolationists, Roosevelt retained the trust of the American people. For the thousands of men and women who gathered outside the White House on the evening of December 7—and for the millions who would listen to his declaration of war the next day—Roosevelt was a father figure as well as a national leader. He had seen the country safely through a great depression and the citizens were confident that now he would see them safely through a great war.

THE DAY AFTER THE PEARL Harbor attack, Anthony Eden, the British foreign secretary, was lying in the sick bay of the HMS *Kent* with a bad case of gastric flu when an unexpected piece of news arrived from London. Churchill had decided to go to America at some point in mid-December. Eden immediately protested. He was scheduled to depart for Russia in a few hours, and he felt it would look bad from a political and a public relations perspective if the prime minister and the foreign secretary both left the country in the middle of a war. But Churchill was no more willing to listen to Eden than he was Roosevelt, who had suggested the prime minister put off his visit until January. Cables flew back and forth between Downing Street and northern Scotland, where the *Kent* was docked. When the last cable from London arrived the prime minister was still going to Washington sometime in mid-December and Eden was still going to Moscow in a few hours.

Eden was not looking forward to the trip. The Russian passage was the naval equivalent of the stations of the cross. It involved five days through U-boat-infested waters in howling winds and rough seas to Murmansk on the northern tip of the Soviet Union; then—depending on how often the train crew had to stop to clear the tracks of snow—a five- or six-day trip from Murmansk to Moscow.

As the *Kent* made its way north on the Murmansk leg of the journey the sky fell below the horizon, and the daylight hours shrank to a thin ribbon of cold light that appeared for an hour each day around noon. Farther north the light disappeared completely; the temperature fell to minus-fifteen degrees Celsius; and for four days the *Kent* sailed through a roiling sea in complete darkness. On the fifth day Murmansk appeared and the sky filled with color again. There was a rich, lemony glow on the southern horizon and bloodred Soviet flags flapped over the town's streets and piers. Sir Alexander Cadogan, one of the British delegates, thought the kits of the Russian honor guard looked faintly mauve against the freshly fallen snow.

Five days later an unsmiling Stalin greeted Eden in his Kremlin office with a long list of complaints that included Britain's refusal to open a second front in the west to relieve pressure on the Soviet Union— and the slow trickle of British military aid. Behind these complaints was a more global concern. Churchill had been a vocal anti-communist all his adult life. Could his promises of support be trusted? The Moscow Charter, the document Eden presented to Stalin on December 16, was intended to allay Soviet concerns about British support. It included several proposals for Anglo-Soviet cooperation, including assistance with postwar reconstruction and economic aid. When Eden finished talking, Stalin offered some general observations; then he brought up the subject he really wanted to discuss: Europe's postwar borders. Given that the German army had been at the gates of Moscow two weeks earlier and remained a formidable force, it seemed premature to be talking about postwar borders. Eden said he was not authorized to discuss the border issue, and he guided the conversation back to the safer ground of postwar reconstruction.

The following night Stalin and Eden met again, this time in a Kremlin office decorated with oversize photos of Lenin, Stalin, and Marx. Also present were the witty, abrasive Alex Cadogan, the permanent under secretary at the Foreign Office, and Stafford Cripps, the British ambassador to Russia—and an important figure in left-wing London circles; he acted as Eden's second. The affable Maisky and the sinister Molotov acted as Stalin's seconds. The meeting offered another example of the technique Stalin used on Beaverbrook and Harriman. In her book *Churchill and Eden at War*, historian Elisabeth Barker described it thusly: "At the first meeting with a visiting dignitary, Stalin would be 'pleasing and warm'; at the second meeting 'piercing and icy'; and at the third 'moderate and glowing'—so that the visitor left Stalin's presence 'grateful for small mercies.'"

On his second visit to the Kremlin, Eden met the Stalin of the purges, the pogroms, and the gulags. The issue that had him so agitated was, again, the Soviet Union's postwar borders. In 1939 and 1940—sensing war was imminent—Stalin had created a buffer zone. Before reaching Soviet soil the Germans would have to fight their way through and around the annexed Baltic states of Estonia, Lithuania, and Latvia. Now flush with victory after the successful defense of Moscow, Stalin wanted Britain to recognize the annexed territories as members of the Union of Soviet Socialist Republics. When Eden demurred a second time, saying that Britain and the United States had pledged not to discuss border issues until after the war, Stalin became undiplomatically blunt. He described himself as "surprised and amazed that Mr. Churchill's government refuses to recognize the Soviet Union's claims in the Baltics and eastern Europe," and he said, "If [Britain] can't give us support on this question . . . I think it will be better to postpone our [other] agreements." He added, "If our people were to learn that, after all their sacrifices, Great Britain, our ally, was reluctant to support the claims of the USSR to the Baltic States . . . they would regard our treaties [with Britain] as scraps of paper."

Eden returned to his hotel that night feeling vexed. Roosevelt and Churchill were adamant about leaving border discussions until the end of the war, but they were speaking out of principle; by contrast Stalin was speaking from facts on the ground. In December 1941, 90 percent of the German army was fighting in Russia, and, at a cost of two million dead, the Soviets had fought that army, the best in the world, to a standstill. Eden went to bed that night debating with whom Britain should side—Stalin or Roosevelt—and wondering if there was any truth to the rumors of secret Soviet-German talks.

ON DECEMBER 10, TWO DAYS after Eden left for Moscow, Winston Churchill was reading a packet of dispatches in his bedroom when the telephone rang. The voice on the other end of the line was familiar, but the caller had a "sort of odd cough," Churchill thought. After Admiral Dudley Pound collected himself, which took a few seconds, he announced to the prime minister that he had some bad news. "I have to report to you that the *Prince of Wales* and the *Repulse* [the latter, the ship that carried Churchill to the Placentia Bay conference] have been sunk off the coast of Malaysia." Tom Phillips, the *Prince of Wales*'s commander, went down with the *Wales*. Later Churchill would say that he was grateful he was alone when Pound called. "In all the war, I never received such a direct shock. There were now no British or American capital ships in the Indian Ocean or the Pacific, except the American survivors of Pearl Harbor, who were hurrying back to California. Over all this vast expanse of water Japan was supreme, and we, everywhere, were weak and naked."

When news of the Japanese attack reached the Wolf's Lair, the Führer's headquarters in East Prussia, the Führer "slapped his thighs with delight" and declared, "We simply can't lose the war now. We have a partner who has never been beaten in three thousand years." Goebbels also saw ultimate victory in the news from Pearl Harbor. "It will greatly strengthen our position in the Middle East, the Atlantic, and North Africa," he declared. Joachim von Ribbentrop, the German foreign minister, agreed with Goebbels up to a point: Japan's entry into the war would strengthen Germany's international position. But Ribbentrop saw no benefit in declaring war on the United States. Germany was already facing two major powers. Furthermore, a declaration of war was unnecessary to keep America out of Europe. Pearl Harbor, the Philippines,

Guam, the Midway Islands—the United States' interests in the Pacific would keep the Americans tied down in the that region for years. Hitler could not be persuaded. "If we don't stand on the side of Japan the pact is politically dead," he told Ribbentrop. On December 10 Germany declared war on the United States. The next day Hitler thanked providence for entrusting him "with the waging of a historic struggle which will decisively fashion not only our German history for the next thousand years but also the history of Europe." He chided Roosevelt for running up America's national debt, and he declared that the Japanese attack "at Pearl Harbor fills all . . . decent people of the world with profound satisfaction." He blamed the "eternal Jew" for Bolshevism, and, in a failed attempt at humor, he likened the Atlantic Charter to "a bald hairdresser recommending his unfailing hair restorer."

Eleven days later—on December 22—the HMS *Duke of York* delivered Churchill to Hampton Roads, Virginia. Plans called for the Churchill party to proceed up the Potomac to Washington by water; but at the last moment the prime minister had a change of mind and ordered up a plane to fly him and his entourage to the capital. Three-quarters of an hour later Churchill's physician, Charles Wilson, along with Lord Beaverbrook and Averell Harriman, were circling above the capital in a Lockheed Lodestar. Looking down at Christmas lights twinkling in the crowded streets, Dr. Wilson was visited by a feeling he had not had since the September morning that the weary voice of Neville Chamberlain announced that Britain and Germany were at war: a sense of security. There were no anxious searchlights scanning the sky, no ambulances screeching through bombed-out streets—just happy shoppers and street-corner Santas. Above Washington National Airport, the Lockheed made a slow circle in the twilight sky, then dipped its nose downward and landed on a restricted section of the airfield, where Roosevelt awaited the British guests. After meeting the president, Wilson concluded that Churchill was right: Roosevelt had a "majestic head." An hour later an annoyed Eleanor Roosevelt was asking an aide why no one had told her that the prime minister was coming for a visit—and Churchill was standing atop a table in the White House press room, puffing on a cigar and exchanging snappy barbs with the Washington press corps. "That night I went to bed and slept the sleep of the saved," Churchill wrote later. "The United States was in the war up to its neck and to the death." Thus ended the first day of what would be called the Arcadia Conference.

The smooth working relationship that Churchill and Roosevelt developed owed something to personal chemistry. Roosevelt kept his deeply forested interior hidden under layers of irresistible charm, and Churchill, aware of the importance of establishing a personal relationship with the president, assumed the role of a Sancho Panza to Roosevelt's Don Quixote. In the evening, after cocktails, the prime minister would sometimes wheel Roosevelt from the drawing room to the elevator. In the days following Pearl Harbor, the public outcry for a Japan-first strategy briefly strained Anglo-American relations; even the isolationists were demanding vengeance. But Roosevelt stood by the pledge that the United States had made to Britain the previous spring: if America entered the war, it would fight a holding action in the Pacific until Germany, the more dangerous enemy, was defeated.

On the evening of his arrival at the White House, Churchill proposed an amendment to the Germany-first strategy: keep Germany as the main enemy but move the battlefield from Europe—where the Anglo-American forces could easily become ensnared in another long, bloody war of attrition—to North Africa, where the terrain offered room for maneuver, lessening the prospect of heavy casualties, and where the Germans only had a few panzer divisions and a weak Italian ally. Roosevelt was intrigued by—even enamored of—Churchill's idea. Henry Stimson and George Marshall were not. Neither man could see much value in sending hundreds of thousands of troops to North Africa to fight a war that could only be won in Europe, and neither was shy about sharing his opinion with the president. The following evening, the prime minister found Roosevelt less enthusiastic, but this was only the beginning of the Anglo-American discussion on strategy—and Churchill's powers of persuasion were formidable.

On Christmas Eve afternoon Churchill and Roosevelt put aside the war for a few hours and attended a ceremony on the White House lawn. The next day the Washington papers would credit the unseasonably warm weather for the large crowd, estimated at twenty thousand, that gathered on the White House lawn. But fear and loneliness also helped to swell the numbers. Five days earlier the term of military service had been extended to the duration of the war plus six months, this at a time when even the president's sons were disappearing into the training camps across the country at a rapid rate. A few days before Christmas Eleanor Roosevelt was speaking to a young friend, Joseph Lash, when she suddenly broke down and burst into tears. Lash thought Mrs. Roosevelt was upset by some difficulty in her work at the Office of Civilian Defense, but that was not it. She and the president had just said goodbye to their duty-bound sons James and Elliott. They had to go to service, of course; she said seeing them take the risk in leaving was hard. "If only by the law of averages not all her boys would return," Lash understood.

As the final fragments of light disappeared behind the Virginia hills, the president appeared on a balcony, pressed a button—and the White House lawn turned a shimmering white. Roosevelt's speech was brief. "Our strongest weapon in this war is the conviction of the dignity and brother-hood of man, which Christmas Day dignifies," he told the crowd gathered outside the White House gates. By the time he introduced Churchill to the crowd as "my old and good friend," there was a slight chill in the air and a crescent moon overhead.

"I spent this anniversary and festival," the prime minister began, "far from my country, far from my family. Yet I cannot truthfully say that I feel far from home. . . . Here, in the midst of war raging and roaring all over the lands and seas, creeping nearer to our hearts and homes, here, amid all the tumult, we have tonight the peace of the spirit in each cottage home. . . . Here then, for one night only, each home . . . should be a brightly lighted island of happiness and peace."

In a speech to Congress the next day, Churchill demonstrated his ability to make even anger sound eloquent. "What sort of people do they think we are? Is it possible they don't realize that we shall never cease to persevere against them until they have been taught a lesson which they and the world will never forget?"

IT WOULD BE AN EXAGGERATION to say that George Marshall enjoyed a deity-like status in 1940s Washington—but not a large exaggeration. Six feet tall, sturdy of build, with sandy hair, chilled features, and cobalt-blue eyes, Marshall was variously described by newspapers of the era as intimidating, aloof, and Olympian. But the word that most often attached itself to the general was *authoritative*. Gerald Johnson, a War Department official, once noted that "seeing Marshall in civilian cloth-ing, a newspaper boy might not know *who* he was, but the boy would know *what* he was: Lawful Authority." Even the president, who rou-tinely addressed subordinates by their first names, made an exception for Marshall, having once addressed him as *George* and been chastised by the indignant stare of Lawful Authority thereafter. Roosevelt made it a practice to address him as *General Marshall*. The Arcadia Conference would catapult the general from national to international prominence. Each morning during the conference he—along with Admiral Harold Stark, the chief of naval operations, and General Henry "Hap" Arnold of the US Army Air Corps—would walk over to the Federal Reserve Building, north of Foggy Bottom, to meet with their British counterparts: Admiral Dudley Pound, Air Chief Marshal Sir Charles Portal, and Field Marshal Sir John Dill. Officially, Marshall's charge was to represent the American point of view; but, after the initial meeting at the Federal Reserve Building, he came away convinced that the first order of business had to be imposing unity on an Anglo-American coalition deeply divided by differences about how and where to fight the war, as well as doubts about each other's military competence.

In the Great War the cream of the British Empire had marched into the mud of northwest France and Flanders, and they were slaughtered—there was no other word for it. At the end of that war nearly a million British and Commonwealth soldiers were dead, and in every corner of the empire the cry went up: "Never again!" The peripheral strategy that Britain adopted after Dunkirk was a weaponized version of "Never again!" Sea power and airpower, bolt-and-run raids on the European continent, a land campaign in peripheral regions like the Middle East and Italy—all of these would so weaken Germany, the theory went, that the culminating campaign—the invasion of Europe—would be a walkover. The American war plan was more audacious. As part of his new victory program, in the early autumn of 1941 Roosevelt asked army and navy planners to determine how large an arsenal the United States would need to defeat the country's potential enemies. The planners answered that question and then addressed a question that Roosevelt had not asked: How large a force would be required to defeat Germany in the field in Europe? Major Albert Wedemeyer, a senior American planner, estimated that a campaign of that scale would require 215 divisions, which worked out to an army of nine million men, including support troops. And that force would have to be heavily armored.

Field Marshal Dill summarized the British view of Wedemeyer's plan in a few pithy sentences: the Americans "have not, repeat 'not,' the slightest conception of what war means, and their armed forces are more unready for war than it is possible to imagine." Dill was not alone in thinking that the inexperienced Americans had little understanding or experience of real war. "Of uncertain value" and "unfit for current operations" was the general British view of the American soldier, while the American view of the British soldier could be summed up in a single word: *Dunkirk*. There was a measure of truth in both assessments. During a December 26 meeting at the Federal Reserve Building, Marshall proposed a solution. "I am convinced there must be one man in command of the entire theater: ground, air, and ships," he said. "Cooperation is not enough." During the Great War the French, British, and Belgians (and eventually the Americans) had conducted their own campaigns, and for four years Allied gains were measured in kilometers and Allied deaths were counted in the hundreds of thousands. Only in 1918, when Marshal Ferdinand Foch became overall commander of the Allied forces, was victory finally attained.

Later that afternoon, Marshall summoned one of his subordinates, a brigadier named Dwight Eisenhower, and gave him a blunt order: write a paper so persuasive it would put to rest the primary military objection to unity of command. The Eisenhower whom Marshall summoned that afternoon was not yet the Eisenhower of history. He was still Ike Eisenhower with a smile as big as the Kansas sky he was raised under, a little self-conscious about his lack of combat experience, and full of funny stories about Douglas MacArthur, under whom he had "studied drama" in the Philippines. He was also a quick study: on the morning of December 27 Secretary of War Stimson and Roosevelt approved Eisenhower's paper on unity of command. The British were slower to embrace unity of command, but by the end of the conference Churchill had given it his imprimatur. The culminating event of the Arcadia Conference was the Declaration of the United Nations. The principal author was Roosevelt, and the name was provided by Churchill. Its principal goal was to extend the pledges that Britain and America had made to include a wider swath of humanity.

On the evening of January 1, 1942, the United States, Britain, the Soviet Union, and China signed the charter. The next day twenty-three other nations pledged to "defend life, liberty, independence and freedom of conscience" to foreswear a separate peace and to use all available resources to defeat the Axis powers. The declaration made no mention of international peacekeeping, but that would be one of its legacies. Seventy-five years of peace, however fragile, would be another.

6

THE WORST OF TIMES

THE BATTLE OF MOSCOW WAS GERMANY'S FIRST EXPERIENCE OF serious defeat. Army Group Center arrived at the gates of Moscow as a coherent unit, capable of assembling its constituent parts into a single, powerful strike force. But by December 10—the fourth day of the Soviet counteroffensive—the strike force had fragmented into dozens of individual combats, fought in isolation by units frostbitten, riddled with dysentery, and half-drunk on schnapps. On December 10, with the temperature fallen to minus-sixty-three degrees Celsius, many men died while performing their natural functions in the open.

Out of the 100,000 cases of frostbite that Army Group Center sustained, 14,357 cases—in other words, the strength of a German division—were classified as major. In these cases the patient sometimes required one or more amputations. Sixty-two thousand were listed as moderate—the patient was totally incapacitated but did not require amputation. The men who were not classified in the major or moderate categories were considered fit to return to service within ten days.

The German officer corps underwent an amputation of a different kind. Thirty-five corps and divisional commanders were sent home in varying states of disgrace. Hitler made many grave strategic errors during the war, but, in retrospect, the stand-your-ground order he issued during the German retreat from Moscow seems not to be one of them. "Any attempt to withdraw from positions . . . without fuel or service-able vehicles, to retreat across the drifting snow fields at a rate that could not be more than three or four miles a day would have resulted in the whole German army being cut to pieces," says historian Alan Clark. "Better to stand and fight it out, relying on the innate tenacity and disci-pline of the German soldier."

The German defeat had another important consequence. It made Stalin overconfident. At a meeting on January 5 he outlined his auda-cious plan for 1942 to an audience that included Zhukov, Timoshenko, and several other generals and members of the Politburo. "The Germans are in disarray," Stalin told his guests. "They've prepared badly for the winter." He continued, "Our task is . . . to give [them] no time to draw breath. [We must] drive them to the west and force them to use up all their reserves before spring comes." He wound up his speech by saying, "This is the time for a general offensive!"

For all their differences, Hitler and Stalin did share one common-ality: both men overrated their military skills. A few defeats down the road Stalin, though not Hitler, would recognize his limitations and begin listening to the professional soldiers. But at the beginning of 1942 that time was still far off. The plan he outlined on January 5 ignored the large losses the Red Army had sustained in front of Moscow, the exhaustion of the survivors, and the continuing German superiority in weaponry. Grandiose in scale, Stalin's plan would play out in phases, across a thou-sand miles of snow-covered front. Following the liberation of Leningrad, one Soviet force would encircle a wounded Army Group Center and destroy it while a second attacked German positions in the Ukraine. In a private conversation with Stalin on the fifth, Zhukov had warned him that the Red Army was too weak to sustain a general offensive in the height of winter. The defense of Moscow had left the army short of armor, artillery, aircraft, and ammunition. Focus on a single goal, Zhukov urged: the destruction of Army Group Center. It was the most powerful component of the German war machine. Marshal Boris Shaposhnikov, the Red Army's chief of staff, agreed with Zhukov, but he framed the readiness issue in a different way. Russia, he said, "still needed to assim-ilate the experience of modern war. Neither here nor today will the out-come of the war be decided. . . . The crisis is still far off."

On January 10 the Red Army went over to the offensive, and a war of animation descended upon a thousand-mile front. Offensives were launched to relieve Leningrad and the Ukraine and to complete the destruction of Army Group Center. Initially, the results were promising, but then German troops from Norway, Belgium, France, and other regions of the Reich descended on the Red Army, and the German front stabilized. In February, when Stalin announced that Germany had lost the advantage, the citizens of Leningrad were facing the white death of starvation, and a snowfall of exceptional heaviness and steel-hard frozen ground had made it difficult for Russian units to create even rudimentary defensive positions. For the men fighting it, the war was no longer about victory, honor, territory, glory, or a sense of duty. It was about a roofed cabin to sleep in or a slab of meat from the corpse of a ten-days-dead horse.

In the Crimea, where the weather was more temperate, the fighting continued unabated through the winter and into the spring. In the ancient port town of Feodosia, where the Black Death entered Europe from Asia in 1347, the fighting swung back and forth for several months. The Germans captured the town; then the Red Army recaptured it; then the Germans captured it a second time. By March the coastal roads around Feodosia were heaped with the dead, their faces frozen in the shocked expression of sudden death. "We used to say whoever survived the winter will survive a long time," one young Russian soldier said; but after the Germans seized the town the second time, that soldier lost hope. "I'm ready for death of any kind," he wrote home. On the Kerch Peninsula at the easternmost tip of the Crimea, the fighting continued into the summer—and its tragic conclusion was a by-product of one of those bureaucratic squabbles that cost lives in every war. In the spring of 1942, a displeased Stalin told his senior commander in the Crimea, Army Commissioner First Class Lev Mekhlis, that his leadership "positively stinks." Stung by the rebuke, Mekhlis—who was a political apparatchik, not a professional soldier—issued an order forbidding the use of trenches. The day the Germans arrived on the peninsula, the war correspondent and novelist Konstantin Simonov did not see Mekhlis or any other Soviet officers. There were just the soldiers, most Georgians, far from home, marching forward the way the British had at the Somme, across a flat open field under a hot sun into the German guns.

THE NEXT DAY MEKHLIS ORDERED another group of Georgians to march into the German guns, and he got the same result. In twelve days of fighting almost 200,000 Soviet troops were killed. For his part in the fiasco, Mekhlis was demoted two ranks to become a corps commissar, a humiliation. However, he left the Crimea with his head still on his shoulders.

The fighting in the winter of 1942 and the spring of 1943 cost the Germans 80,000 men and the Red Army 444,000. But the Russian numbers did not include the tens of thousands of civilians stripped of their shoes, coats, and mufflers by the retreating enemy and then shot or pushed half-naked into the cold. Nor did those numbers include the thousands of peasants who had their supply of potatoes and firewood rifled by a German raiding party. At the Tolstoy estate, a German unit burned the great man's manuscripts for fuel and then buried their dead around his grave site. Brutal as the winter of 1942 was, however, it taught the Russian soldier he was fighting for something far greater than his personal survival, says British historian Richard Overy. During the early weeks of the winter advance Soviet troops passed "village after village torched or blown up, peasant women and children scrambling for scraps of food in snowbanks, the frozen bodies of the executed hanging from a post in village squares."

The German soldier was also deeply affected by the fighting. In January the suicide rate in the Wehrmacht began to rise, and Berlin found those numbers worrisome enough to forbid the photographing of German suicides—though not the execution of Jews and partisans. As winter deepened and the suicide rate continued to rise Berlin's response became surreal. In a sharply worded order the German soldier was warned that his life was not his own; it was the property of the fatherland. Hence "suicide in field conditions [was] tantamount to desertion." Black humor seemed the only appropriate response to such madness. "Christmas," one German joke went, "will not take place this year, for the following reasons: Joseph has been called up for the army; Mary has joined the Red Cross; Baby Jesus has been sent to the countryside with the other children; and the three Wise Men could not get visas because they lacked proof of Aryan origin." Another black joke instructed the German soldier how to behave on leave, point by topical point. "You must remember that you are entering a National Socialist country. You must be tactful with the inhabitants." For example, regarding the quest for food: "Do not rip up the parquet or other kinds of floor because potatoes are kept in a different place. Curfew: If you forget your keys, try to open the door with a round shaped object. Only in cases of extreme emergency use a grenade. Defense against animals: Dogs with mines attached to them are a special feature of the Soviet Union. German dogs, in the worst cases, bite but they do not explode."

At the end of March the Soviet offensive sputtered to a close with some gains made, but key objectives like Leningrad and the Ukraine were still in German hands. Within a month Europe would be abuzz with rumors about a new German offensive coming that summer.

AFTER A SERIES OF GOODBYES at the White House, during the late afternoon of January 14, 1942, a Boeing flying boat carrying Winston Churchill and his entourage made a slow, lazy loop in the Virginia sky and turned southward. The United States had been at war for seventeen days now, but so far a general blackout had not been imposed. Washington, Richmond, Charlottesville: the twinkling lights of a dozen Southern cities illuminated the Boeing's journey southward. The night air grew warmer, the prime minister grew sleepier, and then, just above Fort Lauderdale, the Boeing turned eastward, and in twenty minutes it landed at the Bermuda International Airport. Enthralled by the smoothness of the trip, Churchill proposed a change of plans. Instead of returning to London on the *Duke of York*, which was awaiting the Churchill party off the coast of Bermuda, why not fly home in the Boeing? Could it be done? the prime minister asked Captain Kelly Rogers, the Boeing's pilot. Indeed it could be done, Rogers assured his guest. However, a weekend stopover in Bermuda offered the prime minister time for reflection. The ocean was vast, the weather treacherous—and the Boeing's ability to withstand such conditions untested. "I thought perhaps that I had done a rash thing," Churchill later recalled. "But the die was cast."

The prime minister's fears were not entirely unwarranted.

Approaching England from a southeasterly direction, a navigational error put the Boeing on a course that would have carried Churchill over the German guns at the town of Brest, France, within six minutes. Fortunately, Air Marshal Portal caught the navigational error in time—and a half hour later the Boeing was circling above an RAF airfield in the port city of Plymouth. The city had gotten its first taste of the current war on July 6, 1940, when a Luftwaffe raid killed three civilians. Now—59 bombing raids and 1,172 deaths later—Plymouth "was wasting away in reddish trails of smoke," one observer noted. The population had shrunk from about 200,000 to almost half that number; the city's two main shopping centers lay in ruins; and 26 of its schools, 8 of its cinemas, and 41 of its churches had been reduced to rubble.

The landscape improved only marginally on the journey up to London. The prime minister's train passed buildings black with soot, as well as abandoned shops and farmhouses and untended fields. Below every sky on the journey, clusters of silver balloons bounced up and down in the wind like elephants dunking for water. In the London suburbs, the rank smell of coal smoke penetrated the damp winter air. In heavily bombed areas the smell of the smoke was so acrid people said they could almost taste it.

The winter of 1942 was the best and worst of times for Britain. The country now had two powerful allies, Russia and the United States; a formidable air force; and a growing army. But from Egypt to Hong Kong the empire was at bay. The arrival of Erwin Rommel's Afrika Korps had put General Claude Auchinleck's Eighth Army on the back foot in the Middle East, and in the Pacific the Japanese would be disassembling Britain's Eastern Empire, the work of centuries, in a matter of weeks. Already gone were Burma and Hong Kong and the HMS *Prince of Wales* and her sister ship, the *Repulse*. Both were sunk on December 10. Now a new Japanese force was workings its way down the Malayan peninsula toward the British naval base at Singapore, the lynchpin of Britain's eastern defense system. Except for the *Daily Mail*'s intrepid girl spy cartoon character Jane, who daily saved the British Empire in her underwear, the country did not have much to cheer about in the winter of 1942.

In 1940, the danger had been more immediate, but Churchill's rhetoric and a spirit of defiance had pulled the country together. Now, two and a half years later, the tunes of glory had faded, replaced by government posters explaining how to prepare National Wheat Meal Bread and why wasting food was unpatriotic. For millions of Britons the war had become a daily slog of ration cards, fuel shortages, twelve-hour workdays, unheated bed-sitting rooms, and gloomy BBC reports. Averell Harriman, who was in London that winter, described the national mood as "embarrassed, unhappy, and increasingly baffled"; and no group of

Britons was more baffled than the Great War generation, which had seen the sacrifices it had made at Passchendaele and Vimy Ridge a generation earlier frittered away at Munich. The generation still numbered in the millions. Its male members were identifiable by their scars, limps, and missing limbs; its female members, by their collective indignation at the name the tabloids had given them—"surplus women"—and their veil-shrouded presence at memorials for dead husbands and for sweethearts who had gone to an early grave in France.

Finally, and overwhelming all else that winter, was Singapore, the British island fortress on the southern tip of Malaysia, where the White Man's Burden died an ignominious death on February 15, 1942. The Japanese arrived in northern Malay the day after Pearl Harbor and for the next several weeks fought their way down the peninsula, through sweltering jungles and across dense rain forests, outflanking and outfighting the superior British, Australian, and Indian forces who had been sent to check the Japanese advance. By mid-January the Japanese were closing in on Singapore, and London was beginning to realize that the island's reputation as an impregnable fortress owed more to magical thinking than to reality. Not the least of Singapore's flaws were the heavy naval guns in the harbor, which could only be fired outward toward the sea and thus were useless against a Japanese army advancing southward on Singapore from the landward side of the peninsula. In February, as the Allied position continued to crumble, John Curtin, the Australian prime minister, warned London that his government would view the evacuation of Singapore and Malaysia as an "inexcusable betrayal." But the war cabinet saw no alternative to withdrawal other than to save what it could of British honor. Churchill ordered what amounted to a last-man, last-round defense. In a cable to Lieutenant General Arthur Percival, Singapore's commander, he spoke of the immortal glory that awaited the island's defenders and of the heroic Russian stand before Moscow and the dogged American defense of the Philippines and Guam.

General Archibald Wavell, the senior British commander in the Pacific region, also weighed in with a brief lecture on history and honor. "I look to you to prove that the fighting spirit that won our empire still exists," Percival, who evoked a headmaster at a second-tier British public school, replied to Wavell. There would "come a time," he continued, "when further bloodshed will serve no useful purpose."

On February 8 a Japanese force of twenty-three thousand burst into Singapore and murdered several dozen patients at the Alexandra Hospital. On the streets outside the hospital British and Australian troops threw down their weapons and marched into captivity with fear in their eyes and their hands above their heads. On the fifteenth, the Japanese received the surrender of a hundred thousand British and Commonwealth troops. Films of the surrender show Percival holding an oversized Union Jack in his hand and wearing the expression of a man who already knows what the first sentence of his obituary will be. "God knows we did our best," he told an aide before he was marched off to captivity.

The Singapore fiasco and most of the British setbacks that preceded it were the by-product of a miscalculation that dated to the beginning of the war. Confident that the French would provide most of the troops for the ground war and desperate to avoid another Great War–size butcher's bill, in 1939 Churchill, Neville Chamberlain, and other senior British officials concluded that, this time, Britons would fight in the air and on the sea and leave the land battle to the French. Now, nearly two years later, France was in German hands and Britain was scrambling to transform several million raw recruits into fighting soldiers—thus far with mixed results. A few days before the Singapore surrender Churchill's old friend Violet Bonham Carter found him depressed and fearful. "In 1915," Churchill said, "our men fought on even when they had only one shell left and were under fierce barrage. . . . Now they cannot resist dive-bombers. We have so many men in Singapore, so many men. They should have done better."

Three days later, feeling overwhelmed by the rush of events, Churchill unburdened himself to Captain Richard Pim, who oversaw the map room in the Downing Street annex. The list of grievances that the prime minister cited that morning was long: the unfair press criticism, the impatience of the British people—in the summer of 1940, had he not warned them that many months of blood, sweat, tears, and toil lay ahead? Then there was "the lack of real fighting spirit" in the British and Commonwealth armies and—his most immediate concern—the rebellious mood in Parliament. On January 31 Churchill won, by a wide margin, a vote of confidence in the House of Commons. The victory was, however, not as overwhelming as it seemed. The vote was not intended to be a death threat but, rather, a parliamentary shot across the bow.

There was a growing sense in the country that the war effort had lost definition and purpose. For the past two and a half years the same group of ministers had pursued the same set of policies and had produced the same result. Even the Royal Navy, the pride of the British nation, had lost it edge. In the midst of the Singapore fiasco, three German cruisers—the *Scharnhorst, Gneisenau,* and the *Prinz Eugen*—had slipped out of the Brest harbor and sailed up the English Channel in broad daylight, under the nose of the Royal Navy.

As the news from Singapore worsened, a cry went up for "new men with new ideas." The new man who attracted the most attention to Churchill was Sir Stafford Cripps, until recently the British ambassador to the Soviet Union. Cripps was Woodrow Wilson with a British accent, but he was even more high-minded and self-righteous than Wilson. As historian Angus Calder has noted, in one sense Cripps was a throwback to the last of the great Victorian reformers. "He was a devout Anglican and the scion of a noble family devoted to the rigors of public service." Yet in another sense Cripps was the embodiment of things to come: of the postwar Britain, of the National Health Service, of nationalized industries, and of the egalitarian socialist tomorrow that the British public craved in 1942. And the higher Cripps's star rose, the more Churchill looked like yesterday's man. Working-class Britons had put up with the prime minister's antediluvian ideas in 1940 because he inspired them, made them feel brave and noble, and because there was no credible alternative available. Now, with Cripps on the scene, there was. Sensing danger, in February Churchill swallowed his dislike of Cripps's socialism, his anti-imperialist sanctimony, and—what may have been the hardest swallow for the prime minister—Cripps's vegetarianism; and he offered his rival a seat in the war cabinet. Cripps had to know he was being presented with a poison chalice. As a member of the cabinet, he would have to bear part of the blame whenever things went wrong and bear none of the credit when things went right. However, confident that Churchill would eventually make a fatal stumble, Cripps decided to bide his time and suffer the slings and arrows that came his way while awaiting destiny's call.

Roosevelt was also creating difficulties for the prime minister. In late February Stalin again pressed Britain to recognize the Soviet Union's claim on the Baltic states. Public opinion in the United States ruled out an American endorsement of Russia's claims in the Baltics. Churchill was more accommodating; the Soviet Union was popular in Britain. After giving it some thought he decided to drop the ban on discussing border issues until the postwar period had begun and to recognize Soviet claims on the Baltics. But, fearful that the decision would open him up to charges of caving in to Stalin, he sought the cover of an unofficial presidential endorsement. In a March 7 cable to Roosevelt he wrote: "The increasing gravity of the situation has led me to feel the principles of the Atlantic Charter [which forbade the discussion of border issues until the end of the war] ought not be construed to deny Russia the borders she occupied when Germany attacked her. I hope therefore that you will be able to give us a free hand to sign the treaty."

Roosevelt's response was informed by a new piece of intelligence; the United States' close relationship with Britain had made the Soviets distrustful of America. On March 12—five days after the Churchill cable—Roosevelt summoned Maxim Litvinov, the Soviet ambassador, to Washington, and he instituted what historian Gabriel Gorodetsky has described as a "coup in relations with Russia." The president told Litvinov that, henceforth, he should deal directly with him on the border issue since it is "difficult to do business with the English." The president also wrote an unusually sharp letter to Churchill. "I know you won't mind my being perfectly frank when I tell you I think I can handle Stalin better than either your Foreign Office or my State Department," he began. "Stalin hates the guts of all your top people. He thinks he likes me better, and I hope he will continue to do so." Every once in a while the president's forested interior would open up and the real Roosevelt would make a brief appearance.

Later that spring, with European capitals abuzz with rumors of a coming new German summer offensive, Roosevelt softened his stance on the border. He said he would offer no objection if the British government were to sign a secret agreement with Russia, provided the British did not inform him. However, by the time Roosevelt made the offer, Stalin had lost interest in the border issue, which raised two possibilities as to why. The first one: with a new German attack looming, he did not want to damage relations with his Western allies. The second possibility: he had decided to explore a détente with Hitler. This would not be the first such Soviet-German arrangement. In 1917 Lenin and Trotsky had come to terms with the kaiser's armies, and in 1939 Stalin had signed a nonaggression pact with Hitler. So why not a third time?

By late March there was reason to believe that Stalin might be wondering that himself.

The Soviet winter offensive, which was going to win the war in 1942, had ground to a halt, with little to show for the effort except more weeping wives and fatherless children. Six million Soviet soldiers were killed or captured, the Russian tank and air forces were crippled, and a third of the national rail network was in German hands. In addition heavy industrial production had shrunk to a quarter of its June 1941 level, and there was little prospect of help from Russia's Western allies, who were besieged on three continents.

ON THE FIRST EVENING OF Churchill's White House visit in December, he and Roosevelt found themselves in agreement on where the Allied road to victory should begin. An invasion of North Africa would preempt the rumored German invasion of the region through Spain and Portugal, and it would set the stage for an Allied assault on the continent to come later—in 1943. In late January 1942 the plan received a name, Gymnast, but not much attention.

In the dark winter of 1942 British and American forces were fighting hundreds of individual battles along an arc that ran from Singapore to the North Atlantic, and they were losing almost everywhere. In the Western Desert Erwin Rommel's Afrika Korps was launching a new offensive. In the Mediterranean, Malta, the crucible of British dominance in the Middle East, was under heavy attack by the German and Italian air forces. In the Atlantic German U-boats prowled the sea-lanes from Murmansk to the Caribbean. And in the Pacific the Japanese had isolated the Philippines, seized Singapore, and were looking eastward.

For imperial reasons the British remained committed to launching the Allied counteroffensive from North Africa, and Churchill would be very unlikely to budge on the issue. All of Britain's oil—and much of its food supply—flowed through the Suez Canal. The Middle East was also the gateway to Britain's empire and to the dominions, Australia and New Zealand. Churchill, who thought in imperial rather than in national terms, had considered North Africa such a vital interest that, in 1940, at the height of the Battle of Britain, he had dispatched a large tank force to defend the region. American army and navy planners, who thought in national terms, were baffled by the British strategy. Why travel 2,500 miles to a desert to fight an enemy whose main force sat 30 miles away on the other side of the English Channel? However, except for their shared bafflement at the British way of war, American commanders agreed on little. The navy favored a Pacific-first strategy and had a powerful spokesmen in Admiral Ernest King, the chief of naval operations.

A legendary figure in naval circles, King had the face of a hard drinker, the vocabulary of an old sea dog, and a volcanic temper. King's daughter once described him as the most consistently tempered man in the navy thusly: "He's always angry." She was exaggerating, but not by much. Roosevelt likened King to a human blowtorch, and the historian John Ray Skates rated him the most disliked Allied leader of World War II, with the possible exception of Field Marshal Bernard Montgomery. In a talk with Roosevelt in early March, King made the case for a Pacific-first strategy on racial as well as strategic grounds: if they allowed the Japanese to capture "the white man's countries of Australia and New Zealand," he told Roosevelt, "there would be dangerous repercussions among the nonwhite races of the world."

The army's Germany-first campaign grew out of a series of staff talks in early 1941, and it rested on a straightforward premise. To win the war the Allies had to defeat the most dangerous enemy first—and that was Germany. Japan had a formidable army and navy, but Hitler had the industrial might and manpower of Europe at his disposal. With the resources of France, Belgium, Holland, and Czechoslovakia, Germany could complete the conquest of Britain and Russia, then pivot west to the Americas. In late January 1942, Eisenhower, now chief of the army's War Plans Division, wrote in his diary: "We've got to stop wasting resources all over the world . . . and go to Europe and fight." His warning went unheeded.

In January Roosevelt was still considering the North African option. Then, in early March, the mounting crisis in the Philippines sucked up the last reserve of trained American troops, and the North Africa plan was shelved and might have remained shelved but for a twisted series of events.

Roosevelt was determined to get American troops into the war somewhere in the European theater in 1942. As to where, he was more flexible. Two days after the Gymnast postponement, he told Churchill he was interested in establishing a "new front in western Europe, this summer." But a few weeks later he seemed to change his mind. At a meeting with Marshall, Secretary of War Stimson, and several other advisers on March 25, Roosevelt spoke almost wistfully about Gymnast. Officially the plan had been dead for a month, but Hopkins may have encouraged the president to keep the North African option open; an opportunity might present itself. After several minutes of confused back-and-forth and a cranky complaint about Roosevelt's "dispersion debauchery" from Stimson, whose smiles were as warm as the winter solstice, Marshall presented the latest version of what would become known as the Marshall Memorandum. The plan had two versions: the first envisioned a cross-channel invasion by a forty-eight-division force—thirty American, eighteen British—in 1943. In the second version a nine-division Anglo-American force would make a cross-channel attack in 1942 in the event that the Red Army was facing collapse or, though more unlikely, if the Germans were. To ensure that the Marshall Memorandum enjoyed the unanimous support of the American military Hopkins made certain that Roosevelt and Marshall were present on the day he asked Admiral King, "Do you see any reason why this [plan] cannot be carried out?" King gritted his teeth and replied, "No, I do not."

Eight days later, on April 8, General Alan Brooke, chief of the Imperial General Staff, was standing by his staff car at Hendon Aerodrome in north London, awaiting his American guests. Earlier in the war the Aerodrome had been badly mauled, but, with the Luftwaffe increasingly focused on Russia, it had regained some of its prewar character. The only visible mementos from the Spitfire summer of 1940 were the unfilled potholes that crossed the field. As chief of the Imperial General Staff, etiquette required that Brooke personally greet the prime minister's American guests, George Marshall and Harry Hopkins. Upon their arrival there were the customary smiles and handshakes, but that morning Brooke's mind was on the other side of the world. Two days earlier a large Japanese naval force had slipped into the Indian Ocean, raising the prospect that the sea, which had carried Arab and Persian traders between Asia and the Middle East for millennia, would in the next few weeks be carrying the Japanese fleet to a rendezvous with Rommel's forces in the Middle East.

Brooke had only been chief of the Imperial General Staff for four months. Churchill turned to him in December, after concluding his current CIGS, Sir John Dill, lacked a fighting spirit. That was a failing that Brooke was never accused of. A subordinate described his first encounter with the new CGIS thusly: "The hurricane-like eminence of a thick-set general burst from a flagged staff car, tore up the steps, exploded through the door . . . and an extraordinary current of energy, almost of electricity" flashed through the room. An Ulsterman by birth, Brooke was a member of the Fighting Brookes—a family famous for its centuries of military service to the Crown. Brooke had been an artillery officer in the Great War, and, as a corps commander, in 1940 he was instrumental in getting the British army safely off the beaches at Dunkirk. It would be hyperbole to say that Brooke was a war lover, but he stood up to war better than most men. During the Dunkirk retreat, he stumbled into a scene out of the medieval allegory the Dance of Death. In a corpse-ridden field forty miles east of the Dunkirk beaches he found himself surrounded by patients "from a bombed out 'insane asylum' standing in a field"—singing and dancing and grinning at one another with the "flow of saliva running from the corners of their mouths and noses." Later, when he was asked how he held his nerve at such moments, Brooke shrugged and said that at a certain point "one's senses become numb in the face of catastrophe." That was evident in his diary entries. A typical entry for the winter of 1942 began: "Lost another part of the Empire today."

On the drive in from Hendon the American guests made no mention of the Marshall Memorandum, and Brooke gave no indication that he had read the memorandum a few weeks earlier. Brigadier Vivian Dykes, a British liaison officer in Washington, had come across a copy and passed a summary on to London. Hopkins knew nothing about Dykes, but when the conference convened that afternoon it quickly became apparent to him there had been a leak. He and Marshall were not telling the British anything they didn't already know. But Churchill had a broader concern that afternoon: how to satisfy Roosevelt's desire to get Allied forces into action in 1942 without making a commitment to do so. This was not easy to do, but Churchill was a wizard with words. After Marshall laid out his plan, which was a replica of the one he had presented to Roosevelt and Stimson in late March, Churchill responded with a dazzling piece of verbal gymnastics: he said he did "not take the proposals as seriously as either the facts warranted or as did the United States. [Nonetheless] in spite of all the difficulties he . . . was prepared to go along with it."

Brooke, who had concluded that Marshall was "a pleasant man" with a plan whose implications he had not yet "begun to realize," was lying in wait the next morning when a group of senior British commanders convened to hear Marshall present a detailed version of his plan. After Marshall finished, Brooke stepped forward and proceeded to shred Sledgehammer, the emergency 1942 invasion. A force that had "landed to relieve the Russians," Brooke said, "could not exceed seven infantry and two armored divisions," and such a force would not be strong enough to maintain a bridgehead against the scale of attack the Germans could bring against it. Furthermore, "it was unlikely that we could extricate the force if the Germans made a really determined effort to drive us out."

Admiral Lord Louis Mountbatten also had serious reservations about Sledgehammer. For one thing, he noted, the small size of the French ports would make it difficult "to maintain the invasion force over open waters for an extended period of time." Air Marshal Portal, who spoke next, cautioned that even if the landings succeeded it would be extremely difficult to provide fighter cover over the assault beaches for an extended period of time. Later that day Hopkins launched a counterattack. During a visit to Downing Street, he reminded Churchill of the "serious weight the President and Marshall [give] to our proposals [the Marshall Plan]. Our military leaders have, after canvassing the whole world, made up their minds that this plan was by far the most advantageous."

While Hopkins kept an eye on Churchill, Roosevelt kept an eye on him. "Please put Hopkins to bed," he instructed Marshall. "And keep him there under twenty-four-hour guard by army or marine corps. Ask King for additional assistance if required." Hopkins somehow managed to slip out of the hotel anyway. He spent the weekend at Chequers. It was spring now, and even for an Iowa boy accustomed to lush green springs the greenness of the English countryside felt overwhelming. "It is only when you see this country in spring that you begin to understand why the English have written the best goddammed poetry in the world," he said. Hopkins was still admiring the views at Chequers on Sunday afternoon when Churchill cabled Roosevelt that in principle the British chiefs of staff were now in "entire agreement" with the Marshall Memorandum.

The next few days unfolded like a Henry James novella about American innocents abroad. After listening to Churchill and his military advisers give a detailed description of Britain's contribution to Marshall's plan, at a meeting on the fourteenth, Hopkins and the general returned to the United States, confident of British support. However, *in principle* can mean almost anything—from a commitment with details to come to a polite way of saying no. In this instance it was the latter. A few days after the Americans departed Brooke announced that his support for Marshall's plan was limited to only one aspect of it—the 1943 invasion. He would not countenance a "sacrificial" landing in 1942 to save Stalin. To varying degrees this was also the position of Churchill, Eden, other members of the war cabinet—and of most senior British politicians and military leaders.

Nine days earlier, in a forest in the wilds of East Prussia, Adolf Hitler issued Directive Number 41, the German war plan for 1942. In early March, during a visit to the Wolf's Lair, Propaganda Minister Goebbels had been shocked by the change in Hitler's appearance. The bold, strutting Hitler of the propaganda posters had become "quite gray," and "merely talking about the cares of winter made him seem to have aged very much." Usually a shrewd observer of his Führer, in this instance Goebbels misjudged. Moscow did age Hitler, but it also vindicated his belief in his genius. His hold-your-ground order had been central in preventing a collapse that could have broken the German army, physically and mentally. Moreover, most of European Russia, including the Ukraine and Leningrad, remained in German hands—and hot food, generous leaves, and a fresh supply of men and matériel, especially tanks, had improved morale. "We were in a good state," one officer recalled later.

The new war plan Blue would be less than half the size of Barbarossa: 68 divisions instead of 153, 8 panzer divisions instead of 17, 7 motorized division instead of 13. The 52nd Division—Italy, Romania, and Hungary—would make up some of the manpower difference, though German officers regarded the average Italian or Romanian soldier as about half as good as his German counterpart. In some important ways, however, Germany's situation was more favorable than it had been in 1941. In the Middle East Rommel's Africa Korps was now within striking distance of the Suez Canal and all the oil riches of Arabia; in the Pacific the Japanese had the British and Americans on the back foot in the Philippines, Singapore, the Dutch East Indies, Burma, and the Indian Ocean. In these individual victories Hitler saw a historic opportunity; if Germany gained control of the oil-rich Caucasus and the southern steppe of Russia, the armies of the Axis powers could link up in the Middle East and launch a super Blue, an "animating sweep" northward behind Soviet lines to Moscow and the Urals.

When spring arrived, both sides began to prepare. In May the German 6th Army recaptured the city of Kharkov in preparation for an assault on Stalingrad, an important communications center as well as namesake of Russia's leader, and Stalin sent his foreign minister, Vyacheslav Molotov, to the west to meet with Churchill and Roosevelt. Thickset, with a facial expression that rarely changed, Molotov was a perfect embodiment of the Soviet ruling class circa 1942. His woolen suits always looked half a size too small, his smiles were infrequent, and his conscience was elastic enough to countenance all manner of misdeeds. During the 1930s Molotov approved 372 execution lists, and in the late 1940s when his Jewish wife, Polina, was sentenced to a year in prison for taking an unauthorized meeting with her childhood friend, the Zionist activist Golda Meir, Molotov made no attempt to intervene on her behalf. To the extent that Molotov was known in the West, it was as the Soviet diplomat who had signed the German-Soviet Nonaggression Pact in 1939. The morning after the signing a photo of Molotov and his German opposite number, Joachim von Ribbentrop, adorned the front page of newspapers across Europe and North America. On this visit there were no photographers. When he arrived at Downing Street on the afternoon of May 20 there was just a skeptical Winston Churchill, chomping on a cigar. Molotov's brief was to persuade Britain and the United States to open a second front this summer, and he arrived at Downing Street with what he thought would be an attractive quid pro quo. The Soviet Union would temporarily withdraw its request for recognition of its 1941 borders in return for a British promise to reexamine the second front issue.

Molotov's cause was not helped by his diplomatic style. After a first meeting with him Alex Cadogan observed that Molotov "has all the grace . . . of a totem pole." The next day Molotov made an even more remarkable proposal: an Allied invasion of the continent large enough to draw forty German divisions west. Churchill was polite but blunt. "It is unlikely that any 1942 attack, even if successful, would draw off a large number of German troops from the eastern front," he said. Disaster for the sake of action would not aid anyone except the Germans. Failing to get anywhere on the second front, Molotov returned to the border question. But unlike last December he had no great victory to wave in front of the British. The Soviet Union was the supplicant now. Molotov did get an agreement from the British before leaving for Washington and a meeting with Roosevelt, but it did not include an agreement to recognize Russia's 1941 borders.

The Churchill whom Molotov said goodbye to the next morning was a politician past his prime. During the heartbreakingly glorious summer of 1940 the prime minister had been the hope of the world. But two and a half years of air raids, food shortages, and parliamentary challenges had rendered him mortal again. He was an aging politician whose policies were increasingly challenged and whose leadership of the war was quietly slipping into the hands of the new leader of the Allied cause, Franklin Roosevelt, whom Molotov was flying across the Atlantic to meet.

In the spring of 1942 the American president was sixty and still in relatively good health. He had a secret scribe, George Elsey, a member of the staff of the White House Map Room, who wrote an insightful portrait of him that spring. "Congress," Elsey began,

> has generally—not always, but generally—done what [Roosevelt] wanted. The American people had supported him. He simply felt he knew what the country needed, what it ought to have, and that he could get his way with what he wanted. Had he not been in his third term, his attitude might have been very different. . . . But here he was, an unprecedented third term president—and of course he knew better than anyone else what was good for the United States: that was his attitude. . . . 'I'm in control. This is the way it's going to be. . . . It's going to be the way I want it.' And everyone accepted that he was the boss: Stimson, Knox [Frank Knox, the navy secretary], Marshall, King, Arnold [Hap Arnold, the army air force chief]—everyone.

On May 29 Molotov arrived in Washington without ceremony and unaware that his arrival coincided with a decisive moment in the Pacific war. Earlier that morning naval intelligence reported that a large Japanese task force was bearing down on Midway Island, a US protectorate 1,100 miles northwest of Honolulu. The navy pilot who spotted the task force counted four aircraft carriers, two battleships, three cruisers, and twelve destroyers. There could only be one explanation for such a large force:

Japan was preparing to mount a challenge to America's naval supremacy in the western Pacific. Upon greeting Molotov, Roosevelt made a brief reference to events in the Pacific; then—accompanied by Hopkins and Molotov's interpreter, a large pockmarked Ukrainian with a gold front tooth—the president and his Russian guest vanished into the Oval Office.

Ten minutes into the conversation Hopkins looked across the table. Roosevelt seemed restless. He was drumming a pencil on his desk and gazing out the window. The interpreter's thick Ukrainian accent made it hard for Roosevelt to understand anything he said. But: no, Roosevelt told Hopkins that night; it was not the interpreter's thick accent—it was Molotov. Roosevelt said he had "had dealings with all kinds of people but never before had he encountered anyone like Molotov."

The next morning, at a meeting with Marshall, Stimson, and the president, Molotov was unusually candid about Russia's position. The Soviets "hoped to hold on and fight all the way through 1942," he said. "But Hitler might throw in such reinforcements as to make that impossible." In such a situation, since Britain and the United States both thought time was on their side, "no development would become beyond the range of possibility." But "it is not," he said emphatically. Time was on Hitler's side. If the Red Army collapsed that summer Hitler would follow the example of Imperial Germany in 1918 and transfer his armies to the western front for a final blow. If there is a slaughter on the beaches of France, said Molotov, it would occur in 1943, when the Allied forces faced a German army of almost four million—not in 1942 when Germany only had twenty to twenty-five reserve divisions in northwest Europe, most made up of boys and middle-aged men.

After Molotov finished talking, Roosevelt turned to Marshall and asked, "Can it be done?"

"Yes," Marshall said; a second front could be established that year. Later that day, in a speech to a group of West Point cadets, the general doubled down on the commitment. American troops were landing in England and "will land in France," he declared. The pledge marked the high point of the Molotov visit. Within a few days, American planners would produce a half dozen objections to a cross-channel invasion in 1942, including insufficient shipping to support the invasion force. General Eisenhower, recently returned from London, believed even 1943 might be out of the question. The British were moving very slowly, he said. On June 3, when the departing Molotov asked for a public commitment to a 1942 date, Marshall objected vehemently and told Hopkins not to include a date in the public communiqué. Roosevelt overrode him. The 1942 reference stayed.

On a stopover in London on his way home, Molotov presented Churchill and Eden with a communiqué stating that Britain and the Soviet Union had reached "full agreement in regard to a second front in 1942." The statement was a fabrication, but, like Roosevelt, Churchill believed that in war "truth requires a bodyguard of lies." The aide-mémoire Molotov received on his departure laid out the British government's true position. "We can give no promises" about a second front, as "we believe an invasion in 1942 is likely to fail." With a new German offensive looming and Anglo-American support critical, Stalin took a step back and dropped the border issue—for the time being.

As historian James MacGregor Burns noted more than a half century ago, Pearl Harbor did not just anger Americans—it unified and excited them: "The air raid scares, the war rallies, the bond drives, the smart new uniforms, the exhilarating sense of being part of a great national effort: it all combined to take some of the sting out of the early defeats."

Yankee swagger took out the rest of that sting. Yes, America was suffering defeat after defeat, people acknowledged; but (and there was almost always a *but* because the "Japs" had resorted to a sneak attack) "We'll teach them a lesson" became the national mantra in January and February 1942. Then came the Japanese victories in Singapore, in the Java Sea, in the Indian Ocean, and in the Philippines. White men were not supposed to lose wars to yellow men. By early April the long queues, the food rationing, the shortages of nylon stockings, the canceled sporting events—those small inconveniences that had unified the country in January—were losing their power to unite. Women missed their nylons, men their cigars. The worst blow of the spring was the fall of Corregidor. In a letter to the president on the eve of the surrender, General Jonathan Wainwright, commander of the Corregidor garrison, wrote: "With broken heart and head bowed in endless sadness but not in shame, and with continued pride in my gallant troops, I go to meet the Japanese commander."

The victory at Midway in early June helped restore American confidence. On the fourth an outnumbered US Navy fleet of three carriers fell on a much larger Japanese force northeast of Midway Island and sank four frontline Japanese carriers at the cost of one American carrier, USS *Yorktown*. In an official communiqué on June 6, Admiral Chester Nimitz, commander of the Pacific fleet, declared Pearl Harbor had been "partially avenged." Nimitz was right to include a qualifier. More than sixty thousand American soldiers marched into captivity after the fall of Corregidor—and seven thousand of them would never see home again.

7

THE LONGEST SUMMER

——————

IN EARLY JUNE 1942 TWO NEW NAMES ENTERED THE AMERICAN vocabulary—the Alaskan islands Kiska and Attu. The islands owed their sudden notoriety to Midway. Before the battle a large Japanese task force had sailed north to draw off the marines and airmen defending Midway. The ruse failed, but Kiska and Attu were now occupied, giving Japan a back door into the Soviet Union. In a cable to Stalin on June 9 Roosevelt warned that "the situation in Alaska and the Northern Pacific area is developing in such a way" as to indicate Japan is "preparing to conduct operations against the Soviet Union's Maritime Provinces." He added that he believed "an immediate exchange of detailed information . . . is essential to our common security." In London and Moscow there was also a growing sense of urgency. Except for Midway and the Moscow victory the Allied nations had not had a single major success in the first half of 1942. In 1941, a British garrison with a large Australian component had withstood an eight-month-long siege in the Libyan port city of Tobruk. In June 1942, fighting the same enemy over the same terrain and enjoying a superiority in armor and artillery, a British force, made up largely of Anglo South Africans and Afrikaners, collapsed. At the end of the battle thirty-three thousand men marched into captivity, hands over their heads, leaving behind undulating plains littered with abandoned artillery pieces and shattered tanks with names like Valiant and Crusader painted on their sides. In Russia that June the siege of Sevastopol, the storied playground of czars, was entering its final days. At the height of the fighting in June the Luftwaffe dropped 20,528 tons of bombs on the city, and the army deployed a new class of artillery superweapons, including a 283-mm railway gun and two new 600-mm mortars nicknamed Thor and Odin.

As summer set in, the fighting moved across the city like a ballet: street to street, then house to house, then hand to hand—and finally underground into the sewers. Subsisting on month-old bread and rat meat, the defenders held out until mid-July. To boost morale, a few weeks before Sevastopol fell, Molotov gave a fairy-tale version of his visits with Roosevelt and Churchill in a speech to the Supreme Soviet. "Naturally serious attention was given to the problem . . . during [our] talks both in London and Washington. The results of these talks can be seen from the identical Anglo-Soviet communiqués. This has a great importance for the people of the Soviet Union because the establishment of a second front in Europe would create insuperable difficulties for the Hitlerite armies on our front."

Later that day on the other side of the world, General Brooke pushed back the curtain next to his seat and gazed out at the twinkling Washington sky. In the hazy evening light the Potomac looked like a silvery ribbon. While Brooke debated whether anything as big as the Boeing could land on anything as small as that ribbon, the big seaplane made a slow arc in the fading light, then swept down and landed on the water with a swanlike grace. Inside the plane Churchill; Brooke; Brigadier Stewart, chief of war plans at the War Department; Pug Ismay, the prime minister's military assistant; and Sir Charles Wilson, the prime minister's physician, grunted their approval.

Churchill came to Washington determined to solve the still unresolved second front issue. At various times during the past six months tentative agreements had been reached about a cross-channel assault in 1943, and a somewhat more tentative agreement was reached about a sacrificial nine-division assault in 1942, if Russia faced defeat. But Churchill—and to a lesser extent Roosevelt—had never quite given up on Gymnast, the assault on North Africa, though they supported it for different reasons. Eager to avoid the carnage of another Great War Churchill did not want to enter Europe until the German army had been weakened by several years of peripheral battles in places like North Africa and Italy. Roosevelt's priority was to get the American troops into action quickly—and under the current plan the American soldier was not likely to enter Europe until 1943.

On the morning of the eighteenth, as the Churchill party breakfasted thirty thousand feet above the Atlantic, the seventy-four-year-old secretary of war, Henry Stimson, and the sixty-one-year-old General George Marshall drew up plans for what could be described as a gentlemanly coup. Stimson wrote a strong defense of the current war plan: a major cross-channel invasion in 1943 and, if events warranted it, an emergency invasion in 1942. Marshall endorsed the plan and distributed copies to his chief advisers, including Dwight Eisenhower, who was about to take command of the American forces in Britain, and Hap Arnold, who circulated a letter saying that Stimson had the support of all the officers who had read the letter. Later in the day a copy was rushed to Hyde Park.

Aware that a final decision on the second front would be made during his visit, Churchill had come prepared for battle. On June 19, after a peaceful night's sleep at the British embassy, he set off for Hyde Park in a US Navy plane. When it set down at New Hackensack Field Roosevelt was waiting in a car at the far end of the runway. The prime minister got in, expecting a leisurely drive along the sun-dappled summer roads. But the president had something more adventurous in mind. Of the episode that followed, Churchill later wrote, with uncharacteristic understatement, that "it gave me some thoughtful moments. . . . Mr. Roosevelt's infirmity prevented him from using his feet on the brake, clutch and accelerator: an ingenious arrangement which allowed him to do everything with his arms, which were amazingly strong and muscular. He invited me to feel his biceps, saying that a famous prizefighter had envied them. This was reassuring, but I confess that when, on several occasions, the car paused and backed on the grass verges of the precipice over the Hudson, I hoped the mechanical devices and brakes would show no defects." Churchill continued: "All the time we talked business and, though I was careful not to take his attention off of the steering, we made more progress than we might have done in formal conference."

A lifetime of disagreements had taught Churchill that the best way to say no was to start with a yes. During a talk with Roosevelt later that afternoon he went into considerable detail about the effort that British planners had made to come up with a feasible cross-channel attack in 1942; but no matter what angle they looked at it from, the conclusion was always the same: the channel would run red with American and British blood. Then he turned the tables on Roosevelt. "Have the American planners devised an invasion scheme?" he asked. "If so, what is it? At what points would the American forces strike?" More questions followed: How many landing craft and how much shipping were available to support the landing? What American general would command the invasion force? What British forces and assistance would be required? Churchill concluded by reiterating the British position: His Majesty's government would welcome "any scheme that offered a reasonable chance of success."

The next day—Sunday, June 21—the second front debate took an unexpected turn. Roosevelt and Churchill had come back to Washington earlier in the day and were in the Oval Office talking to General Brooke when Marshall appeared and handed Roosevelt "a pink piece of paper"; the president scanned the message and then, without comment, handed it to Churchill, who announced to the other guests that Tobruk had fallen. When he finished, Roosevelt asked, "What can we do to help?"

That warm summer afternoon ended with an extended debate about the second front. Present were Roosevelt; Churchill; Marshall; Brooke; Stimson; Mackenzie King, the Canadian prime minister; and several Dutch, Chinese, and other foreign officials. The debate—perhaps the most consequential held on the second front—lasted deep into the night and appeared to end on a note of triumph for Marshall and Stimson. The press release the White House issued the next morning dwelled on the strategic opportunities offered by "operations in France or the Low countries." But the final sentence—"If the success of an operation [on the European mainland] appeared improbable, an alternative must be ready for execution"—was ambiguous. Was that just another generic assertion of Anglo-American resolve? Or was the sentence a temporary placeholder for Roosevelt and Churchill's "secret baby," the North African operation?

Distraught by the Tobruk defeat and facing a noisy, embarrassing second Parliamentary vote of confidence on July 2 Churchill was eager to return home after the Sunday evening debate. But Marshall was not going to let the British delegation leave until they had inspected the new American army he was forging. After some back-and-forth, a date (June

25) and a place—Fort Jackson, South Carolina—were selected for the demonstration. This was not the first time that Marshall had staged such an event for visiting British military and civilian dignitaries, but the earlier events at Fort Bragg and Fort Benning had not gone as well as the general had hoped. In Marshall's eyes—and in the eyes of most of the other American officers who were present—the Fort Jackson event did do as well as they hoped. Ten thousand men and several dozen tanks marched through burning Carolina heat in perfect military order. Publicly the British guests were full of praise, but privately the story was different. General Brooke left Fort Jackson thinking the Americans still had much to learn, and Pug Ismay thought it would be "murder" to put these young men up against "continental professionals."

At the end of June Churchill returned to London—and to a blistering editorial in the *Manchester Guardian*, one of the most influential papers in the country. The editorial listed all the British defeats since the start of the war—Norway, Dunkirk, Singapore, and Greece—and noted that in each instance there had been a defensible explanation for the defeat. But for Tobruk there was none. "Here at least we were supposed to be strong," the editorial said. The *Guardian* was not alone in its criticism. Another paper predicted TOBRUK FALL MAY BRING CHANGE IN GOVERNMENT. A few days later Churchill survived a second parliamentary vote of confidence, but the margin of victory was smaller. In January only one MP had voted against him. This time there were twenty-five and they all carried the same message: the country needs a victory.

So did its prime minister. On July 8 Churchill removed Gymnast from its placeholder, weaponized it—and sent it to Washington via cable. Roosevelt was in his bedroom that evening when an aide appeared and handed him a copy of the prime minister's note. It began in an uncompromising way: "No responsible General, Admiral, or Air Marshal is prepared to recommend Sledgehammer"—the code name for a cross-channel invasion of France that year. "The lodgement would have to be nourished and the bomber effort on Germany greatly curtailed. All our energies would be involved in defending the bridgehead on a very narrow front. It may therefore be said that premature action in 1942 . . . would decisively injure the prospect of a well-organized, large-scale action in 1943."

Having said no to an operation he had little faith in, Churchill turned to North Africa with a more optimistic attitude. "I am sure myself that

Gymnast"—which he described as the American invasion of North Africa—"is by far the best chance for effective relief to the Russian front in 1942." He continued, "This has always been in harmony with your ideas. In fact, Mr. President, it is your commanding idea." That was an overstatement. Roosevelt's "commanding idea" was to put American troops on the battlefield in 1942, while Churchill's commanding idea was to put them on a North African battlefield, a relatively safe place to bleed an untried army. The only European professionals in the region were the four divisions of Rommel's Afrika Korps and a handful of disgruntled French divisions that might or might not resist an American landing. There was also an Italian army fighting with the Germans, but it was poorly led, poorly equipped—and, disheartened, it did not represent much of a threat. After giving Churchill's cable some thought, Roosevelt signaled his approval. Conspicuously, Marshall and Stimson did not. At Gallipoli from 1915 to 1916, and in Norway in 1940, Churchill had sent thousands of young Britons to an early grave after they had fought battles of little strategic consequence. Marshall and Stimson believed that decisive victory could only be achieved on decisive battlefields, and in this war, as in the last, those battlefields were located in the fields and hamlets of France, Belgium, and Holland, in the heartland of western Europe.

On the afternoon of July 10 relations between the War Department and the White House reached a new low. At the weekly chiefs of staff meeting Marshall dismissed the proposed North African campaign as "expensive and ineffectual" and accused the British of double-dealing. "If the British position must be accepted," Marshall said, then "the US should turn to the Pacific for decisive action against the Japanese." Admiral King immediately seconded Marshall's proposal. For the past few weeks, the admiral had become increasingly agitated by the thought of sacrificing a portion of the Pacific fleet to feed the North African campaign. General MacArthur, who had recently established an American command in Australia, was also pleased by Marshall's decision. He predicted that the Pacific-first plan would have the greatest effect on relieving pressure on Russia in the coming summer. However, since Japan and the Soviet Union were not currently at war, it was difficult to see how.

The president received a copy of the memorandum on the Pacific-first strategy from Marshall and King before leaving for Hyde Park for the weekend. Roosevelt kept his silence for two days; then on Sunday morning, July 12, as Washington awoke to a sultry summer day and the wire services reported that the British Eighth Army had fallen back on the Egyptian border, the telephone rang in the War Department. Roosevelt told the nervous junior officer who answered the phone that he wanted the War Department to provide him with a full statement of the Pacific-first plan, including how many planes, ships, and men would be transferred to the theater, what their transport needs would be, and how the withdrawals would affect the buildup in the Atlantic theater and the defense of the Soviet Union and the Middle East. He said he wanted an answer to these questions on his desk that afternoon. It was an impossible request, and it was meant to be impossible. The document that went out to the president that afternoon had the feel of a very rough draft. It reported that an offensive in the Pacific would relieve pressure on the Russians, but it failed to explain how, as the Germans were not fighting in the Pacific, and the Soviet Union and Japan had recently signed a nonaggression pact. The memorandum also failed to address the likely public reaction that would ensue when Americans learned their sons were fighting and dying to liberate the colonial holdings of the Dutch and British.

Upon receipt of Marshall's draft Roosevelt fell silent again. Then on the fourteenth he summoned Marshall and ordered him to London. King and Hopkins were to accompany him. Their brief was to reach final agreement with the British. The president said he was still open to a cross-channel invasion, but Marshall left the Oval Office feeling he was leaning more and more toward North Africa.

When the American visitors arrived in London on July 18 the British government was still in shock over the loss of the PQ 17 convoy. Two weeks earlier, in the Icelandic port of Hvalfjordur, PQ 17, the largest convoy ever to chance the Russian passage, had received a solemn farewell. The convoy's route would take it past the German naval installations and airfields in Norway and Finland, and casualties were expected to be heavy. King George, who came up from London to wish the crews good fortune, gave a short, rousing speech the afternoon that PQ 17 set sail. But most of the sailors in the audience were thinking about the hundreds of miles of angry sea and bitter cold that lay ahead. The younger men, going into battle for the first time, wondered what the experience would be like. The older men, who had sailed on two or three previous convoys, wondered how well they would hold their nerve this time.

To the king's surprise, one of the faces in the audience that afternoon was familiar: the Hollywood actor Douglas Fairbanks Jr. "Well, what are you doing up here?" the king asked. "I have not seen you since we played golf at Sunnydale about five years ago." Fairbanks, who had helped Cary Grant save India in the 1939 movie *Gunga Din*, was now a lieutenant on the USS *Wichita*. An hour later, PQ 17, which was bound for the ports of Murmansk and Archangel, slipped into the open sea, where its escort—six destroyers, four corvettes, three minesweepers, four trawlers, and two submarines—and one German U-boat, U-456, awaited. Two additional Allied naval units—one composed largely of cruisers; the other, an aircraft carrier task force—would join the convoy at sea. Below and above deck the merchantmen groaned with the sinews of war: 297 aircraft, 594 tanks, 4,246 trucks and gun carriers, crated bombers, and 156,000 tons of general cargo, enough equipment to arm a Russian army of 50,000 men. Twenty-two of the merchantmen in the convoy were American; eight were British. The rest were Dutch, Russian, and Panamanian.

The first few days at sea were quiet enough to allow time for contemplation. On the decks of the merchantmen there were lively discussions about what was more treacherous—the winter passage to Russia, when the cold could kill a man in a few minutes, or the summer passage, when the sun never set and every ship was a target every hour of every day. Off Stromness Point in the Orkneys, the convoy paused to assemble into battle formation: nine columns, four ships to a column. U-456, hidden just below the horizon, continued to keep Berlin abreast of the convoy's progress. Entering German-patrolled waters on the twenty-ninth, the crew of the USS *Melville* broke the seal on one of the M3 tanks strapped to the deck; a hurrah went up when its 37-mm gun spit out a burst of fire. On other merchantmen, crates of armor-piercing shells were carried up to the deck and cut open.

Late on the twenty-ninth the admiralty warned that the enemy's main units were massing. "Hi-yo, Silver!" a lookout shouted two days later. Above him, the sky was suddenly full of Germans fighters. For the next few days the escorts and the merchantmen gave a good account of themselves. On July 2 they fought off an attack by seven Heinkel dive-bombers with no casualties, and on the third they beat back a second air attack with only one major loss, the Liberty ship the SS *Christopher Newport*. But the intelligence reports were growing more ominous. The battleship *Tirpitz* and its escort, the cruiser *Admiral Hipper*, were reported to be at sea—and two U-boat packs were believed to be assembling to the north of the convoy. The *Tirpitz* report was an error; it was changing berths and would not enter the battle until it was almost concluded.

It is impossible to know what went through the mind of First Sea Lord Admiral Dudley Pound when he was told that the *Tirpitz* was as sea, but it had only been a few months since the *Prince of Wales*, the Royal Navy's newest battleship, and her escort, the *Repulse*, were sunk off the coast of Malaysia. At the end of a late-night meeting Pound asked each member of his twelve-man staff if PQ 17's escort force should be withdrawn. Only one officer raised his hand in support of the motion. One was enough for Pound. At 2111 hours he signaled the escorts: "Most Immediate and Secret: Cruiser force to withdraw westward at high speed." At 2123 hours he sent a second cable: "Immediate: Owing to threat of surface ships, convoy is to disperse and proceed to Russian ports." At 2133 hours there was third cable: "Most Immediate: Convoy is to scatter." Stripped of protection and trapped in the open sea under a twenty-four-hour sun, its casualties quickly mounted. On July 5 the Luftwaffe sank six ships and the Kriegsmarine sank the same amount. The next day the Germans scored two more kills, and on the seventh and eighth, a further five. On the tenth, two more. After each encounter the wind would collect the dead, human and animal (mostly walruses)—and send them whistling northward in a sloping arc toward Bear Island, a deserted spur of land on the Barents Sea.

As the fighting intensified, the radio rooms on the retreating destroyers crackled with messages from abandoned crews. In an attempt to lure the U-boats away from the undefended ships, a signalman on the *Wichita* began sending out false messages; but most of the replies that came back were from American and British seamen. "On fire in the ice. Abandoning ship. Six U-boats approaching on the surface," said one man. "Am being bombed by a large number of planes," said another. "The radio room was bedlam," Fairbanks recalled later. "The bridge could not keep up with all the reports." When the *El Capitan* passed a German crew burning to death inside the bubble of a downed bomber, the sailors jeered. But by the end of the battle most of the jeering was on the German side. Only eleven of the thirty-five merchantmen in the convoy survived long enough to deliver their goods. Everything and everyone else was dead or underwater: twenty-four merchantmen and two-thirds of the planes, tanks, and other matériel the ships carried were at the bottom of the sea.

On July 17 Churchill, contrite but resolute, informed Stalin that he had suspended PQ 18, the next scheduled convoy, and he said the suspension would remain in force until a way was found to make the northern sea as dangerous "for German warships as they make it for ours." A few days later the American government sent a similar note. Stalin's reply was bitter. He called the suspension "wholly unjustified." But the rebuke was ignored. In mid-July, in Anglo-American circles, resolution of the second front remained the most important issue. The debate was now in its sixth month, and the clock was running out. In another month or two, weather and logistics would make a strike anywhere in 1942 impossible. A final decision had to be made now.

General Brooke expected the new round of Anglo-American talks to be contentious, and events proved him correct. Upon arriving at Prestwick air base on the afternoon of the eighteenth, Marshall, Admiral King, and Hopkins ignored the prime minister's invitation to join him at Chequers and instead proceeded directly to London. While the American party was on the train south Churchill and his generals gathered to examine the cross-channel operation a final time. No minds were changed. It still looked like a suicide mission to every senior British officer who examined it. On a visit to General Eisenhower's London headquarters the next day Marshall got a very different perspective. All the young officers he spoke to were bursting with optimism. Not only was the invasion of northern France feasible this year, they were confident that the invading force would be able to secure a permanent lodgment, enhancing the chances of success for Roundup, the 1943 attack.

During three days of debate, Marshall made the case for Sledgehammer several times, and each time he was defeated by superior British planning and experience. By the end of the third day he was down to his last argument. For logistical reasons canceling Sledgehammer might make a 1943 invasion impossible. A few days later the war cabinet, Britain's ultimate authority on issues of war and peace, voted unanimously to kill the 1942 invasion plan.

In retrospect, the British were right about Sledgehammer: it would have failed at a great cost in human life and without drawing a single German soldier from the eastern front. In June 1942 there were twenty-seven German divisions stationed in the west, more than enough to defeat a nine-division assault by an Allied force. However, Marshall was right about Roundup. Because of the logistical difficulties the main

Allied attack would have to be moved back from 1943 to 1944. There were no tears in the White House when the British war cabinet administered the final blow to Sledgehammer. Roosevelt had waited patiently on events. Now his patience had been rewarded: the North African campaign was put on the schedule for November 1942.

IN THE SPRING OF 1942 the war in the east moved from the central front to southern Russia, surprising Stalin, who had expected another assault on Moscow, and alarming Field Marshal Bock, the commander of Army Group South. The previous winter, as Army Group Center's commander, Bock had looked on helplessly as division after division was chewed up in the Moscow meat grinder because Hitler refused to acknowledge the limits of German power. Now, six months later, Bock feared an even greater catastrophe was gathering.

In theory Operation Blue was a continuation of Barbarossa, but in reality it was more like Barbarossa's feisty younger brother. It was up for a fight, but even reinforced by ten Hungarian, six Italian, and five Romanian divisions, it lacked the punching power of Barbarossa. Hitler was aware of this shortcoming, but he was convinced of the superiority of the German soldier, and he believed the special powers that the gods of war had endowed on him would carry Germany to victory. The new southern strategy was unveiled in May as a series of softening-up assaults. On the nineteenth a German force seized the Kerch Peninsula in the Crimea after driving three Soviet armies into the sea. Then, nine days later, a second German force seized Kharkov, a vital rail junction in the southern Ukraine. At a particularly dangerous moment in the Kharkov battle General Friedrich Paulus, the new commander of the German 6th Army, whose name would forever be linked with Stalingrad, had a twinge of doubt and requested permission to stage a fighting withdrawal. Bock refused, and the next day a bold assault by the 1st Panzer Army saved the situation and Paulus's hesitation was forgotten.

A few weeks later there was another telling incident, this one involving Stalin. A Russian soldier discovered a copy of the Operation Blue plan on the body of a dead German pilot, but seeing only what he wanted to see, Stalin, who had dismissed rumors of a German invasion in June 1941, dismissed the document as a German plant. On the morning of June 28, 1,370,287 German troops began marching eastward into the rising day under an umbrella of 2,035 aircraft and an escort of 1,934 tanks.

As the Germans pushed deeper into the empty, featureless steppe, villages became oases and feeding stations. Turnips, onions, ducks, chicken, and geese were particular favorites, but after a day of fighting, hungry soldiers would eat anything. On a June afternoon Clemens Podewils, a German war correspondent attached to the 6th Army, came across a unit that had hit the culinary jackpot. "Black figures jump down from tanks and half-tracks," he said of it. "Suddenly a great execution is carried out, and the poultry, with bloody ruffs, and furiously beating their wings, are carried back to the vehicles. The men jump on board. The tank tracks ground the soil and the vehicles move on again."

In the early days of Blue, when morale was high, the war regained some of the dark glamour it had lost at the gates of Moscow. "As far as the eye can see," wrote one young officer, "pennants float in the shimmering afternoon air. And commanders stand fearlessly erect in their tank turrets, one arm raised high waving their companies forward." Another young soldier, a former seminarian, was so swept up by the sights and sounds around him—staff cars rushing forward in the dust; the sweaty smell of the tank crews sunning in the steppe grass; the exploding shells hanging in the night sky like young moons—that he wrote a love note to his country. "Germany, you country of strong hearts. You are my home. It is worth one's life to become a seed for you." In a few weeks the young man would get his wish.

Eager to follow the fighting closely, on July 16 Hitler arrived at Werewolf, his headquarters in the Ukraine. Located in a wood seven and a half miles from the town of Vinnytsa, the complex was austere in character. It consisted of Führerhaus, Hitler's modest log cabin, and an adjoining private courtyard. The complex also had twenty guest cabins, a swimming pool, a barbershop, a teahouse, a bathhouse, and a cinema. Bunkers, barbed wire fences, and attack dogs provided protection. As a further safeguard, the Führer's food was chemically analyzed before being cooked and sampled by a taster prior to it being served to him. The water at Werewolf was examined daily for poisons, and the laundry was x-rayed for contaminants.

Hitler did not occupy the complex until the Jewish population in neighboring Vinnytsa had been removed. As the war continued to slip southward from Voronezh to Kharkov to Rostov, Hitler grew increasingly infatuated with his military genius, and in so doing he made a fatal error. As originally conceived, Blue called for the 6th Army and the 4th

Panzer Army to launch a joint strike on Stalingrad and then turn south into the Caucasus. As reconceived by Hitler, Blue became a tale of two armies, each acting independently: the 6th in the Stalingrad region; the 4th Panzer, 455 miles to the south in the Caucasus. With the stroke of a pen Hitler had transformed one powerful striking force into two vulnerable ones.

However, months would pass before the Kremlin could exploit the error. Patriotic fervor and love of country had kept the half-trained, half-equipped Red Army in the field in the summer of 1941. In July 1942 exhaustion, fear, hopelessness, and apathy were the principal emotions in many parts of the Soviet Union. In mid-July Rostov, the gateway city to the Caucasus, was the most vital strategic point along the thousand-mile German-Soviet front. On the twenty-third the Red Army abandoned the city with barely a fight. "The majority of our commanders are cowards," a young Russian soldier wrote in disgust. "Surely we did not need to run away. We could have stood our ground and fought. The hell with retreating. I'm sick to death of pulling back from places where I grew up." The words were the last the young man would write.

In another village in the Rostov region, the local peasants invited a Russian officer to share in their "last crusts." After the meal the officer walked away in shame. "I ate the bread and knew that in an hour I'd be retreating," he wrote, "but I said nothing. I didn't have the right."

Stalin was aware that morale was weakening. "They've forgotten my Stavka order," he told General Aleksandr Vasilevsky, the army chief of staff. It was the morning of July 28 and ever since the previous August the order that Stalin was referencing had served as a reminder to wavering soldiers that there were worse things than death. Under its provisions a soldier could be executed for a host of infractions, but what made the order singular was its provision on families. If a soldier removed his insignia in battle and surrendered, he would be shot and his family would be arrested. If he surrendered during an encirclement, he would be punished "by any means," and his family would be deprived of all state allowances and provisions. "They've forgotten the order," Stalin said, adding, "Write a new one."

"How soon do you need it?" Vasilevsky asked.

"Today," Stalin replied. "Come back as soon as it's ready."

The document that Vasilevsky presented that evening was officially known as Order 227, and within days Russian soldiers across the Soviet

Union were standing at attention in the sweltering August heat in various locations, listening to a commissar or an army officer read its provisions. "Each position," the order began, "each meter of Soviet territory must be stubbornly defended to the last drop of blood. . . . Anyone who surrenders is a traitor. We must cling to each inch of Soviet soil and defend it to the end." Panic-mongers and cowards were to be executed; commanders who permitted troops to retreat would be stripped of their rank and sent to a penal battalion. The order also contained enforcement provisions. In General Zhukov's armies soldiers judged wanting in valor were as likely as a German was to be killed by fellow Russians. In other units sharpshooters positioned themselves behind the advancing troops and sorted out the weak and wavering with a bullet to the head. Not One Step Back—as Order 227 came to be known—had some effect, but the greatest mobilizing force that summer was the same force that had mobilized the country in 1812 when Napoleon invaded: an abiding love for the eternal Russia, celebrated in the poem "Smolensk Roads."

> *Remember the Rain and the mud and pain,*
> *The woman exhausted who brought milk in pitchers*
> *And pressed them like babies at breasts in the rain*
> *The road disappearing past hills in the distance*
> *Its length we measured with tears on the run*
> *And villages and villages, churches and churchyards*
> *As if all of Russia was gathered as one*
> *It seemed in each Russian Village we passed*
> *The hands of our ancestors under the sod*
> *Were making the sign of the cross and protecting*
> *Their Children who no longer believe in God*

In "Courage," another much-read poem in the summer of 1942, the poet Anna Akhmatova wrote:

> *We know what today lies in the scales*
> *And what is happening now.*
> *The Hour of Courage has struck on the clock*
> *And Courage will not desert us*
> *It is not frightening to fall dead under enemy bullets.*

Alert to the change in public mood, the Kremlin began to recast the war as a patriotic struggle. References to communism and the Union of Soviet Socialist Republics grew more infrequent. Transforming Soviet Russia back into Mother Russia required a heroic act of hypocrisy, but hypocrisy was a specialty of the Soviet state. In 1938, sensing war was imminent, Stalin had ordered the director Sergei Eisenstein to make a film about Alexander Nevsky, the Muscovite prince who defeated the Teutonic knights in the thirteenth century. In 1939, after signing a non-aggression pact with Hitler, Stalin withdrew the film. Then, in 1942, with the 6th Army hurtling toward Stalingrad, he released it, and it played to large audiences across the Soviet Union.

It is likely that Stalingrad was also a factor in the more lenient attitude the Soviet state took to the Russian Orthodox church. The state also mobilized two other forces that summer—hate and grief. In the case of grief, by the second year of the war millions of families had lost a loved one and many families had lost more than one son or daughter. As for hatred, it was stoked by Soviet war correspondents. But the hate that the correspondents trafficked in was not the synthetic hatred of the propaganda sheet. Rather it was the boiling hate born of lived experience, of passing the bodies of disemboweled children in a ditch or seeing a raped woman hanging from a scaffold, her severed breast lying in the mud below her dangling feet. "Now we know," wrote Ilya Ehrenburg, perhaps the most famous of the Russian war correspondents. "The Germans are not human. Now the word 'German' has become the most terrible swear word. Let us not speak. Let us not be indignant. Let us kill. If you do not kill one German he will kill you. If you have killed one German . . . kill another."

"There is nothing jollier than a German corpse," wrote Konstantin Simonov, the author of "Wait for Me," the tenderest poem of the war. Simonov was a more sensitive man than Ehrenburg, but when he spoke of the Germans, he spoke Ehrenburg's language. "If you don't want to give away all that you call your country, then kill a German. Kill a German every time you see one." After the war the writer Vyacheslav Kondratev would correctly criticize the Soviet state for taking credit for the revival of morale that summer. That revival, as he rightly noted, was born out of love of country; but hate and the burning desire for vengeance had come first—before love.

JULY 28, 1942, IS NOTEWORTHY not only for being the second coming of the Not One Step Back order but as the day that Stalin invited Churchill to Moscow for talks. The invitation was arranged by Clark Kerr, the British ambassador in Moscow. "It's time to soothe the bear," he wrote in a cable suggesting the visit. Churchill was hesitant. The meeting was certain to include a great deal of unpleasant talk about sunk convoys and nonexistent second fronts, but Kerr was persistent.

Two weeks later the prime minister was gazing down at a ridge of volcanic cones from the window of a B-24. Tabriz, an industrial city in northern Iran, would be coming into view momentarily. An hour later the oil capital of Baku came into view. Then the B-24 lurched sharply to the west; due north lay Stalingrad. For the next few hours a vast expanse of featureless steppe swallowed up the war. During this phase of the journey, General Archibald Wavell kept his fellow passengers amused with a witty little poem about the second front. After he recited it a few times the other passengers chimed in.

> *I do not like the job I have to do*
> *I cannot think my news will go down well*
> *Can I convince them of our settled view?*
> *No Second Front in 1942*
> *Things are stickier than glue*
> *Stalin and Molotov simply hate the tale I have to tell*
> *Can I convince them of our view?*
> *No Second Front in 1942.*

Toward Moscow the war reappeared. The roads were tattooed with bomb craters and the Caucasus littered with burned-out tanks; here and there an upturned staff car offered its belly to the sun. The B-24 set down around 5:00 P.M. on the afternoon of August 12. When a crew member swung open the plane door Molotov; Marshal Shaposhnikov, the chief of the Soviet General Staff; and an honor guard were standing on the tarmac, waiting to greet the prime minister and his party. An aide-de-camp—an enormously tall, splendid-looking officer whom Churchill believed had been of a princely family under the czarist regime—was put at his disposal. For the next few hours the prime minister bathed in "totalitarian lavishness." Veteran servants in white jackets and wearing beaming smiles served caviar, vodka, and rare wines from France and

Germany. Later, Molotov's driver took Churchill to his quarters, State Villa Number 7. It was a warm day and the prime minister wanted to let some air into the car, but, to his surprise, opening the window was like lifting a heavy weight. The glass was more than two inches thick. When Churchill expressed surprise at this, Molotov's driver said, "The minister [Molotov] says it is more prudent."

That evening, when Churchill, Harriman, and Clark Kerr arrived at the Kremlin, their host was seated at a conference table near his office. Molotov and Marshal Kliment Voroshilov, a Stalin crony, were also present. Churchill came to the meeting with a plan. He would give Stalin all the bad news first. Then when that was out of the way he would pacify him with a piece of news that Stalin was certain to like—the North African invasion had been given a green light. Stalin also seemed to have had a plan, and it was a variant of the Mr. Hyde–Dr. Jekyll routine that Beaverbrook and Harriman had experienced in December. Good first meeting; dark, torturous second meeting—and reconciliation at a third or fourth meeting.

Stalin opened the conversation on a sober note. "The Germans seem to have drained the whole of Europe of troops," he said. They have "raised an additional fifty-two divisions in Hungary, Romania, and Italy." (This was an exaggeration; twenty-one divisions was closer to the truth.) He also said that Germany was making a tremendous effort to reach the oil capitals of Baku and Stalingrad. When Stalin finished, Churchill delivered the bad news: the British and American governments had decided to forgo a cross-channel invasion in 1942. It was almost September, and a cross-channel invasion in rough autumn seas would be too dangerous to risk. A record of the meeting was made in real time, and it noted that, after Churchill had delivered his bad news, Stalin "looked very glum." What about the Pas-de-Calais or Cherbourg? Stalin asked. Churchill said a landing at either site would be too high risk. Frustrated, Stalin asked why the British were so hesitant to act, adding that there was "not a single German division in France."

"There are twenty-five," Churchill corrected him. The prime minister's source were the Ultra transcripts, but he kept that to himself.

Stalin recast his argument: there might be twenty or twenty-five German divisions in France, but they were all at half-strength. Again relying on Ultra transcripts, Churchill said that at least nine of the divisions were at full strength. Failing to get anywhere with arguments about landing sites, Stalin switched to personal attacks. Why were the British so afraid of the Germans? The answer: "Experience shows that troops must be bloodied in battle." The meeting continued in this vein for some time; then Churchill arrived at what he hoped would be the turning point of the evening. He took out a map of southern Europe, the Mediterranean, and North Africa. The three regions would feature prominently in the soft-underbelly strategy the prime minister championed later in the war: an attack on Germany through Italy. But this evening he used the map to sell Stalin on Gymnast, now code-named Torch. The argument he made was essentially the same argument he had made to Marshall, King, and Hopkins a few weeks earlier in London. Securing North Africa in 1942 would help ensure the success of Roundup, the main Anglo-American cross-channel attack, which was scheduled for 1943.

Next Churchill turned the conversation to the air war. He said the British "hoped to shatter twenty German cities, as we have already shattered Cologne, Dusseldorf, and Lübeck." If need be, he added, the RAF would "shatter almost every dwelling in almost every German City." The meeting was being recorded, and the transcript notes that after the prime minister finished describing the RAF's plans for the air war "Stalin smiled" and offered a piece of advice. The new four-ton bombs "should be dropped with parachutes," he said. "Otherwise, they dig themselves into the ground and fail to explode." With the atmosphere warming, Churchill returned to Torch and gave his host a detailed picture of the assault plan. General George Patton would lead a Western task force of thirty-five thousand American troops, and Major General Lloyd Fredendall would lead a Central task force of thirty-nine thousand. A British naval force would also participate in the landings, but ten thousand of the thirty-three thousand troops in the force would be American. Churchill was not exaggerating when he told Roosevelt that Torch would be an American operation. The transcript notes that, as Churchill described the details of the Torch, Stalin's "interest quickened" and at one point reached "a high pitch."

CHURCHILL, HARRIMAN, AND KERR WALKED into the warm Moscow night, pleased with the meeting, which closed with Stalin reciting Torch's virtues back to his British guest. It would take the enemy in the rear, make the Germans and French fight each other, put Italy out of action, and keep Spain neutral. Churchill's golden tongue had transformed Torch into the military equivalent of the miracle of the loaves and fishes. The first inkling he had had that things might not be as he had imagined came the next morning during a conversation with Molotov. After a discussion of the military situation, which Molotov described as "far worse than it had been in May or June," he began interrogating the prime minister about Torch, and in the voice of a man who doesn't quite believe what he is being told.

Worse was to come.

That evening, when Churchill arrived at the Kremlin for the second meeting, there was no transcriber waiting to take notes—just a blank-faced Stalin. When Churchill took his seat Stalin handed him a memorandum enumerating the various ways that Britain and America had failed to honor their responsibilities as Allies. The list of grievances in the memorandum was long and began with a complaint that Churchill thought he had resolved the previous evening: the cross-channel invasion. According to the memorandum, the failure of the Anglo-Americans to open a second front in 1942 would "deliver a mortal blow to the whole of Soviet Public opinion . . . complicate the situation of the Red Army at the front, and prejudice the plans of the Soviet Command." While the memorandum was being translated, Stalin continued his harangue. What had the British and Americans contributed to the war? Stalin asked. The British had just given time; the Americans, only money. Russia was providing the blood of her people. The Anglo-Americans treat the eastern front as if it were of "secondary importance," he said.

Then he brought up the PQ 17 fiasco. This "is the first time in history that the Royal Navy has ever turned tail and fled from the battle," he declared. "You British are afraid of fighting. You should not think the Germans are supermen. You will have to fight sooner or later; you can't win a war without fighting." A few moments later Stalin abruptly announced that he could carry the argument no further and invited the confused and agitated Churchill to dinner.

The next morning, when the British delegation convened to discuss Stalin's outburst, Harriman, a target of Stalin's ire the previous autumn, said he thought the outbursts were designed to confuse and intimidate visitors and to put them on the defensive. Churchill had a different theory: perhaps Stalin's power was not as absolute as outsiders assumed;

perhaps he answered to unseen forces in the Kremlin, and they wanted to take a hard line against the Anglo-Americans. Neither theory made the prospect of another visit to the Kremlin more attractive. But this was the magical third meeting in the cycle. Upon arriving that evening the British and American guests were surprised to find themselves ushered into a large room where a sumptuous dinner party was getting under way. Colonel Ian Jacob, Churchill's military assistant secretary, counted more than a hundred guests, including all the leading Soviet generals who were not at the front. "We had barely sat down," Jacob recalled later, before Molotov sprang to his feet and proposed a toast to the prime minister's health. Jacob continued, "Churchill then proposed [a toast] to Stalin's health, then Stalin offered a toast to the health of Roosevelt and Harriman and concluded by toasting his generals and admirals, making a speech of three or four sentences after each toast."

The next day, August 15, Stalin and Churchill met again, this time alone except for their translators. The prime minister was frustrated. He had come to Moscow hoping to establish a personal relationship with Stalin and had ended up arguing with him for three days over second fronts and convoys. Tonight, the night before his departure, Churchill had decided to make a final effort to put his relationship with Stalin on more human terms. He arrived at the Kremlin at seven, just as he had on the previous three days; and he was greeted by Stalin's bodyguard, who led him up a flight of steps to a large conference room, where Stalin was waiting for him under portraits of Marx and Lenin. Outside the window the Moskva River shimmered in the fading August light.

The first few minutes were difficult. Stalin looked down at the floor when he shook Churchill's hand, doodled on a notepad as the prime minister spoke, and launched into yet another tirade about the second front. The atmosphere in the room became so heated that Major A. H. Birse, Churchill's interpreter, thought the evening might end in rancor and bitterness. But then Churchill began to speak. He "realized what I had to say about a second front would be painful, so I thought it would be my duty to come myself to see you, Premier Stalin, that it would be more friendly and proof of my sincere feelings if I came myself—rather than communicate through our ambassador. I asked for plain speaking, and I should like to say I have no feeling in my heart about anything [negative] that has been said. . . . I hope nothing stands between us. I came here, apart from direct business, with an earnest wish for personal understanding."

It was a brave speech, and Stalin was impressed. "The fact that we have met is of very great value," he said. "We have gotten to know each other. Obviously, there are differences between us, but differences are in the nature of things. That personal contact has been established means that the ground had been laid for future agreement . . . I am inclined to look upon things with optimism."

Four days later Churchill fulfilled a promise he had made to Stalin. At first light on August 19 a British-Canadian force assaulted Dieppe, a French port town to the south of the Pas-de-Calais. The operation had a checkered history. First proposed in June, it was canceled in July by General Bernard Montgomery, who deemed it too risky; and it was resuscitated later in the summer by Vice Admiral Mountbatten, an officer of great dash and questionable judgment. The plan, which was presented as a trial run for a cross-channel invasion, was also a sop to Stalin. It called for the attackers to seize Dieppe for a day, kill as many Germans as possible, and take prisoners. But the operation was so poorly thought out and so poorly executed that the principal beneficiary was Hitler. The Germans, who had intelligence on the raid, were in place when the men of the Royal Regiment of Canada poured off assault craft at first light on the nineteenth. Startled by the intruders, cawing seagulls filled the sky.

In the homes along the shore, lights flickered on and faces peered through curtains. Then, abruptly, the bluffs above the beach began to spit machine-gun fire. Men screamed. Hands, legs, and arms flew into the air. Pools of blood formed in the damp sand. Shouts of "Finish me off!" and "Kill me!" drowned out the barking of the local dogs. Of the six thousand men who reached the beaches that morning, over three thousand were killed, wounded, or captured. The RAF, which provided air cover for the raid, also suffered grievously. A hundred Spitfires and thirty-three Hurricane fighters were shot down and a destroyer was sunk—a heavy price to pay for a day at the beach.

When news of the raid arrived at Hitler's advance headquarters in the Ukraine that afternoon, Joseph Goebbels, who was visiting the Führer, wrote in his diary: "Under pressure from Stalin, the British have clearly

undertaken an attempt to open a second front." Later in the day, he and
Hitler discussed the postwar fate of the three Allied leaders. Hitler said
Churchill and Roosevelt would be executed, but he would spare Stalin.
The Soviet leader had shown himself to be a worthy enemy and would
be treated as Napoleon had been: exiled to a remote but not unpleasant
island to live out his final years.

8

WE'VE GOT TO FEEL
WE HAVE VICTORIES IN US

IN THE SUMMER OF 1942 THE WAR DOMINATED ALMOST EVERY aspect of American life. Jukeboxes across the country were playing "Praise the Lord and Pass the Ammunition," "Der Fuehrer's Face," "He's 1-A in the Army and He's A-1 in My Heart," and "You're a Sap, Mr. Jap." The most popular movies of the season were *Wake Island*, *One of Our Aircraft Is Missing*, and *Flying Tigers*. Billboards featured a pretty young member of the Women's Army Corps (WAC) pitching underwear for Munsingwear foundation garments. In Washington the population swelled as thousands of young men and women arrived seeking war work; and Shangri-La, President Roosevelt's new weekend retreat in the Maryland hills, had become a favorite source of gossip. There were rumors that Roosevelt had tired of Hyde Park, but Shangri-La (which President Eisenhower renamed Camp David) owed its existence to proximity. It was only a two-hour drive from the capital—close enough for the president to get to his office relatively quickly in an emergency.

As the summer White House, Shangri-La was a relatively modest affair: a simple woodland lodge with four bedrooms and two bathrooms, one for the president, the other for his guests. A series of cottages near the main house were set aside for secretaries, Secret Service personnel, and a telephone exchange. On a typical summer weekend Roosevelt would work on his stamp collection, serenaded by a screen door banging back and forth against the porch. Then he would play solitaire and gossip with old friends like Daisy Suckley, Hopkins, and his speechwriter Robert Sherwood. For a man who had as much on his mind as Roosevelt did that summer, Shangri-La offered a much-needed sanctuary. Despite all the patriotic fervor the war was not going well. On August 8, in one of the first major American operations of the war after Midway, a marine task force of eleven thousand men was abandoned on the beaches of Guadalcanal by its naval escort, which withdrew to avoid an encounter with the Japanese fleet. At home work was plentiful and salaries were rising, but food rationing, price controls, caps on pay, and a ban on car sales (which left automobile dealers across the country with a half million unsold cars) ensured that a good portion of the average paycheck was funneled into war bonds.

The summer also saw a rise in racial tensions; the war was drawing more African Americans into the workforce, and in many parts of the country their arrival was unwelcome. In July Eugene "Bull" Connor, of Birmingham, Alabama, wrote a letter of complaint to the United States government. Connor charged that the Fair Employment Practices Committee (FEPC), which was created to assist African Americans' transition into war work, was causing disunity in the country. Connor, who in the 1960s would become an international face of American racism, also described venereal disease as the number-one "Negro problem"—and he urged that "the Ku Klux Klan be revived to oppose racial change." Connor concluded his 1942 letter with a taunt: "Don't you think one war . . . in the South is enough?" The following year a confrontation between black and white war workers did lead to a major race riot that produced thirty-four deaths, but the confrontation occurred in Detroit, not the South.

Roosevelt's attitude about racial issues was paradoxical. He was quick to respond to acts of personal injustice. When a noted African American tenor, Roland Hayes, and his wife were assaulted in a store he spoke up—and he spoke up again when the War Department labeled black soldiers serving overseas as "service troops." But on broader issues of racial justice he tended to remain silent. In 1942 African Americans accounted for 10 percent of the selective service entrants, but the army had only three hundred black officers, and only three of the three hundred held the rank of colonel. In the main, the president's views on race reflected those of his fellow New Yorker, Secretary of War Henry Stimson, another wealthy, privileged member of the city's elite. In the world that the two men inhabited the "Negro" was seen largely as a cause: someone to be supported by attendance at charity balls and the funding of soup kitchens. Like many men of his class Stimson found it difficult to see the African American as a fighting man. "The Negro," he wrote a friend, "still lacks the particular initiative which a commanding officer of men needs in war . . . Also the social intermixture of the two races is basically impossible." However, by the standards of 1942, Stimson's views were relatively enlightened. In London General Eisenhower was collecting "reports on colored troop problems," and senior commanders in the South and in multicultural Hawaii were protesting the assignment of "colored troops" to their commands. The Australian government, the president of the Republic of Panama, the governor of Alaska, the government of Bermuda, the British authorities in Trinidad, and various South American leaders were also reluctant to accept black troops. To his credit Stimson did refuse to honor most of the governmental requests to remove black troops.

For African Americans the war at least broadened employment opportunities. For Japanese Americans there were no offsets. The war was a zero-sum game played out in the interior of the American West against a backdrop of big skies and bleak flatlands. In the spring of 1942 Milton Eisenhower, director of the War Relocation Authority and brother of General Dwight Eisenhower, reported that currently eighty-one thousand Japanese Americans were in temporary assembly centers, twenty thousand in permanent relocation centers, and fifteen thousand frozen in place in eastern California. Eventually most of the detainees were funneled to one of the eleven internment camps in the interior. During a visit to the White House in the spring of 1942, Milton Eisenhower briefed the president on the camps; but what he did not tell Roosevelt and what the president did not ask him about was the situation of the detainees: "the sad departures from hard-won homes and farms, the 'hurry up and wait'" journey through the detention centers; the shock of arrival at a camp in Poston, Arizona; Heart Mountain, Wyoming; or Topaz, Utah. The burning heat and numbing cold of the region; the endless rows of barracks; the one-room-to-a-family accommodations; the red tape and boredom; the barbed wire fences; and the machine guns staring down at the detainees at morning roll call. The camps were not a state secret. Anyone who could read a newspaper knew about them, and polling showed they had public support. Even the American Civil Liberties Union gave the camps its imprimatur.

In the late summer and early autumn of 1942 there was a great deal of polling done on public attitudes toward the war. The findings revealed that the average American's understanding of what the country was fighting for did not go much beyond the popular vocalist Kate Smith singing "God Bless America." In a fiery speech that autumn, the anthropologist and public intellectual Margaret Mead warned that casual patriotism was insufficient. Victory required "an impassioned effort by every individual in this country," Mead said. "The Government must mobilize people not just to carry out orders but to participate in a great action . . . [and] to assume responsibility. We've got to feel we have victory in us."

That autumn Franklin Roosevelt was thinking along similar lines, and that thinking resulted in one of the most unusual trips in presidential history: a two-week tour of America free of the pomp and circumstance that usually attends presidential travel. There was to be no publicity about the trip until Roosevelt returned to Washington; no parades or speeches in the cities he visited, no advance notice to the workers in the war plants he inspected, and no large traveling press—just three reporters and eight photographers. Eleanor would accompany him as far as Chicago; his other traveling companions were his cousins Daisy Suckley and Laura Delano, his old law partner Harry Hooker, and his dog Fala for the entire trip.

On September 17 the president left Washington and set out to look for America. In Detroit he was surrounded by cheering workmen as he watched hundreds of metal sheets materialize into a tank before his eyes. At the Great Lakes Naval Training Station outside Chicago he watched a company of marines jump over obstacles and in and out of trenches. At Fort Lewis in Washington State he inspected ski troops and watched while Fala had his picture taken. At Henry Kaiser's shipyard in Portland, Oregon, he joked with the workers. "You know," he said, "I'm not supposed to be here today. I hope you will keep [his visit] a secret." In California he made surprise appearances at aircraft factories, and he visited a naval hospital in San Diego. In New Orleans he spent a day at the Higgins boat company, which was creating a new assault craft that would carry American soldiers onto the beaches of Normandy, Okinawa, and dozens of battlefields in between. And in Texas he visited army air force training stations.

Within a few months many of the young men who had exchanged wisecracks with him would be flying combat missions over France and Germany. Roosevelt set out to answer two questions, and he returned to Washington satisfied that the United States possessed the technical and manufacturing skills needed to win the war and that, beneath their breezy, bebop exterior, the young men and women of the country understood how high the stakes were and the sacrifices that would be demanded of them.

On September 18, while Roosevelt was inspecting a defense plant in Detroit, 1,400 miles to the north a flight of Heinkel dive bombers and Junkers Ju 88s were sweeping out of the arctic sky. The planes dropped to wave-top level, released their torpedoes—and the ships of Convoy PQ 18 began to explode like piñatas in the cold arctic air. Cautioned by the horrific experience of its predecessor, PQ 17, the Royal Navy had gone to great lengths to safeguard PQ 18: fifty escort warships, including an air-craft carrier and two submarines. Yet the best all this naval might could achieve was a Pyrrhic victory. On September 21 PQ 18 limped into the port of Archangel, with thirteen of the forty merchantmen in the convoy destroyed: a lower rate than that of PQ 17, but still unsustainable.

Initially, Roosevelt and Churchill agreed that the next convoy, PQ 19, should be postponed. Then the president had second thoughts. Russia was in a perilous position. With the North African operation mere weeks away the only concession Churchill was prepared to make was sacrifi-cial in nature. He proposed that ten unescorted merchantmen chance the Russian run in October, relying on the dark autumn moon to carry them to safety.

OVERSHADOWING EVERYTHING THAT SUMMER WAS Stalingrad. "Its sur-vival became not just a military and economic necessity," writes his-torian Richard Overy, "but a symbol of defiant nationalism." The city began life in the sixteenth century as Tsaritsyn, a Volga port town, and it was reborn as Stalingrad in 1925 to honor an alleged act of heroism by its namesake. In the 1930s the city grew into a major industrial center. By the beginning of the war Stalingrad was home to the Red October, the Red Barricades, and a dozen other factories whose names would forever be linked to Stalingrad. For different reasons the German 6th Army's link to the city would also become immortal.

At the start of the campaign in late July of 1942, the 6th Army held the advantage in men and matériel: 250,000 troops versus the Red Army's 100,870; 700,400 tanks versus the Red Army's 300,860; and 1,200 aircraft versus the Soviet Air Forces' 300,300. Passing through the lush countryside of the Cossack region that summer the German soldier was reminded of what he was fighting for. Five years hence the war would be over, Russia Germanized, and the neat whitewashed cottages and green meadows he was passing would be homesteads for thousands of young Germans like himself. Later, one German soldier would remember the final days of July 1942 as the last "happy time" of the war.

In early August the army crossed the Don River, and the landscape changed—from welcoming to ominous. Stalingrad lay to the east on the Volga River, and in between the Don and Volga lay what Overy described as "a barren, naked, lifeless steppe without a bush, without a tree, for miles without a village." It was, a German soldier later recalled, "the most desolate and mournful region to come before my eyes." It was also good panzer country. The steppe was flat and straight, and Hitler, pacing back and forth at his forward headquarters in the Ukraine, was impatient for good news.

The war came to Stalingrad on August 23. It was announced by the screech of loudspeakers. There had been several false air-raid alarms over the summer, so people were not immediately frightened. Then anti-aircraft guns began to boom in the distance, and people ran for cover. On Mamayev Kurgan, the Tartar burial ground in the center of the city (and a favorite picnicking spot), parents swept up their children and rushed for shelter. Along the long, broad streets parallel to the Volga panicked crowds pushed and shoved for a space in one of the trenches built by the city's block committees. Overhead squadron after squadron of Stuka bombers swept across the silvery afternoon sky. Upon reaching a target the planes would dip into a dive, and the streets and factories below would disappear into balls of fire. The members of a female anti-aircraft crew watched in horror as the wind caught a German pilot who had just worked free of his burning plane and deposited him into the belly of a blazing department store.

That evening the military commission in Moscow informed Stalingrad's beleaguered defenders that the city was to be held at all costs.

"Keep after the enemy not only in daytime but also at night," the commission ordered. "Above all, do not give way to panic. Do not let the enemy scare you. Keep faith in your own strength." A few days later an "at all costs" order was issued. "We shall never surrender the city of our birth," it began. "Let us barricade every street. Let us transform each district, each block, each building into an impregnable fortress." The attackers would prove as faithful to the "at all costs" order as the defenders. Visiting Stalingrad in early September the journalist and novelist Konstantin Simonov was reminded of an ancient burial pit. "It seemed as though the houses had sunk into the ground and grave mounds . . . had been heaped over them."

On September 12, a heavyset man with a swarthy Slavic face, hard eyes, and a smile full of gold teeth arrived in Stalingrad to assume command of the 62nd Army, one of the two Soviet armies charged with defending the city. Vasily Ivanovich Chuikov was a man between youth and middle age who had just returned from China, where he served as a military adviser to Chiang Kai-shek, and arrived in Stalingrad with a simple plan for victory: "Make every German feel he is living under the muzzle of a Russian gun." It is not uncommon for soldiers to boast that they have no fear of death, but Chuikov was among the few men who could make the boast honestly. He was not the kind of officer that soldiers came to love, but he inspired respect and trust. Almost every Russian soldier who entered Stalingrad that autumn expected to die there. Chuikov's troops at least had the consolation of knowing that if they did die in the city at least they would die a purposeful death, rather than because their commander wanted to impress Moscow.

On September 13—the day Chuikov arrived in Stalingrad—the 62nd Army had been reduced to twenty thousand men; the streets crackled with the sound of gunfire; and the sky had been turned a dull brown by explosives, dust, and the constant cannonade. In the dugout near the Tartar burial site where Chuikov had set up his command center, soil dislodged from the shelling seeped down through the roof logs onto the floor. Chuikov, who had seen almost every kind of death in his twenty years of soldiering, did not rattle easily, but what he saw that day on the way to his new command post unnerved him. *Everything has perished,* he thought. The city was "dead."

In September, as the fighting grew savager, Chuikov would be forced to move his command post several times. Frequently, the Germans held the central railway station by day; the Red Army by night. The Mamayev Kurgan also changed hands numerous times. One of the most critical moments in the battle occurred on the fourteenth, when a German assault came within a few hundred yards of cutting off Soviet access to the Volga River, the city's lifeblood. Men, matériel, oil, weaponry, rations—every vital element of war—flowed across the river to the docks, which changed hands three times on the morning of the fourteenth.

Overmatched and outgunned, Chuikov's decimated 62nd Army fought a slow, bitter rearguard action, contesting every street and every ruin, fighting amid the corpses of children, decapitated bodies, and the wild barking of feral dogs. Then, on the afternoon of the fourteenth, the Volga produced a miracle. The 26th Guards Division—commanded by General Alexander Rodimtsev, hero of the Soviet Union—arrived from the Russian side of the river. The first wave of guardsmen were so eager to get at the enemy, they did not even bother to fix bayonets. "They leapt from their boats into the shallow water and charged up a steep sandy bank," said Anglo-Russian correspondent Alexander Werth. A third of the guards suffered casualties that day, but they held the riverbank. Of the 10,000 guardsmen who fought at Stalingrad, only 320 would still be alive at the end of the campaign. Asked about this sacrifice, one replied, "There is no land for us behind the Volga!"

The challenge that Stalingrad posed to both sides was elemental: to achieve victory, the German commander would have to the push the Red Army into the Volga; to avoid defeat, at a minimum, the Russian commander would have to hold the region around the river to keep the supply line open. Chuikov mastered his challenge more effectively than General Paulus had managed his, by recognizing that in the close combat of Stalingrad what mattered was not strategy but tactics: the dozens of small individual actions that pave the way to victory. Thus, to neutralize the German advantage in firepower, Chuikov ordered his troops to keep their front line close to the enemy's, which had the effect of making the Germans hesitate to fire—for fear of killing their own men. Chuikov also encouraged his soldiers to take advantage of the terrain and to make use of their skills in close-quarter and night fighting. Often, after dark, Soviet units would fall upon an isolated German unit, startle them with a fearsome barrage of yells, then kill them. By late September the Russians owned the night. An advantage in firepower, in the air and on the ground, made the Germans masters of the day. The Soviet T-34 was the best tank on the battlefield in 1942, but there were not many T-34s in Stalingrad, and the skill of their crews was often wanting. Other serious deficits also hobbled the defenders. The Soviet aircraft defending the city were a generation behind their German counterparts, and many of the Russian troops thrown into the Stalingrad cauldron were thrown in after a four- or five-day ride in an unheated train from Siberia or Kyrgyzstan: untrained and unarmed and often dependent on the dead to provide weapons.

By late September the German advantage in weaponry and training was beginning to appear. Paulus held most of the central city, including the iconic Univermag department store, which was defended to the death by a Soviet unit holed up in the store's basement. In the southern part of the city a giant grain elevator was in the first stages of what would become a fifty-six-day siege, the Soviet defenders fighting floor to floor under constant bombardment by German tanks and artillery.

On September 25—as Roosevelt was inspecting an aircraft factory in Los Angeles—Paulus turned his attention to the factory complex in the northern district of Stalingrad. Three understrength German infantry and two panzer divisions attacked the district along a three-mile front. After a bitter battle most of the surviving Soviet units were driven back from their original positions to the Red Barricades factory near the banks of the Volga, or they found refuge in a dugout along the river. The 62nd was not fighting alone. Its sister unit, the 64th Army, though badly mauled, continued to maintain an active defense. Its Katyusha rocket launchers were particularly effective in preventing a German breakthrough.

By early October bitter fighting raged from every ruin, street, factory, house, basement, and staircase in Stalingrad. Even the sewers became scenes of vicious fighting. Germans called the underground war the Rattenkrieg—the rat's war—and they joked about capturing a kitchen but still having to fight for the living room and bedroom. Buildings, in particular, saw a great deal of close combat. Men would fight room by room through the bombed-out debris of homes and offices. In some of the taller buildings, reduced to roofless shells in the fighting, the Germans would take a position on the third floor, the Red Army on the fourth floor, and then the two sides would shoot at each other through a staircase or through holes in a wall. How could men survive under such conditions? The ubiquitous presence of the NKVD was a factor, but not the only one. Alexander Werth, who interviewed a number of Stalingrad veterans, believed a kind of natural selection was at work along the Volga. "Men arrived shocked and fearful on the riverbank under continuous German fire," he said. "A quarter might be dead before reaching the front line a few hundred yards beyond the bank." But the rest, said Werth, developed a tough survival instinct. Konstantin Simonov, who visited the city during the fighting, offered a different explanation. In the unique conditions of the Stalingrad battlefield, "the dour determination of the ordinary Russian" was a more effective weapon than the superior weaponry and training of the German soldier.

On September 12, Zhukov and Aleksandr Vasilevsky, Stalin's chief of staff, returned from Stalingrad, gravely concerned. The force currently defending the city was too small to sustain a viable defense, and pouring more troops into the cauldron would only produce more casualties. The day after their return, Zhukov and Vasilevsky presented Stalin with a new plan—a flank attack. Rather than strike the Germans where they were strongest, inside the city, the Red Army would assault the German flanks to the north and south of the city, areas that were defended by poorly led, poorly trained Italian, Romanian, and Hungarian units. One Soviet force would strike the Axis-flanking divisions to the north of the city; the other, the flanking divisions to the south—and then link up and drive into Stalingrad. Stalin made a few changes to the plan and then approved it. Now everything would depend on time and on the steadfastness of the Russian soldier. Zhukov and Vasilevsky would need forty-five days to prepare a new battle plan. And the Russian soldier would have to provide the time, if necessary, by sacrificing himself.

9

GENERAL DETERMINATION AND GENERAL "THEY WILL BEAT US!"

<hr />

B Y OCTOBER STALIN'S FORBEARANCE WITH HIS WESTERN ALLIES was wearing thin. While the Stalingrad cauldron was consuming hundreds of young Russians daily, the Americans and British, distressed by convoy losses, were temporarily suspending deliveries to Murmansk and Archangel. In *A Meeting of Military Experts*, a cartoon that appeared in the October 6 edition of the Soviet newspaper *Pravda*, Stalin voiced his anger at the decision. The two Red Army officers in the cartoon are young and vigorous. Their names are General Determination and General Courage. Their Anglo-American counterparts are General They Will Beat Us; General Is It Worth the Risk?; General No Need to Hurry; and General Something May Go Wrong.

The hands on the clock above the generals was set at 11:30 P.M. Roosevelt, who was now back in Washington, did not need General Courage to tell him Stalin was angry or where the anger could lead. In the summer of 1941 Stalin had toyed with the idea of making a separate peace with Germany. Fearing that Stalin might revisit that option, Roosevelt and Churchill made a peace offering—Operation Velvet. At the beginning of 1943 an Anglo-American air force of twenty squadrons would be dispatched to the Caucasus to help the Soviets check the German advance into the oil fields of southern Russia. A few days after the cartoon appeared Churchill presented Stalin with a second peace offering—the long-promised Anglo-American second front. On October 23 a British force of almost 200,000 men would attack the Afrika Korps at El-Alamein, an Egyptian town near the Libyan border. Two weeks later—on November 8—an American force of 100,700 men would seize Algiers, Oran, and Morocco and link up with the British units advancing west from El-Alamein.

Geographically, the Torch plan had great sweep. It encompassed the thousand-mile-long shoulder of land, rock, and mountain that stretched across the Middle East from Casablanca on the Atlantic coast to Tunisia. But the landings would put the Anglo-American forces two thousand miles from Stalin's preferred target, northern France. After being briefed on the Allied plan, Stalin brooded for a few days and then sent Churchill a cable. It was brief—but there was a world of meaning in those words: "I received your message of October 9. Thank you."

Churchill's first reaction to the note was anger. Hundreds of thousands of men and thousands of tanks, planes, and artillery units had been assembled for the campaign; more than a thank-you seemed in order. However, upon thinking it over, the prime minister decided it would be a great mistake to run after the Russians in their present mood. "The only thing that will do any good is fighting hard and winning victories," he told Eden. Roosevelt's response was breezier. "I am not unduly disturbed by Moscow's response," he told his aides. "I have decided that they do not use speech for the same purposes as we do."

IN MID-OCTOBER TORCH AND LIGHTFOOT, the code name for the British assault at El-Alamein, took center stage, and Russia briefly slipped into the background. The military risks posed by Torch, the American assault, were particularly daunting. The towering waves that thundered across the beaches of Casablanca could play havoc with the men and matériel during the landings. The beaches of Algeria were calmer, but if, as some rumors were suggesting, a German force lunged down through Spain during the landings, the American troops on the beaches could be cut off.

Beyond these dangers there were the political risks. North Africa was not a domain of France, it was a domain of Vichy France, and the loyalties of Vichy's leader, Marshal Philippe Pétain, were unclear. The situation was further complicated by a threat developing on the other side of the world. In early October Chester Nimitz, commander of the Pacific fleet, warned Washington that the Japanese were assembling a large strike force to attack the marines on Guadalcanal. "The situation is critical," Nimitz cabled Washington. Alarmed, Marshall asked Douglas MacArthur, commander of US forces in the South Pacific, to provide air support for the beleaguered marines. MacArthur, who had a famously large ego and favored a Pacific-first strategy, balked. The situation was so critical, he told Washington, "the entire resources of the United States [should] be diverted temporarily to (the Pacific) to meet the threat."

Like MacArthur, who was famous for his corncob pipe and gold braided hats, the ferret-faced Bernard Montgomery, commander of the British Eighth Army, had a penchant for trademark clothing. Montgomery dressed for battle as if preparing for a cricket match: jodhpurs, neck scarf, and, his most iconic trademark, a black beret. During the Dunkirk evacuation Montgomery had demonstrated a skill for improvisation and the ability to keep his nerve in dangerous situations. But his specialty was the set-piece battle. He would work out every aspect of a battle plan in great detail, then drill his troops until each soldier understood the plan and the part he played in it. After months of rigorous training, by mid-October Montgomery was confident the Eighth Army could meet the Germans on equal terms and defeat them. In an eve-of-battle speech on October 23 he told his soldiers what would be expected of them. Every man "must be imbued by the desire to kill Germans, even padres." He recommended killing "one German for weekdays and two for Sundays." When he finished, an eight-hundred-gun cannonade lit up the desert sky, and the Tommies began winding their way through the German minefields.

The force facing the British was no longer the Afrika Korps of 1942. Indeed, in some ways it was no longer Rommel's Afrika Korps. In September, before returning to Germany on medical leave, the Desert Fox wrote a long, somber appreciation of the Afrika Korps and its principal ally, the Italian army. The gist of the analysis was that the Axis armies in North Africa were a spent force, and only a victory in Stalingrad or elsewhere in southern Russia could restore the Axis position in Africa. The Battle of El-Alamein proved Rommel right. The British began with an overwhelming advantage in men (195,000 versus the Italo-German defenders' 116,547) and in tanks (over 1,000 versus the defenders' 547), and military pieces: 892 versus the Italo-Germans' 552. (There is still disagreement about the Italians' performance at El-Alamein.) During the first few days of fighting German mines and skillful tactics slowed the British advance and produced heavy casualties. With the campaign threatening to degenerate into a battle of attrition, the usually cautious Montgomery threw caution to the winds and ordered a New Zealand and Australian division, supported by British armor, to attack strongpoints along the German line. The force of the assault and the sudden death of General Georg Stumme, Rommel's replacement, rattled the usually resolute Germans, who now began a general retreat under a new commander, General Wilhelm Josef Ritter von Thoma. The ten-day battle left Germany with 30,000 casualties; Britain, 13,000; and it dented Rommel's reputation as a military wizard. Except for his success at the Kasserine Pass and a few minor victories, he would spend his remaining months in North Africa organizing retreats.

THE COLLAPSE AT EL-ALAMEIN CAME as a blow to German radio listeners. The security services, which monitored public opinion, found that as the situation in Stalingrad darkened, more and more German civilians had come to rely on Rommel and the Afrika Korps for good news. In Britain and America the newspapers and newsreels covered the landings as if the battle had already been won, not just starting. The film footage featured tanned young soldiers playing soccer and baseball and smiling before dozens of clicking cameras. North Africa also made Dwight Eisenhower, recently promoted to supreme commander of Allied forces, instantly more famous than John Wayne and Errol Flynn combined. In addition, it introduced him to French politics in the form of Admiral François Darlan, whose titles included that of vice president of the council, the French equivalent of prime minister.

A member of a distinguished French military family—one of Darlan's ancestors had fought the British at Trafalgar—the admiral's service record had been exemplary until 1940. He had led a French naval unit at the battle of Verdun, and after the Great War he represented the French Navy at the London Naval Conference. Intelligent and blessed with more than his fair share of Gallic charm, Darlan's star rose steadily during the 1930s. But beneath the smooth engaging exterior there was a complicated personality with at least three different faces. There was Darlan the fierce French patriot, who had fought at Verdun and would never forgive the British for turning their guns on the French fleet in 1940. There was Darlan the politician, who worked diligently to ingratiate himself with Adolf Hitler. And there was Darlan the silky fixer, whose services were for sale.

A few weeks after the landings Darlan and Eisenhower, who was new to international politics, reached an agreement: the Allies would recognize Darlan as the French high commissioner, a post that made him governor of North and West Africa; in return the admiral would order the French forces under his command to lay down their arms and facilitate relations between American commanders and local French officials. In Britain and the United States, where Darlan's reputation had preceded him, the appointment produced an uproar. The admiral was a fascist, a quisling, an amoral opportunist who had looked the other way when the Germans began sending French Jews to the camps. On November 17, with anti-Darlan feeling growing in Britain, Churchill cabled Roosevelt, "I ought to let you know very deep currents are [being] stirred up [here] by the arrangement with Darlan. The more I think about it, the more I am convinced it can only be a temporary expedient justified solely by the strain of battle." In a reply the next day Roosevelt said, "I too have felt the deep undercurrent of feeling about Darlan. I felt I should act fast, so I have just given out a statement at my press conference, which I hope will be accepted. . . . People in the United Nations . . . would never understand the recognition or reconstitution of a Vichy government."

By early December 1942 the question roiling through Allied capitals was not: Should Darlan go? It was: How should he go? The consensus view was by assassination. In early December Sir Alexander Cadogan, permanent under secretary at the British Foreign Office, told colleagues, "We shall do no good until we've killed Darlan." At a lunch with Anthony Eden a few days later Charles de Gaulle, the leader of the Free French, made a similar proposal—as did Carleton Coon, an OSS operative; a special operations executive of the British Secret Operations Unit; Abbot Cordier of the Church of Saint Augustine; and Bonnier de La Chapelle, a royalist whose great ambition was to make France a monarchy again. The final scene in the Darlan drama followed the conventions of 1940s gangster movies. At a meeting two days before Christmas 1942, Abbot Cordier persuaded La Chapelle to kill Darlan. The next day, Christmas Eve, La Chapelle entered the admiral's hotel room and shot him at point-blank range with a Colt Woodsman pistol.

Reactions to the assassination varied. De Gaulle was relieved, as was SOE, but Eisenhower and Marshall came away from the incident chastened. Even in war, they concluded, a nation should not employ methods that undermine the values it was fighting for. However, by the beginning of January the Darlan killing had already become yesterday's news. All eyes were on Stalingrad, where the titanic struggle between Russia and Germany was reaching a tipping point.

AT FIRST LIGHT ON THE morning of November 19 a Romanian unit to the north of Stalingrad warned the 6th Army that a major Soviet attack was imminent. Under other circumstances the German officer who received the message would have immediately awakened his superior, the 6th Army chief of staff, General Arthur Schmidt. But the Romanians were considered an excitable people with more false alarms to their credit than the Italians, Hungarians, and the other Axis armies fighting with Germany. The officer hesitated for a moment, then decided not to wake up Schmidt. It was a cold autumn morning, and the general had been up late the previous evening. Whatever was in the Romanian's note could wait until Schmidt awoke. Around the same time hundreds of thousands of Russian soldiers were gathering in the fields and villages and squares across European Russia to hear an officer read a message from Stalin: "Dear generals and soldiers, I address you as my brothers. Today you start an offensive and your actions will decide the fate of the country: whether it remains an individual country or perishes." Stalin's delivery was wooden, but that morning "the villages and the hands of our ancestors under the sod" made it feel "as if all Russia had gathered as one" to hear Stalin speak. "I was close to tears when the meeting was over," one Red Army officer recalled later.

In 1941 the Russian soldier's willingness to sacrifice himself, and not much else, had stopped the Germans at the gates of Moscow and Leningrad. In 1942 a million-man Soviet force would go into battle with better logistics and intelligence, as well as 1,400 heavy guns and 979 tanks. Initially the attack had been scheduled to begin on the eighteenth, but nine days before the starting date the battle-weary German 6th Army made a last attempt to seize the city. General Kurt Zeitzler, the German army chief of staff, had grave reservations about the assault, but Hitler had been adamant. "I won't leave the Volga," he told Zeitzler. At dawn on November 9, thousands of German soldiers—their faces unshaven, their eyes red with fatigue—emerged from rat-infested dugouts and bunkers and roofless buildings into the bitter November morning. The Germans cut Chuikov's 62nd Army in half for a second time, then punched a corridor five hundred yards wide down to the Volga. But the gains proved unsustainable. Photos of the city taken in this period are reminiscent of the photos of Hiroshima in 1945: vast swaths of empty space intersected, here and there, by a ruined building or a woman on her knees searching through the "harvest of death" for a scrap of food.

On a map, Operation Uranus resembled an elongated cell. In the first two days of the offensive the Red Army made two incisions. On the nineteenth the Romanian forces guarding the 6th Army's northern flank were destroyed, and over the next two days the Romanians guarding the army's southern flank were also destroyed. On the twenty-first, seven thousand Romanians marched into captivity with nothing to sustain them but the tattered photos of wives and children they would never see again. In 1941, before the start of Operation Barbarossa, Hitler had boasted to his commanders, "All we have to do is kick in the door and the whole rotten structure will collapse." In November 1942 the prophecy came true but the rotten structure on the edge of collapse was the German army. By November 24 the Soviet offensive was in its fifth day and Hitler was concerned enough about the reports from Stalingrad to consult two of his most trusted advisers. Both men told him what he wanted to hear. Field Marshal Erich von Manstein promised to break through the Soviet cordon around Stalingrad and relieve the 6th Army, and Hermann Göring, the Luftwaffe chief, promised to deliver five hundred tons of supplies to Stalingrad daily.

Neither man kept his promise. On December 19 the Luftwaffe delivered 262 tons to the besieged city, roughly half what Göring had promised. Initially, Winter Storm, Manstein's attempt to relieve Stalingrad, had some success, but his force was still thirty miles from the city when a heavy snow and biting winds made a further advance impossible. The collapse of the German positions in the Caucasus in December and

January swelled the number of troops in the Stalingrad cauldron from about 270,000 to 300,300.

Fate now offered General Paulus an opportunity to enter Valhalla as a hero of national socialism. A heroic death on a Stalingrad street would win him a state funeral attended by Hitler, Göring, and Goebbels. There were officers who would have embraced such an opportunity, but Paulus was not among them. He was the antithesis of his predecessor at the 6th Army, the flamboyant, swaggering Walther von Reichenau, who had died suddenly six months earlier. Even-tempered, well-mannered, a Beethoven devotee, he was—according to an officer who served with him—quietly vain. "He was always beautifully turned out with a gleaming white collar and immaculately polished field boots," the officer remembered. Five months in, Stalingrad washed away his vanity—and left behind a broken man. In the final stage of the campaign, colleagues remembered Paulus as being chronically "tired, listless, prone to bouts of debilitating illness" and "devoured by an unspoken bitterness at the role fate had assigned him." In late January, as the Red Army was clearing out the remaining German strongpoints, a German staff officer emerged from the Univermag department store and signaled to one of the young Russians standing in front of the store, Lieutenant Fyodor Yelhenko. Yelhenko and two companions followed the German down to the store's malodorous basement, where hundreds of German soldiers were sprawled on the floor in various stages of dying. Amid the groans and weeping, Yelhenko accepted the German surrender from a member of Paulus's staff; then he was led to another part of the store where he found the general lying on a bed, unshaven and listless.

Later Yelhenko remembered saying to him, "Well, that finishes it!" and Paulus nodding in agreement. The previous day—January 30—Hitler had promised to promote Paulus to field marshal in hopes the promotion would stiffen his spine and lead him to choose a soldier's death. The ploy failed, greatly annoying the Führer, who vented his rage in a talk with his cronies a few days later. "In Germany, in peacetime," he noted, "eighteen to twenty thousand people a year choose to commit suicide. Here is a man who sees fifty or sixty thousand of his men defending themselves bravely to the end. How can he surrender himself?" The next day German radio played Siegfried's funeral march from *Götterdämmerung*.

That afternoon in Stalingrad it was snowing. It snowed on the decapitated buildings, the half-dug ditches, and upturned tanks and roofless apartments where men had fought floor to floor, room to room. The snow fell on Chuikov's broken 62nd Army, on the slopes of Mamayev Kurgan, on the Red Barricades factory—and on the tens of thousands of uncoffined Italian, Romanian, and Hungarian dead who congregated in the brilliant white fields under the shadow of the cold February sky.

10

TURN OF THE TIDE

I T WAS TWO O'CLOCK IN THE MORNING, THE NIGHT SKY OUTSIDE the Commando was black and cold, and Winston Churchill had just awoken with a burning sensation in his foot. He recognized the source immediately, a heat point. More than a dozen points had been installed in the Commando's interior to keep the cabin and sleeping bay at room temperature during long flights, but the points were a technology in progress—if one malfunctioned, a fire could be ignited.

Churchill climbed out of his bunk and woke up Air Marshal Charles Portal, who was asleep in the bunk next to his. Outside the window a gust of wind was bouncing the plane up and down in the sky. Flashlights in hand Churchill and Portal walked up and down the Commando's half-lit interior, looking for other malfunctioning points. They found several, and two were located in a particularly sensitive area—next to the petrol engine in the bomb bay. The two men faced a choice: if the points were shut off, the temperature inside the cabin would drop precipitously and the passengers would spend the rest of the flight in a numbing arctic cold. But if one of the points exploded the plane would be brought down.

Choosing safety over comfort, Churchill ordered the points shut off and extra blankets distributed to the passengers. A few hours later the morning sky brought a friendly Mediterranean sun and the first glimpse of Casablanca. A French protectorate, the city had escaped Torch relatively unscathed. There were three days of fighting, just enough to satisfy French honor—and then a formal surrender. The morning that the Churchill party arrived fifteen-foot waves were pounding the broken landing craft and upturned jeeps along the beaches. The prime minister thought it "a marvel anybody could have gotten ashore alive under such conditions."

Two hours later, Churchill was standing at the entrance to the Anfa Hotel in suburban Casablanca, surrounded by palm trees, bougainvillea, and orange groves. In a city famous for its ancient architecture, the hotel stood out as a bold beacon of modernity. Oval shaped, with three swirling deck-like floors and a mast-like roof, the exterior of the hotel suggested a stranded cruise ship, while the sleek interior was the kind of place where a visitor might encounter Humphrey Bogart and Ingrid Bergman at the bar, and in the background someone would be playing "As Time Goes By." Churchill quickly acclimated to his surroundings. He wore a pink dressing gown at breakfast, zippered romper suits at lunch, and between meals, he played games of Basque pelota and took long walks along a nearby beach, stopping to examine interesting seashells and to talk to the young American soldiers who guarded the compound.

During one of his walks Churchill encountered an American sailor carrying a guitar and asked him to play "You Are My Sunshine." Afternoons he would sit in the sun and wait for the day's guests to arrive. Guests of Roosevelt would soon include exiled Dutch queens and Norwegian kings; Churchill's were typically Vichy officials, former Czech foreign secretaries, Polish mayors, and Greek bishops. The prime minister spent most evenings discussing strategy with his commanders, and often the sessions were tumultuous. When an officer said or did something Churchill disliked, he would shout, "You have grown fat from the honors of your country! All you want is to draw your pay, eat your rations, and sleep." Charles Wilson, Churchill's physician, viewed the outbursts as regrettable but necessary to the prime minister's mental and physical health. "When he gets away from the red boxes and leaves London," Wilson noted in his diary, "he puts his cares behind him. It's not only that he loves adventure; he feels . . . at times he must let up, even [for] a week or two. . . . He wants to shed for a little while the feeling that there are more things to do in the twenty-four hours than can possibly be squeezed in."

THE TORCH LANDINGS PUT AN exclamation mark at the end of one of the most successful periods of the war for the Allies. Over the previous ninety days Russia had been victorious at Stalingrad, Britain at El-Alamein, and the United States on the beaches of Algiers and Morocco. What Churchill called the "Hinge of Fate" was beginning to swing in the Allies' direction. In January 1943, when the Casablanca Conference convened, the question before the Allies was how best to take advantage of their victories, and since Stalin had twice turned down invitations to attend the conference, citing the fighting at Stalingrad, the decision would fall on the British and the Americans.

The press in both countries depicted Casablanca as a joint effort by two like-minded democracies to devise a strategy to defeat Nazi Germany. The assertion was true as far as it went, but it did not go very far. Allies often have different ideas about how to achieve a shared goal—and in such cases the views of the best-prepared ally usually prevail. At Casablanca that was the British. They had centuries of experience in international affairs and they knew how to put what they had learned to use. They arrived at Casablanca in large numbers, comprehensively briefed, and supported by a strike force of technical experts, with a six-thousand-ton ship repurposed as a communication center, and a plan. The plan was: avoid an attack on the European mainland, where the Germans were strongest, until they had been weakened by a series of battles on the European periphery—North Africa, Italy, Greece, and the eastern Mediterranean.

The American chiefs—General Marshall, Admiral King, and General Arnold—arrived in Casablanca with a small staff, little guidance from the White House, and divided over American strategy. Marshall remained a tenacious advocate of a cross-channel invasion, but the Dieppe raid had made other senior American commanders wary of putting untested young Americans up against German veterans. Moreover, given the supply demands of a global war only twenty-five trained divisions, at most, would be available for an assault by September 1943; and given the channel weather at that time of year only six of those twenty-five would be available for the initial assault on the beaches.

Admiral King's victory plan was summarized succinctly by a British colleague: King "has his eye on the Pacific. That is his eastern policy. Occasionally, he throws a rock over his shoulder. That is his western policy." General Arnold's victory plan was the B-17 Flying Fortress, an effective bomber but, as time would show, not the war winner that Arnold and many other airmen imagined it to be in 1942. Aware of the strategic differences among his commanders, a few days before the American delegation left for Casablanca Roosevelt summoned Arnold, Marshall, and King to the White House and told them if they found themselves unable to come to agreement on strategy during the conference, they should take the position that the American buildup in Britain and the Mediterranean would continue for the time being, but the United States would make no binding commitments about 1943 until the military situation was clearer.

Most of the decisions made at Casablanca, including the American decision to cancel a cross-channel invasion in 1943 and to invade Sicily at the conclusion of the North African campaign, emerged from the banquet room of the Anfa Hotel, where General Alan Brooke presided over the daily military meetings. Three years of war had left the chief of the Imperial General Staff ill tempered at the best of times and ferocious at the worst of times, and even on his good days he had difficulty finding something positive to say about General Eisenhower, the new commander of the American forces. In a diary entry dated December 28, 1942, Brooke wrote: "Eisenhower as a general is hopeless. He submerges himself in politics and neglects his military duties partly, I'm afraid, because he knows little, if anything, about military matters." Brooke's tone was even sharper on January 15, when Eisenhower presented his plan for Satin, a lunge across Tunisia to the sea. If successful, the plan would cut Axis forces in the country in half, but the plan was complex, and when Brooke began grilling Eisenhower on details—how would he coordinate with Montgomery's forces in Libya? General Kenneth Anderson's forces in the north?—he found Eisenhower's answers wanting. Surprisingly Marshall, King, and Arnold, who were also present, made no effort to come to Eisenhower's defense. It may have been random chance, but the next day, several of the American delegates professed to hear their British colleagues quietly humming "Rule, Britannia!" in the corridors of the Anfa.

The Americans did enjoy some victories at the conference. King got a pledge that 30 percent of the American war effort would be shipped to the Pacific in return for a promise to support an invasion of Sicily. Marshall also muscled a quid pro quo out of the British by threatening to withdraw from the European theater if Britain refused to contribute troops to the upcoming offensives in Burma and the Pacific. Still, the Americans had no illusion about their performance at Casablanca. "We came, we saw, and we were conquered," declared Major Albert Wedemeyer. Most of Wedemeyer's colleagues agreed. They also agreed that before meeting the British again, they had to up their game. There was less unanimity on another subject: how to deal with the Soviet Union. During the Stalingrad campaign, Roosevelt and Churchill had decided to move the date of the cross-channel invasion back a year from 1943 to 1944 and to suspend the Allied convoys to Murmansk and Archangel for a second time.

Concluding that there was no good way to tell Stalin the bad news, and fearing news this bad might tempt him to reconsider a separate peace, the president and prime minister decided to fudge. They would keep the new round of convoy cancellations a secret until it became absolutely necessary to reveal them. In the meantime they would assuage Stalin with reports on the Anglo-American military buildup in Britain, the success of the Allied air war, and promises to implement the cross-channel attack "as soon as tractable." Inter-Allied relations were further complicated on January 24, when, without consulting Churchill or Stalin, Roosevelt announced that the Allies would demand the unconditional surrender of the Axis powers. Later the president would say the idea just popped into his head during a press conference, but he had discussed it with his son Elliott several weeks earlier. Maurice Hankey, one of Churchill's senior advisers, was among the many officials who thought the president's proposal would only stiffen Axis resistance, and the history books supported his view. The last recorded instance of one nation imposing unconditional surrender on another occurred two thousand years earlier, when Rome demanded Carthage surrender unconditionally. Hankey concluded that if unconditional surrender had any military merit, it probably would be employed more than once every other millennium.

SHORTLY BEFORE THE CASABLANCA CONFERENCE convened Harry Hopkins laid out the Anglo-American position on postwar France. "It is," Hopkins wrote, "the duty of the United States and Great Britain to preserve, for the people of France, the right and opportunity to determine for themselves what government they will have." Hopkins seems to have had a kind of stewardship in mind. A group of prominent Frenchmen would oversee the nation's interests until the French people were in a position to resume ownership of the country. It was an interesting idea, but it ran afoul of General Henri Giraud, who replaced Darlan as high commissioner in North Africa, and General Charles de Gaulle. Both men were patriots and authentic heroes. Giraud had escaped from German captivity twice, once in 1914 and again in 1942, while de Gaulle's Free French fought valiantly by the side of the British and Americans throughout the war. However, both also had excessive amounts of amour propre. De Gaulle's Joan of Arc complex was so acute that Churchill once threatened to find a bishop to burn him at the stake, while for reasons best known to himself Giraud arrived in North Africa expecting to be given overall command of the campaign and went into a sulk when he was passed over. Toward the end of the conference Churchill tried to reconcile the two Frenchmen. The Germans and Italians were deeply entrenched in Tunisia, and there was still much fighting to do. Casablanca had been a great success in the prime minister's view, and he did not want it undercut by two egotistical Frenchmen. Thus, at the end of the conference he summoned de Gaulle and Giraud to Casablanca for what amounted to a photo op with Roosevelt and himself. The visit was not a great success. De Gaulle was imperial and aloof; Giraud, still brooding over his demotion to onlooker, the small part he had been given in the North African campaign. After the conference the two men would put aside their differences and joined forces to create the French Committee of National Liberation, but those differences were too deep and their egos too large to sustain a lasting partnership. By 1945 de Gaulle was leader of France and Giraud a retired pensioner. When Giraud died several years later people remembered him as the man who almost saved France—if they remembered him at all.

HOPKINS RETURNED TO AMERICA DISAPPOINTED. He thought Churchill's Mediterranean strategy, which had won the day at Casablanca, "feeble for two great powers." Marshall also returned home unhappy, but had a broader complaint. He thought a campaign in the Mediterranean "would have little value in ending the war." Their frustration was understandable, but given supply needs of the American air force, the navy, the Pacific campaign, the industries producing the sinews of war, and the decision to limit the American army to ninety divisions, the United States would be incapable of fighting a war in the European heartland until 1944.

11

DEATH STANDS AT ATTENTION

THE WORDS WERE WINSTON CHURCHILL'S, BUT THE THOUGHT belonged to the English novelist H. G. Wells. On the eve of the Great War Wells wrote *The World Set Free*, a cautionary tale about the misuse of science. Wells begins his story with an observation: "The history of mankind is the history of the attainment of external power." In the book Wells imagines a world in which atomic energy—still a hypothesis in 1914—ignites a catastrophic war. Decade after decade thousands die. Then, at some point in the mid-1930s, one of Wells's imaginary heroes—Monsieur Leblanc, the French ambassador in Washington—convenes an international conference at which another Wells hero, King Egbert of Britain, abdicates his throne and becomes a champion of world government.

Inspired, the other world leaders embrace the idea, and out of the ashes of death a new utopian world arises. Atomic energy, now tamed and repurposed, eliminates the need for work. Freed from the drudgery of the factory and the shop, humanity's nobler impulses emerge. It was a lovely idea, but by the time the real 1930s arrived Monsieur Leblanc and King Egbert had been replaced by Adolf Hitler and Benito Mussolini. A new world war looming, and the only thing standing between mankind and a superbomb was the knowledge of how to build one. Then one evening in February 1940 Otto Frisch, a young Austrian Jew who fled his native country to escape the Nazis, had a flash of insight on a street corner in Birmingham, England. There were four possible ways to produce an explosive chain reaction in uranium. Upon testing, Rudolf Peierls, Frisch's laboratory partner, found that three of the ways were too weak to produce a powerful explosion. The fourth—U-235—was more interesting. Upon examination, Peierls concluded that something would happen if U-235 was hit by a neutron (a subatomic particle). But what that "something" was he did not know. The answer turned out to be the nuclear age itself. In a follow-up test Peierls discovered that the heat thrown off by a pound or two of U-235 could produce temperatures as hot as the interior of the sun and pressures greater than the interior of the earth, where iron flows as liquid.

In March 1940, Frisch and Peierls began condensing their findings into a memorandum, but they did so with some trepidation. The British thought of themselves as a moral people; sustaining that belief would be difficult if the country were incinerating sixty or seventy thousand people in air raids with a weapon that burned as hot as the sun. But Dunkirk and the Battle of Britain washed away whatever scruples the British had about employing weapons of mass destruction. Frisch and Peierls continued their work on the bomb, though not for the MAUD Committee, which Churchill created in the summer of 1940 to explore the possibility of creating an atomic bomb. Rather, presumably for reasons of national security, the prime minister decided to limit membership in the committee to British-born scientists. The men chosen were given three briefs: 1) consider the problems arising from uranium research; 2) recommend the experimental work that needed to be done; and 3) facilitate cooperation between different groups of investigators.

The committee had a short life span—only a year—but it was a year of great achievement. In July 1941, when the committee disbanded, Britain was the world leader in the military use of atomic energy, an achievement that reflected the intellectual excellence of the committee members. Three of those members were Nobel laureates: George Thompson and James Chadwick of Cambridge and Marcus Oliphant of Birmingham University. The achievement also reflected the excellence of the four universities where the research was done: Cambridge, Oxford, Birmingham, and Liverpool. In July, before disbanding, the committee issued two final reports. The first described in detail how to make a bomb and how much power it would release—the equivalent of 1,800 tons of TNT; the second report examined the possibility of creating a plutonium bomb and pointed to some of the beneficial uses of atomic energy.

Two years later one of the lingering mysteries of the MAUD Committee finally resolved itself: the origins of its name. Most of the scientists who worked for the committee assumed MAUD was an anagram of some sort, but the name turned out to have a more interesting pedigree. The day the German army invaded Denmark, Niels Bohr, the renowned Danish scientist, sent his English maid a cable. Her name was Maude.

LEO SZILARD, THE ÉMIGRÉ HUNGARIAN scientist who became the Paul Revere of the American bomb program, arrived in the United States in 1938, already famous for his pioneering work on nuclear chain reactions. One day in 1933 Szilard was standing on a London street corner when a scene from *The World Set Free* abruptly came to mind: "The bomb flashed blinding scarlet in mid-air, and fell, a descending column of blaze eddying spirally in the midst of a whirlwind." At that moment, Szilard said later, "it suddenly occurred to me that if we could find an element capable of emitting two neutrons when it was absorbed by one neutron; such an element, if assembled in a sufficiently large mass, could sustain a nuclear chain reaction."

Also in 1938 the German chemist Otto Hahn proved uranium atoms could be split, and the German and Russian governments were looking into the potential military uses of uranium. It was in this frenzied period of discovery that Szilard had his second great insight—and this one had a name: Albert Einstein. The most famous scientist of the twentieth century was an old friend. A few decades earlier Szilard and Einstein had collaborated on the most unlikely of projects, a scheme to improve home refrigeration. In the late summer of 1939 Szilard proposed a new collaboration. He would write a letter to President Roosevelt under Einstein's name, outlining the ways atomic energy could change the character of war. Einstein liked the idea, and in October 1939 a letter arrived on Roosevelt's desk. It read: "In the last few months it has been made probable . . . that it might be possible to set up a nuclear chain reaction, by which vast amounts of power and large quantities of new radium-like elements would be generated. Now it appears this could be achieved in the immediate future." Roosevelt responded by creating several committees to assess the wartime uses of atomic energy. But it was 1939; anti-war feeling was strong in the country, and Roosevelt was planning to run for a third term. Politically he could not afford to get out too far ahead of public opinion.

A year and a half later the bomb program was at a crossroads. British scientists lacked the resources to create a large-scale program, and in America, where the war still seemed far away, war work was not popular in the scientific community. Enter Marcus Oliphant: an athletic, straight-talking Australian who was a professor of physics at Birmingham University, and a member of the MAUD Committee. In March 1941, Oliphant began sending minutes of the committee's reports to Washington in hopes the data would energize his American colleagues. Four months later he was still waiting for the Americans to reply. Frustrated, in late August he hitched a ride to Washington in an unheated B-24 Liberator bomber. The alleged purpose of Oliphant's trip was to discuss radar programs with American colleagues. The real purpose was to discover why the Americans were not responding to the MAUD reports. He found the answer in the office of Lyman Briggs, chairman of the US Uranium Committee. Under questioning from Oliphant, Briggs admitted he had not distributed the reports. They were still under lock and key in his office safe. It is unclear whether it was at this meeting that Oliphant called Briggs an "inarticulate unpleasant little man" or whether he made that statement a few days later in a talk with colleagues.

What is clear is that after the meeting Oliphant took matters into his own hands. On August 26 he summoned a group of leading American scientists to a gathering in New York and told them they must concentrate "every effort on creating the bomb and had no right to work on power plants of anything but the bomb. [It] would cost twenty-five million dollars," Oliphant said, "and Britain did not have the money or the manpower; it was up to America."

Oliphant's visit ignited a chain reaction in the American scientific community. Oliphant inspired Ernest Lawrence, a Nobel Prize laureate and professor of physics at Berkeley; by turn Lawrence inspired Karl Compton, chairman of the National Academy of Sciences committee, to evaluate the use of atomic energy in war. And George B. Kistiakowsky, a Harvard scientist and expert in explosives, inspired James Conant, the president of Harvard and an accomplished chemist. G. P. Thomson, the former head of the MAUD Committee, inspired Vannevar Bush, the engineer and science administrator at the Office of Scientific Research and Development. Thomson's report provided American scientists with a road map, but Roosevelt made one major change in it. The British gave their technical people a voice in deciding how bombs would be used; Roosevelt limited decision-making to himself and the small group of advisers who reported directly to him: Marshall, Hopkins, Stimson, Conant, and Vice President Henry Wallace.

By March 1942, Bush had identified the materials needed to make a bomb capable of creating an explosion equivalent to two thousand tons of TNT: five to ten pounds of "active material," a centrifuge plant capable of producing enough U-235 to make one bomb a month, a gaseous diffusion plant to enrich the uranium, and an electromagnetic plant to separate it. After looking at the estimate Roosevelt told Bush, "I think the whole thing should be pushed . . . not only in regard to development but also with due regard to time." However, one key element was still lacking: a leader capable of directing a workforce of 130,000 men and women, spread over thirty-four project sites in more than a dozen states. Such a man would also have to be a highly competent engineer, a skilled organizer, experienced in overseeing large projects—and ill tempered enough to be intimidating, but not so ill tempered as to be unapproachable. Colonel Leslie Richard Groves, a West Point and US Army War College graduate and special assistant for construction to the quartermaster general, met all those requirements.

When Groves was approached about the Manhattan Project in September 1942 he had just finished building the Pentagon, one of the largest construction projects in American history. He had a reputation as a doer, a driver, and a son of a bitch to work for. "Demanding, critical, abrasive, sarcastic, and never willing to offer a word of praise" is how one former subordinate, Colonel Kenneth Nichols, described Groves. Everything Nichols said was true. But Nichols was a soldier. With scientists Groves was more cautious. There were explosions—but not as many and not as loud. Groves also had an eye for scientific talent. In September 1942, during a visit to the science laboratories at Berkeley, his eye fell upon J. Robert Oppenheimer, a brilliant, temperamental young scientist who resembled a Picasso abstract come to life. He was tall, very thin, with long limbs and no definable center. When he met Groves, Oppenheimer was just coming off a major success. The previous summer he had led a much-talked-about seminar on the bomb. Groves invited him to dinner and returned to his hotel, impressed but hesitant. There were rumors about Oppenheimer's youthful ties to the Communist Party; he could be aloof and arrogant; and, unlike several of the other candidates that Groves was considering, Oppenheimer was not a Nobel laureate. However, he was available—and most of the other candidates were already engaged in war work.

When Groves proposed Oppenheimer to the Military Policy Committee, which had the final word on the appointment, he was told to look elsewhere. Familiar with the politics of army life Groves bided his time and let the committee look for other candidates. A few weeks later, when they came back empty-handed, he proposed Oppenheimer again. This time the committee accepted his choice.

IT'S DIFFICULT TO EXPLAIN HOW men as different as Groves and Oppenheimer were able to work so well together, but it may have had something to do with Groves's ability to see something in Oppenheimer no one else had. Beneath his aloof exterior Oppenheimer was a deeply frustrated man who felt his scientific work had not received the attention he believed it deserved. In Groves he saw another opportunity to grasp the golden ring of scientific immortality.

In 1939, if the nations of the world had convened a race to determine which country would be the first to make an atomic bomb, the smart money would have been on Germany. It was home to some of the most brilliant scientists in the world, including Werner Heisenberg, a Nobel laureate at thirty-two, and Otto Hahn, who discovered nuclear fission. Germany also had a strong industrial base and a military prepared to fund scientific projects. In 1941, when Oliphant arrived in Washington demanding the United States act on the bomb, the German nuclear fission program had thirty-two institutes spread out over twelve cities. But a few months earlier Hitler had invaded the Soviet Union, and, as Russian resistance hardened, it became clear that Germany lacked the manpower and military resources to sustain a major war in the east and a large expensive scientific program that could fail.

In December 1941 the German army downgraded the nuclear fission program to focus on weapons that would have a more immediate impact on the war, such as jet aircraft and rockets. For the remainder of the war the German program would be treated like a neglected child, moving willy-nilly from one government agency to the next. At one point it ended up in the Reich's Ministry of Science, Education, and Culture, where it fell under the jurisdiction of SS lieutenant Bernhard Rust, a former provincial schoolteacher. Not knowing what to do with it, in February 1942, Rust transferred the program to the Reich Research Council, one of few government agencies still interested in pursuing research on a bomb. Hoping to revive interest in the project, later that month the council invited a number of leading Nazis—including Hermann Göring, Martin Bormann, and Heinrich Himmler—to a luncheon to hear Germany's leading scientists discuss their work.

Perhaps forewarned that the experimental luncheon served at the conference included entrées prepared with synthetic shortening, most of the Nazi leaders sent their regrets. It was their loss, for the scientists had some interesting things to say that afternoon, especially the Nobel laureate Heisenberg, who told the hushed audience that the explosive power of "pure uranium" was so great as to be "quite unimaginable." He also noted that the Americans were pursuing the bomb with "particular urgency." Albert Speer, the armaments minister, missed the February luncheon, but that June he and an aide attended a talk that Heisenberg gave on atomic energy. When Heisenberg finished speaking Speer's aide raised his hand and asked how large an atomic bomb would have to be to destroy a city. Heisenberg cupped his hands and replied, "As large as a pineapple." Speer was immediately intrigued, but in a private talk later that evening Heisenberg was less optimistic. While a bomb was feasible, he said it would take years to create a workable weapon.

On August 6, 1945, the day Hiroshima was bombed, Heisenberg was in Farm Hall, a detention center near Cambridge University. As news of the bombing came across the wireless, the incredulous Heisenberg began shouting, "I don't believe a word of the whole thing!"

THE SOVIET BOMB PROGRAM HAD several possible starting times. One was in May 1940, the day a young Soviet émigré teaching history at Yale University came across an article in the Sunday *New York Times* entitled THE VAST POWER IN NUCLEAR ENERGY. Intrigued he sent a copy of the article to his father, Vladimir Vernadsky, a Soviet scientist who had done work on uranium and atomic energy.

Another plausible starting date was in February 1942. Early that month Lieutenant Georgy Flerov, a Soviet physicist serving in the Soviet

Air Forces, noticed that the Western science journals were no longer carrying articles on nuclear fission and that the scientists who had previously filled the journals with papers on the subject were now writing on different subjects. Suspecting these odd developments were related to the British and American bomb programs, Flerov wrote a letter to the State Defense Committee's plenipotentiary for science, an official named Kafanov. But the only evidence Flerov had to support his suspicions was a version of the Sherlock Holmes theory about "the dog that didn't bark." The theory holds that the fact that nothing happened can mean something *did* happen and was being kept secret. In his letter to plenipotentiary Kafanov, Flerov said the sudden silence in the British and American scientific communities was not a random fluke. Just the opposite: "The 'seal of silence' was proof that vigorous work is going on now aboard." When Kafanov failed to reply to his letter, Flerov wrote directly to Stalin, and when Stalin failed to reply to two letters, Flerov proposed that Russia's leading physicists organize a symposium on the bomb. That idea also went nowhere. At the end of 1942, lobbying by Soviet scientists did persuade Stalin to restart the country's prewar nuclear research program, but the all-consuming nature of the war and the refusal of Britain and the United States to share their scientific work made the Russians rely heavily on their spy networks to keep abreast of the British and American research programs. Anatoly Gorsky, the NKVD resident in London, was particularly adept at the spy game.

On September 25, 1941, Gorsky, whose code name was Vadam, sent Moscow two reports on the British bomb. On the basis of the minutes of a September 16 meeting of the MAUD Committee, he concluded that Britain expected to have a workable uranium bomb within two years; and from a mole who was probably John Cairncross, private secretary to Lord Hankey, chair of the Defense Services Committee, he concluded that the MAUD Committee had ordered the creation of a uranium factory. Klaus Fuchs, a German-born naturalized British citizen who worked on the British program and later on the American program, was also an important Soviet asset. Through his handler, Ursula Kuczynski, Fuchs passed on information about two critical elements in the bomb-making process: isotope separation and the gaseous diffusion process.

It would be a year or more before American intelligence became fully aware of Soviet efforts. But by late 1942 Russia's growing strength and how to respond to it was already opening up divisions in the White House and in the State and War Departments. On one side were Roosevelt, Hopkins, and the most vocal advocate of a Soviet-American partnership, General James Burns, chief of the president's Soviet Protocol Committee. "We not only need Russia as a powerful and fighting ally in order to defeat Germany," Burns wrote in a memorandum in late 1942, "but eventually we will also need her in a similar role to defeat Japan. And finally we need her as a real friend and customer in the post-war world." On the other side of the argument were these men: Hap Arnold, who, as he put it, was concerned about where a Soviet victory might lead and was reluctant to continue sending heavy bombers to the Soviet Union, and William Bullitt, the former American ambassador to France, who warned Roosevelt that Stalin was "intent on imperialist expansion, perhaps as far as the Rhine, perhaps beyond."

Colonel Carter Clarke, head of the US Army's Special Branch, went beyond warnings. In early February 1943, Clarke created the Venona project to monitor Soviet penetrations. There was also the letter from an anonymous State Department official who declared that it was time for America to wake up since "a civil war . . . between the Anglo-Saxon powers on one hand and Russia on the other has already begun." Later in 1943 the debate over Soviet intentions would enter the public arena through the work of journalist Walter Lippmann and the British geopolitician Sir Halford Mackinder, who wrote a much-discussed article in *Foreign Affairs* in which he predicted that Russia would emerge from the war as the greatest power in the world.

12

THE END OF THE BEGINNING

T HE BATTLE FOR NORTH AFRICA BEGAN ON JUNE 10, 1940, AND was still raging when the Casablanca Conference concluded in January 1943. The most notable events between the two dates were the Allied landings on November 8, 1942. In Algiers the GIs leaped out of the landing craft and into a sea of clicking cameras and friendly faces. In Morocco and Oran the French units resisted fiercely until December 10, when, a few weeks before his assassination, Admiral Darlan stepped in and brokered a peace agreement between the Allies and the Vichy French. It was also around this time that fate and the United States Army began to sort out the GIs. The lucky ones would spend the winter days unloading cargo, drilling, and marching, and they would spend the winter nights drinking, gambling, and discussing the virtues of North African nightlife.

Algiers was at the top of most soldiers' lists. The cafés were full of lovely Frenchwomen, and the streets were patrolled by friendly gendarmes who could find a soldier almost anything for the right price. The city was also home to famous exotics, like the African American singer Josephine Baker, a recent exile from Vichy, France, and M. Pierre-Étienne Flandin, the former French minister of commerce, who had been a pen pal of Hitler's before the war.

Unlucky troops were sent to Tunisia.

On prewar travel posters Tunisia was depicted as a land of temperate winters, but the British war correspondent Alan Moorehead, who shivered through the winter of 1942/43 in the hills of Tunisia, found no evidence to support that claim. Often it rained for days on end, and Tunisian rain was unlike any that Moorehead had ever encountered. It was "wild torrential African rain as cold as a snake," Moorehead wrote, and so dense it produced a thick, sticky, bottomless African mud that made it difficult to bury the dead and left the living wet and shivering in the winter cold "all day and night."

The only redeeming feature of the Tunisian winter was its egalitarianism. All ranks suffered equally. Brigadier General Theodore Roosevelt Jr., son of a former president and cousin of the current president, complained to his diary, "It is still bitterly cold. . . . Our military, with its customary dumbness, did not envisage this and considered Africa a tropical country." Shortages of eyeglasses, machine guns, and spare parts for jeeps and tanks, and the lack of hot food, further enhanced the miseries of the Tunisian winter. Morale fell, and concerns about the quality of the American military grew. Marshall, who rarely raised his voice, returned from one trip to the front so upset he shouted at his staff, "No more goddamn drugstore cowboys standing around!" And Eisenhower had yet to win the complete trust of his president. "Not until there is some reason to do it," Roosevelt replied when Marshall proposed promoting Ike a rank.

In February Rommel arrived in Tunisia weeks ahead of the British, armed with Germany's most advanced tanks and combat aircraft and reinforced by more than a dozen of the best divisions and brigades in the German army. Hitler knew North Africa could not be held indefinitely, but if it could hold for another seven or eight months the logistical problems created by the delay would make an Allied cross-channel invasion in 1943 impossible, and it would buy time to strengthen Germany's defenses in the east. Upon arriving in Tunisia, Rommel's eye fell on the Kasserine Pass, a two-mile gap in the Dorsal Mountains along the route to Tunis, the national capital and Rommel's target. The pass and the region surrounding it were defended by the American II Corps, an inexperienced unit led by General Lloyd Fredendall, who had a well-deserved reputation as a trainer of men and who looked like a *Life* magazine version of an American general. He was a little chunky, but he knew how to hide his paunch from the cameras, which always seemed to catch him staring into the middle distance as though thinking through some brilliant new battle plan. Marshall, whose judgment was good but not infallible, called Fredendall "one of the best." Eisenhower agreed. "I bless the day you urged Fredendall upon me," he told Marshall. As things turned out so would Rommel.

There are two possible explanations for Fredendall's command style. Either he was so confident of his leadership it never occurred to him that his troops might not trust him—or, alternately, he was so consumed by his own safety he did not care what anyone else thought. What can be said about Fredendall with certainty is that no other senior Allied officer in Tunisia went to such great lengths to protect his person. Happy Valley, the nickname for Fredendall's command center, was located seventy miles from the front and was protected by a bomb-proof shelter, which took an engineer battalion a month to build. It was ringed by antiaircraft guns. Fredendall's troops had several names for Happy Valley; favorites included "Lloyd's very last resort" and "Shangri-La, a million miles from anywhere."

By early February it had become clear to General Orlando Ward, one of Fredendall's subordinates, that the Germans were massing for an attack. At a meeting on February 13, he warned Fredendall that the hill-top defense positions he was relying on to hold the Germans were spread too far apart. "We need to concentrate our forces into a tight fist," Ward said. It was good advice, but it came too late.

The next morning at first light German tanks swept down onto the Tunisian plain and caught an American infantry squad in the midst of its morning ablutions. Moments later every man in the squad was either dead or captured, and the squad's radio, intended to alert Happy Valley to the enemy's intentions, had become the property of a German sergeant. Within minutes calls began flooding into Happy Valley. An American tank unit was obliterated in an explosion so loud one dazed survivor "likened it to the sound that would be made if half of the Krupp Iron Works suddenly blew up and flew out of the Ruhr Valley." The low point of the day came in midafternoon when the American units on the hills waiting their turn to be attacked watched in horror as the panzers obliterated their comrades on the flats.

Of the nine hundred men who awoke to the day on the hill only three hundred would still be alive by late afternoon. Panic began to spread. Men broke and ran, and many kept running until they reached the Kasserine Pass, a grim expanse of treeless hills and twisting, unpaved roads fifty miles from where the American infantry squadron had been ambushed on the fourteenth. Rommel seemed back in form after several months of playing hide-and-seek with the British Eighth Army, but the brutal fighting on February 21 and 22 would raise questions about his fitness. On the afternoon of the twenty-first, after days of humiliating retreat, an American counterattack led by artillery and tanks halted a combined German-Italian force of forty panzers and German and Italian infantry four miles short of their target.

Expecting a long day, on the morning of the twenty-second, death got up early. The British, who had been badly mauled the previous day, were feeling particularly vulnerable that morning, but help was already at hand. The previous evening, Lieutenant General Stafford LeRoy Irwin, a soft-spoken Virginian with a reputation as a master artilleryman, arrived in the British sector with a 2,200-man force. Lacking the equipment required to guide his shells to their target, Irwin improvised. He created a three-mile arc and began firing artillery into it. It was a primitive defense, but it worked.

Later that day, Field Marshal Albert Kesselring arrived in Kasserine Pass after a bumpy ride in a spotter plane from his headquarters in Rome. "Smiling Albert" was a hard man to depress, but after an hour of listening to Rommel's complaints about the Italians, the Luftwaffe, his fellow officers, and his demands to end the campaign and withdraw, the field marshal returned to Rome depressed and worried. The Desert Fox seemed to have lost the "passionate will to command." He was "physically worn out and psychologically fatigued." By this point so were many of the officers who worked with Rommel and the soldiers who worked under him. After Kasserine, the Afrika Korps would fall into a downward spiral that continued until the end of the campaign.

On February 23, the day after the Rommel-Kesselring conference, General Ernest Harmon arrived in Happy Valley with a letter for Fredendall. After reading it, Fredendall turned to Harmon and said, "The party is all yours."

On a warm May afternoon three months later, on a road trodden by Roman centurions two thousand years earlier, the German and Italian forces in North Africa drove themselves into captivity—the German officers in blunt-nosed little Volkswagen staff cars, the Italians in Fiat

Topolinos and flashy Lancias. It would be many hours before the last Axis staff car offered itself up for surrender. The tail of the surrender line stretched back eighty miles, past unmarked graves, lost opportunities, and a sense of hopelessness. Rommel was only a memory now; he had been recalled to Germany in March, ostensibly for health reasons but in reality to preserve his reputation as an undefeated German paladin. His successor, Colonel General Hans-Jürgen von Arnim, an eastern front veteran, fought a skilled rearguard action, but by the end of April he was down to two options: flee to Sicily, over two hundred miles away, across an Allied-dominated sky and sea, or surrender.

Arnim chose surrender. For the British and American soldiers who watched 150,000 Axis troops march into captivity that May afternoon, the North African victory had different meanings. For the British, who had been fighting in the Middle East since 1940, the victory was a testament to national grit; for the Americans it was vindication for the humiliation at Kasserine.

WILLIAMSBURG, VIRGINIA, HAS BEEN INVADED three times in its long history: in 1775 by the British, in 1862 by the Union Army, and in May 1943 by the British again. But this time it was invaded at the invitation of General George Marshall. Hosting was an unusual role for the chief of staff, whose many virtues did not include conviviality. Still, as a veteran of several Anglo-American conferences, he had experienced the unnerving effects produced by long days of argument in conference rooms that smelled of stale cigarette smoke. Thus, when plans were made for the Trident Conference, the first Anglo-American meeting since Casablanca, Marshall made it a point to include a weekend recess so that the American chiefs of staff and their British counterparts could get to know one another on a personal level.

Marshall chose Williamsburg as the meeting site because it still retained an eighteenth-century English character, thanks to John D. Rockefeller, who had made a large contribution to the town's recent restoration. The crabmeat, fried chicken, Virginia ham, terrapin à la Maryland, and the fruit and cheeses that the British and American guests feasted on—as well as the butler who delivered the food to Williamsburg—were also provided by Rockefeller.

The British party arrived by plane at around ten o'clock on a sunny May morning and upon landing were amused to learn that Yorktown, where Lord Cornwallis surrendered to a ragtag American army in 1781, was only a twenty-mile drive from Williamsburg. "Now what was the name of that chap who did so badly here?" Pug Ismay asked at lunch. Later that afternoon the guests dispersed to private pleasures. General Alan Brooke, a dedicated bird-watcher, rambled through the Virginia countryside looking for interesting American species. General Archibald Wavell, who was about to take up a new command in India, took dozens of photographs. Sir Charles Portal, the RAF chief, went for a swim in an oversize bathing suit and emerged from the pool stark naked, and Admiral Sir Dudley Pound, who had badly botched the PQ 17 convoy several months earlier, lost his way in a maze and a search party had to be sent out to find him.

After dinner, the British guests visited the newly restored Governor's Palace. For men who had spent the better part of the past three years living in the squalor and ruin of war, the palace's brilliantly lit rooms were a thing of awe and wonder.

Brooke in particular was relieved to be on land again. The Mid-Atlantic Gap, the undefended stretch of sea that had claimed hundreds of ships and thousands of sailors earlier in the war, had recently been declared closed, but a hundred German U-boats still prowled the North Atlantic, and every commander in the U-boat fleet would have given a year's pay to claim a prize as big as the *Queen Mary*, the ship carrying Brooke and the other members of the Churchill party to America. In theory the heavy screen of escorts trolling the choppy waters around the *Queen Mary* would make a penetration difficult to impossible. But after an hour of training on one of the ship's flimsy rafts Brooke concluded that was nonsense. If a U-boat commander got off his torpedoes, the lucky passengers would get a quick death by a torpedo blast, and the unlucky ones a long, freezing death in one of the *Queen Mary*'s rafts.

At dinner Brooke's black thoughts faded away. Churchill had been in rare form that evening. As the big ship had cut its way through a tumultuous sea he'd regaled Brooke, Harriman, Beaverbrook, and Ismay with stories of his exploits in India as a subaltern and as a correspondent in the Boer War. It was almost midnight by the time Brooke had gotten to bed. The next morning when he awoke the war had returned and was knocking at the door. Overnight the U-boat packs had claimed sixteen Allied merchantmen in the icy waters between Newfoundland and Greenland. On May 10 the *Queen Mary* reached the safety of American waters and Churchill cabled the president: "Since yesterday, we have been surrounded by the US Navy and we all greatly appreciate the high value you put on our survival. I look forward to being at the White House with you tomorrow afternoon."

The next day, May 11, Harry Hopkins traveled to Staten Island, New York, a working-class place long on pizza shops, jukeboxes, and landfills and short on diplomatic pomp, to greet the Churchill party. After the German and Italian prisoners of war disembarked—for security reasons POWs were taken off first—the Churchill party emerged into the warm afternoon sun and a welcoming smile from Hopkins. As at Casablanca, the prime minister's goal at Trident was to safeguard British interests and in particular to persuade the Americans to embrace his peripheral strategy—North Africa to Sicily and from Sicily up the Italian boot. To that end he had brought along a fearsomely large entourage, including almost a hundred clerks and typists.

At the opening of the conference the British visitors noticed two changes. Roosevelt's interest in further Mediterranean adventures had waned, and their American colleagues displayed a new professionalism. There were more officers on hand to present the American point of view, and they were better informed about the issues, more skilled in defending American interests, and less polite about poking holes in British operational plans. The transformation was largely a by-product of the debacle at Casablanca. Determined not to be outmatched again, in the run-up to Trident, American officers spent hours practicing how to war-game British proposals, how to employ a strategy called *aggressive argumentation*, and how to take the initiative in conversations.

Trident opened on May 12, with overviews from the two principals. Roosevelt, who spoke first, acknowledged the most logical step after North Africa would be Sicily but added that a victory in Italy would not have much strategic resonance beyond Italy, and the casualties it produced would decrease the force available for a cross-channel invasion. Roosevelt also questioned Churchill's claim that an Italian campaign would relieve pressure on Russia. Hitler would not move twenty or thirty divisions west to save Mussolini. An air offensive from Sicily or the Italian boot might achieve the same result as an invasion but at a much lower cost in lives, Roosevelt said, then turned to the second front. Churchill was still talking of a cross-channel invasion in 1943, but his predicate was so impossible—the Germans would have to be on the edge of defeat—it was just the prime minister's polite way of saying no to the proposal.

Roosevelt was also a master of double-talk; one of his most famous boasts was that his left hand often didn't know what his right hand was doing. But about the second front he was straightforward and single-minded. The armies of the United States and Great Britain would invade the European continent in the spring of 1944, and in the months prior to the attack Overlord, as the plan was called, would have the highest priority on men and matériel.

The Italy Churchill conjured up after Roosevelt finished bore little resemblance to the president's Italy. It was the "first prize, the great objective in the European-Mediterranean theater," the spring in the trap that would draw thousands of German troops west to a cold, wet death in the November mountains of Monte Cassino and Mont Vélan. And the prime minister was just getting started. The collapse of Italy might also "mark the beginning of the doom of the German people," relieve pressure on Russia, drive the Italian forces out of the Balkans, eliminate the Italian fleet, make Turkey favorably disposed to join the Allies, and provide Britain and the United States with "the air bases to attack the Balkans and southern Europe." The differences between Roosevelt and Churchill were echoed by their subordinates. On many occasions an American and British officer would look at a problem and find themselves coming to completely different conclusions about how to solve it.

In the spring of 1943, the Joint Strategic Survey Committee, a policy arm of the Joint Chiefs of Staff, looked into the source of these differences and concluded many arose from the peculiarities of British history, geography, and demography. As a small island nation Britain was better served by a peripheral strategy. Fighting along the edges might drag out the war a year or two, but it was less likely to produce catastrophic Great War casualty rates of 50–60 percent. The strategy also had residual benefits. Prolonging the war increased the likelihood Germany and the Soviet Union would exhaust themselves, allowing Britain to resume its traditional role as arbiter of the balance of power in Europe.

The committee also came up with an explanation for an aspect of the British character that particularly puzzled Americans: a fixation with the Middle East. The committee concluded it arose from a fear of being caught between empires at the end of the war. India, where the hot winds of nationalism had been blowing for decades, would declare independence immediately after the war ended, and within a few years, Malaysia, Burma, and Britain's other eastern colonies would follow suit. In Libya, Palestine, Syria, Iran, and Iraq, the British saw the raw materials for the making of new empire, one that would provide markets for its goods and soldiers for its wars.

The British were annoyed and puzzled by the committee's findings. Britain did have designs in the Middle East, but not on the scale their American colleagues imagined, nor were the British as diabolically clever as some the Americans seemed to think. One British delegate at Trident attributed the perfidious Albion charge to a misreading of national character. "The British did so many stupid things," he said, the Americans could not take their behavior at face value and so attributed it to some dark design.

After the war the British historian D. C. Watt did a study of the Trident Conference that, among other things, demonstrated the fickleness of human nature. Watt concluded that five different wars were waged at the conference. The war that received the least attention was the war with Germany and Japan; the war that received the most, the war between Britain and the United States. Somewhere in between the two was the long-running war between the American army and navy. In Watts's scheme the Williamsburg interlude emerged as a temporary armistice, and the days of frustration and discussion that followed the interlude, a lesson in the virtues of compromise. After two years of trying, by the end of the conference Marshall had finally got the British to commit to a cross-channel invasion. It would begin on May 1, 1944, and be proceeded by a combined bomber offensive against Germany's military, its industries, and its economy. In turn the Americans made two concessions. Operations in the Mediterranean would continue, but with the proviso that in November 1943 the Allies would begin transferring men and matériel back to Britain to prepare for Overlord. The second concession restored Britain's access to the bomb program.

During a meeting in May 1942, Churchill and Roosevelt agreed to share research on the bomb on a coequal basis and that most of the work would be done in Britain. Shortly thereafter the British project received a code name, Tube Alloys, and an overseer, Sir John Anderson, a trusted Churchill adviser. But nothing was put in writing. It was a gentleman's agreement between the emperor of the East and emperor of the West. A few months later, when it became clear that Britain lacked the resources to do a big science project and fight a global war, Anderson, anxious to safeguard Britain's coequal status, proposed that the British scientists working on the bomb relocate to the United States, where the most advanced research was being done. "We must . . . face the fact that the pioneering work we have conducted in this country is a dwindling asset," he told Churchill. "Unless we capitalize on it quickly we shall be rapidly outstripped. We now have a real contribution to make to a merger. Soon we will have none." The next morning Churchill scribbled, "As proposed," on Anderson's memo. There matters stood until the Casablanca Conference, when an alarmed Anderson cabled Churchill that the Americans were preparing to sharply reduce their information-sharing agreement with Britain. The pretext for the downgrade was security, Anderson said in his cable, "but one cannot help suspecting that having benefited from our endeavors the US military authorities will not suffer unduly by casting us aside." In a March memorandum the Americans reintegrated their intention to limit British access to the bomb program and said the downsizing would extend "over the greater part of the Tube Alloys field." Anderson found one of the last sentences particularly galling. "Apparently the United States authorities expect us to continue to exchange information 'on the parts where our work is ahead of theirs.' This is quite intolerable." The prime minister said he quite agreed. At the Casablanca Conference Hopkins had promised "all would be made right," when Churchill complained about the restrictions the Americans had placed on what was now called the Manhattan Project. In March Churchill wrote Hopkins again. "Time is passing," he said. "No information is being exchanged." Two weeks later, in yet another appeal to Hopkins, Churchill sharpened his tone. "I am much concerned about not hearing from you about Tube Alloys." In early April, frustrated by Washington's continuing silence, Churchill asked Anderson for an estimate of how much it would cost to build a British bomb, and his scientific adviser, Lord Cherwell, how long it would take to create such a weapon. Even given the highest priority, Cherwell said, it would be six to nine months before Britain could even begin construction. Whatever remaining hopes Churchill had of building a British bomb were quashed on May 13, when the United States bought the entire output of the Canadian uranium mines for the next two years.

However, Churchill did receive a consolation prize. Britain's access to the Tube Alloys program was restored and with it a pledge from

Roosevelt that henceforth the project would be conducted as a joint venture. Not all the president's advisers were happy about the decision. Broadly speaking, by mid-1943 two different visions of America's place in the postwar world were beginning to take shape. One camp, led by men such as James Conant, envisioned a postwar Pax Americana, based on the United States' position as the world's sole atomic power. Roosevelt's vision was more expansive: a postwar world overseen by the "Four Policemen": the United States, China, Britain, and the Soviet Union. But China could barely govern itself, and the Soviet Union could not be trusted. Roosevelt's decision to restore Britain's access to the Tube Alloys program was not an act of charity but of realpolitik. At the end of the war he wanted a trustworthy ally, militarily strong enough to assist America in patrolling the peace.

13

THE POLISH AGONY

I N THE SUMMER OF 1942, A GROUP OF POLISH RAILWAYMEN WORK-
ing on a German construction site in Smolensk heard rumors about
a mass execution of Polish soldiers and civilians in the months after the
Polish surrender in 1939. During a visit to the site one afternoon the railwaymen came across the remains of a Polish soldier but found no evidence to support the claim that the Russians had executed thousands of
Polish soldiers and civilians at the site. The railwaymen passed on their
findings to the Polish underground—and there matters stood until January 1943, when Rudolf Christoph Freiherr von Gersdorff, a German
intelligence officer, heard rumors about a mass grave in the Katyn Forest,
several miles to the west of Smolensk. He passed on the information to
Berlin propaganda minister Joseph Goebbels, who immediately recognized the value of Gersdorff's discovery.

The executions had all been conducted in eastern Poland, the Soviet
sector. Stalin would have a hard time shifting the blame to Germany,
which controlled the western sector of the country. On April 13, 1943,
German radio announced that the bodies of three thousand Polish officers, piled up in twelve layers, had been found in the Katyn Forest,
twelve miles to the west of Smolensk. Time and weather had decayed
the remains, but the tattered snapshots on the forest floor suggested

that most of the dead had been in their twenties and thirties and had been killed by a single shot to the head. When the death toll rose to twelve thousand, Goebbels could hardly contain himself. "We are now using the discovery of twelve thousand Polish officers, killed by the GPU"—a Soviet agency—"for anti-Bolshevik propaganda on a grand scale," he said.

Seeing a rare opportunity to put Germany in a positive light, he invited a European Red Cross committee made up of forensic experts from Belgium, Bulgaria, Sweden, Norway, Croatia, Denmark, and several other countries to inspect the execution site. Tours were also arranged for neutral journalists and even an American POW, Colonel John H. Van Vliet. The Kremlin immediately dismissed the German accusations as lies, and when the Polish government in exile in London demanded its own Red Cross investigation, Stalin broke ties with the London Poles and created his own Polish government in exile, the Lublin Poles.

Unbeknownst to the thousands of Poles who marched into captivity in autumn of 1939, they were about to be forced into a real-life version of Russian roulette. Over the winter the Poles were subjected to frequent interrogations and political agitation by their NKVD masters. Prisoners deemed to have displayed a proper "pro-Soviet" attitude during these interchanges would live. Those deemed "uncompromising enemies of authority" (i.e., lacking in the proper proletarian spirit) would not. It was not happenstance that most of the 25,700 Poles deemed uncompromising were members of the Polish elite. Stalin and Lavrentiy Beria, who oversaw the executions, were intent on creating a new Soviet-style Poland, but before fashioning the new order the old order had to be destroyed.

Over the summer of 1940 twenty-two thousand Polish generals, admirals, professors, physicians, lawyers, engineers, journalists, pilots, and other accomplished citizens were executed. The executions were carried out at several sites in eastern Poland—not just the Katyn Forest—and varied in character. In outdoor executions the prisoner often was brought to the killing ground from another location, bundled in a coach, its windows smeared with cement to obscure the passenger inside, who often arrived at the execution site badly bruised. Upon arrival at the execution site, an alert prisoner might get a final glimpse of the forest light before the crack of the executioner's pistol. Indoor executions were conducted in Smolensk or a nearby abattoir and had a "darkness at noon" character. As the prisoner stood at attention an NKVD officer would examine his paperwork to ensure everything was in order. The Soviet state compiled statistics on executions as carefully as it did statistics on agricultural production.

Next the prisoner would be led to a cell adorned with stacks of sandbags. The bags were intended to muffle sound, but often they blocked the light streaming in through the windows. Finally the prisoner was instructed to get down on his knees. Except for a May Day break the 1940 killings went on without interruption until the liquidation was completed. When the Red Army recaptured Smolensk in the autumn of 1943 Stalin brought in his own medical experts, who concluded the Poles had been killed by the Germans in the early stage of Barbarossa. True to his aphorism, "In wartime truth is so precious that she should always be attended by a bodyguard of lies." Churchill took Stalin's side in the dispute. "We shall certainly rigorously oppose any investigation by the International Red Cross or any other body," he declared. Roosevelt was also prepared to look the other way. He told an interviewer, "I am inclined to think that Prime Minister Churchill will find a way of prevailing on the Polish government in London to act with more common sense."

Hitler was kept abreast of the accusations and counteraccusations swirling around the Katyn massacres, but it was Kursk, an industrial city in the farming country of southwest Russia, that preoccupied his thoughts in the spring of 1943. After the catastrophe at Stalingrad just the thought of attacking another large Russian city made Hitler's stomach churn. Germany had lost almost two million men in the past few years, and the dead included a large contingent of the twenty-five- and thirty-year-olds who had brought Germany to the edge of victory in 1941 and again in 1942; increasingly, fifty-year-old men and sixteen-year-old boys were taking their place on the line.

The German high command was also divided about launching a new summer offensive. Heinz Guderian, the panzer commander who drove the British and French into the sea at Dunkirk and who was currently general of armored troops, opposed the operation. During a talk with Hitler in May he warned that the Red Army had strengthened its position around Kursk in the past few months, bringing in more antitank guns, tank traps, barbed wire, land mines, and artillery pieces. "How many people do you think even know where Kursk is?" he asked Hitler.

"It's a matter of profound indifference to the world whether we hold Kursk." Other opponents of what was now called Operation Citadel pointed to North Africa, where a German defeat was only weeks away, and to the staggering losses of Barbarossa and Operation Blue. A failure at Kursk could leave the German army too weak to mount future offensive operations.

Erich von Manstein's weak chin deprived him of Guderian's swaggering physical glamour, but nature compensated by endowing Manstein with one of the best military minds in the German army. In 1942 he overcame months of suicidal Soviet resistance in a rats' war of streets and cellars and captured Sevastopol, home of the Soviet fleet. In March 1943 he checked Stalin's counteroffensive, and in between the two victories he came within a few dozen miles of liberating the beleaguered German forces in Stalingrad. Given a free hand, Manstein would have launched Operation Citadel in April or May, when the Soviet defenses were still relatively weak. But the Panthers, the new generation of tanks Hitler was relying on to restore Germany's primacy in the east, were experiencing teething difficulties and would not be ready until late June or early July. The delay made Hitler's stomach churn again, but in the end he concluded that the opportunities that a success at Kursk would open up were too great to ignore. The German army could swing south and seize the oil fields that had been beyond its reach the previous summer or swing northeast up behind Moscow. Success might also make it possible to move troops to the western front. From North Africa the next logical steps for the Anglo-Americans would be Sicily, then up the Italian boot to Rome.

In early June Armaments Minister Speer arrived at the Wolf's Lair, Hitler's redoubt in East Prussia, with some good news and some bad news. The good news was that the 324 Panther tanks Speer promised had overcome their teething difficulties. The bad news was that, due to logistics and other difficulties, the tanks would not be ready for active service until June 13. Hitler's stomach churned again, and when the June 13 date became sometime in early July there was another churn. Unlike Hitler, Stalin was learning from his mistakes. In April, when Zhukov questioned his plan to launch a preemptive strike against the German line at Kursk, instead of threatening him with the gulag, as the Stalin of 1941 might have done, he polled his generals, and when all but one supported Zhukov's plan—a defense in depth followed by a counterattack—Stalin did not challenge the decision.

The target at Kursk was a Soviet bulge in the German line 120 miles wide and 60 miles long. The resources each side mustered constituted a measure of the importance each attached to the bulge. To expand it the Russians had mustered 1.3 million men, 1,600 tanks, and 1,000 planes. To close the gap the Germans fielded an army of 900,000 men, 2,700 tanks, and 2,700 planes. On a warm summer evening in early July a young panzer officer surveying the terrain in his sector was seized by a sense of fatalism. If the enormous amalgam of tanks, men, and matériel that Germany had assembled proved incapable of breaking the Russian salient at Kursk, could anything do that? In dutiful adherence to security regulations, on the evening before the assault, a group of panzer commanders made a final recognizance. In the distance lay an enormous plain broken by numerous valleys, small groves, and irregularly laid-out villages, some intersected by little brooks; of these the most notable was Pena, which ran in a swift current between two steep banks. Even in the half-light it was clear that the ground favored the defender. It rose slightly to the north and was intersected by high cornfields that limited visibility.

On July 2, Stavka—the Soviet high command—alerted its commanders on the Kursk front to expect an attack between the third and the sixth. Two days later, in the midst of a Russian artillery barrage, German troops received a personal message from the Führer:

SOLDIERS OF THE REICH

This day you are to take part in an offensive of such importance that the whole future of the war may depend on its outcome. More than anything else your victory will show the whole world that resistance to the German army is hopeless.

One German officer found some irony in Hitler's choice of dates. July 4 is "Independence Day in America," he told a fellow officer, then added, "and the beginning of the end for Germany."

The attack at the northern end of the Soviet salient began at 4:30 A.M. on the morning of July 5 and was led by a Hitler favorite, Field Marshal Walter Model. Short and heavily built, Model had a well-deserved reputation for aggressiveness and was noted for his skill on the defense; on this early July morning he would lead the offense, a role less familiar to him. The brown smoke that rolled across the sky at first light reminded some of the older men of Mons and Vimy Ridge a quarter of a century earlier.

The challenge Model faced that morning was formidable. To get at the enemy his troops would have to navigate a series of strongpoints that stretched back deep into the Russian line. For the first few days skill and luck kept the Russians at bay. Model advanced four miles on the first day of the attack, and, supported by three thousand guns and a thousand tanks, he advanced three miles on the second. Then, on July 7, he was checked near the town of Ponyri, a nondescript collection of cottages surrounded by two state farms and a grove of apple trees. Looking for a softer target, the next morning Model moved south several miles and attacked Olkhovatka. By evening the sky above the town was bloodred and dozens of the new Panthers lay in ruins along the roads. By the ninth Konstantin Rokossovsky, one of the Soviets' ablest and most charismatic generals, had Model "reeling backward" over "the pits and trenches" the Germans had breached a week earlier. The war in the northern salient was effectively over, and Russia had prevailed. On the southern wing of the salient, Manstein's sector, the Germans continued to hold their own and in some instances more than held their own. The commander that Manstein selected to lead the attack in the south—the sleek, silver-haired Hermann Hoth—had an advantage denied Model: nine of the finest panzer divisions in the German army, including three elite SS panzer divisions—the Death's Head, the Das Reich, and Leibstandarte SS Adolf Hitler—and an ample supply of Panther and Tiger tanks.

Hoth's advance began well. In the first few days of fighting, his units made fifteen to twenty miles; then as Soviet resistance stiffened, the panzers rolled themselves into a ball and fought their way through to the Psel River, frightening the local wildlife and tattooing the lush meadows along the riverbanks with miles of tank tracks. The river was the last natural barrier before Kursk, but there were still miles of man-made obstacles to be surmounted. Hoth looked for a less formidable line of attack and settled on the region around Prokhorovka, an administrative center fifty miles to the south of Kursk. The Germans settled down and waited for the enemy. In the early hours of July 12 flares announced the arrival of the Soviet 5th Guards Tank Army. Neither side expected a head-on clash that morning. The tank was an offensive weapon designed to slash and cut, to move swiftly across the battlefield; street fighting was the province of the infantry. Estimates of the number of tanks that fought at Prokhorovka on July 12 vary widely. The most frequently cited number is 1,200 tanks and self-propelled guns.

About the nature of the fighting, there is more agreement. Even by the standards of the Russian campaign, the battle of Prokhorovka was savage. The day was hot and humid, and the occasional thunderstorm proved a mixed blessing. The rain offered temporary relief from the sweltering heat and kept the mosquitoes at bay, but then the steaming summer sun would reappear from behind a cloud, and, soaked to the skin, the soldiers would slug forward through fields of thick mud. For the tank crews the rapid fire of their guns was a constant threat to limbs, and the lack of sanitary facilities caused men to soil themselves mid-battle. No quarter was given at Prokhorovka, and none was asked. When a shell immobilized a tank the crew would fight from inside the vehicle; then, when shells were exhausted, they would leap to the ground and hurl petrol bombs and grenades at the advancing enemy. Men began the day fighting for country, honor, and the future; but in the melee that ensued a wild intoxication seemed to take hold on both sides, and soldiers began to grab death by the waist and dance her across the sodden fields just for the thrill of it.

Estimates of the losses that day vary. Historian Richard Overy puts the tank losses at about seven hundred. Whatever the exact figure, Hitler found it unbearably high. Three days earlier the Allies had invaded Sicily. On the thirteenth, he summoned Manstein to the Wolf's Lair and ordered him to close down Citadel. Manstein protested, "On no account should we let go of the enemy until [our] mobile reserves are beaten." It was a startling inversion of roles. Usually it was Manstein urging caution and Hitler embracing risk. That evening, as night fell across the battlefield, German units began withdrawing. A few days later Manstein retreated to his bed with a case of dysentery.

The note of congratulations Roosevelt sent Stalin after Kursk also included an invitation to meet one-on-one. This was not the first time the president had gone around Churchill in his dealings with Stalin. Unbeknownst to the prime minister in May he attempted to arrange a meeting with the Soviet leader in Alaska through Joseph Davies, a slick Washington lawyer with a thousand-watt smile and a talent for self-promotion. As ambassador to Moscow in the 1930s Davies had been one of few

Western diplomats to defend the Soviet show trials, and such were his skills at persuasion and self-promotion that, upon his return to Washington, Metro-Goldwyn-Mayer turned him into a secular saint in *Mission to Moscow*, a film about Davies's Moscow years. At Roosevelt's request Davies returned to Moscow in 1943 to arrange a one-on-one meeting between the president and Stalin in Fairbanks, Alaska. Initially Stalin showed interest. A tentative date was even set; then a few weeks later he abruptly backed out, citing the pressures of war. After Kursk Roosevelt made another attempt to arrange a meeting with Stalin but got another no. In part Stalin's rudeness may have been a response to two years of broken promises about second fronts that never materialized and convoys that never sailed; but he was also feeling less dependent on his Western allies in the summer of 1943.

The victories at Stalingrad and Kursk transformed the Soviet Union into the greatest land power in the world. And the master of the castle felt he and his country were entitled to the prizes attendant with such high rank. If the Red Star was ascendant in the summer of 1943, the Union Jack was looking frayed. On the eve of the Sicilian invasion Roosevelt gave a stirring speech on America's commitment to liberty, but he failed to mention Britain's role in the campaign. "In all fairness to our friendship," a wounded Churchill wrote in a sharp but dignified response, "the impression might grow among the British people and their forces that their contribution has not received equal or sufficient recognition."

Even by the standards of summertime Washington, July 25, 1943, was unusually hot and humid. By 9:00 A.M. fans were twirling furiously across the city, and the thermometer gave every indication that the temperature was headed in only one direction: up. About 10:00 A.M., a sleek black Packard emerged from the White House driveway and headed north to Shangri-La, the president's new weekend getaway in the Maryland hills. The White House log for the twenty-fifth mentions only three visitors—the president, Eleanor Roosevelt, and their son Elliott—but Robert Sherwood, a playwright turned presidential speechwriter, and Samuel Rosenman, a longtime Roosevelt aide, were also in the car that carried the Roosevelts up to Shangri-La. At around four that afternoon the two wordsmiths were working on a presidential speech when Steve Early, the White House press secretary, called. Mussolini had been deposed, he said in a thick South Carolina accent. Sherwood braced himself. Two hours from now half the Washington press corps would be standing on the lawn at Shangri-La, shouting questions at Roosevelt. Then the unexpected happened: nothing. Except for Early's call and a bulletin from Rome radio, there was no further news on Il Duce's downfall. "Oh, well," Roosevelt said, "we'll find out about it later."

The rest of the afternoon passed uneventfully. After Sherwood and Rosenman finished the speech they were writing they had a long, leisurely dinner with the Roosevelts. Then, as the light disappeared behind the Maryland hills, the president and his entourage climbed into the Packard and drove back to Washington. The next morning Sherwood was still wondering how a story as big as Mussolini's fall could go unnoticed in Washington. Then, quietly, the gears of Roosevelt's deeply forested interior began to grind; a few days later he announced that the implications of Mussolini's downfall were sweeping, not just for the United States, Britain, and the Soviet Union but for morale in Germany, Austria, and the lesser Axis countries—and that a conference must be convened immediately. A few days later the conference had a name, Quadrant, and a venue.

A few days before the conference convened Daisy Suckley, the president's cousin and confidante, spent a languid Hyde Park afternoon studying Mr. Churchill as he and Roosevelt sat on a porch talking. This was the first time Daisy had had an opportunity to study Mr. Churchill in detail. He was "a strange looking little man," she decided. "Fat and round, with clothes that bunched up on him, and practically no hair." Later that afternoon when Churchill appeared in a pair of bathing shorts, Daisy was reminded of a Kewpie doll, then much to her surprise, the sixty-nine-year-old Kewpie doll made a nearly perfect dive into the Roosevelts' swimming pool. Daisy's inspection also included an assessment of the prime minister's personality. She found him difficult in conversation when he didn't want to talk and perfectly delightful and witty when he did.

Watching his attentiveness to Roosevelt, Daisy concluded that Churchill adored him and "loves him as a man, looks up to him, leans on him." However, the observation said more about Daisy than about Churchill. The prime minister admired and respected Roosevelt, but he had been the target of the president's high-handedness on a number of occasions and that had left a mark. The historian Max Hastings has suggested that it was not just the press of the war that kept Churchill from attending Roosevelt's funeral in 1945.

Churchill's Hyde Park visit also included a discussion of the Russian alliance. Despite their public defense of Stalin, Roosevelt and Churchill knew who was behind the Katyn massacres, and privately both men had been appalled by the savagery of the killings. It was enough to make "one's blood boil," Churchill told Roosevelt—then added that at some point a break with Russia would probably become inevitable. There was too much blood on Stalin's hands. A continued association with him would make a mockery of every value Britain and America claimed to represent. However, neither he nor Roosevelt thought now was the time to act. An immediate break would throw the weight of the war on the Anglo-American forces and put hundreds of thousands of American and British lives at risk.

The next day, as Churchill was preparing to leave for Quebec, he told Roosevelt, "We ought to make a renewed final offer to 'Uncle Joe' to meet him in Fairbanks [Alaska] as soon as the military conference is over. If he accepts, it will be a great advantage, if not we shall be on very strong ground" vis-à-vis future Soviet demands and requests. That evening, as the prime minister's train wound its way north through the peaceable August countryside, a garbled copy of the Italian surrender terms was threatening to blow up all his plans for Quebec.

How the mistake was made is unclear, but the copy of the Italian surrender terms Stalin received failed to provide a place for Russia in the new commission. Perhaps because he thought that was a slight to the Red Army, which had fought the Italian troops Mussolini sent to the east, or for some other reason, Stalin fell into a fury. He ordered his ambassadors in Washington and London to withdraw immediately and demanded Soviet representation on the commission. Churchill had encountered Stalin's anger before—but nothing like this. "Stalin is an unnatural man," he told a colleague after reading Stalin's note of protest; then added solemnly, "There will be grave troubles." Roosevelt's response was breezier. He dismissed Stalin's note out of hand, calling it "rude, stupidly rude," though secretly he feared the oversight might tempt Stalin to seek a separate peace. "It is what I have feared all along," he told Daisy. Then just as the Grand Alliance appeared about to crash and burn, Stalin received a correct copy of the surrender terms and all was instantly forgiven. In his next cable Stalin congratulated Roosevelt and Churchill for endorsing a course "in line with the aim of the unconditional surrender of Italy."

•

ON THE MORNING BEFORE THE opening of the Quebec Conference—code-named Quadrant—General Alan Brooke stood on the shore of a lake forty miles to the north of Quebec, taking in the view. After the filth and noise of wartime London the scene seemed almost miraculous. Lovely pine tree–covered hills met the water, and the morning wind caught the sound of a bleating fox where Brooke was fishing.

That evening he returned to his lodgings, feeling he had had one of the most perfect days in his life. Two days later he would have one of the worst. The setting on this occasion was the Citadelle of Quebec, the iconic fortress where the conference was being held. It was mid-morning, and Brooke and Churchill were taking a constitutional on the Citadelle's terrace when, without forewarning, the prime minister announced that an American commander would lead the cross-channel invasion. It was part of a trade, Churchill said. Britain appointed the supreme commander in Southeast Asia, and the price was giving Eisenhower Overlord. Normally Brooke kept his feelings under lock in a safe-deposit box, but on this occasion his disappointment was too deep. As Churchill talked, Brooke was "swamped by a dark cloud of despair." On three separate occasions, Churchill had promised him Overlord. "Not for one minute did he realize what this meant to me," Brooke recalled later. "He offered no sympathy, no regrets. [He] dealt with the matter as if it were of minor importance." Brooke would not be the only British officer to leave the Quadrant meeting feeling a little smaller than he had when he had arrived.

THE QUEBEC CONFERENCE, WHICH BEGAN on August 17, a month after the Allies seized Italy, was more far-reaching than its predecessors. Between August 17 and 24 Churchill, Roosevelt, and senior American and British officers discussed the air war against Germany, the buildup of American forces in Britain, the atomic bomb, the war against Japan, and the weakening British position in Palestine.

But the subject that dominated the conference was the one that had dominated earlier conferences: the Anglo-American differences over strategy. Though Churchill continued to pay lip service to a cross-channel attack, the American delegates believed he remained wedded to the soft-underbelly strategy: keep the war in Italy, the eastern Mediterranean, and other peripheral regions, and avoid the European heartland until the German army was small enough to fit into the Führerbunker. Anticipating a confrontation at Quebec, Marshall made sure every member of the American delegation was thoroughly briefed, including the president, who received two briefings, one before he left for Quebec and one en route by General Thomas Handy, chief of the army's operations division, and Harry Hopkins.

The confrontation Marshall was anticipating occurred on August 16, the day before the official opening of the conference. During an exchange between senior British and American officers the atmosphere became so heated the junior officers were ordered to leave the room. Eventually the two sides reached a compromise. The Americans agreed to fight up the Italian boot, but only as far as Rome and only under the condition that in the autumn of 1943 British and American troops would begin returning to Britain to prepare for the cross-channel invasion in the spring.

RUSSIA DID NOT OCCUPY A large place in the official Quadrant agenda, but Hopkins arrived in Quebec with a study called "Russia's Position," which he passed on to several of the delegates. Hopkins did not provide many details about the origins of the report, only that it was drawn from a recent "very high level" US military strategic assessment. It made for a somber read: the authors began by noting Russia would emerge from the war as the dominant power in Europe. With Germany crushed, no other nation on the continent would be strong enough to oppose her tremendous military forces. It was true, the report continued, that Great Britain was currently holding up a position in the Mediterranean, but the authors doubted she would be able to oppose Russia unless otherwise supported. "The conclusions from the foregoing are obvious," they noted. "Since Russia is the decisive factor in the war, she must be given every assistance, and every effort must be made to win her friendship. Likewise, since without question she will dominate Europe on the defeat of the Axis, it is even more essential to develop and maintain the most friendly relations with Russia."

A few weeks later Stalin accepted Churchill and Roosevelt's invitation to meet in the Iranian city of Tehran.

14

MR. CHURCHILL AT HARVARD

―――――――

"NOTHING, CLEMMIE! CHARLES GOT NOTHING!"
Until that moment it had never occurred to Dr. Charles Wilson that his ignorance of fly-fishing was an infirmity, but the Churchills clearly regarded it as such. Thus, on August 25, the day after the Quebec Conference concluded, on a Canadian lake four thousand feet above sea level, the prime minister of Great Britain resolved to give his doctor a lesson. As Wilson stood on the porch of the Churchill cabin that morning, he could hear his instructor shout to his wife, "Clemmie, where is my fishing rod?" In between lessons to Dr. Wilson—who was proving to be a disappointing student—the Churchills daily sallied forth on Snow Lake in search of trout. They enjoyed such success that in his memoirs he boasted, "We did not run short of fresh trout at our meals."

Churchill was in no hurry to return to Britain after Quadrant. He paced the ramparts of the Citadelle; he went fishing with his daughter Mary when his wife was unavailable; he attended a meeting of the Canadian cabinet. He addressed the Canadian people in a radio broadcast. He packed his prize catch, a two-foot trout, and sent it to Hyde Park. He attended another meeting of the Canadian cabinet. He complained that he was finding writing more difficult. One evening Dr. Wilson found him standing at the window of his railway car, "giving the V for victory salute to a group of workmen, who could see nothing but a train rushing by in the August night." Colleagues noticed that the prime minister seemed out of sorts, but they proffered different diagnoses. Dr. Wilson thought Churchill was "depressed." Anthony Eden feared he might be ill. "He does not look well and [has] bad color," Eden told a friend. When Churchill complained of tiredness, Eden urged him to extend his sabbatical, Churchill recalled.

At the beginning of September the Churchill family visited Washington. The first Allied landing in mainland Italy—an assault on Salerno, a beach town near Naples—was only a few days away, and the prime minister wanted to go over the invasion plan with Roosevelt. From Washington the Churchills traveled up to Harvard University. The only public notification of the visit was a mysterious announcement in the press a few days earlier saying that the prime minister would give a speech on September 6 at an unnamed American university. The visit was Roosevelt's idea. Earlier in the year he had suggested to James Conant, the president of Harvard, that the university ought to bestow an honorary degree on Churchill. Roosevelt—who was an alum: Harvard 1904—envisioned a ceremony rich in pomp and circumstance, and Conant, who was also deeply involved in the bomb project that summer, made every effort to comply, including providing wardrobe tips. He suggested that the prime minister receive his honorary degree in the scarlet academic robe of Oxford rather than austere American cap and gown, and he scoured the academic world until he found, at Princeton, facsimiles of the Oxford cap and gown. Princeton agreed to a short-term loan.

Clementine Churchill once observed that her husband was never "pleasant company" when drafting an important speech. The journey up to Boston on September 5 reaffirmed that family truism. Churchill boarded the train grunting and soured by the thought of all the blank pages he would have to fill that night. By Baltimore most of the clerks, typists, and advisers who followed him onto the train had given up hope of getting any sleep that night. Meanwhile Churchill had retired to his compartment to work on his speech. It grew out of an idea he had been thinking on for a while but had been unable to put into words. As he sat in his berth, listening to the rumble of the trains passing in the night, the words began to come.

The Harvard community that greeted Churchill the next morning included the university's military formations, which gathered in rows under the elms in the old part of Harvard Yard. It also included alumni, many of them men of Churchill's age, who took their places next to the Memorial Church that the university built to honor Harvard's 370 Great War dead. The four German Harvard men who died fighting under a different flag had their own memorial in a discreet section of the campus. Churchill began the day by reading his speech to James and Grace Conant at their home; then he proceeded to Sanders Theatre, where he would be awarded an honorary degree and give his speech. John Martin, an aide who encountered the prime minister on his way to the theater that morning, thought he looked like "a genial Henry VIII in his bright scarlet Oxford robe and black velvet hat." At noon a crowd of 1,300 gathered in the theater to watch Churchill receive a doctor of laws degree. Several minutes of applause followed, then he stepped to the microphone.

Churchill began his speech by painting a word picture of Britain's bombed-out cities and fields. Then he started slowly edging toward his master theme, each sentence building on the power of its predecessor. "Twice in my lifetime," he said, "the long arm of destiny has reached across the ocean and involved the entire life and manhood of the United States in deadly struggle. There is no use in saying we don't want it, we won't have it. . . . The long arm reaches out remorselessly and everyone's existence undergoes a swift, irresistible change. We have reached the point where . . . it must be world anarchy or world order."

Having sketched out his supporting themes, Churchill moved on to his master theme: an Anglo-American world order: "The Great Bismarck, for there were once great men in Germany, is said to have observed that the most potent factor in human society at the end of the nineteenth century was that the British and American peoples spoke the same language. . . . Nothing can go forward without the united effort of the British and American people. If we are together, nothing is impossible. If we are divided all will fail. Therefore, continually preach the doctrine of the fraternal association of our peoples—not for territorial aggrandizement, or the vain pomp or earthly domination but for the honor that comes from those who faithfully serve great causes."

The speech was widely praised in the press the next morning, but the cheers may have said more about the power of the moment than anything Churchill himself said. After the war Robert Sherwood wrote that the prime minister would never have gotten away with the Harvard speech at a "less propitious" moment in the war—or, for that matter, Sherwood added, "at any previous time since the Declaration of Independence."

ON SEPTEMBER 9, THE DAY Italy surrendered and a 70,000-man Allied force swept down on Salerno, General Marshall presented his biennial report on the nation's military forces. Under his leadership the army had increased by 5 million men since 1941; the officer corps, from 93,000 to 521,000; the air force, to 182,000 officers and nearly 2 million enlisted men; and the Army Corps of Engineers by over 4,000 percent. The United States had also created a communications network that spanned the globe from the Persian Gulf to the Aleutian Islands to Australia.

Marshall took particular pride in the amount of aid the United States had given to Russia. Since the beginning of the war it amounted to over 3,000 airplanes, 2,400 tanks, 80,000 trucks, 109,000 submachine guns, 130,000 field telephones, and mountains of munitions. However, by the autumn of 1943 Marshall's indispensability was becoming an issue. Like Churchill, Roosevelt had promised his most trusted military adviser command of Overlord. But after a talk with British general Sir Frederick Morgan in September, the president had second thoughts. It would be difficult to find another officer who could match Marshall's talents as an organizer, a leader, and an adviser. It would be impossible to re-create the bond of trust the two men shared. The chaotic Allied assault on mainland Italy in late September further strengthened the president's conviction that he needed Marshall by his side in Washington.

Marshall had never put much credence in Churchill's song of Italy. The country's soft underbelly was attached to a mountainous iron spine. Still the easy Allied victory in Sicily suggested that the mainland might offer opportunities for low-risk, high-reward operations—and there were tens of thousands of idle British and American troops in North Africa and Sicily. Maps were consulted in Washington, London, and at Eisenhower's headquarters in Algiers and a target selected, Salerno, a raffish little beach town on the Bay of Naples that could have served as the set for a Fellini movie. The invasion, code-named Avalanche, would be led by General Mark Clark, a tall, lanky Virginian who was renowned for his skills as a staff officer and for the size of his ego. Behind his back subordinates referred to Clark as Marcus Aurelius Clarkus. Avalanche would be Clark's first experience as a commander. Three assault divisions— two British, one American (the latter, the 36th: a Texas outfit)—would lead the attack. On the voyage across the Mediterranean under a warm September sun there was much chest-thumping among the twenty-one- and twenty-two-year-old British and Americans who would storm the beaches. But Radio Algiers's September 8 announcement that Italy had surrendered produced what Churchill would later describe as "an unfortunate psychological effect" on the troops.

Instantaneously, martial order gave way to unabashed relief. On the HMS *Duchess of Bedford* news of the Italian surrender produced "dancing, kissing, and backslapping." On the USS *Mayo* there were shouts of "The war is over!" Chaplains offered up prayers of thanksgiving; soldiers, expecting a walkover, jettisoned their bandoliers and grenades to make room for an extra carton of cigarettes in their kits. One British officer said, "I never again expect to witness such scenes of pure joy." But the joy was short-lived.

Twenty-four hours later, in the half-light of the rising day, British and American assault troops began scrambling into landing craft a few thousand feet from the beaches. Above them exploding flares hung in the early-morning sky like young moons. Clark, who was watching the scramble from the deck of a ship, wrote in his diary, "All out of my hands." Above the beaches, the defenders, many veterans of Moscow and Stalingrad, waited. As the Texans of the 36th Division approached the beaches, a German loudspeaker welcomed them in guttural English. "Come on in and give up! We have you covered." A moment later, the first wave of landing craft reached the beaches; ramps splashed down, and men leaped into the morning sea. In some units the cacophony—the *rat-a-tat-tat* of machine-gun fire, the thump of mortars, the screams of the wounded, the whiz of the 88 shells overhead—produced near panic. Men flung themselves behind decapitated tanks. They overturned jeeps and the bodies of the dead—anything that offered refuge from the ring of fire. Listening to shell fragments ping against the wall that he was sheltering behind, one soldier was reminded of "spring rain on a taxi window." Another man recalled the sweat and fear that hung in the air that morning. "I could feel the damp sand squelching beneath my feet, sticking to me as I ran and all I could hear was the *thump thump* of my heart beating through my head."

On the first day the fighting ended in a draw. Some of the British and American units progressed inland several miles, but in many places the gains could be measured in yards, and the casualties were heavy. One query from the beaches began, "On what beach shall we put our dead?" For the next few days the fighting swung back and forth across a battle-field drenched in the smell of cordite and blood. On the ninth the British X Corps seized Montecorvino Airfield, denying the Luftwaffe a critical air base. The next day, the tenth, the Germans countered with a thirty-six-hour air assault on the USS *Ancon*, the fleet's flagship. During their extended visit the Luftwaffe flew 450 sorties over the *Ancon*, and Admiral Henry Kent Hewitt, the ship's commander, issued thirty red alerts.

On the twelfth, with the outcome of the battle still in doubt, General Harold Alexander, commander of British forces in the Mediterranean, cabled Brooke, "I am not satisfied with the situation with Avalanche. The buildup is slow and the [troops] are pinned down to a bridgehead which has not enough depth. . . . I expect a heavy German counterat-tack to be imminent." It came the next morning—Black Monday—to the men who survived the onslaught of panzers and the German grena-diers who emerged out of the mist that morning. In the three-day battle for supremacy that followed, both sides suffered terrible losses. By the sixteenth the Anglo-American advantage in men and matériel began to show, but the price of victory was higher than expected. The British X Corps suffered six thousand casualties; the Texans of the 36th Division, almost four thousand; and several other units had comparable casualty rates. Having taken a bite at the soft Italian underbelly, the Allies had found it as hard as a kick in the teeth.

IT MAY HAVE BEEN HAPPENSTANCE, but Stalin's choice of the first day of the Salerno campaign, to finally accept Roosevelt and Churchill's often-voiced request for an invitation to meet is open to another interpreta-tion. The rapid Allied buildup in Italy had raised questions in Stalin's mind about the Anglo-American commitment to Overlord. The Ameri-cans were solidly behind the 1944 date, but Stalin had less faith in Mr. Churchill's commitment to the operation—and the prime minister had great powers of persuasion. With the Red Army on the offensive almost everywhere, after Kursk Stalin concluded now was the time for a face-to-face meeting with his Western allies.

In his cable of acceptance Stalin proposed Tehran as the venue. Its proximity to the Soviet Union would allow him to remain in daily con-tact with his generals. Roosevelt and Churchill countered with offers to meet in Cairo, Basra (Iraq), or Baghdad: settings easier for them to reach. Stalin balked. If Tehran was unacceptable Molotov would represent him at a venue chosen by the Western allies. The threat put an end to the back-and-forth about venues. A date was set for the meeting—December 1943—and, at Stalin's suggestion, the Tehran meeting would be preceded by a foreign secretaries' conference.

On a blustery October afternoon a month later, a C-54, the military version of the DC-4E—a high-end prewar passenger plane—circled the sky above Moscow. The Luftwaffe had been driven from the city's skies several months earlier, but the scorched remains of the German and Russian fighters that littered autumn streets were a reminder of how bitter the air war over the city had been. A red warning light flicked on in the cabin, and the passengers buckled their seat belts and braced for a landing. The American delegation to the Moscow Conference was led by Secretary of State Cordell Hull, a Tennessee gentleman born six years after the end of the Civil War, frail in health and jealous of his prerogatives. The other delegates included Averell Harriman, the newly appointed American ambassador to the Soviet Union and his daughter Kathleen, a recent Bennington graduate who served as her father's aide-de-camp, and General John Deane, the new chief of the US military mission in Moscow.

The Soviet welcoming committee included Molotov, who was wearing a fur cap against the bitter Moscow wind, and two former ambassadors, both currently under a cloud: Maisky, who had been recalled to Moscow for going a little too native in Britain, and Maxim Litvinov, the former ambassador to the United States, who was rumored to have leaked information to Sumner Welles, the American under secretary of state. Upon landing, the Anglo-American delegates were treated to several minutes of vigorous handshakes and badly translated small talk, followed by a slightly off-key rendition of "The Star-Spangled Banner." Then the American delegation piled into several waiting cars and were driven to the US embassy, Spaso House, which had begun life in 1913 as the home of a wealthy Russian textile magnate and which, two world wars later, had been reduced to what Kathleen Harriman described to an American friend as "a sort of slum. Our garden consists of some leafless shrubs and a couple of dead trees. The walls are dirty" and painted with pictures of fish and women, and "the vestibule is generally so dark you can't tell who let you in, a Russian, a Chinaman, or a Finn."

•

THE MOSCOW CONFERENCE, WHICH BEGAN a day later, marked the beginning of a happy time in the Grand Alliance. In the early years of the war Stalin's American and British visitors often found him difficult to deal with. They would come to Moscow wanting to discuss a broad array of political and strategic issues, but Stalin would keep bringing the conversation back to the second front—or, more accurately, to the lack thereof. At the beginning of the Moscow Conference, Cordell Hull had an epiphany: give Stalin an absolutely ironclad agreement on the second front and he would be more receptive to the issues that the British and Americans wanted to discuss. Complex problems rarely lend themselves to simple solutions, but this one did. Suspecting the Russian hosts would be more amenable to discussing the Anglo-American agenda if Stalin received an ironclad agreement on a cross-channel invasion in 1944, Hull urged John Deane, the new head of the US military mission, and Pug Ismay, Churchill's chief military aide, to give the Soviets a detailed briefing on Overlord.

The briefing was conducted on October 19, and, as historian Mark Stoler has noted, on the twentieth Molotov approved almost every major request that Hull made, including that Germany surrender unconditionally, that postwar occupation duties be shared by the Big Three, and that Britain, the Soviet Union, and the United States would assist in creating a new international organization to replace the dormant League of Nations. During the conference Stalin also made an informal pledge that the Soviet Union would enter the war in the Pacific, upon Germany's surrender.

The Russian change of tone had a powerful effect on General Deane. In a November letter to the Joint Chiefs of Staff, he wrote that he arrived at the conference believing "the Russians were unwilling to cooperate . . . and interested only in their own views" and that he left confident that the Soviets had no interest in seeking a separate peace with Germany and were self-critical enough to admit to their unresponsiveness in the early years of the war, which they blamed on the unrelenting nature of the fighting in 1941 and 1942. Deane left the conference confident that the Russians would join the Pacific war as soon as Hitlerism was destroyed.

RELATIONS BETWEEN THE BRITISH AND American delegates at the Moscow Conference were less smooth. The British delegates were mildly horrified by Harriman's instruction to the American delegates at the beginning of the conference: "If we want to earn the Russians' trust, we must give them our full military position on the Mediterranean submarines, bombing, the Pacific"—and must explain "why the tentative promise we made to develop an offensive from England . . . was impossible to fulfill." Upon learning of Harriman's instruction, an irritated Clark Kerr, the British ambassador to Moscow, buttonholed Harriman and told him, "Now is not the time to be talking about second fronts." Ismay was also annoyed by Harriman's apologetic tone. The Western allies already had a second front, he pointed out—Italy—and a third front: the air war.

A few days later Constantine Oumansky, the Russian ambassador to Mexico, warned Joe Davies, Roosevelt's adviser, that Stalin believed Churchill "was not concerned with beating Hitler in the most direct way so much as he was in directing a political offensive which would enable Britain to dominate the Balkans and all of Europe." That was an exaggeration, but one that had some truth in it. After the Italian surrender, Churchill assembled a British battle group to seize the Dodecanese, a chain of Greek islands that had been under Italian control, until Italy surrendered. A race ensued, and the German units from Greece reached the islands first; a very agitated Churchill demanded units training for Overlord be diverted to seize Rhodes, the main island in the Dodecanese chain, and Marshall told him, "Not one American soldier is going to die on that goddammed island!"

In late October Churchill again aroused concern in certain precincts of Washington by backing away from several of the pledges he had made at the Quebec Conference and proposing that he and Roosevelt settle on a unified Anglo-American strategy before conferring with Stalin at the Tehran Conference in late November. The suggestion never went anywhere—but fearful Churchill's next suggestion might, in a November 10 letter to Hopkins, Secretary of War Stimson wrote that "the chief task before the President was . . . to hold the situation firmly to the straight road. He should tolerate no departures from the program. . . . So the one prayer I make for the Commander in Chief is steadfastness—a very difficult virtue, but one more needed than any other in this particular problem."

Roosevelt seems to have sensed his staff's concern. A few days before departing for Cairo, where he would make a brief stopover to confer with Chiang Kai-shek, Roosevelt summoned Hopkins, Marshall, King, and the other members of the Joint Chiefs of Staff to Shangri-La and assured them that British attempts to postpone the cross-channel invasion would be firmly resisted.

On the other side of the Atlantic that autumn other diarists were also ruminating on the upcoming meetings in Cairo and Tehran. "There is still a very distinct cleavage of opinion between us and the Americans as to the correct strategy in Europe," Major General Sir John Kennedy, Brooke's director of military intelligence, wrote in his diary in late October. "[Our] main points are to continue—the offensive in Italy, to increase the flow of supplies to the partisans in the Balkans . . . to induce Turkey to enter the war and to accept a postponement of Overlord." A few days later Kennedy added a coda to that entry: "The [Cairo] Conference will be a difficult one. The Americans seem to think we have acted in an underhanded way over the Mediterranean [campaign]. This is curious because we have felt almost the same about them. . . . The time has come for plain speaking on both sides."

15

COMMANDER IN CHIEF

O N ARMISTICE DAY 1943 THE COLD GRAY SKY ABOVE ARLINGTON National Cemetery held the promise of rain, and a sharp wind whipped across the rows of headstones, catching the damp leaves and twirling them upward into the frosty air. At the entrance to the cemetery, a directory led the living to the graves of the dead. At a little before 11:00 A.M. an open car bearing the hatless president of the United States arrived in Arlington and was directed to the Tomb of the Unknown Soldier. The dark navy dress cape wrapped around Roosevelt's shoulders complemented his aristocratic profile and added a flash of color to his colorless cheeks.

The president was recovering from an extended bout of what his doctor described as the grippe, though it was uncommon and dangerous for the grippe to produce a temperature of 104 in an adult. Still, it was wartime; thousands of young Americans were dying on battlefields across the globe. It was the duty of the president of the United States to publicly honor their sacrifice. Roosevelt's car stopped in front of the Tomb of the Unknown Soldier, where the dead of the Great War awaited him on the twenty-fifth anniversary of the end of the war that was supposed to end all wars. A soldier holding a wreath of chrysanthemums stepped forward. An army band struck up "The Star-Spangled Banner";

Vice Admiral Wilson Brown, the president's naval aide, placed a wreath at the grave; the somber ruffle of drums followed—and then the cold November air filled with the lonely sound of a single bugle playing taps.

The following day Roosevelt; Admiral William Leahy, his chief of staff; Hopkins; Admiral King; and General Marshall all boarded the fifty-eight-thousand-ton battleship USS *Iowa* in Hampton Roads, Virginia. It was a perfect sailing day: the sky blue, the wind becalmed. But an old sailor's suspicion held that Friday departures brought bad luck, and the president was not inclined to challenge that superstition. The *Iowa* sat at anchor until a few minutes after midnight on the thirteenth. Then it hoisted anchor and disappeared into the night. Two days later an incident at sea proved that bad things can also happen to ships that sailed on Sundays. That afternoon Roosevelt and Hopkins were up on deck watching a live-fire exercise when the *Iowa*'s loudspeaker suddenly came alive: "Torpedo defense! This is not a drill!"

An officer on the bridge two decks above Roosevelt and Hopkins leaned over a rail and shouted, "It's the real thing! It's the real thing!" Amid furious shouting and the blurting of the loudspeaker, Hopkins asked the president if he wanted to be taken back to his cabin. "No," Roosevelt said—and asked to be taken to the starboard side of the *Iowa*, which offered a better view. The *Iowa* boasted 157 guns, and by the time the president reached his new position all 157 were pointed at a silvery object splashing through the rough sea toward the *Iowa* with a dolphin-like grace. "Target, six hundred yards!" a voice shouted. A furious volley of gunfire followed; the torpedo swerved, missing its target, and exploded. The hull of the *Iowa* rocked back and forth for a few moments, then steadied.

The only real damage inflicted that afternoon was to the reputation of USS *William D. Porter*, the destroyer that mistakenly fired a live torpedo round at the president of the United States and the chiefs of staff—and a $100 million battleship. Furious, Admiral King immediately ordered the captain and crew of the *Porter* placed under arrest, a first in naval history. At the trial in Bermuda several of the *Porter*'s officers were sentenced to shore duty, and the quick-fingered torpedo man responsible for the incident was sentenced to hard labor. Roosevelt later commuted his sentence.

The rest of the 3,800-mile journey from Hampton Roads to Oran was peaceful nautically but tumultuous politically. From Moscow

General Deane cabled that "the Russians wanted to end the war quickly and think they can do it." And from Molotov, via Harriman, came a claim that there was so little fighting in Italy, the Germans were sending some of their panzer divisions back to the eastern front. In between cables, the president ruminated on Overlord and who should lead it. There were many competent officers in the armed forces, men of steady nerve and long service who had mastered the logistics of beach landings against hostile fire. There were others with a deep knowledge of personnel who knew which of their fellow officers were fit to lead men into battle—and which were better suited to a desk job in Washington. By general agreement, though, George Marshall was the only officer who possessed all these qualities. Even colleagues who opposed his appointment to the Overlord command—like Admiral King—opposed it for the same reason that Roosevelt hesitated to appoint Marshall. The war was made up of a million different parts, and George Marshall's brain was one of the few places where all the parts formed into a coherent picture. He could speak with equal fluency on MacArthur's New Guinea campaign and the Salerno beachhead. Stoic by nature Marshall kept his personal feelings about the Overlord command to himself. On one occasion he sat quietly at a table while King tried to talk Roosevelt into keeping Marshall in Washington.

The president began thinking seriously about the Overlord appointment during the Quebec Conference, and he had made up his mind by the time he arrived at Eisenhower's handsome villa on the Gulf of Tunis a month later. The villa had a storied history; its last occupant was General Erwin Rommel, and prior to Rommel it had been host to a long line of soldier-warriors, dating back to antiquity, when Tunis was an appendage of Carthage and Carthage challenged Rome for dominance of the ancient world. The purpose of Roosevelt's visit to the villa was to deliver some bad news; during a sightseeing tour with Hopkins and several other aides the day after his arrival Roosevelt pulled Eisenhower aside. "Ike," he said, "you and I know who the chief of staff was during the final years of the Civil War, but practically no one else does. . . . They know the names of the field generals—Grant, of course, and Lee and Jackson and Sherman, Sheridan and the others: every schoolboy knows them. That is one of the reasons I want George to have the big command; he is entitled to establish his name in history as a great commander. I hate to think fifty years from now practically nobody will know who George

Marshall was." Eisenhower could not have been happy about the decision since it meant he'd probably be recalled to Washington to replace Marshall as chief of staff, a position he did not covet, but he kept his feelings to himself.

On the flight from Tunis to Cairo a few days later the remains of the three-year-long North African campaign unfolded below the C-54 carrying the presidential party. Toward the Atlas Mountains in the north a clutch of Matilda tanks sat half-buried in a sheltering valley. Toward Tobruk the land flattened and the plane passed over a shattered Daimler armored car, a decapitated German Ju 52 bomber, and a battery of German 88s, their barrels pointed downward into the sand. An hour later Cairo came up over the horizon. The meeting in the Egyptian capital, the first of the two conferences that the Allies would hold in the final weeks of 1943, had a breezy public relations feel to it, but beneath the friendly smiles there was a good deal of tension. On the first day of the conference Churchill complained that the Overlord buildup was hollowing out the Italian campaign, "gravely weakening our ability to force the enemy back."

General Chiang Kai-shek's visit to Cairo was also not the success his American friends had hoped it would be. Officially Chiang was in the Egyptian capital to discuss China's role in the Pacific war. Unofficially he was in Cairo because Roosevelt wanted to take his measure. In the postwar world the president envisioned each of the four policemen delegated to keep the peace would have a beat. China's was Asia, but the Americans who worked with the generalissimo were divided about his fitness for the post. General Joseph Stilwell, Chiang's American military adviser, believed he was more interested in fighting the Chinese communists than the Japanese and that he wasn't all that eager to fight communists if he could avoid it.

Henry Luce, the media baron and Chiang's most influential American supporter, championed the generalissimo in his magazines—*Time*, *Life*, and *Fortune*. Chiang's other big asset was his wife, Madame Chiang Kai-shek. A Wellesley graduate and movie-star glamorous, Madame Chiang enjoyed celebrity status in the United States. She was the first Chinese—and only the second woman of any ethnicity—to address the US Congress. Dr. Moran—the knighted name of Dr. Charles Wilson—who spent a good deal of time in Madame Chiang's presence during the conference, found her "very intelligent." However, her husband made a less favorable

The war in the east is in its second month and an uneasy Stalin, in July 1941, awaits the arrival of Harry Hopkins, the American envoy whose decisions will have a deep effect on Allied relations over the next four years.

In the summer of 1941, the Germans cross the Soviet border; eighteen days later they would advance three hundred miles to Smolensk, a key Russian city on the way to Moscow.
Bundesarchiv

At the Atlantic Charter Conference in 1941: Standing behind FDR, Admiral Ernest King, the Navy Chief of Staff, demonstrates that it is perfectly appropriate for an officer to enjoy his reputation as the worst son of a bitch in the United States Navy. *US Navy*

Death moves a day closer. August 1, 1941—the Russians are in the middle of their defense of Moscow. *Russian International News Agency (RIA Novosti)*

Molotov: During this 1942 meeting, Churchill (third from right) refuses the request of Soviet Minister for Foreign Affairs, Vyacheslav Molotov (front left) for thirty divisions to strengthen Russia's positions in the East.

Department of Foreign Affairs and Trade, Australia

In the autumn of 1941, the people of Leningrad kept their nerve and defended the city of their birth for 872 days. Nearly 100 years later their children, grandchildren, and great grandchildren come to the city's museums on Saturday and Sunday mornings to honor their sacrifices.

Russian International News Agency (RIA Novosti)

Anthony Eden was every mother's dream of the man her daughter should marry: an authentic war hero who'd spent most of his military service at the front and possessed of the kind of good looks found only in movie stars. He was also a good Number 2 to Churchill—though it remained to be seen what kind of Number 1 he would make.

Imperial War Museum

Lord Beaverbrook: The British press baron—William Maxwell Aitkin—and the Soviet dictator comprised a kind of story of unrequited love. Beaverbrook wanted Stalin to like him personally; Stalin held the cards and played with him and Averell Harriman.

Dutch National Archives

George Marshall: The best description of the Army Chief of Staff was made by a colleague who observed that even a boy who knew nothing about the general would know—just by looking at him—that he was lawful authority incarnate.

US Army

Marshal Zhukov: Khalkhin Gol is the Mongolian group of battles fought around the Soviet-Japanese border that would bring General Georgy Zhukov to international fame. He proved himself in that May-to-September 1939 testing ground.

Russian International News Agency (RIA Novosti)

On a visit to the Kremlin in the summer of 1942, Stalin inflicted a trick on Churchill and Averell Harriman that neither man would forget: On the first day he was gracious to his guests; on the second day, angry and rude; and on the third day he would act as if nothing had happened. *National Museum of the US Navy*

Almost a hundred years on, the Battle of Stalingrad still speaks for itself. Losses for the German armed forces and its allies: more than 840,000 soldiers killed, wounded or missing. Soviet losses likely exceeded one million casualties. Daily losses of Russian soldiers and civilians: 19,000. *Russian International News Agency (RIA Novosti)*

The Casablanca Conference in January 1943 was Britain's final appearance on the world stage as a great power. The change was so consequential, it took Britain and the rest of the world time to grasp that the center of the universe was now three thousand miles to the west of where it had been for the past several centuries.

Franklin D. Roosevelt Presidential Library and Museum/NARA

A mis-call: General Zhukov (center) finally halted German advances at the Battle of Kursk in the summer of 1943. By the spring of 1944, victory was growing beyond Germany's reach, but Erich von Manstein, one of Germany's most talented officers, insisted that it was still possible. In theory it may have been, but later a large Russian tank force broke through the German lines, and the remnants of the German units fled: some toward to Italy, to join the Axis forces in the region; some, south to Bavaria.

Russian International News Agency (RIA Novosti)

Rumors had it that Roosevelt was so eager to meet Chiang kai shek that he summoned the Chinese general to Cairo in 1943 for talks with him and Churchill, with whom he did not wish to meet. Other versions of the story had a slightly different viewpoint: Roosevelt was so eager to avoid the British prime minister, he was prepared to spend two days along with the general and his wife.

National Archives

General Leslie Grove (left), the hot-tempered Army engineer who built the Pentagon during the war, would lead the Manhattan Project; nuclear physicist J. Robert Oppenheimer (right) was in charge of the Los Alamos Laboratory that designed the atomic bomb.

US Army

At the Tehran Conference in December 1943, Churchill presents Stalin with the Sword of Stalingrad to honor the heroism of the Russian people during one of the bloodiest battles of the war.

Library of Congress

A buoyant Churchill receives an honorary degree from Harvard in September 1943. He brought his wife and daughter to the celebration. Churchill loved getting attention— and here the attention was avid.

Harvard University

Operation Shingle: Poor training and poor leadership turned the Anzio landings in January 1944 into one of the bloodiest fiascos of the war. By February, the Americans, led by General John P. Lucas, and British forces, commanded by General Harold Alexander (far right), had not been able to breakout from the landing zone.

Imperial War Museum

Harry Hopkins's eighteen-year-old son Stephen was killed in action during combat with a Japanese unit. He was in combat for less than an hour. Churchill would write a moving commemoration.

Harry Hopkins' Son Killed on Namur

KWAJALEIN, Feb. 2 — (UP) — Private first class Stephen Hopkins, 18, son of Harry Hopkins, adviser to President Roosevelt, was killed a few hours after landing with marines on Namur Island in the invasion of the Marshals.

Hopkins, a rifleman who was popular among the marines, landed with a unit which bore the brunt of fighting in a tree to tree pursuit of the enemy. He was killed in a sniper melee.

En route to Kwajalein, before the attack, Hopkins' company commander described him as a "good marine."

(facing page, top) Operation Overlord: Planning for the D-Day invasion started in London and then moved across the channel, after which came four months of dead-serious war. Fourth from the left is General Dwight Eisenhower; to his left is General Bernard Montgomery. *National Archives*

(facing page, bottom) Churchill and Eisenhower (second from left) on an inspection tour of American troops in the weeks before the Normandy landings. *US Army*

To General Ist-Brooks,
Second Army Service Command,
par excellence.
Sidney R. Hinds.

Winston S. Churchill
Dwight D. Eisenhower

Polish women and children are led away by German troops during the Warsaw Uprising in early August 1944. The Germans brutally crushed the rebellion and systematically massacred tens of thousands of civilians. No one knows how many children died in the resistance, but estimates range as high as four or five thousand. *Bundesarchiv*

Dumbarton Oaks: In the final months of the war, representatives from the United States, Britain, the Soviet Union, and China met at Dumbarton, one of the most renowned estates in Washington, to discuss what would become the United Nations. *Dumbarton Oaks Archives*

The War Refugee Board, established to aid people who had fled Europe and were trying to get help in the U.S., had several meetings. Here, at their third, in March of 1944, are, right to left, Secretary of War Henry Stimson, Treasury Secretary Henry Morgenthau Jr., and Secretary of State Cordell Hull. *Franklin D. Roosevelt Presidential Library and Museum/NARA*

At the second Quebec Conference in autumn 1944, FDR, Churchill and Allied chiefs of staff discussed the post-war Europe. Henry Morgenthau and Henry Stimson had a sharp disagreement over how Germany should be punished. Morgenthau, a Jew, favored a harsh punishment; Henry Stimson, a member of the New York elite, agreed that punishment was necessary, but also said it had to be kept in mind that Germany was one of the wealthiest, best educated nations in the world. Roosevelt was present, but he seems to have kept his thoughts to himself. *US Army*

At a meeting of generals on December 7, 1944, sharp disagreements arose over the best use of Allied forces as they made steady progress advancing toward the Reich. On the eve of Germany's counteroffensive, Allied unity was at a low point. *National Army Museum*

As the Allies argued, Hitler ordered Field Marshal Gerd von Rundstedt (center) to plan a massive German counterattack through the Allied lines in the Ardennes forest. The Battle of the Bulge was Germany's last gamble and its failure hastened its collapse. *Bundesarchiv*

Roosevelt and Churchill have an intimate conversation at Yalta, a few months before the president's death. *US Army*

At the Yalta Conference in the winter of 1945, Churchill, Roosevelt and Stalin decided to set the perimeters for the new Europe: what boundaries and positions other countries besides the big three would enjoy—or not enjoy. *National Archives*

The war has been over since May. In celebration of Hitler's surrender and suicide, Churchill, at the Reich Chancellery two months later, relaxes on a on a chair that the Russians declared had been taken from Hitler's bunker.

impression. Roosevelt came away from his first meeting with Chiang on November 23 disappointed. The generalissimo struck him as "weak, grasping, and indecisive." To stiffen his spine Roosevelt offered Chiang a series of promises, including permanent membership in the Big Four and the return of Manchuria, Taiwan, and the other regions of China currently occupied by Japan—and he pledged to give serious consideration to China's postwar economic needs and to take Chiang's side in Sino-Soviet territorial disputes.

A few days before departing for Tehran, Roosevelt, Churchill, and the Combined Chiefs of Staff gathered in a Cairo conference room to discuss the future of Allied operations in Europe. When the prime minister's turn came he made another pitch for his soft-underbelly strategy, speaking of Allied successes in Italy. Ignoring the high casualty rates and the urgent need to decide what part of the soft underbelly should be targeted next (southern France or the Balkans?), toward the end of his presentation the prime minister turned to the second front but almost as an afterthought. Overlord, he said, should not be such a tyrant as to rule out every other activity in the Mediterranean. To Hopkins that sounded like a wobble on Overlord. After the meeting he buttonholed Moran and complained that Churchill "never stopped talking and most of what he said was about his bloody Italian war. Some of us are beginning to wonder if the invasion will ever come off."

That evening Moran noted in his diary that a certain hardening of purpose had become evident in the American camp. They left Quebec in great heart, assured that everything was settled for good. And here was the British prime minister at his old games again: "There is an ominous sharpness in the Americans' speech when they say they are not going to allow things to be messed about in this way indefinitely." The hardening of purpose Moran sensed manifested itself a few days later when Admiral King and General Brooke almost came to blows during a strategy discussion. According to Hap Arnold, the American air chief, "Brooke got nasty and King got good and sore. And almost came over the table at Brooke. God, he was mad!"

16

THE CITY OF
A HUNDRED PROMISES

———

THE TEHRAN CONFERENCE PRODUCED A NUMBER OF FIRSTS, beginning with the amount of time it took to arrange. Roosevelt had been attempting to set up a meeting with Stalin for more than a year, but every time he broached the subject in their correspondence Stalin would cite the demands of war and beg off. During a visit to Moscow in the summer of 1943 Joe Davies, Roosevelt's former ambassador to Russia, got Stalin to agree to meet with Roosevelt, but he refused to commit to a date. In October, when Hull and Harriman visited the Kremlin, Stalin was still saying no. "The opportunity to defeat the Germans decisively was at hand," he told his American visitors. However, toward the end of the conversation he intimated that he might be open to a conference provided it was held in Tehran. The Iranian city was relatively easy to reach from Moscow, and the Red Army controlled the local telephone and telegraph lines, which would allow him to keep in touch with his generals. Hull left the meeting grumbling about Stalin to Harriman, with a sense of urgency.

In a cable to Roosevelt, Harriman stressed, as Harriman put it in his memoirs, "the extreme importance of meeting Stalin even if it meant going to Tehran." The president was hesitant. His duty to veto or approve legislation promptly was not suspended during trips abroad, and the mountainous terrain around Tehran would make communication with the outside world difficult. Given the fragile state of his health Roosevelt also may have feared that the 1,000-mile-plus journey from Cairo to Tehran on top of the 6,318-mile trip from Hampton Roads, Virginia, to Cairo would exhaust him. He sent Stalin a polite no, but almost immediately his conscience began to nag at him. Final decisions had to be made about landing craft, bomb sites, invasion beaches, and a host of other issues too complicated to resolve by cable. On November 22 he told Stalin he was looking forward to their meeting in Tehran. Five days later the Sacred Cow, Roosevelt's plane, left Cairo for Tehran.

Stalin was already in the city. At 8:00 A.M. the previous morning, November 26, he arrived at an aerodrome in Baku, a port city on the Caspian Sea. The Tehran trip would be his first flight and he was not looking forward to it. For a moment, Stalin stood on the tarmac in the morning cold gazing back and forth at the plane assigned to him and the plane assigned to his NKVD chief, Beria. Colonel General Alexander Golovanov, his pilot, was among the highest-ranking officers in the Soviet Air Forces; Beria's pilot, a Colonel Pavel S. Grachev, a relative nobody in political terms. But unlike Golovanov, who was fighting the war from a Moscow desk, Grachev was an experienced combat pilot. After a few moments of further reflection Stalin turned to Golovanov and said, "Don't take it badly, but colonel-generals don't often pilot aircraft. We'd better go with the colonel." An escort of twenty-seven fighters appeared overhead and Stalin's plane lumbered up into the morning sky. Unlike his British and American colleagues Stalin was traveling light. His entourage included Molotov, whose Olympian capacity for negotiation could exhaust even the most determined opponent; the sinister NKVD chief, Beria, whose small, untrusting eyes would scan the conference for security breaches; and General Kliment Voroshilov, a Stalin crony since the revolution. In the summer of 1941, Voroshilov bungled the defense of Leningrad—given the urgency of the situation that summer, a capital offense, but in a rare act of kindness Stalin absolved him of his sins. The other members of his entourage included his physician, Professor Vladimir Vinogradov, and twelve Georgian bodyguards who looked almost as ferocious as the swarthy, turbaned, gun-wielding Sikhs who would arrive in Tehran the following day with a disgruntled Mr. Churchill.

The prime minister's journey to Tehran had not been smooth. On waking on the morning of the November 27 flight, Churchill found himself too hoarse to speak and required an 8:45 A.M. whiskey and soda to restore his powers of speech. The five-and-a-half-hour flight to Tehran was uneventful, but the landing at Mehrabad Airport, a few miles outside Tehran, was so inept Churchill whacked the pilot across the legs with his stick and snapped, "Bloody bad landing!" The Sikhs got out of the plane and took up positions around the airfield, then the prime minister emerged and walked across the field to a waiting Rolls-Royce. Churchill was a man of steady nerve, but Tehran had a restive population, a history of assignations, a cadre of German operatives, and a primitive idea of security. The Persian cavalrymen stationed at fifty-yard intervals on the road into Tehran were armed with gleaming swords, pretty to look at but useless against a serious attack; and the police car stationed a hundred feet ahead of the prime minister's slow-moving Rolls offered a would-be assassin an alert that his target was approaching. Toward the center of the city the cavalrymen disappeared, replaced by noisy crowds four and five deep. Most of the faces pressing against the window of the Rolls seemed friendly enough. A few were even waving Union Jacks; still, any one of the welcoming faces could be carrying a weapon. A few minutes later the British legation came into view, and Churchill returned to brooding about the Italian campaign, which had ground to a halt in the winter mud.

The Americans considered Tehran so dangerous that even the young shah was not permitted to greet the president. The Roosevelt party arrived in the city the same day as the British, November 27, but landed at a Soviet airfield to the south of the city guarded by a ring of Iranian soldiers. Inside the ring a sprawl of lend-lease tanks and trucks sat in piles and boxes awaiting shipment north to Russia. In his final preconference cable to Stalin the president had ended with a question: "Where should I stay?" Mikhail Maximov, the Soviet chargé d'affaires in Tehran, discerned a message in the request. Roosevelt wanted an invitation to stay at the Soviet embassy, which Maximov promptly issued. But by the time Roosevelt arrived on November 27 the Russians were so worried that he might ignore the invitation, Molotov turned its acceptance into a matter of life and death. That evening he told Harriman and Clark Kerr, the British ambassador, that the Germans knew Roosevelt was in the city and were planning a "demonstration," Harriman recounted. When

Harriman asked "what he meant by 'demonstration,'" Molotov said there might be "an assassination attempt, which, even if it failed, would lead to shooting and might even result in the killing of innocent civilians." Though Molotov presented no evidence to support his warning, the next morning, in a near-unanimous vote, Roosevelt's aides agreed he should accept the Russian invitation. Later, under interrogation by Harriman, Molotov admitted Soviet intelligence never had any hard evidence of a German plot. But he said there were German operatives in the city, which, in the world Molotov lived in, amounted to the same thing.

The president of the United States and the leader of the Union of Soviet Socialist Republics met for the first time the next day, November 28, in the president's rooms at the Soviet embassy. Stalin arrived a little after 3:00 P.M. dressed in a mustard-colored marshal's jacket with red epaulets and white stars. The only vestiges of the baggy-trousered Stalin whom Hopkins had met in the black summer of 1941 was the pockmarked face, the yellow teeth, and the powerful frame Hopkins described as "a football coach's dream." Mike Riley, Roosevelt's Secret Service agent, recalled that on arriving Stalin "walked toward the boss very slowly, sort of ambled across the room to Roosevelt grinning." Then "the boss grinned back and as they shook hands, he said, 'It's good to see you, Marshal.'" Then Stalin "burst into a very gay laugh." Historian Susan Butler attributes the instant chemistry to the famous Roosevelt charm. "This man, this cripple who did not look or act like a cripple, whose clothes hung on him so well that . . . seated on the couch, he appeared not just physically normal but elegant, was famous for his charm. He could make a casual visitor believe nothing was so important to him, that . . . he had been waiting all day for this hour to arrive." In Stalin's case that feeling had the added virtue of being true. Otherwise Roosevelt would not have risked his fragile health to travel across a thousand miles to an unsafe city rumored to be swarming with German agents to meet a man a sizable number of his fellow Americas viewed as abhorrent.

Roosevelt opened the discussion with an apology. He said he wished it were in his power to bring about the removal of thirty or forty German divisions from the eastern front. "It would be of great value," Stalin said. The remark invited a reply but Roosevelt offered none. He had said everything he intended to say on the subject for the present. Coming from Churchill a response that abrupt would likely have ignited a spirited exchange, but Roosevelt commanded Stalin's respect in a way the prime minister did not. Next Roosevelt turned to a subject that would please his visitor. At the end of the war, he said, Britain and the United States would find themselves with more transports and merchant ships than they needed and suggested some of the surplus vessels would be given to the Soviet Union. "That would be a fine thing," Stalin replied, "not only for Russia but for the United States and Britain, as they would receive Russian raw materials in exchange."

France was discussed next. Free French divisions were fighting valiantly in Italy, and members of the French underground were daily attacking German supply trains and radar sites, at great risk. Still, with American casualties in the hundreds of thousands and Soviet casualties in the millions, Roosevelt and Stalin were not inclined to waste much pity on the French. "The trouble with de Gaulle," said Stalin, "is that he behaves as if he is a great leader and France still a great power and he is wrong on both accounts. The real France collaborates with Germany and must pay a price for that after the war." Roosevelt agreed and proposed that "Frenchmen over forty and, in particular, Frenchmen who have served Vichy [should] not be allowed to hold public office."

There was also general agreement on two other sites, French Indochina and India. As to the former, French Indochina should be made a United Nations trusteeship after the war in preparation for its independence. "Paris has been in [Indochina] for a hundred years," Roosevelt said, "and the people are worse off than they were at the beginning." On India Roosevelt and Stalin agreed; discussions about its future should be avoided during the conference for obvious reasons. Privately, though, Roosevelt had been ruminating about India's future and had concluded that the best solution would be reform from the bottom up. Stalin agreed but made a point Roosevelt had overlooked: "Reform from the bottom would mean revolution."

While Stalin and Roosevelt talked Churchill brooded. It had been evident for months that the Big Three was becoming the Big Two plus One, and Churchill was having difficulty acclimating to the change. He looked so unhappy the afternoon that he arrived in Tehran Moran broke his rule about avoiding personal questions and, according to Moran, he asked the prime minister whether anything had gone wrong. "A lot has gone bloody wrong," Churchill replied, but he refused to elaborate. The next day Harry Hopkins was all smiles when Moran crossed paths with him at the conference. "Harry told me 'with the broadest grin' how the president had asked Stalin whether he would like to discuss the future peace of the world," and Stalin had answered that "there was nothing to prevent them from discussing anything they pleased."

The first plenary session of the conference began after the Roosevelt-Stalin meeting on the twenty-eighth and was preceded by a gifting ceremony. To honor the great Russian victory at Stalingrad, a little after noon a contingent of forty soldiers marched into the great hall of the Soviet embassy in perfect order. Twenty British soldiers, bayonets gleaming in the afternoon light streaming through the window, moved to one side of the hall, twenty machine-gun-bearing Russians to the other side. Roosevelt sat on a chair in between, Stalin to one side of him, Churchill on the other. When all the parties were in place a Russian band played a rousing rendition of the "Internationale" and a not entirely credible version of "God Save the King," then Churchill stepped forward and presented Stalin with the gleaming four-foot-long Sword of Stalingrad. The inscription on the sword read: "To the steel-hearted citizens of Stalingrad the gift of King George VI in token of the homage of the British people." Genuinely moved, Stalin raised the sword to his lips and kissed it, then handed it to his crony Marshal Voroshilov, who promptly dropped it on the floor.

A few hours later Roosevelt opened the first session of the Tehran Conference with a witticism. As the youngest member of the alliance, he said, it was a privilege to welcome his two elders. After the laughter died down the president offered the delegates a tour d'horizon of the war as he saw it. In the Pacific, he said, the United States was bearing most of the burden and sinking more ships than Japan could replace. About China he expressed concern. The most important Allied nation in the Pacific theater was dominated by a scrum of warlords more interested in accruing power and wealth than fighting Japan. Next he turned to Europe. After five major conferences—Casablanca, Trident, Quadrant, Cairo, and Moscow—the second-front issue had been definitively resolved. The plan Roosevelt described that afternoon was essentially an updated version of plan General Marshall had been promoting since 1942—a cross-channel invasion through France into the German heartland. To appease the British the plan left a place for small actions in the Aegean and Adriatic in 1944, provided they stayed small. When Churchill's turn to speak came he said that Overlord was absorbing most of

Britain's and America's resources but both countries were resolved to implement the cross-channel invasion. The statement seemed to conflict with the orders Anthony Eden received before leaving for the Moscow Conference: "Tell Stalin the British pledge on Overlord was contingent on the exigencies of the battle of Italy."

DURING CHURCHILL'S TOUR D'HORIZON STALIN took out a piece of paper and pencil and began drawing pictures of wolves. According to Stalin scholar Butler the doodling was a legacy of his time in Siberia. Imprisoned by the czarist regime nine times, the young Stalin escaped eight times. The ninth time he was sent to an escape-proof back of beyond called Kureika, a remote peasant village near the Arctic Circle. In 1917 the Russian revolution freed him from Kureika the place but not Kureika the memory. Often when Stalin was upset, fearful, or just bored the memory of wolf packs crossing the tundra in the morning cold would come back and he'd pick up his pen and begin doodling.

On the afternoon of the twenty-ninth the Soviet leader was the last of the three principals to address the conference, and he began with an announcement. Russia would join the war against Japan at the end of the German conflict; then, turning to the situation on the eastern front, he offered snapshot accounts of the Stalingrad and Kursk battles, briefly described the Red Army's plans for 1944, and concluded with another announcement. For the first time in the war the Red Army had achieved numerical superiority over the Axis powers in the east. When he turned to the second front, Stalin's voice, formerly matter-of-fact, attained an edge. He dismissed the Italian campaign as too small and unimportant to deliver a knockout blow to Germany; Hitler was only using Italy to buy time for his armies in the east. The road to victory required closing directly on the enemy's strongpoints. The Anglo-Americans must get into the heart of Germany with an attack through northern or northwest France. When Stalin finished, an affronted Churchill rose from his chair to defend the Anglo-American strategy. Battle by battle the prime minister gave a detailed account of the British and American victories in North Africa, predicted Rome would fall within a month (January 1944), and "dwelt at length on the possibility and desirability of Turkey entering the war" on the Allied side. Time and events would prove all the predictions wrong. Rome was not captured until July 1944, Turkey refused to enter the war, and British and American troops would still be fighting in Italy when the war ended in May 1945. But all that was in the future; the task at Tehran was to properly sort out the present.

ON THE EVENING OF NOVEMBER 29 Churchill attended a dinner party hosted by Stalin. Earlier in the day the two men had had a sharp exchange over the second front; when Churchill arrived at the dinner party that evening Stalin seemed eager to pick up the fight where it had left off. As Churchill noted in his memoirs there was a kind of hierarchy in Tehran. Roosevelt was the "American Eagle" and first among equals, Stalin the "Russian Bear," and he was the "little English Donkey." What Churchill left out of his memoirs is how much the bear enjoyed taunting the donkey. Charles Bohlen, a young foreign service officer who served as a translator at the conference, said Stalin "lost no opportunity to get in a dig at Mr. Churchill." Harriman also noticed the bullying. "When the president spoke, Stalin listened closely and with deference, where . . . he did not hesitate to interrupt Churchill." The issue the two men clashed over at the dinner party was not the second front but how to treat a defeated Germany, and they had a large audience—Hopkins, Harriman, Marshall, Brooke, and a host of other senior British and American officials. Stalin instigated the fight by offering a toast "to the swiftest possible justice for Germany's war criminals—justice before a firing squad." Then, raising his glass a little higher, he proclaimed, "I drink to our unity in dispatching them as fast as we catch them, and there must be at least fifty thousand of them."

Outraged, Churchill said that the British Parliament and the British people would never stand for such mass murder. "I take this opportunity," he said, "to say most strongly that . . . no one, Nazi or not, shall be summarily dealt with by a firing squad without proper legal trial and proven evidence against them." At that point Roosevelt attempted to lower the temperature with a joke. Turning to Stalin he said, "Clearly there must be some sort of compromise between your position . . . and that of my good friend the prime minister. Perhaps we could say, instead of summarily executing fifty thousand war criminals we should settle on a smaller number. Shall we say forty-five thousand, five hundred?" Churchill was not amused. While war criminals must be made to pay for their crimes, he averred, "soldiers should not be randomly thrown up against a wall and executed because of the uniform they wear." Next, and more unusually, the prime minister turned on Roosevelt, proclaiming, "The

British Empire now and the British Empire forever!" Britain would keep most of its overseas colonies and territories after the war, and if challenged, Britain would fight to defend her territories. As he finished, Churchill felt a hand clapping on his back. When he turned around Stalin and Molotov were standing behind him, wearing big grins. It was all a joke, Stalin said. They were just playing.

What began as a difficult evening ended as a frightening one. In the midst of a discussion on postwar borders with Stalin, Roosevelt's face suddenly lost color, molecules of sweat bled on to his shirt, and he was rushed to his living quarters. For long minutes the dinner guests chattered back and forth in nervous whispers, then Vice Admiral Ross McIntire, Roosevelt's physician, appeared and announced the president had a mild case of indigestion. That may have been true, though for political and personal reasons McIntire often downplayed the president's medical problems.

The next morning—the thirtieth, the final day of the conference—Roosevelt felt well enough to shop for souvenirs and knickknacks at an exchange in the Soviet embassy. Other delegates took advantage of the fine weather to take long walks, to lunch at an outdoor café, or shop for souvenirs. Nonetheless, one important piece of business was conducted on the thirtieth: Churchill awoke that morning still uneasy about Overlord and resolved to make a final effort to persuade Stalin of its risks. During a talk at the Soviet embassy he warned that the current Allied estimates of German strength could be wrong. The French beaches could be heavily defended. Stalin kept his thoughts to himself until Churchill finished speaking, then allowed himself a flash of anger. Russia "was counting on an Allied invasion of northern France," and needed to know now if the operation was going to be canceled. At a lunch with Churchill and Stalin later in the day, Roosevelt brought the second-front debate to a final and conclusive end with two announcements. Overlord had received the imprimatur of the Joint Chiefs of Staff and had been given a definitive date: June 1, 1944. When Roosevelt finished, Stalin said the Red Army would support the invasion with a series of simultaneous attacks, then asked the president if the Overlord commander had been selected. Marshall had been promised the post, but the closer the invasion date came, the more reluctant Roosevelt was to lose him. "I need a few more days," he told Stalin, then changed the subject.

WHEN THE THIRD AND FINAL plenary session of the conference convened an hour later Stalin expanded on his offer to support Overlord: "The period of greatest danger will be the moment when the assault troops leap from the landing craft onto the exposed beaches." From the other side of Europe it was impossible to reduce the moment of maximum danger directly, he said, but it could be minimized indirectly from a distance by ensuring the landing beaches were thinly defended. Therefore, in May, the Red Army would organize an offensive to hinder the movement of Germans troops from the eastern to the western front. Next the conversation turned to the prizes that victory would bring. Stalin expressed an interest in Dalian, a port city; Roosevelt in Bremen, Lübeck, and Hamburg; and, in a portent of things to come, both men expressed interest in the strategically important Kiel Canal. Stalin's bargaining style was blunt. He announced his interest in Darien by asking, "What can be done for Russia in the Far East?" The final item on the agenda was the conference communiqué, which Churchill oversaw. "The notes to be struck," he told the drafters, were brevity, mystery, and a foretaste of impending doom for Germany.

NOVEMBER 30 WAS ALSO CHURCHILL's birthday, and at the beginning of his seventieth year he was given two birthday parties. That afternoon the British and Indian troops in Tehran were summoned from their barracks and the employees of the Anglo-Iranian Oil Company from their office desks for a march-by. Together the soldiers and the oilmen barely filled the small field where the ceremony was held, but they gave Churchill the best birthday present he could hope for: a sense of home. As he walked down the thin red line accepting salutes tears streamed from his eyes. The birthday party the prime minister hosted for himself that evening was a more spectacular affair. A light breeze had taken the edge off the afternoon heat and the guest list was a who's who of the Allied war effort. In attendance were Roosevelt, who presented the prime minister with a Persian bowl; Stalin, who came with two gifts, an astrakhan hat and a large Chinese sculpture depicting Russian folktales; Brooke, who came bearing a rare smile; Churchill's daughter Sarah and Roosevelt's son Elliott; Admiral William Leahy; General Voroshilov; and Pug Ismay, who recalled later "that the speeches started directly as we sat down and continued almost without stop until we got up."

In his toasts Churchill praised Roosevelt, "who, by his courage and foresight, prevented a revolutionary upheaval in the United States in 1933, Stalin, who he predicted would be ranked with the great heroes of Russian history and had earned the title Stalin the great." As the evening progressed and the alcohol flowed more freely Stalin and Churchill began teasing each other. When the prime minister said Britain was becoming pinker, Stalin interjected, "It is a sign of good health." Several drinks later Churchill raised his glass in salute to "the proletarian masses," and Stalin responded with a toast to "the Conservative Party."

Two weeks after the end of the Tehran Conference, Bohlen wrote, in an assessment of Soviet aims and their likely consequences, "Germany is to be broken up and kept broken up. The states of eastern, southeastern and central Europe will not be permitted to group themselves into federations and associations. France is to be stripped of her colonies and strategic bases beyond her borders and will not be permitted to maintain any appreciable military establishment. Poland and Italy will remain approximately at their present size, but it is doubtful if either will be permitted to maintain an appreciable armed force. The result [will] be that the Soviet Union [will] be the only important military and political force on the Continent of Europe. The rest of Europe [will] be reduced to military and political."

17

A WALK IN THE SUN

IN DECEMBER 1943 THE GERMAN ARMY IN THE EAST WAS AFFLICTED by a sense of doom. The year that began with the catastrophic defeat at Stalingrad was ending with Kursk, Smolensk, and Kiev, the Ukrainian capital, all in Soviet hands, as well as with the German army again retreating westward in a heavy winter snow. Even the Führer, as fierce an advocate of "not one step back" as Stalin, recognized that the defeat at Kursk had left German forces too weak to hold their current positions and ordered a general retreat to the Dnieper, a strategically important river that flows through the Ukrainian capital down to the Black Sea. The heavy fighting in 1943 had also take an heavy toll on the Russians. The 5th Guards Tank Army, which went into the battle of Kursk with five hundred tanks, emerged with fifty. But German intelligence that earlier in the war underestimated Soviet strength was now overestimating it, and Soviet commanders were quick to take advantage of the mistake.

General Pavel Rotmistrov, commander of the 5th Guards Tank Army, conjured up a tank army out of thin air and with a technical sleight of hand convinced the Germans the army was real. The year ended in a crescendo of death. Between September and December 1943 almost 4 million men—2.6 million Russians and a German force of roughly half that size—clashed over an 870-mile battlefield in a campaign that began in the mud and rain of a wet September, with both armies racing southward to take up positions along the Dnieper, the Germans scorching the earth behind them to slow down the pursuing Soviets. According to one historian, "Whole armies slithered through fields of sugar beets, tanks sank through mats of sledge, asphyxiating their crews. Infantrymen from central Asia, lacking swimming skills, drowned crossing the river and whole Red Army penal brigades were sacrificed to defuse a single minefield or storm a forward position." But fortune was now fighting on the Russian side. Slowly, inexorably, the autumn battle swung toward the Red Army. By early November Kiev, which intersects with the Dnieper, was in Soviet hands and there were Russian bridgeheads along the western (German) side of the river.

The Dnieper campaign ended ignominiously for one of Germany's most renowned generals: on December 19, Field Marshal Erich von Manstein destroyed what he believed to be four Soviet corps, but it was a deception force created to mask a Soviet buildup. On Christmas morning, as Manstein sat in his quarters contemplating his recent success, the Soviets launched a massive attack, ripping open a gap in the German defenses and demonstrating that the Red Army was now capable of launching multiple offensives simultaneously. In January the Germans retreated westward in a heavy snow, leaving behind burned villages, shattered fields, slaughtered livestock, and human remains. By late January the dead were everywhere. They assembled in the snowy fields, hung from the naked trees, lay stacked like cordwood along winter roads, peered out of barnyards and roofless shops. They frightened children, were fed upon by rats, dogs, and a half dozen other species, and became a source of conflict between the local people who wanted the corpses removed immediately and the local authorities who wanted to wait until the spring thaw.

In May, when the migratory birds returned to their nesting grounds along the Dnieper, they seemed unsettled and confused. All the familiar markers that had oriented the birds in previous years were gone. There were no trees, no meadows, no crickets chirping, no frogs croaking— just a scorched black earth and the heavy sound of silence. In February 1944 a Russian soldier wrote his wife, "Sometimes there are moments of such strain the living envy the dead. Death is not as terrible as we used to think. Truth is that we fight for its future."

On February 7, 1943, five days after the fall of Stalingrad, Hitler summoned his gauleiters—Nazi Party district leaders—to his headquarters and told them, "If the German people fail, they do not deserve that we fight for their future." He needn't have worried. Despite the nightly bombing raids and food shortages, despite the hundreds of thousands of dead sons and husbands, despite Stalingrad and Kursk as 1943 slipped into history—despite all of that the German people continued to stand by the Führer.

The same could not be said of Germany's allies. By the end of the year Italians were fighting alongside Britain and the United States in Italy. And Finland, Hungary, Romania, and Slovakia—Germany's other allies—were considering peace. Cracks had also begun to appear in the German leadership. In an October 1943 speech to a group of SS generals, Reichsführer Heinrich Himmler again swore allegiance to the "final solution." "In front of you here," he said to the SS men, "I want to refer explicitly to a very serious matter. . . . I mean here the annihilation of the Jewish people. Most of you know what it means when one hundred corpses lie side by side, or five hundred or one thousand. . . . This page of glory in our history will never be written. We have the moral right. We are obliged to our people to kill these people which wanted to kill us."

Notwithstanding the hard words, Himmler was not blind to Germany's increasingly desperate military situation. To visiting neutral diplomats he presented himself as a man not unlike themselves, a senior bureaucrat who saw communism as anathema and wanted to return Germany to the family of nations. To that end he had begun exploring peace through third parties. Two months before the SS speech German intelligence came into possession of an Allied cable that said, "Himmler's lawyer confirms the hopelessness of Germany's military position and has arrived in [Switzerland] to put out peace feelers," but when the cable came to light all the blame fell on the Reichsführer's emissary Dr. Carl Langbehn, a noted jurist, who was arrested on his return to Berlin and sent to an SS facility where his testicles were torn out. Then he was thrown against a wall and shot. Himmler protected his other emissary, Johannes Popitz, a senior German bureaucrat, until the final days of the war in the mistaken belief that friendship with a senior government official was tantamount to having a get-out-of-jail-free card. On discovering this was not the case Himmler had Popitz executed.

At various times three other men in Hitler's immediate circle—Joseph Goebbels, the propaganda minister; Heinz Guderian, inspector general of armored troops; and Hermann Göring, commander in chief of the Luftwaffe—were approached by interlocutors seeking a negotiated end to the war. All three men refused to breach their oath to the Nazi state, yet, significantly, not one disclosed the name of the interlocutors who approached him, though the name of one eventually came to light: Baldur von Schirach, leader of the Hitler Youth, who was the gauleiter of Vienna and the husband of Henriette von Schirach, who claimed Hitler had tried to kiss her when she was twelve years old. Frau Schirach was present the evening that Göring and her husband met, and she wrote a brief account of the meeting later. The setting was a "secluded, velvet room of a high-end Vienna restaurant and the evening began in an atmosphere of Gemütlichkeit [warmth and good cheer]." One of the guests, a famous composer, played the piano; then Göring played improvisations from *Der Freischutz*. Afterward, the Reichsmarschall (this was another of Goering's titles) showed the Schirachs two purchases he had made during a shopping expedition earlier in the day. One was a leather briefcase decorated in Luftwaffe blue, the other a bottle of Jean Desprez perfume, which Göring claimed was only available in Vienna. Schirach, who had become disillusioned with Hitler's leadership, let Göring go on for several minutes. Then, judging the moment right, he brought up the war—but gingerly and in a manner that would appeal to the Reichsmarschall's vanity and patriotism.

Schirach began by urging Göring to have a private conversation with Hitler, which both men knew would lead nowhere. Then the gauleiter got to the point: "I and my Hitler Youth are with you, the Luftwaffe is strong and there are plenty of men who are prepared to act. . . . We must make this a common cause. . . . As Reichsmarschall, it is expected of you." Göring knew what Schirach was asking but could not do it. Maybe once, but not after Stalingrad, not after failing to honor his pledge to feed the German army, trapped inside the city, by air. "To speak to Hitler alone!" Göring said. What an idea. "I never see him alone these days! Bormann [Martin Bormann, who had replaced Göring as Hitler's number two] is with him all the time. If I could, by God, I would have gone to Churchill a long time ago. Do you think I am enjoying this damned business?" At that point Emmy Göring put her hand to her husband's mouth and said, "Let's not talk about it anymore; all will be well in the end."

IN THE WINTER OF 1939/1940 Khasan Israilov, a young Chechen Muslim, had an epiphany. In the hierarchy of the Soviet state Muslims like himself and his brother Hussein were viewed as third-class citizens. Seeing no recourse, the brothers accepted their fate stoically. Perhaps Allah would reward them in the afterlife for their suffering. Then in late 1939 Finland, a country not much larger than Chechnya, fought an invading Russian army to a draw for several months. If Finland could repel Stalin's tanks and planes, why couldn't Chechnya? Over the next year Khasan and Hussein recruited like-minded young Chechens and built a base of operations in the mountainous southeast of the country. A failed NKVD attempt to obliterate the Israilovs' little army further enhanced the brothers' prestige—and the support of the German army, which arrived in 1941, deepened Khasan Israilov's conviction that, with the Soviet state fighting for its life, now was the moment to break free and create an independent Chechnya. A five-thousand-man army was formed and the new state given a name: the Provisional Popular Revolutionary Government of Chechen-Ingushetia (Ingushetia was a neighboring Muslim enclave).

In early 1944, with the Germans in retreat, Stalin decided it was time to tidy up the home front. The Israilov brothers were hunted down and killed; then Stalin turned to the larger question of what to do with the millions of Turkish and Chechnyan peoples who inhabited the Caucasus. When the Germans arrived in the region in 1941, they were welcomed as liberators in some villages, though in the main the members of the ethnic groups in the region remained loyal to the Soviet Union. Nonetheless, in late 1943 Stalin concluded the most effective way to avoid further outbreaks of nationalism and other dangerous ideas was punishment. The pogrom of the Caucasus peoples, which began in late 1943 and continued into the postwar years, was reminiscent of the Trail of Tears, Andrew Jackson's forcible removal of the Cherokees from their homeland east of the Mississippi to what is now Oklahoma. On February 20, 1944, Beria and his deportation expert Ivan Serov, a short stocky man with ice-cold blue-gray eyes, arrived in Grozny, the capital of Chechnya, with a hundred thousand NKVD troops and nineteen thousand Chekists, members of the Soviet secret police. Three days later the local population was ordered to gather in the city's squares. The Chekists and NKVD units emerged from the shadows and arrested everyone in sight.

On March 7, 1944, Beria informed Stalin that eight hundred thousand Chechens were on their way to resettlement in remote areas of

Siberia and central Asia. By the time the program concluded almost two million people had been caught up in its net, including the Tatars of the Crimea and the Volga Germans, who had escaped arrest during a 1942 roundup.

But the principal victims were the peoples of the Caucasus. The region was peppered with obscure races, small in number and mysterious in origin, like the Balkars, an agricultural people whose population numbered 42,600 in 1939. Concluding the Balkars were "bandits," on February 25, 1944, Beria wrote Stalin, "If you agree, before my return to Moscow, I can take necessary measures to resettle the Balkars." Twenty percent of the population would be dead by the time the Balkars reached their new homeland. The Karachays, a north Caucus people with a population of 80,000, lost a third of its population en route to a new settlement in the back of beyond. The Kalmyks, a Buddhist people of 93,000 who did collaborate with the Germans, were singled out for particularly harsh treatment. At 6:00 A.M. on December 28, 1943, several thousand NKVD agents descended on the Kalmyks' settlement and announced to the dazed villagers who had been pulled from their beds that the president of the Supreme Soviet had found the Kalmyk people guilty of collaboration.

Families were given twelve hours to collect their belongings and prepare for deportation. At six that evening 93,000 Kalmyks of all ages were put into unheated railway cars. Upon arriving in Siberia, they were dispatched to camps where the workday was twelve hours—and the workweek seven days. Exhaustion, malnutrition, and frostbite shrank the Kalmyks' population 20 percent by 1945. Pleased by the success of the pogroms Stalin presented the 413 Chekist officers who participated in the resettlements with medals.

In the early hours of December 13, 1943, General Brooke had been asleep in a guest room in Eisenhower's Carthage villa when he was awakened by a voice that kept repeating, "Hullo. Hullo. Hullo."

"Who the hell is that?" Brooke shouted—and then turned on the light next to his bed. Winston Churchill was standing in the doorway in a dragon dressing gown, a brown bandage wrapped around his head.

"I am looking for Dr. Moran," the prime minister said, adding that he had "a bad headache." News of Churchill's affliction spread quickly to Eisenhower's other guests—and the villa filled with the sound of footfalls and whispers.

By daylight the pain had passed, but Moran was worried. Churchill had just turned sixty-nine, ate and drank in excess, and the back-to-back Cairo and Tehran Conferences had strained him both physically and emotionally. Moran summoned a pathologist and two nurses from Cairo and borrowed a portable x-ray machine from a hospital in Tunis. The pathologist, Lieutenant Colonel Robert Pulvertaft, declared Churchill's blood count normal, but his temperature had risen to 101, and the ominous dark shadow on the x-rays Pulvertaft took indicated a serious case of pneumonia.

Over the next few days the prime minister's condition worsened. When Harold Macmillan, the British resident minister in the Mediterranean, visited Churchill's villa on the thirteenth, Churchill looked "weak and drowsy," Macmillan recalled. The following evening a new complication arose: the prime minister's heart exhibited signs of strain. On the evening of the fifteenth an inflection point was reached. Churchill's lungs became congested and his heartbeat "very" irregular. "I knew we were right up against things," Moran recalled later. "A heart attack on top of pneumonia makes a man feel pretty awful."

For the next four hours a tense Moran sat by his patient's bedside waiting for Churchill's heart to return to a normal beat. At 10:30 that evening the palpitations stopped and he fell asleep. The next morning his pulse steadied and his lungs were clearing. At 3:00 A.M. on the eighteenth, the palpitations reappeared but only briefly. That afternoon, the prime minister felt well enough to sit up in his bed and read the get-well cards from his many admirers. As Christmas approached color returned to his cheeks and purpose and energy to his actions. He was particularly buoyed by a cable from the British chiefs of staff on December 22. The chiefs declared themselves "in full agreement: the present stagnation in Italy cannot be allowed to continue."

The Italian campaign was shaped by a directive from the Combined Chiefs of Staffs—in other words, the British and American chiefs of staff. The directive outlined two goals. The first goal—knock Italy out of the war—was achieved almost immediately. In September 1943 Mussolini was removed from office in a coup, and shortly thereafter Italy capitulated. But the victory came with an asterisk: there were still thousands of German troops in the country.

The second goal—draw German troops away from the eastern front—remained in force. The Joint Chiefs' directive made no mention of Rome, but the Eternal City was rich in glamour and history and had a powerful advocate in Winston Churchill, who very much wanted to capture Rome. Roosevelt was more focused on Overlord, now only six months away; nevertheless, he thought that Italy was important enough to encourage Mark Clark, commander of the American Fifth Army, to "keep on giving it all you have, and Rome will be ours."

As a prize of war Rome was hard to resist. The liberators would march into the Eternal City under a blanket of bouquets, pretty young women would throw kisses at them, old men would serenade them with accordions, old women would offer up rosaries on their behalf, and children would run alongside the marching soldiers, waving the Stars and Stripes and Union Jack, and at parade's end there would be the prospect of a night of great decadence.

In time a version of this vision would come to pass, but achieving victory would take longer and claim more lives than anticipated because the Allied planners failed to fully grasp what Albert Kesselring, the German commander in Italy, already knew: in the mountainous terrain of southern Italy the advantage falls to the defender. As a result the British and American formations in Italy spent the autumn of 1943 slogging from hill to hill, mountain to mountain, river to river: their boots covered with mule dung, their hands red from the cold. They stepped over bodies flattened by passing tanks, subsisted on Spam and C rations, went weeks without a change of clothing, were tormented by the cold, wet rains of October, and fell prey to pneumonia in the sleet and snow of November. On the rare days when the sun came out, German planes would appear overhead and the fill the sky with leaflets that taunted, "The road is long."

The road was also heavily defended. During the autumn of 1943 Kesselring constructed a network of defensive lines to check the Allied advance. By late autumn the British and Americans had breached two, the Barbara and Bernhardt Lines, but victory brought little relief. To the north, the sullen mountain ranges seemed to spread out to infinity, and behind the final range, waiting patiently for the GIs, was the Gustav Line, which spread across Italy from the Mediterranean Sea in the west to the Adriatic in the east and was defended by a network of interlocking defenses that guarded the road north to Rome. German propaganda claimed the Gustav Line was impenetrable, and the GIs slogging through the snowy mountain passes toward the Eternal City were not eager to test the German boast.

But for a cruel piece of luck, the Allied troops might already have been in Rome. Initially the Germans had planned to abandon the capital, but as the autumn fighting progressed and German commanders began to realize what a valuable ally the mountainous Italian terrain was, a sharp argument broke out between the two senior German commanders in the country. Erwin Rommel, who led a nine-division force in northern Italy and was losing faith in Germany's ability to prevail, wanted to abandon Rome and fall back to a more defensible position in the Po River valley, several hundred miles to the north. Kesselring, who commanded an eight-division force in the south, had no illusions about Germany's future in Italy, but blessed with an optimistic temperament he was confident he could make the British and Americans pay a heavy price for every foot of Italian soil they seized. One of Germany's most versatile generals, "Smiling Albert" had played a major role in the Battle of Britain and a year later in the aerial campaign at the opening of Barbarossa. In Sicily Kesselring demonstrated his skills as a field commander. Under the nose of a vastly superior Anglo-American force, he evacuated 40,000 Italian and German troops, 93,000 vehicles, 970 tons of fuel, and 15,000 tons of stores to mainland Italy.

In the autumn of 1943, when Hitler began searching for a supreme commander to lead the Italian campaign, the choice quickly narrowed down to Kesselring or Rommel. Hitler equivocated for a while but finally chose Kesselring. He was not as well known as the Desert Fox, whose exploits in North Africa had become the stuff of legend. But Hitler was not looking for a German Lawrence of Arabia. He believed that military success without optimism was impossible and that Smiling Albert, an optimist by nature, could find a streak of sunlight in the darkest cloud, while Rommel, though an "extraordinarily brave and able commander," could not.

Kesselring proved an inspired choice. By early December the Allied advance had slowed to a crawl, and frustrated British and American planners were searching for a way to seize back the initiative. The search led to a reexamination of an idea that had been kicking around in various iterations since October. It was initially proposed by General Alexander, the senior British commander in the Mediterranean. Alex, as friends called him, was born in Northern Ireland, the cradle of the British officer class. He was glamorously handsome and, in his smooth, well-mannered, gentlemanly way, a warrior. While other soldiers rushed home after the Great War, Alexander had gone looking for another war and found one in eastern Europe. In 1940 he was among the last, and may have been the last, of the British officers to leave the beaches at Dunkirk. Frustrated by the stalemate in Italy, in late autumn Alexander proposed a solution: a two-pronged attack. The first prong would center on the town of Cassino, which sits beneath the ancient abbey of Monte Cassino, and was the most heavily defended sector of the Gustav Line. Under the plan, the American Fifth Army would engage the Germans forces in Cassino, while a five-division force would sail north and establish a beachhead in Anzio, an Italian town thirty-five miles south of Rome. When Alexander's plan was bigfooted by Overlord, which had first priority on landing craft, General Clark proposed a scaled-down version of the Alexander plan. A single, reinforced division of twenty-four thousand men would seize the beaches at Anzio and hold them until the Fifth Army breached the Gustav Line and came to their rescue.

A week later Clark killed the plan. The most optimistic estimates had the Fifth Army arriving at Anzio in seven days, and Clark doubted a twenty-four-thousand-man force could hold the beachhead for more than a day against a determined German attack. Almost immediately, Churchill resuscitated the operation. Italy was central to the prime minister's soft-underbelly strategy; moreover, a victory at Anzio would restore some of the prestige that the empire had lost at Dunkirk and Singapore. On Christmas Day 1943 Churchill, still ailing from pneumonia, called Roosevelt and asked if a portion of the landing craft scheduled for Overlord could be kept in the Italian theater until February to support what was now called Operation Shingle. Roosevelt agreed, although he was not happy about the British sideshows in the eastern Mediterranean.

In its final iteration, Shingle resembled an expanded version of Clark's plan except instead of one, two assault divisions would rush the Anzio beaches. The plan's advocates described it as a win-win proposition. If Kesselring chose to challenge the landings he would have to pull troops from the Gustav Line, increasing its vulnerability to attack; conversely, if he chose to ignore the Anzio threat and husband his resources for the coming battle at Cassino, the assault force could seize the Alban Hills, the gateway to Rome, with relative ease. As December faded into January the weather worsened and the fighting grew bitterer. Camino, Rotondo, Lungo, San Pietro, and dozens of other obscure little Italian towns the world had never heard of became miniature Sommes and Passchendaeles for a few days. Replacement troops were chewed up so quickly that men often died never knowing the names of the other soldiers in their squadron. The dead were packed into 1940s-version body bags to protect them from the feral animals prowling the roads, and the only emblem of their service was a bloodstained dog tag. Battalions sustained casualties of one hundred to two hundred men daily. Exhausted stretcher-bearers fell asleep in the bitter cold and awoke with hacking coughs. On January 16, at a cost of sixteen thousand casualties, American troops pierced the Bernhardt Line, the next-to-last German line. But the victory brought little cheer. Directly ahead lay the Gustav Line, the most formidable of the German positions. It stretched a hundred miles across the belly of Italy, but its most muscular point was the town of Cassino and the rivers that snake around it—the Rapido and the Garigliano. The town sits directly southwest of the abbey that bears its name and less than half a mile from where Saint Aldemar the Wise and Saint Benedict of Nursia prayed a millennium earlier.

Four hundred German heavy guns and rocket launchers guarded the approaches to Cassino, each battery linked to an observer who sat shivering behind a tree or rock, monitoring activity in the town. Every foot of Cassino that could be weaponized was. For two months "German engineers and press-ganged Italian workers blasted gun pits from rock faces, reinforced bunkers with telephone poles then reinforced the roofs of the bunkers with more poles, oak beams, and several feet of dirt," a historian wrote. In the town of Cassino fields of fire were cleared around the fortified railway station and the Hotel Continental. The Allies responded by bringing in Polish and New Zealand troops. In homes beneath the abbey old women took out their rosary beads and offered up Hail Marys. Hitler countered by promising Kesselring more mines, barbed wire, antitank guns and engineers, slave laborers, and three-ton armored turrets with charcoal burners to keep the crews warm. As both sides rushed to mobilize more men and matériel the looming battle began to feel like a dress rehearsal for Armageddon.

•

OPERATION INSTRUCTIONS NUMBER 34, THE plan of attack General Alexander drew up, did not lack for ambition. French, British, and American forces would launch assaults along the Rapido and Garigliano Rivers in the Cassino region on January 12, 17, and 20, then, having punched a hole in the Gustav Line, the troops would march seventy miles north to Anzio, where on January 22 they would be reinforced by a second contingent of British and American troops carried north by sea. Then the two battle groups would join forces and march on Rome, thirty-five miles to the north, and from there farther up the boot to Pisa and Florence. General Lucian Truscott, commander of the American 3rd Division, was appalled when he reexamined Alexander's plan. Before it could be implemented, the Anglo-American forces at Cassino would have to breach the Gustav Line, and Truscott warned General Clark there was "little chance" any assault would succeed unless the heavy German guns guarding Cassino were silenced first.

General Fred Walker, commander of the 36th Division, a hard-luck division badly mauled at Salerno then again at San Pietro, was even more apprehensive. On January 8, Walker confided to his diary: "I don't see how we or any other division can possibly succeed in crossing the Rapido." A week later Walker's dreams were still full of corpses flowing facedown in the winter surf. "This is going to be a tough job and I don't like it," he wrote in his diary. "There is nothing in our favor." As the day of attack approached, there was also debate about the wisdom of landing a force seventy miles north of the nearest Allied soldier. The analysts at Alexander's Fifteenth Army Group were confident Kesselring would fall back to the north upon encountering the heavily muscled Anzio strike force, which boasted two divisions of VI Corps, three Ranger battalions, two commando battalions, a parachute regiment, a parachute battalion, and the promise of a steady stream of reinforcements across the beaches. However, G2, military intelligence, thought Kesselring would stand and fight. The assessment was based on Smiling Albert's military record, but there were also personal reasons why he might choose to make a stand. He came to Italy believing the Italians would stand by Germany; and when Italy changed sides he felt a personal sense of betrayal.

To a large extent the success of the Alexander plan would depend on who had read Kesselring's intentions clearly, Fifteenth Army Group or G2. On the moonless night of January 19, in a town a dozen or so miles to the south of Cassino, an answer suggested itself. The British

46th Division was attempting to breach a line when German engineers opened the sluice gates of a local river. If it had been fifteen degrees colder the water might have frozen immediately and the 46th could have continued its assault, but on the nineteenth the air was only cold enough to sting the hands and face. As the Tommies took up position the night air filled with the sound of splashing water, machine-gun fire, the shouts of dying men, and the cries of frightened women.

The next morning, what remained of the 46th was taken off the line. On the twentieth it was the Americans' turn. The lead division, General Walker's 36th Division, was ordered to walk into the January night and throw itself upon the German line below Cassino. Expecting a blood-bath, a day earlier, General Clark had armed himself with a series of rationalizations. "It is essential," he wrote, "that I make the attack fully expecting heavy losses in order to hold all the German troops on my front . . . thereby clearing the way for Shingle [the Anzio assault]." Clark was right to expect heavy casualties. Between Thursday evening, when the battle began, and Sunday afternoon, when the fighting petered to a conclusion, the 36th and several sister divisions sustained casualties at the same rate as the troops at Normandy would experience six months later. There was one important difference, though.

At Normandy the results justified the high casualties. Clark's decision is harder to support. In the weeks following the fighting, the War Department sent out thousands of death notices to families, informing them that a son, a husband, or a brother had died on the banks of two rivers they had never heard of near a town they had never heard of in a campaign that would have no effect on the outcome of the war. The hard 36th Texas Division ended the battle with 2,019 casualties and little to show for it. A few days after the fighting ended, the Germans sent a mocking note across the lines to the Americans via carrier pigeon: "We look forward to your next visit." Still the sacrifice of American and British lives was not totally in vain. A few days earlier an Ultra transcript had reported that Kesselring was concerned about the attacks on the Rapido and that he had moved two of his best divisions south to reinforce the Gustav Line.

Thanks to that unexpected piece of good luck, Anzio was virtually undefended on January 22, 1944, when the VI Corps arrived offshore, muscled up with commando and parachute units. Since Mussolini's fall the previous autumn Anzio's experience of war had been akin to that of living with an ill-tempered German shepherd. The shepherd bared its teeth frequently but rarely bit, and that attitude carried through the landings. A few German antiaircraft batteries opened fire and the Luftwaffe made a few nervous visits to the beaches, but it was for show. On the twenty-second, British and American planes flew over twelve hundred sorties during the landings. Alexander and Clark were on hand to watch the VI Corps storm the mostly empty beaches, but only as observers. Operation Shingle was in the hands General John Lucas, a favorite of General Marshall's.

Born in West Virginia and educated at West Point, Lucas had an experience of war typical for a professional soldier of his generation; in 1916 he was part of the force that routed Pancho Villa on the Rio Grande, and in 1918 he was wounded in the final days of the Great War. He spent the interwar years rotating between college ROTC programs and the US Army Command and General Staff College, was an observer during the Sicilian campaign, and received his first combat command at Salerno, where he relieved the overmatched General Ernest Dawley and brought a troubled campaign to a victorious end.

In January 1944, Lucas was fifty-four but looked a decade older, was fatigued by months of fighting from mountain to mountain, and had a bad feeling about the Shingle operation. How much the feeling had to do with Mark Clark's final warning to him—"Don't stick your neck out"— and how much to Lucas's fear that the goals were greater than the forces he had been given is unclear, but on the eve of battle he was in a melancholic mood. "They will end up putting me ashore with an inadequate force and get me in a serious jam. Then who will take the blame?"

Under Shingle Lucas had two options. If the VI Corps met light opposition on the beaches he was to immediately march on the Alban Hills twenty miles inland and from there to Rome. If the VI Corps met heavy opposition he was to form a perimeter and defend Anzio and its immediate environs. Though opposition was light on the twenty-second Lucas chose the second option, to form a perimeter. The decision emboldened Kesselring. Concluding his opponent was overly cautious Smiling Albert decided to contest the landings. By late afternoon he had summoned the Hermann Göring Division from Rome, the 714th Light Motorized Division from southern France, the 114th Light Jäger Division from the Balkans, the 3rd Panzergrenadier Division, the newly formed 16th SS Panzer Division, the 26th Panzer Division, elements of the 1st Panzer

Division, several division-size formations from Germany, and at least a half dozen other units from other parts of the still formidable German Empire. On the early evening of the twenty-second, as Lucas was brooding, Kesselring's confidence was swelling. Later that evening he informed the German 10th Army that the possibility of a large-scale expansion of the Anzio beachhead was no longer a risk. Privately he thought he might be able to push the Allied strike force back into the sea.

During the next few days Lucas remained cautious. The port of Anzio remained in German hands, and until it was liberated he believed it would be dangerous to move men and matériel inland. On January 25 an unhappy Clark arrived in Anzio. Shingle, created to relieve pressure on the Cassino front seventy miles to the south, was having the opposite effect. While the VI Corps cautiously expanded its perimeter, the rivers and flats around Cassino were filling with British, American, French, Polish, and New Zealand blood. The fighting in the region was the bloodiest yet seen in the war. After Clark left that afternoon, Lucas confided to his diary, "This is the most important thing I have ever tried to do and I will not be stampeded." Two days later, after another visit from Alexander, he wrote: "Had I been able to seize the high ground around the [Alban Hills] immediately after landing nothing would have been accomplished except to weaken my force . . . the only thing to do is what I did do; get a proper beachhead and hold it." Coincidentally, that same day, January 27, Alexander told Clark that Lucas was moving inland too slowly. Churchill was also losing patience: "We thought we had thrown a wild cat on shore. Instead, all we got was a stranded whale." By the beginning of February, Lucas seemed emotionally exhausted: "My head will probably fall in the basket but I have done my best. There were just too many Germans here for me to lick. They could build up faster than I could. I was sent on a desperate mission, one where the odds were greatly against success."

In fairness to Lucas he was not the only frustrated Allied commander in the Italian theater that winter. By early February the VI Corps had grown to a hundred thousand men, giving it a ten-thousand-man advantage over the German forces facing it. Yet progress remained slow because a key element in the Shingle plan was still missing. The Allied troops designated to drive north and link up with the Anzio force for the assault on Rome were still fighting around Cassino. There was also a growing consensus within the military and in the British and American press about why Cassino was proving so impenetrable.

During a flyover of the abbey earlier in the winter General Ira Eaker, the senior US Army Air Forces commander in the Mediterranean, and Lieutenant General Jacob Devers reported seeing German uniforms hanging in the abbey courtyard and machine-gun emplacements fifty yards from the abbey wall. Shortly thereafter C. L. Sulzberger of the *New York Times* claimed there were German observation posts and artillery positions in the abbey. General Francis Tuker of the 4th Indian Infantry Division was of the opinion that the abbey should be bombed, even if it was empty, to prevent the Germans from occupying it. There were a handful of skeptics. Lieutenant General Geoffrey Keyes, who had flown over the abbey several times, told Fifth Army intelligence staff that he had seen no evidence to suggest a German presence in the abbey. More surprisingly Mark Clark, the senior American commander in Italy and a man not known for shying away from cameras, also felt an assault on the abbey was unjustified and told his superior, Alexander, the senior Allied commander in Italy, he would not take a part in the assault unless given a direct order. Alexander gave it to him. On February 15, 142 B-17 Flying Fortresses, 47 B-25s, and 40 B-26s flew out of the morning sky and dropped 1,150 tons of high explosives and incendiary bombs on the abbey, reducing its top to a ruin and thrilling the hundreds of soldiers and newspaper correspondents who gathered in the streets and fields below the abbey to watch the assault. According to one estimate, 230 of the civilians who took refuge in the abbey were killed in the air assault; the following morning those who were still physically fit fled the abbey.

Later that day Cardinal Luigi Maglione, the Vatican secretary of state, summoned Harold Tittmann, the American ambassador to the Vatican, and told him the air assault was "a piece of gross stupidity." By the evening of the sixteenth there were only forty people left in the abbey; the seventy-nine-year-old abbot, Gregorio Diamare, six monks, several children, and a few local farmers and their families. Unbeknownst to the Allies, on arriving at Monte Cassino the Germans had pledged not to use the abbey for military purposes. After the bombings the promise was broken, and German paratroopers set up defensive positions in the abbey's ruins. But for political or personal reasons the Germans seemed eager to retain the monks' goodwill. On February 17, two days after Cassino was bombed, Abbot Diamare and several monks arrived at a German aid station, bearing a group of sick and wounded civilians. The German medics sent the most serious cases away in a military ambulance, and a German officer arranged transportation to the monastery of Saint Anselm for the abbot and his monks. The following day the abbot met with the commander of the XIV Panzer Corps, Fridolin von Senger Etterlin. In the months that followed, the abbey hollowed out. By spring there was only one resident monk, Carlomanno Pellagalli, a spectral figure who wandered the monastery to the crackle of German machine-gun fire, until he disappeared into the ether sometime in early April 1944.

There remained the war. On February 22 Lucas was relieved of command but without prejudice, a designation that left the door open to future commands. After reading the landing reports Clark, Alexander, and Marshall concurred. Lucas's decision to consolidate his position in Anzio before rushing the Alban Hills was the correct choice. Had he attacked the hills immediately he would have been thrown back within a day or two. Between January and May 1944, the Allies launched four major assaults in the Cassino and Anzio regions. In May 1944 the Cassino-Anzio one-two punch finally bore fruit, and an opportunity arose to justify the terrible suffering of the previous five months. However, instead of cutting off the German retreat and seizing the opportunity to deliver a decisive blow Clark, for reasons that may have had something to do with personal glory, chose to liberate the Eternal City. His moment of glory was short-lived. The day after the Allies entered Rome the D-Day invasion began and the Italian campaign became an afterthought.

The high price of victory at Anzio—29,000 casualties, including 4,400 dead—reawakened concern about what became known as "ninety-division gamble." In 1941, with Britain and the Soviet Union fighting for survival, and the prospect that one day the United States might find itself facing Germany alone, American planners considered building a two-hundred-division army. In mid-1943, with the Germans on the back foot and the navy and air force expanding rapidly, the planners revisited the manpower issue and concluded a ninety-division force would be sufficient. The effect of the decision was felt almost immediately.

IN EARLY JANUARY 1944 GENERAL Lesley McNair, commander of the army ground forces, told Marshall the shortages of men and matériel had become so acute that it might be necessary to cannibalize units training in the United States to keep the forces in the field at fighting strength. Marshall exploded and told McNair he was "damned tired" of listening to that kind of talk. Events would prove McNair, who was killed in Normandy, more right than wrong. By late 1944 the army's manpower shortage would be so acute that when the Germans launched the Ardennes offensive in December the army had to throw in its last reserves. "If they failed to stop the Germans, and the Russians don't come to our side," Marshall told Stimson, "we will have to assume a defensive position in Europe and let the American people decide whether they want to go on with the war enough to raise new armies which [it] would be necessary to do."

HOWEVER, AT THE BEGINNING OF 1944, the Ardennes battle was still almost a year away, and despite the seemingly constant strikes of John L. Lewis's United Mine Workers, the complaints of the anti-Roosevelt Hearst papers, and the ten-hour workdays and ration cards, in the main America was in a salutary mood. A Gallup poll found 98 percent of the country regarded themselves as middle class; another indicator of the national mood was the growing popularity of the Soviet Union. Americans still disliked homegrown communists, but, notes historian Ralph Levering, by 1942, "criticizing Russia had become like criticizing one's son when he was struggling to recover from a crippling paralysis."

By 1943 even rock-ribbed Republicans like Wendell Willkie, Roosevelt's 1940 opponent, were hailing Russian courage and determination. *One World*, Willkie's account of his trip to the Soviet Union, sold over a million copies and was favorably reviewed in conservative-leaning magazines, including the *Saturday Evening Post* and *Reader's Digest*. Henry Luce, another conservative press baron, gave the Soviet Union pride of place in his American Century. In a cover story on Stalin in March 1943, Luce's *Life* magazine noted that "Russia and the United States were likely to emerge from the war as the two greatest powers of the postwar era. Without their full and honest cooperation there can be no stable, peaceful world," *Life* warned.

OF ALL THE MARKERS THAT defined the national mood in the early months of 1944, none was more powerful than the sense of purpose that united the country. High, low, and in between, people felt themselves engaged in a great and noble endeavor and were prepared to play their part, even when birth and wealth and fame provided them other options. Among them was eighteen-year-old Stephen Hopkins, Harry Hopkins's son. In early February, while a troop ship was carrying the younger Hopkins across the broad expanses of the Pacific to his first experience of combat, his father posted a letter to him. "You can imagine how much my thoughts have been with you during the last few days and I hope that all is going well. I am sure it is. The Japs can never withstand the force we are throwing at them in the Marshalls." The letter was never delivered. While Hopkins was en route to Florida to recover from a lingering illness he received a telegraph from Roosevelt. "I am terribly distressed to have to tell you that Stephen was killed in action at Kwajalein [an atoll in the Pacific]. We have no details yet other than he was buried at sea. . . . I am thinking of you much. FDR." A few days later Churchill sent his condolences in the form of a passage from *Macbeth*. It began:

> *Stephen Peter Hopkins, Age 18*
> *Your son, my Lord, has paid a soldier's debt.*
> *He only lived but till he was a man,*
> *The which no sooner had his prowess confirmed*
> *In the unshrinking station where he fought,*
> *But like a man he died.*

It would be the epithet of a generation.

18

"NICE CHAP,
BUT NO GENERAL"

———————

I N ONE FORM OR ANOTHER, THE SECOND-FRONT QUESTION WAS
almost as old as the war itself. Stalin was the first to propose opening a second front. A few weeks after the start of Barbarossa, Stalin told
Churchill the military position of the Soviet Union and said that Great
Britain would improve substantially if a front against Hitler were established in the West (northern France) and the North (the Arctic). Churchill
demurred, citing the "limitations imposed on us by our resources and
geography." But the exchange ignited a strategic debate that lasted three
years and would not be completely settled until the cold gray morning
of June 5, 1944, when British and American troops assembled in ports in
west and southwest England for the passages to Normandy.

In their most fundamental form the British and Americans opening
a second front were experiential in nature. Combined, Britain and its
empire suffered a million dead in the Great War—and the United States
a tenth of that number. On the eve of that earlier conflict Churchill told
his wife, "Everything is as ready as it has never been before. And we are
awake to the tip of our fingers. But war is the unknown and the unexpected." A generation later, escorting John McCloy, the American assistant secretary of war, through the House of Commons, the prime minister

turned his mind back to that earlier war. "I am," he told McCloy, "a sort of sport of nature in the sense that most of my generation lay dead in the fields of Passchendaele and the Somme. An entire generation of British leaders were cut off and Britain cannot afford the loss of another."

The "Never again!" spirit allowed the British to carry the day at Casablanca against the American delegation that favored a cross-channel attack; but, new to coalition politics, they arrived at Casablanca poorly prepared and at odds with their president, who favored an assault on North Africa. "If I had written down beforehand what I hoped the conclusion [of the conference] would be," one British officer wrote, "I could never have written down anything so sweeping, so comprehensive and so favorable to our ideas." To their credit, the American delegates acknowledged their poor performance and went about finding ways to improve it.

Several months after Casablanca, the cross-channel plan was resuscitated, and General Frederick Morgan—an Englishman with a lively sense of humor and an impressive combat record in two world wars—was selected to, as his instructions put it, "coordinate and drive forward plans for a cross-channel invasion this year and next year." Shortly thereafter the planners widened Morgan's brief. Morgan was now instructed to plan a "full-scale assault on the Continent in 1944 at the earliest feasible date, in order to take advantage of the full summer fighting season."

That was easier said than done. Morgan's staff was small; his second-in-command was General Ray Barker, an American. Beyond that he had a handful of junior British and American staff officers. There were also sharp differences about the scale of the invasion force. The Americans favored a plan based on the maximum forces available; the British favored one based on the forces available at the time of the assault. "Well, there it is," Brooke is alleged to have said, upon handing Morgan his brief. "But you must bloody well make it work." Morgan named his new organization COSSAC, the initial constituted letters of his title (Chief of Staff to the Supreme Allied Commander)—and went to work.

The most immediate challenge was the shortage of landing craft. The first wave of troops would have to get on the beaches in large-enough numbers to sustain themselves until reinforced; planners estimated that that would require a five-division force—and currently there were only enough landing craft for a three-division landing. Unless directly ordered

Admiral King was unlikely to release landing craft from the Pacific for the Normandy landings. The ninety-division gamble also made manpower a problem. The current plans called for seven Allied divisions to be transferred from Italy to Britain in the autumn of 1944 to prepare for Overlord, but Churchill would fight to keep a large Allied force in the Mediterranean. There was also the question of when and where the landing should take place. The right landing site had a very specific profile. It had to be within range of the Allied fighters in the United Kingdom, situated near a major port, and the port had to be invulnerable to attack from the landward side and large enough to accommodate the offloading of LSTs (landing ship, tanks) and other large amphibious vessels. There also had to be enough exits on the beaches to permit vehicles and men to move swiftly off the beaches and onto the roads. The 1942 raid on the French beach town of Dieppe was a reminder of how quickly things could go wrong if these specifications were not met. In the course of a summer day half of the largely Canadian force that landed at Dieppe was killed, wounded, or captured—and the RAF lost over one hundred aircraft.

The Pas-de-Calais, only forty miles to the east of Canterbury, was a perfect landing sight, but its perfection was so evident on the day of the invasion that a large German force was certain to be waiting on the beaches—machine guns and mortars at the ready—when the doors of the landing craft splashed open. There were also suitable landing sites in Holland and Belgium, but their proximity to the fatherland would allow the Germans to bring up reinforcements quickly. Le Havre, Brest, and Cherbourg were also considered, but, for one reason or another, they were all ruled out. This left Normandy.

Normandy was 170 miles from Britain, a long way for a large invasion force to travel without attracting attention. Still, Caen, the most important city in the Normandy region, had a good port, an airfield nearby, and, once seized, the invasion force would be able to cut the railway and highway traffic between Cherbourg and Paris. Caen also had the virtue of being a city the British knew well. Shortly after Dunkirk, the BBC asked listeners to send in postcards gathered during prewar vacations on the continent. Ten million Britons responded to the request; RAF air-reel photos and the French underground also provided valuable intelligence about landing sites and German troop disposition in the region. However, in December 1943, one critical question still remained unanswered: Could the beaches to the west of the Orne River, which flows through Normandy, bear the weight of the tanks, trucks, and other heavy equipment that would land with the troops? The question was answered with a piece of daring that would have thrilled the readers of *Boy's Own*. Armed with pistols, daggers, wrist compasses, waterproof watches, and a dozen twelve-inch tubes, on New Year's Eve 1943 Captain (later, Major) Logan Scott-Bowden and Sergeant Bruce Ogden-Smith emerged from a midget submarine, rode a big breaker into the shore, dodged their way through the searchlights sweeping the beaches, and moved inland, careful to keep below the high-water mark so that the sea would wash away their footprints before first light.

Sand samples were gathered, and the location of each sample was carefully noted on underwater writing tablets. All went well until Scott-Bowden and Ogden-Smith returned to the shoreline. The sea had grown heavier in their absence, and on their first two tries to reach the submarine, the breakers threw them back on to the shore. Before making a third try, the two men paddled in place for a few minutes, studying the rhythm of the waves. On the next try they breached the wall of breakers, and a waiting submarine emerged out of the darkness. Suddenly Ogden-Smith remembered the date and shouted, "Happy New Year!" at the moon. While Scott-Bowden and Ogden-Smith were sailing back to Britain Hitler was summoning up the apocalypse in a New Year's Day speech. He promised the German people war without end until there were "no victors and vanquished, only survivors and the annihilated."

If everything had gone according to plan, on that New Year's Eve George Marshall would have been sitting in a London office, waiting for Ogden-Smith and Scott-Bowden's report—and Dwight Eisenhower would have been in Washington, settling in as chief of staff, Marshall's former post. But as 1943 came to an end the prospect of losing Marshall continued to weigh heavily on Roosevelt. Thus, on December 7, 1943, Eisenhower learned he would lead Overlord and Marshall would remain in his current position, army chief of staff. The British had mixed feelings about the appointment. Eisenhower had spent the latter half of 1943 overseeing the Allied assaults on Sicily and Italy, and in neither campaign could his leadership be described as outstanding. "Nice chap, but no general" is how Bernard Montgomery, the hero of El-Alamein, described Eisenhower's military talents. That was also Brooke's view, though he saw a silver lining in the decision. "We [are] pushing Eisenhower up into the stratosphere of supreme commander," he said, "where he [will] be free to devote his time to the political and inter-allied problems, while we insert under him our own commanders to deal with the military situation." In the British version of Eisenhower's rise to supreme commander of the Allied forces, he is "a genial, good-natured Chairman of the Board plucked from obscurity by General Marshall and placed in a leadership position." But as Carlo D'Este, Eisenhower's most perceptive biographer, has argued persuasively, the "good natured, charming" Eisenhower that his British detractors poked fun at was a façade. The real Eisenhower was a "ruthless, ambitious officer who thirsted to advance his career" but who also possessed the self-control to keep that part of himself to himself. The commander who led the Anglo-American coalition to victory was governed by two precepts: 1) the key to military success is teamwork; and 2) no matter how grave the situation a commander must preserve optimism in himself and in his command.

Eisenhower was less faithful to another precept he had learned as a young officer: the importance of resting. On May 22 he stayed up late talking to Elliott Roosevelt, who had just returned from Moscow, where he had heard a lot of complaints about the disparity of sacrifice between the Soviet Union and the Western allies. During a visit to the Soviet high command Elliott's hosts told him that the Red Army suffered more casualties before breakfast than the Allied armies suffered in a month. "Stalin is a stickler for keeping his word," Elliott told Eisenhower. Then he added, "The test for Britain and the United States will be keeping their word on the second front." The next day—May 23—Eisenhower took a long horseback ride through Richmond Park, one of the shrinking number of London landmarks that still bore a resemblance to its prewar self. That evening, in a letter, he gave his wife, Mamie, a detailed description of the ride, including the rabbits and partridges he encountered.

After months of subtle and sometimes not-so-subtle opposition, Churchill had committed to Overlord. But on bad nights he was still visited by ghosts of the Somme and Passchendaele. In a talk with Brooke on May 21 he complained about the comparatively small size of the invasion force, in particular the small infantry component. He was also worried about a German gas attack. It seemed unlikely, given the international outrage that would ensue. Still Hitler did not think like other men. When his scientific adviser, Lord Cherwell, told him about a deadly new biologic called N *spores*, which had no cure or prophylaxis, Churchill ordered a half million N-bombs from the United States.

Toward the end of May an American officer cresting a hill in southern England was stunned by the panorama that greeted him. The little country roads in the flatlands below were dense with the sinews of war: troop carriers, trucks, assault tanks, jeeps, and marching men, in mile-long formations. As the armada wound its way southward past the fish-and-chips shops and the Tea for Sale signs, the roads filled with well-wishers waving Union Jacks. Some of the soldiers smiled and waved back; others had the somber look of men going into battle to kill or be killed. The procession lasted until late afternoon. Then troops' ships were sealed, and the soldiers were left with their thoughts.

ON MAY 28 CHURCHILL INFORMED Stalin that "everything here is centered on Overlord." Four days later the seventy-two-hour countdown to the June 5 invasion date began on an uncertain note. Group Captain James Stagg, the senior meteorologist on the Anglo-American meteorological team, warned Eisenhower that if current trends continued, the fifth could be a day of heavy weather. A deep depression was developing between Newfoundland and Ireland. In a cable to Marshall that evening Eisenhower put a positive spin on Stagg's warning. "While still indefinite," he said, "the weather is generally favorable." The following morning, with the American and British meteorologists at odds over the latest batch of weather reports, and a fine spring sun shining through the windows of Eisenhower's headquarters at Southwick House, Stagg refused to commit himself to a forecast. On June 3, the sun was still shining, but the latest weather reports indicated the situation was full of menace from the British Isles to Newfoundland. "Gentlemen," Stagg said that evening in an address to senior British and American commanders, "I'm afraid the fears of my colleagues and I have been confirmed. For the next few days, the English Channel will be battered by heavy winds, rough seas, and low clouds."

When Stagg finished, his listeners looked perplexed. The evening sky outside the window had a lovely pinkish hue. Eisenhower ordered a temporary postponement, but his announcement came too late. The Associated Press was already reporting that Eisenhower's forces were landing in France. The AP pulled the story twenty-three minutes later, but by then CBS and Radio Moscow were reporting that the invasion had begun.

Churchill, who spent the day reviewing troops, was relieved when he came home to a wireless report that the Allies were in Rome; but as the early June night wore on, his thoughts kept coming back to the tens of thousands of young men sitting in ships and camps across England, wondering if they would be alive in a week. The next morning Churchill was working in bed when his wife, Clementine, appeared, handed him a letter, and then vanished. The letter read, "I feel so much for you at this agonizing moment—so full of suspense, which prevents one from rejoicing over Rome." Brooke was also in a somber mood that morning. "I am very uneasy about the whole operation," he said. "At best it will fall very, very short of the expectations of the bulk of the people—namely, those who know nothing. At worst it may well be the most ghastly failure of the war."

Eisenhower had already written the note he would release if the worst happened: "The landings in the Cherbourg-Havre area have failed to gain a satisfactory foothold and I have withdrawn the troops. My decision to attack at this time and place was based on the best information available. The troops, and air and navy did all that bravery and devotion to duty could do. If any blame or failure attaches to the attempt it is mine alone."

It was raining lightly on the morning of June 4, when several hundred young American soldiers gathered on a dock in the channel town of Weymouth to hear Father Edward Waters say Mass. Farther to the east in Southampton that morning, a Tommy from Liverpool scribbled, "Liverpool: best football team in the world," on a billboard before disappearing into an LST. In the Hampshire town of Lepe, a construction crew was finishing work on one of the Mulberrys, the artificial harbors that would be towed across the channel on D-Day and assembled on the Normandy beaches. Farther to the east, in Dover, a convoy of freighters was embroidering frothy white patterns on the sea with their propellers. Above the ships a group of Spitfires was making lazy circles in the half-light of the rising day while waiting for their charges to clear the straits.

In Suffolk, Norfolk, Cornwall, and Surrey, the mood swung back and forth between fear and excitement. It was still raining in early afternoon when Eisenhower arrived in Portsmouth with General Charles de Gaulle. A few days earlier Eisenhower and King had joined forces to keep Churchill from sailing with the invasion force. Now the second-most imperious man on the planet was refusing to give an address on the BBC on the morning of the invasion.

De Gaulle had no objection to the speech he had been asked to read, but he strongly objected to the speech that Eisenhower was scheduled to give following his own. It made no reference to de Gaulle as leader of the Provisional Government of the French Republic, and, in the general's view, it intimated that the Vichy government of General Philippe Pétain would remain in control. It took almost a full day, but Bedell Smith, Eisenhower's chief of staff, and General Marie-Pierre Koenig, one of de Gaulle's aides, cobbled together a compromise: the general would address the French people on invasion day but limit his remarks to a request to "observe the orders given by the French government and the French leaders appointed by the government."

On the evening of June 4, dozens of transports and landing craft were circling the Isle of Wight, waiting for a break in the weather. In the channel town of Weymouth, "hundreds of recalled ships" bobbed up and down in the harbor. In Portsmouth so many ships had returned to anchor that it was possible to walk across the vast harbor going from boat to boat. Eisenhower's cigarette consumption was a reliable barometer of his mood, and by early June he was up to four packs a day. The most vexing issue that morning was the weather. The planners were relying on airpower to make up for the shortage of infantry divisions, but airpower was weather dependent. In a heavy rain the troops on the beaches would have to rely on grit and luck to counter a German attack.

Stagg arrived in Southwick House on the evening of the fourth with his final weather report of the day in hand. The mood in the library, where the principals—Eisenhower, Montgomery, Admiral Bertram Ramsay, Air Marshal Arthur Tedder, Vice Air Marshal Trafford Leigh-Mallory, Eisenhower's chief of staff Bedell Smith, and several other senior commanders—had gathered, was tense. Should the heavy weather continue Overlord would have to be postponed until June 19, the next date a full moon would be available to guide the first waves across the beaches without losing contact with their units and providing enough visibility to dodge the German booby traps. The rain pelting the window kept expectations in the library low, which made Stagg's announcement all the more dramatic. He said the rain would taper off in the early-morning hours and be followed by a day and a half of moderately good weather.

Intermittent periods of scattered clouds were likely, though not on a scale large enough to interfere with air operations on June 5 and 6.

To Leigh-Mallory and to Tedder, Stagg's report sounded more like a guess than a forecast. Leigh-Mallory proposed a postponement until the nineteenth. Eisenhower paced back and forth for a moment, then stopped in front of Montgomery's chair. Montgomery said, "What do you say? I would say go." Eisenhower nodded. A few moments later he asked, "How long can you hang this operation on the end of a limb and leave it?" and then resumed pacing. There were about 150,000 men in the first two waves; landing them on the beaches before the weather closed in again would be a riverboat gamble. Yet waiting would give German intelligence more time to discern where the Allies were likely to land: Pas-de-Calais or Normandy?

After the bomber barons finished speaking the conversation descended into small talk, and Eisenhower decided to return to his camper for a few hours' sleep. When he returned to Southwick House around 3:30 Stagg said, "Well, I'll give you some good news." It was now clear to a certainty that the weather would improve by daybreak. The rest of Stagg's forecast remained unchanged: two days of decent weather, then the sea and sky would boil up again. Montgomery, Admiral Ramsay, and Bedell Smith wanted to go now; Tedder remained a tentative no; and Leigh-Mallory was a strong no.

Eisenhower began pacing again. The options available to him shared one commonality: they could all end in disaster. Eisenhower stopped pacing and said, "Okay! Let's go!"

It would be several hours before Major John Howard learned of Eisenhower's decision. Howard was something of a rarity in the British army, a working-class London boy whose leadership skills had won him a place in the officer corps. Tonight he and his commandos would lead the first assault of the night. In the hours before the assault force left Britain Howard went through the ranks, steadying nerves with small talk about sports, wives and children, and postwar plans. His diary entry for June 5 suggests he may also have been trying to steady his own nerves: "What cruel luck. I am more downhearted than I dare show. Wind and rain—how long will it last? The longer it goes the greater the chance of obstacles on the LZ [landing zone]. Please God, it'll clear up tomorrow."

Howard's prayers were answered a few hours later. Weapons were checked a final time, letters were written; faces were charcoaled to a commando black. Then a little after midnight on June 6 D Company of the 2nd Battalion of Oxfordshire and Buckinghamshire Light Infantry climbed into six Horsa gliders at an airfield in southern England. The men strapped themselves into the metal seats, the engines on the Halifax bombers that would tow the gliders to their target roared to life, and D Company disappeared into the night, carrying with it the uncertain honor of being the first Allied force to land in Normandy.

Howard's targets were two heavily defended bridges: Pegasus Bridge on the Orne River, the other on the Caen Canal, on the far side of the river. British intelligence viewed the bridges as a double threat. The Germans could drive tanks and tank destroyers down to the beaches and attack the landing force, which would arrive lightly armed. Or they could blow up the bridges, leaving the British 6th Airborne Division, which was due to jump into the region in a few hours, stranded between the Orne and Caen Canal. But luck was with the Oxford and Bucks that night. There were casualties: a Lieutenant Brotheridge was mortally wounded crossing Pegasus Bridge, and two glider pilots were knocked unconscious during the landings, but, miraculously, their glider drew to a halt only fifty feet from the bridge on the Caen Canal. Within five minutes the roughly fifty Germans defending the bridges had fled—and Howard was master of both bridges.

Shortly thereafter pathfinder units appeared overhead and marked the drop zones for the parachute troops, then an armada of twin-engine C-47s emerged out of the darkness. Each of the 7,000 British and 13,400 American paratroopers waiting for their drop zones to come up had received hundreds of hours of training. But as historian Stephen Ambrose has noted the pilots carrying the troopers had not had that training. They had no training in night fighting, no knowledge of how to navigate in heavy weather, no understanding of how to avoid flak, and no directional devices to guide them, except the thin blue light flickering on the plane directly ahead. Upon reaching the drop zones the pilots had been instructed to throttle back to 90 miles per hour to reduce the shock on the troopers preparing to jump. Knowing the lumbering C-47 was an easy target at that speed some of the pilots ignored the instruction and sped up to 150 miles per hour, sending the troopers in the plane doors hurtling out into the black June sky.

In the madness of gunfire and screaming planes one pilot looked out the cockpit window and saw a trooper flapping on his wing. "What should I do?" he shouted into his radio. "Slow down and he'll fall off," another pilot replied. As the night deepened the sky became a ballet of twisting, soaring, diving planes, antiaircraft fire, and silver tracer bullets. In the chaos thousands of paratroopers were tossed helter-skelter out into the night, and upon landing they found themselves five, ten, or fifteen miles from their drop zones. Expecting chaos in the hours after the landings every paratrooper was armed with a dime-store clicker that allowed him to signal his presence in the blinding darkness. Quickly three men would become six, then six would become fifteen and fifteen thirty: enough to organize "Kraut hunts."

In the strategically important town of Sainte-Mère-Église one paratrooper landed on a burning building and was incinerated; another landed on a church steeple and spent the night swinging back and forth as American and German troops beneath him fought ferociously for possession of the town. Around 9:00 A.M. on the morning of June 6 Sainte-Mère-Église became the first town in western Europe to be liberated.

Roosevelt was awakened at around 3:00 A.M. Washington time by a phone call from General Marshall, who told him that the landings had begun. After Marshall rang off, Roosevelt asked his valet to bring him his cardigan sweater, then he propped himself up in his bed and began to direct the war. He called the War Department at fifteen- and twenty-minute intervals for updates, summoned White House staffers back to their offices, and conferred with his aides. Eisenhower's office also sent a reassuring cable: "All preliminary reports are favorable."

The East Coast awoke to the news first. In Philadelphia the mayor tapped the Liberty Bell with a wooden mallet for a nationwide radio hookup. In Boston drivers honked their horns on the way to work. In Winsted, Connecticut, and in a thousand places in between, flags were raised and schoolchildren sang "God Bless America." And everywhere across the country people prayed. It just seemed the right thing to do on such a solemn day.

Churchill spent most of the night of June 5/6 in the map room at 10 Downing Street. By the time Washington awoke he had already made a speech in the House of Commons. "I cannot commit myself to any details," he told an edgy Parliament. "Reports are coming in in rapid succession." Nonetheless, "this vast operation is undoubtedly the most difficult and most complicated that has ever taken place. It involves tides, winds, waves, and visibility both from the air and the sea, and the combined employment of land, air, and sea forces. The battle now begun will grow constantly in scale, in intensity for weeks to come. I shall not speculate on its course. This I may say, however: Complete unity prevails throughout the Allied Armies. There is a brotherhood of arms between us and our friends in the United States. . . . The ardor and spirit of the troops [is] splendid to witness. Nothing that equipment science or forethought could do has been neglected. The whole process of opening this great new front will be pursued with the utmost resolution."

Later that day, in a reply to a cable from Stalin, he wrote: "I have received your communication regarding to the opening of the Overlord Operation. It gives joy to us all and hope of further success."

More than a year in the making, Overlord was unparalleled in scale and ambition. Five divisions—two British, one Canadian, and two American—would attack along a sixty-mile front that stretched from the Caen Canal in the west to the Orne River estuary in the east. In the British sector the terrain, generally firm and flat, favored the invader; in the American sector the ridgelike precipice looming over Omaha Beach favored the defender. In one of the first actions of the day, at a little after 7:00 A.M., the British 3rd Division stormed Sword Beach under a low gray sky. Like the other German beaches Sword was heavily mined, but Percy Hobart, an inventive armored warfare specialist, had devised a way to neutralize the threat: the Crab—a modified tank that crawled across the battlefield exploding mines with the flail attached to its snout. Stunned by the heavy preinvasion bombardment and the reptilian Crabs crawling out of the surf, the Germans initially fell back; but as the day progressed the invasion shock wore off. The defenders regrouped in the fields and villages behind the beaches and launched a late-afternoon counterattack that reached the beaches in one sector before being checked. By nightfall Sword was securely in British hands.

The 50th Division and the elite 47th Marine Commandos arrived at Gold, the second British beach, at about the time that the 3rd Division landed—a little after 7:00 A.M. But the weather in the Gold sector was rougher. On the hour-long ride to the beach heavy waves splashed over the landing craft, soaking men and matériel. The German units defending Gold were also more alert than their compatriots at Sword. The moment the metal doors on the landing craft opened, machine-gun fire spat through the ships, and the sea began to fill with blood and floating bodies. Only accurate fire by American and British naval units and aircraft saved the situation. By late afternoon Gold had been secured and the 50th Division was marching inland.

The fighting at Juno, the Canadian beach, was among the bloodiest of the day. During the spring the Germans had installed firing positions in the homes above the beach and in the little hamlets strung out along the dunes below the beach, and the heavy early-morning weather on D-Day minimized the accuracy of the preinvasion bombardment. "All the softening up accomplished was to alert the enemy to the landings," one soldier said. In addition the rising tide half hid the mines and other booby traps the Germans installed in the sector. For some men the price of crossing the beach that morning was an arm or leg. In the first hour of the battle a Canadian soldier had a little more than a one-in-two chance of avoiding death or dismemberment. As the morning progressed the steady stream of reinforcements dramatically increased the soldiers' odds. The seawall at Juno, unlike the seawall at Omaha Beach, had no bluff behind it. As historian Stephen Ambrose put it, "Once across the wall and through the surrounding villages, the country was relatively flat. The trick was getting there in one piece." Over the course of a June day, 1,220 young Canadians were killed or wounded.

At a little after 6:00 A.M. on the morning of the sixth a senior officer with a storied name and taste for adventure removed a map from his jacket pocket, studied it for a moment, then pointed to a quadrant on the map and said, "We're in the wrong place, but we'll start from here." Despite the navigational error the men of the 8th Infantry Regiment considered themselves fortunate to be in the presence of Brigadier General Theodore Roosevelt Jr. Roosevelt's unpretentious manner and courage had made him a favorite of the common soldier. A major who jumped for cover upon landing was surprised to see Roosevelt calmly walking along the beach wall when he raised is head above the hole he was crouching in.

The assault at Utah Beach was the most successful American action of D-Day. The demoralized German defenders put up little resistance, and in the few places where the defenders did choose to fight the price of glory was an agonizing death under the wheels of an amphibious DD tank. The fighting ended in late morning, but the killing continued. According to a soldier in the 8th Infantry his unit was instructed not to take SS troops alive as they "were deemed untrustworthy and might be concealing a weapon." A soldier from another unit said that civilians found along the beaches and for a certain distance inland were also to be dealt with as enemy soldiers and shot or rounded up. However, nowhere that morning was life squandered as cheaply as it was on Omaha Beach.

At a little before 5:00 A.M. on the morning of June 6 Captain Scott-Bowden and Sergeant Ogden-Smith, the two-man amphibious team that spent New Year's Eve 1943 reconnoitering the Normandy beaches, were tossing back and forth in a pilot boat five thousand yards off Omaha Beach when an LST emerged out of the half-light, dropped its ramp, and began disgorging DD amphibious tanks into the water. Scott-Bowden was horrified. The beaches were almost three miles distant, and the morning sea was very rough. The tanks "should be landed closer to the beach!" he shouted. Either the wind carried the warning out to sea or the crew of the landing craft chose to ignore Bowden. Of the thirty-two tanks that went into the water that morning, all but three would disappear into the sea with their crews.

Early in the planning for Overlord it became evident that Omaha would be the toughest beach to breach. The beaches were guarded by twelve strongpoints, and each point had many heavy weapons, including the 88s, the most powerful piece of artillery on the battlefield in 1944; 75-mm Pak 40s; an array of machine-gun emplacements; and a network of trenches that allowed the defenders to move from position to position in relative safety. In some landing zones the bluffs above the beaches were 100–150 feet high. The unique challenges of the terrain on Omaha Beach prompted both the defenders and attackers to adopt unorthodox strategies. General Leonard Gerow, commander of V Corps (the unit that would lead the attack on D-Day), wanted to launch his troops at low tide under cover of darkness to reduce the threat from the German heavy guns guarding the beaches. But Gerow's request for divers to clear channels through the booby-trapped shallows was denied. The operation would disrupt the invasion schedule, and Eisenhower, Montgomery, and Bradley were adamant about keeping to plan.

The first wave would go in at 6:30 A.M. as scheduled. Eisenhower was confident that the forty-minute bombardment that preceded the landings would neutralize the booby traps on the beach. But recent experience suggested that that might not be the case. After the Army Air Forces bombed the abbey at Monte Cassino into oblivion, the Germans turned the abbey's ruins into a formidable defensive position.

Watching the landings from a bluff above the beaches, all the younger German soldiers could see was a five-thousand-ship armada bearing down on them at ten to fifteen knots per hour. It was like "watching a gigantic town on the sea," one teenage soldier said later. However, the veterans of Moscow, Kursk, and Monte Cassino knew an opportunity when they saw one. As the first wave of landing craft approached the beaches a Lieutenant Frerking—seated on a high bluff—shouted into his phone, "Landing craft on our left!" The sergeant who took the message looked out the window and could hardly believe what he was seeing. "Are they going to swim ashore right under our guns?" he asked. Next a colonel of artillery came on the line and said, "Hold your fire until the enemy comes up to the waterline."

For a few moments fingers moved restlessly back and forth, massaging triggers. Then Frerking came back on the line: "Target Dora! All guns range, target four, eight, five, zero. Basic direction twenty plus, impact fuse!" A moment later a shell exploded, and a hundred American mothers lost their sons.

Many of the men in the first waves arrived on the beaches physically exhausted and emotionally paralyzed. Jumping from landing craft, men were hit by rifle and machine-gun fire, and they were often too weak to swim—they disappeared into the rising tide. Other soldiers were frozen by fear. A surgeon from the 1st Division said that many of the men in this group did not seem to be "functioning at all mentally. . . . They could move their limbs but would not answer or do anything." One of the most haunting sights of the day was a group of wounded men hanging from the carcass of a landing craft beached on a sand dune about fifty yards from the shore. As the morning tide rose one by one the men disappeared into the sea. Later that morning a naval officer came across a landing craft filled with bodies floating in rusted water. Days later he was still wondering who or what killed the men. The chaos that spread across the beaches that morning was, in part, the result of intelligence errors. One report had the beaches defended by the 716th Infantry Division, a second-rate unit with a large complement of disgruntled Russians. But half of the 352nd Infantry Division, one of the most formidable German units in Normandy, was wrongly placed; it was already on the beaches when two of its infantry battalions and a light artillery battalion were there as well.

Poor sea-to-shore communications made it difficult for senior commanders to follow the fighting from the cruisers and battleships offshore, but the scattered reports that did arrive painted a bleak picture. Many of the men in the first wave had taken refuge behind beach obstacles and sand dunes and were making no effort to move forward. A little before noon General Omar Bradley, who was following the battle from the USS *Augusta*, ordered an aide, Major Chester Hansen, to the beaches to assess the situation. Hansen returned an hour and a half later with bleak news: the first wave was trapped on the beaches—and the second, third, and fourth waves were stacked up offshore.

Hansen did have one piece of good news, however.

As at Anzio the Luftwaffe made a brief appearance over the beaches to satisfy honor, then disappeared into the morning sky. As the hours passed the steady *rat-a-tat-tat-tat* of machine-gun fire and fear and exhaustion took their toll. Some men burst into tears; others cursed; a few went mad, leaped to their feet, and were sawed in half by machine-gun fire. The mortally wounded, huddled in the shallows, looked like sea creatures that had crawled up to the shore to die.

The senior German commander in Normandy—Field Marshal Gerd von Rundstedt—was the scion of a family that had been providing Germany with soldiers for centuries. Slim of frame, coldly handsome, and haughty in manner, Rundstedt had spent the better part of the war in the twilight zone where mass murder and doing one's duty for the fatherland become indistinguishable. The high point of Rundstedt's career was Dunkirk, where his panzers had come close to trapping the British army on the beaches. The low point was Russia, where his flexible moral code allowed him to split the differences on mass murder, endorsing anti-Jewish propaganda but keeping his troops out of the pogroms conducted by the Nazi death squads.

Russia was also where, as commander of Army Group South, Rundstedt ran afoul of Hitler and was sent back to France as OB West, a position that sounded more important than it was. Final decisions on strategy were the province of Hitler and the OKW, the German high command. When Rundstedt arrived at his office in the medieval castle of Saint-Germain on the evening of the sixth the situation was confusing. The wireless was reporting attacks in Cherbourg and Le Havre, but the Allies had been conducting nuisance raids along the French coast for months. Rundstedt's initial instinct was to dismiss the radio traffic as erroneous but as the night wore on and reports of Allied activity grew more frequent and ominous, he ordered two panzer divisions to Caen, the principal British target on D-Day. By daybreak events would settle the long-running argument between Rundstedt, who favored massing men and matériel in the interior and allowing the invasion force to move inland before attacking, and Rommel, who believed that if the Allies were not defeated on the beaches they would not be defeated. The German response was further clouded by Hitler, who was still asleep and had given orders not to be disturbed. The men piling into landing craft that morning also owed a debt of gratitude to Colonel General Alfred Jodl, chief of operations at the armed forces high command. Jodl spent the night examining the reports and by 5:00 A.M. had concluded Normandy was a feint; the Allied target was the Pas-de-Calais farther to the north. Jodl ordered Panzer Lehr and the 12th SS Panzer Divisions, two formidable units, back to their posts.

While Jodl's decision probably saved hundreds of British and American lives, it did not change the overall picture. Every aspect of the landings was fraught with danger, starting with the skill of coxswains who delivered troops to the beaches. Some were experienced seamen of steady nerve; others, untested twenty-one- and twenty-two-year-olds whose knowledge of how to land assault craft under fire was thin and mostly book-learned. Captain Ettore Zappacosta of the 29th Division drew a young English coxswain who panicked when the beach came into view and shouted, "We can't go in!" Zappacosta put a .45 pistol to the coxswain's head and declared, "By God, you will!" The boy gathered his courage and brought the landing craft in; but when the ramp swung open, German machine-gun fire ripped Zappacosta's chest apart. He was already dead when his face hit the bottom of the ramp.

LIEUTENANT WILLIAM B. WILLIAMS, ONE of Zappacosta's junior officers, had more luck that morning. He drew a boat commanded by one of the most experienced coxswains in the invasion fleet, an old sea dog, steady of nerve and wise in the ways of the sea. After Zappacosta was killed the coxswain swung the landing craft around, sailed six hundred yards down the beach, and deposited Williams and his platoon on a dry, uncrowded patch of sand. For a moment it seemed like the safest place on the beach. Then German artillery shells demolished the landing craft and killed the coxswain. A German machine gun followed Williams and his men across the beaches. In the mayhem six of his men were killed and five gravely wounded. In between bursts of machine-gun and mortar fire Williams and what was left of his command, seven men, climbed the bluffs and entered the fortified town of Les Moulins. Exit three on the Allied maps, the town had one of the five roads that led over the bluffs into the relative safety of the Norman countryside, but Williams would never see its bocage or narrow little country roads. During fighting around Les Moulins a grenade bounced back on Williams and cut his shoulders in three places. A few moments later a second grenade cut him in five places. Crawling to safety a burst of machine-gun fire hit him on the buttocks and right leg. As he was being evacuated he gave his men a final order: "Get moving."

There almost seemed to be a chain of being at work on Omaha that morning. Williams's place was taken by one of his sergeants, William Pearce, who got into an hour-long firefight with a German unit. Later in the morning it ended with seven Germans dead and Pearce and his men entering Vierville-sur-Mer, one of the little seaside towns with a road that led over the bluffs. Lieutenant Walter Taylor was standing in the main street of Vierville-sur-Mer when Pearce arrived. Taylor would later become one of forty-seven immortals of Omaha Beach, the group of men whose grit, courage, and skill prevented the landings from failing. Upon arriving in Vierville-sur-Mer Pearce told Taylor, "Williams has been badly wounded."

"I guess that makes me company commander," Taylor said, and he told Pearce to take a head count. There were 28 men left in Baker Company (at full strength a company runs from 80 to 150 men). "That ought to be enough," Taylor said, then he turned to his men and shouted, "Follow me!"

Baker Company's target was the Château de Vaumicel, an imposing rock wall about five hundred yards inland. The château was honeycombed with artillery-proof tunnels, but the first group of Germans that Taylor's force encountered did not have much stomach for a fight. By sheer chance a grenade thrown by a Baker Company man bounced off the helmet of one the Germans and gave him such a fright that he leaped to his feet and shouted, "*Kamerad, Kamerad!*" Within seconds twenty-four of his colleagues emerged from the hedgerows, hands in the air. Taylor put his prisoners on "parole," then moved his men forward to a crossroads beyond the château. The exit road was not far beyond it, but as Taylor and his men approached it, three truckloads of German infantry suddenly appeared and what had begun to look like the kind of story an old soldier would tell his grandchildren turned into a bitter fight for survival.

One American was killed instantly and three others seriously wounded. "Back to the château!" Taylor shouted, then stood in the street and provided covering fire as his troops fell back. Counting Taylor, Baker Company was down to twenty men, and now, well beyond the landing beaches, Taylor and everyone else in the company had no idea whether the invasion had succeeded or failed. The château's fire slots allowed what was left of Baker Company to hold the Germans off through the afternoon, but toward evening, as ammunition ran low and the possibility of a night attack loomed, a unit from the 5th Rangers appeared out of the twilight, the Germans fell back, and Baker Company learned it was almost half a mile ahead of any other unit in the US Army. Over the next few days tens of thousands of men would pour over the bluffs and into the Normandy countryside.

THE FIVE-HOUR TIME DIFFERENCE BETWEEN London and New York meant that Americans would be awake when the news bulletins began coming in. On a day of public jubilation the *Los Angeles Times* printed a detailed map of the Allied landing zone. The *Philadelphia Inquirer* published bulletins throughout the day. Large crowds gathered in Madison Square Garden to pray. The sixth was also a day of prayers in the United Kingdom. From Westminster Abbey to the little seaside towns that the great armada had sailed from, pews were full on the evening of June 6.

Franklin Roosevelt gave the most moving speech of the day:

My fellow Americans, last night when I spoke to you about the fall of Rome I knew at that moment that the troops of the United States and our allies were crossing the channel in another great operation. It has come to pass with success so far. And so, in this poignant hour, I ask you to join with me in prayer. Almighty God, our sons, pride of our nation this day, have set upon a mighty endeavor, to preserve our republic, our religion, our civilization and to set free a suffering humanity. Lead them straight and true, give strength to their arms and steadfastness to their faith.

19

THE TWO FACES OF WAR

N A WARM JULY MORNING A FEW WEEKS AFTER D-DAY, GENERAL
Bernard Montgomery was standing on a road in the Norman
countryside when a staff car pulled up next to him and a powerfully
built Polish officer emerged and introduced himself. Stanisław Maczek,
commander of the 1st (Polish) Armored Division, had been fighting from
the first hour of the first day of the war. In September 1939 he defended
his native Poland against the Germans and the Russians; in 1940 he
fought alongside the British and French in the Battle of France; and in
1942 he convinced the British government to create what would become
the 1st Armored Division. He and Montgomery exchanged small talk
for a few minutes over the rumble of the artillery fire farther up the road.
Then Monty, whose many virtues did not include charm, said, "Tell me,
General, in Warsaw these days do people speak Russian or German?"

No doubt Montgomery would have been outraged if Maczek had
turned the question around and asked what language was spoken in London these days: French or English? But therein lay the difference between
what Churchill called "giant countries" and "pygmy countries." As a
"giant country," even in crisis Britain received assistance and respect. As
a long-standing "pygmy country," Poland was partitioned whenever the
whim struck one of its larger neighbors. At various times in the eighteenth
century, Poland was ruled by Russia, Austria, and Prussia—sometimes in

a kind of condominium, other times individually. In the nineteenth century and early twentieth century there were four more partitions: 1815, 1832, 1836, and 1939—and, again, the main players were Russia and what had been Prussia but was now Germany.

During 1940 and 1941 thousands of Polish soldiers like General Maczek made their way across Europe and began the fighting to reclaim their homeland from an army base in the British midlands or an aerodrome in Scotland. Initially the pressures of war drew the two nations together. The Poles had a far larger stake in the European war than the Indians and the Burmese did—or, for that matter, than the Canadians and Australians. And the closeness was evident at every level of the alliance: diplomatic, political, and military. The point at which things began to change is difficult to say with certainty, but the summer of 1941 is a good guess. In various forms Russia has been tormenting Poland for the better part of three centuries, but, with the Germans approaching Smolensk and the Poles eager to liberate the Polish soldiers sitting in Soviet prison camps, in the summer of 1941 the Poles put aside their grievances about the 1940 massacres and signed a series of treaties with the Soviets. Under the terms of the military agreement the Polish POWs would provide the nucleus of a new Polish army. The army would be under the titular command of the exiled Polish government in London, but it would fight in Russia under Soviet commanders. In theory the London Poles would be allowed to choose the commander; in practice the Kremlin would have the final say on the choice of commander.

The diplomatic agreement that the two sides signed was less straightforward. In initial talks the Soviet delegates had strongly suggested that at the conclusion of the war Poland's prewar borders, nullified by the German-Soviet pact, would be restored. But when the border issue arose during talks later that summer the Soviet delegates refused to make any commitments about Poland's postwar status. That probably didn't surprise the Polish delegates, but those delegates were likely surprised when the British foreign secretary, Anthony Eden, told Parliament that His Majesty's government had made no guarantees to Poland about its postwar borders.

America's entrance into the war also had an effect on Poland's standing in what became the Grand Alliance. From a psychological point of view, notes historian Norman Davies, America's entry changed the emotional climate in the alliance. The Americans wanted to present the war as a moral crusade, the victory of good over evil—and to a degree it worked. By 1943 even the ironworker in Pittsburgh had the occasional good word to say about "Uncle Joe," while in working-class Britain Stalin enjoyed something like movie star status. When the Women's Land Army, known commonly as the Land Girls, in Leeds and Dorset spoke of the war they were likely to speak first of the heroism of the Red Army and its leader, the former mass murderer Uncle Joe. As Russia's standing rose, the Poles fell into the background, though they remained an important military asset. In various iterations, the Poles fought in North Africa, and a year after the Katyn massacre, in Monte Cassino, where the 2nd Polish Corps did what the American, British, French, New Zealand, and Indian troops had been unable to do: capture the abbey at Monte Cassino. Within the alliance, though, Poland continued to be viewed as a second-tier ally—a Norway or a Holland—but with a bigger punch.

Viewed from a thousand feet Roosevelt's and Churchill's perspectives on the Polish question were similar. Viewed from fifty feet, however, differences emerged. Churchill found the Poles exasperating, yet they felt that, as Britain's first ally, they were owed a certain level of support and respect as long as they did not overreach. Roosevelt's affection for the Poles was more limited. In the new world order he envisioned there was little space and not much empathy for a small nation that seemed full of big grievances. A few weeks before the Tehran Conference, the president told a young English friend of his wife, "I am sick and tired of these people [the London Poles]. The Polish ambassador came to me some time ago" asking for help. "I told him: Do you think they [the Russians] will just stop to please you, or us for that matter? Do you expect us and Great Britain to declare war on Joe Stalin if they [the Russians] cross your precious frontiers?"

Stalin's position on Poland was blunt. To avoid more Barbarossa he wanted to expand the Soviet Union's border well to the west of its current position, a change that would require the Poles to renounce their prewar borders and accept new ones. At Tehran Churchill proposed a compromise that also included a threat. He said the Russians' offer was a good one and if the Poles rejected it then the British government would not be prepared to argue against the Soviets at the postwar conference. After Churchill finished, Anthony Eden asked Stalin if his goal was to re-create the old 1939 Soviet-German border. "Call it what you will,"

Stalin replied. Roosevelt and Stalin also discussed the Polish issue on the final day of the Tehran Conference. Roosevelt said there were between six and seven million Polish American voters and that while he personally agreed with Premier Stalin on the Polish border issue, with the 1944 election less than a year away he could not participate in any arrangements or public discussions on the subject. There would also be no statements on the Baltic question for the same reason. In 1940 Russia seized Lithuania, Estonia, and Latvia to provide a buffer against a German attack; now, with the Germans on the back foot, many Americans with ties to the region feared it would fall back into Russian hands. Harriman, who acted as Roosevelt's second at the meeting, shared their fear. The Soviet Union clearly intended to be the hegemonic power in postwar eastern Europe, which meant that the United States and Britain were left with little or no voice in the status of Poland, Hungary, Romania, and the other eastern European and Balkan states.

If Harriman was troubled by that prospect, Roosevelt seemed prepared to accept the Soviet control of Poland, provided that it was peaceful and the nation's institutions were preserved, says historian Susan Butler.

On a warm summer day in late August 1944, the vagaries of war and chance combined to provide the Polish forces on both sides of Europe with a hill to die on. In the west the hill had a name—Hill 22—and a location: eastern Normandy. The Polish soldiers defending the hill were all that stood between the German 7th Army, which had been badly mauled in Normandy and, like dozens of other German units, was attempting to escape into the relative safety of the French interior. The other hill was a city: Warsaw. The Warsaw uprising was in its third week when the fighting on Hill 22 began, and, thanks to a linkup that ran through London, members of the Polish Home Army (the Armia Krajowa, which went by the name AK and was one of the largest underground armies in occupied Europe) were able to follow the battle in real time from cellars and safe houses in Warsaw.

It was a first and a last. The Warsaw uprising, which began on August 1 and ended in early October, claimed the lives of 15,000 Home Army men and women and 150,000 to 200,000 civilians; sent thousands of other Poles to German prisons; and reduced the center of the city to a postapocalyptic ruin.

One important but often overlooked reason for the success of the Normandy campaign was Operation Bagration, the summer offensive that the Red Army launched to support the Normandy campaign. In late June, while the Anglo-American forces were fighting their way through the bocage of Normandy, the Red Army reached the Lithuanian capital of Vilnius and, in a twelve-day battle, destroyed twenty-five German divisions and killed, wounded, or imprisoned over three hundred thousand German soldiers. The sweeping scale of the victory confirmed the Soviet Union's place as the greatest land power in the world and also redoubled Stalin's resolve to recapture those regions of eastern Europe seized by Germany, starting with Poland. To that end he set out to undercut the London Poles, the prewar government that fled to Britain after the fall of Poland.

The most notorious example of the undercutting was the Katyn massacre. Turning the truth on its head, Stalin depicted the Soviet Union as the victim of Polish lies—then used that alleged calumny as an excuse to cut off relations with the London Poles and avoid recognizing the Polish Home Army.

In early 1944 Stalin ratcheted up the pressure on the Poles. Members of the Home Army were targeted by Soviet agents and communist-led Polish guerillas. On July 22, eight days before the Warsaw uprising, Stalin, Molotov, and Zhukov were among the dignitaries who attended the founding of the Committee of National Liberation, the forerunner of the puppet Polish government that would agree to move Poland's borders to the west so that the Soviet Union would have a deeper buffer against future German assaults. "We do not want, nor shall we set up, our own administration on Polish soil," Stalin assured Churchill a few days after the committee came into being.

On July 31 Soviet tanks broke into the German defenses on the eastern side of the Vistula River, opposite Warsaw. The breakthrough confronted the London Poles and the underground Home Army in Warsaw with two options: do nothing and wait on events—or order a general uprising and put a provisional government in place to negotiate with the Red Army when it reached Warsaw.

The Poles chose the second option. During the early afternoon of August 1, 1944, Home Army men and women took up positions around the capital. The attack would not proceed until 5:00 P.M., which gave the insurgents a long summer afternoon to consider two unknowns. The first was time. How long could the lightly armed Home Army hold out unaided? The second was the German response. Given the heavy losses the Wehrmacht had sustained in Normandy and on the eastern front it seemed unlikely that they would make a stand in Warsaw. That illusion was shattered a little after the time of the attack when a collection of prewar cavalrymen and raw recruits poured out of a tenement on a street corner and rushed the complex of bunkers guarding the SS and Gestapo headquarters. When the German machine guns stopped firing only the commander and six men from the battalion were still alive.

That evening a German squad returned to the same street and killed every resident. Any lingering doubts about Germany's intentions were brought to an end the following day when a column of Tiger tanks from the Hermann Göring Division, supported by engineers whose job it was to burn the city, came close to obliterating five companies of the Battalion Parasol, one of the Home Army's most elite units. On August 3 a Red Army force fought its way to within twelve miles of Warsaw, but, aware that every kilometer counted now, the Germans threw them back with a furious counterattack. The next day, August 4, Churchill cabled Stalin: "At urgent request of Polish underground army we are dropping, subject to weather, about sixty tons of equipment and ammunition into the southwest quarter of Warsaw where it is said the Polish revolt against the Germans is in fierce struggle. They also say they have appealed for Russian aid."

Stalin replied to Churchill immediately: "I think the information that has been communicated to you by the Poles is greatly exaggerated and does not inspire confidence."

By mid-August the fighting had become savage. "Hatred of these villains grew with every atrocity," a Home Army soldier recalled later. "They would round up Poles and place them in front of tanks so that the insurgents couldn't shoot. It was a ghastly sight. You couldn't fire on your own and it was even worse to see the bastards pressing on ahead, killing the poor wretches they had captured." As the fighting continued in the burning summer heat Warsaw became bifurcated. The Germans controlled the city aboveground; the Home Army, the sewers. In late August the Warsaw sewer system became the lifeblood through which flowed food, water, the wounded, and the dying. It was where the wounded Polish Jews sheltered and where reinforcements from other parts of the city were sent into the boiling summer streets. The sewer system also housed an ever-expanding rodent population, which feasted on the dying and the remains of the dead. However, the rats had one redeeming feature: they terrified the Germans. The Germans threw hand grenades into the sewers. They sprayed them with poisonous gas and bugged them with listening devices but refused to climb down into the sewers. After the war General Erich von dem Bach-Zelewski, who oversaw the sewer campaign, confessed he could "never convince his soldiers to descend into the sewers and carry on the struggle there."

When Stanisław Mikołajczyk, prime minister of the exiled Polish government in London, had arrived in Moscow in late July, Stalin told him, "We will try to do everything possible to help Warsaw." But, some days later, when Allied officials requested landing rights for British and American planes ferrying food and weapons to the Home Army, they were told that "the uprising was a reckless adventure . . . and the Soviet Command had decided to openly disclaim any responsibility for the Warsaw adventure." Growing increasingly frustrated, on August 20 Roosevelt and Churchill made a direct appeal to Stalin: "We are thinking of world opinion if the anti-Nazis in Warsaw are in effect abandoned. We hope you will drop immediate supplies and ammunition to the patriot Poles in Warsaw or agree to help our planes do it very quickly?" Stalin remained unmoved. "Sooner or later," he wrote in reply, "the truth about this group of criminals, who have embarked on the Warsaw adventure in order to seize power, will be known to everybody." After reading Stalin's note Churchill's first impulse was to ignore its provocative tone and send another flight of planes to Warsaw with supplies; yet when he approached Roosevelt about issuing a joint statement on the Polish agony the president balked. "I do not consider it would prove advantageous to the long-range general war prospect for me to join you in the proposed message to Stalin."

On September 4 Churchill made a final appeal to Stalin and Roosevelt. In the cable to Stalin he described the behavior of the Soviet Union as "at variance with the spirit of Allied cooperation to which you and we attach so much importance both for the present and the future." His appeal to Roosevelt was more emotional: "Warsaw is in ruins. The Germans are killing the wounded in hospitals. They are making women and children march in front of them in order to protect their tanks. There is no exaggeration in reports of children fighting and destroying tanks with bottles of petrol." Roosevelt too was appalled by the German atrocities, which he called "inhuman" but could see no practical way of aiding the insurgents. Poland was on the other side of Europe and Normandy. Italy and the Pacific campaign were absorbing all the Allies' resources. The president also shared the Joint Chiefs of Staff's concern that if pressed on Poland Stalin might think twice about honoring his pledge to join the Pacific war on Germany's fall and about giving the US rights to attack Japan from air bases in Siberia.

The most insightful description of the Polish tragedy was written by George Kennan, the wartime chargé d'affaires at the US embassy in Moscow. After the war two of Kennan's works—the *Long Telegram*, written in 1946, and a 1947 *Foreign Affairs* article written under the pseudonym X—would shape American thinking about the Soviet Union for more than a generation. But both articles had their genesis in "Russia—Seven Years Later," an essay Kennan wrote shortly after the Polish uprising.

> American concepts of collective security can only seem unreal in Moscow. Russian leaders pay lip service to the principles of the US and Britain but with the second front in place they no longer need to observe excessive delicacy. Their priorities are ascendant now and they all amount to one thing, power. The form it takes and the methods by which it is achieved are secondary. Moscow doesn't care whether a given area was Communistic or not. The main thing is that it should be subject to Moscow's control. The USSR is thus committed to becoming the dominant power in Eastern and Central Europe and only then to cooperate with their Anglo-American allies. The first of these programs implies taking. The second implies giving. No one can stop Russia from doing the taking if she is determined to go through with it. No one can force Russia to do the giving if she is determined not to go through with it. . . . We should bow our heads in silence before the tragedy of a people who have been our allies, whom we have saved from our enemies and whom we cannot save from our friends.

DAISY SUCKLEY'S DIARY ENTRY FOR September 6, 1944, reads: "At 4 P.M. the Pres. telephoned from Wash; said he felt miserable—like a boiled owl—his voice sounded heavy and he had a stomach upset . . . I was much worried." Illness crept up on Roosevelt quietly. Daisy first began to worry about his health when he returned from the Quebec Conference complaining of tiredness. Since he looked well she thought he had just overextended himself, but the tiredness persisted and as the weeks passed seemed to worsen. Sometimes Roosevelt felt so tired he couldn't "make his brain work." On one occasion he fell asleep twice while writing a message to Congress. But Daisy and no one else in the country with the possible exception of Colonel Robert McCormick of the *Chicago Tribune*, the Hearst papers, and a few die-hard isolationists wanted to believe the president was seriously ill. Over three terms Roosevelt had become a father figure to the nation, the calm center that carried the ship of state through the storm. Moreover, initially there was no compelling reason to believe he was suffering from a life-threatening illness.

Like Churchill and Stalin, Roosevelt was in his sixties, and the burdens of war were bound to put a heavy stress on a man of that age. Furthermore, compared to Churchill, who had stopped off in Washington after receiving an honorary degree from Harvard, and Harry Hopkins, who had survived a life-threatening stomach disease in 1939 and was now suffering from pernicious anemia, liver disease, and a host of other ailments, Roosevelt seemed relatively healthy. "We all agreed it was extraordinary," Daisy wrote in her diary in the late summer of 1943. "It seems as though the trials and difficulties of the office of the president . . . acts as a stimulant to the P. They take the place of the exercise he can't have like other people."

The euphoria was short-lived. In October Roosevelt fell ill again, and this time the symptoms were impossible to dismiss as a passing infirmity. His body ached, his temperature rose to 104, and his exhaustion became crippling. In the years after Roosevelt's death Dr. Ross McIntire, his personal doctor and the navy's chief physician, would be criticized for downplaying the severity of Roosevelt's condition, and in public McIntire often did. In press conferences he would blame the president's ragged appearance, long absences from public view, and canceled press conferences on a cold or a bout of the flu. Comments about Roosevelt's dramatic weight loss would be met with a smile and a claim that the commander in chief was proud of his "flat tummy."

But neurologist Steven Lomazow, who wrote a paper on the Roosevelt-McIntire relationship, says McIntire was aware of how gravely ill his patient was and on a number of occasions quietly brought in specialists to examine Roosevelt. Lomazow believes McIntire willingly sacrificed his public reputation to protect Roosevelt, who wanted to keep his physical deterioration as far from public view as his polio. And during the early years of the war, that had been possible; but over time the few bad days became a few bad weeks, then the bad weeks became bad months.

On March 20 Roosevelt wrote Churchill: "The old attack of grippe having hung on and on has left me with an intermittent temperature, Ross [McIntire] has decided . . . that it is necessary for me to take a complete rest of two or three weeks in a suitable climate. . . . *I see no way out and I am furious.*" On a visit to Hyde Park a few days later Roosevelt was still full of fury and pain. "I've never done such a thing in my life before," he told Daisy. It's unclear what he meant by that remark, but his next sentence was as clear and sharp as an x-ray of the soul. "Robert Louis Stevenson in the last stage of consumption," he said to no one in particular.

On March 27 Roosevelt entered the National Naval Medical Center, where Dr. Howard Bruenn, a young cardiologist of high repute, examined him. In his report on the examination Bruenn described the president as "a 62-year-old man in severely declining health with symptoms of severely elevated blood pressure, (136/108) classic signs of long-standing hypertension, an enlarged heart, and congestive heart failure." The final symptom Bruenn cited, ashen countenance with blue lips, suggested Roosevelt also may have been suffering from inadequate oxygenation deriving from cardiac insufficiency, which caused persistent, severe anemia. As the president's chief physician, it's likely McIntire, not Bruenn, conveyed the test results to Roosevelt. How much he told the president is unknown, but from Roosevelt's conversations with Daisy it's clear he knew he had heart disease and from his failure to ask questions that he knew all he wanted to know about his condition.

In April, during his monthlong recuperation at the South Carolina estate of Bernard Baruch, Roosevelt was inundated with get-well wishes. Over the years millions of Americans had come to feel a personal attachment to Roosevelt. He was the big brother, the wise father who had seen the country through the bitter Depression years and now the ravages of war. People worried about him the way they would a family member. "You did many fine and wonderful things for the country," a Brooklyn woman wrote him. "Retire to your . . . home. Rest and enjoy the fruits of your endeavors." A letter from a San Diego man was in the same vein: "I don't believe in working a good horse to death so don't try to carry the whole world on your shoulders." But millions of Americans could not envision life without Roosevelt. "Please, President Roosevelt," one woman wrote, "don't let us down in this world of trouble and sorrow. I believe within my heart God put you here in this world to be our Guiding Star."

When Daisy saw Roosevelt in mid-May the recuperative effect of the South Carolina visit had worn off. He looked "worried and tired." But the war was reaching its peak in the late spring and summer of 1944; thousands of nineteen- and twenty-year-olds were dying for their country. As commander, Roosevelt felt compelled to set an example—for them, for their parents, for the country, for the world—no matter what the personal risk to himself. He spent the first part of the summer in Washington dealing with disgruntled allies and preparing for the 1944 elections. Chief among the former was Charles de Gaulle, who was angry at Roosevelt for refusing to recognize his claim to be leader of the French state, and Winston Churchill, who was unhappy about the president's decision to limit the US postwar policing duties in Europe to the Netherlands and northwest Germany. There was also Poland, and Harriman and Kennan were concerned Roosevelt planned to cede the country to Stalin.

On the home front, the president's greatest challenge was the 1944 elections. After an unprecedented third term, how could he explain to the American people that he would seek yet a fourth term? There was probably some truth in Roosevelt's assertion that he was only standing for a fourth term out of a sense of duty; nonetheless, once he made the decision he was cunning in the way he made the case. He provided skeptical White House reporters with a copy of a letter he sent to Robert Hannegan, chairman of the Democratic National Committee. After twelve years of service, he told Hannegan, he did not wish to remain in the White House, but if the American people, "the Commanders in Chief of us all," ordered him to stand for another term, as a good soldier, he would serve. In late July during a conversation with General Douglas MacArthur, Roosevelt was more forthcoming about his decision to stand for office again. At first he demurred when MacArthur asked what he thought of his opponent, New York governor Thomas Dewey, but after a little prodding by the general Roosevelt dispensed with pretense and said, "I'll beat that son of bitch [Dewey] . . . if it's the last thing I do." On July 20, while en route to Hawaii for a conference, Roosevelt received word that the Democratic Party had nominated him for a fourth term. The high point of the Hawaii trip was his visit to a military hospital. He had a Secret Service man wheel him slowly through a ward of armless and legless young soldiers and marines to illustrate that an infirmity need not be a bar to a meaningful and productive life. The young men he spoke to that morning had no way of knowing, but the president was also struggling with his own infirmities.

A few days earlier, in San Diego, he was leaving his train to board the ship that would carry him to Hawaii, when he suffered a severe angina attack. "I don't know if I can take it," he told his son Jimmy, who was accompanying him on the trip. "I have terrible pains." With his son's help he lay down on the floor of his train car, shut his eyes, and let the waves of pain pass though him. Ten minutes later they began to fade. "Don't tell anyone what happened," he told Jimmy; then father and son went down to the beach to watch a military exercise.

There was another alarming episode, this time at the end of the trip. On his way back to the capital Roosevelt stopped at Bremerton, Washington, a navy town about a fifty-minute drive from Seattle. Plans called for the president to address the nation from the deck of a ship during the stopover, but Roosevelt had lost thirty pounds over the past six months, the wind blowing in his face was cold and sharp, the ship under him was swaying back and forth, and the steel braces on his legs were heavy. Roosevelt gripped the lectern for support, but a few minutes into the speech he had another angina attack. The sharp pain began in his chest, moved up to his shoulders, and drenched his face and shirt collar in sweat. This time the episode lasted a half hour, not ten minutes, but unlike the earlier incident help was immediately available. Dr. Bruenn accompanied Roosevelt "on the final stage of his trip."

20

THE GRAND ALLIANCE
AT HIGH TIDE

N THE SUMMER OF 1944, WITH THE END OF THE WAR IN SIGHT, diplomats from the United States, Britain, the Soviet Union, and China gathered at Dumbarton Oaks, the Georgetown estate of diplomat Robert Woods Bliss, to consider the shape of the postwar world. The estate had an impressive pedigree. In 1702 Queen Anne bequeathed it to Colonel Ninian Beal, and over a century later it became the home of Senator and Vice President John Calhoun. But in none of its previous iterations had the estate played such an important role in the history of the world. The diplomats gathered in Dumbarton's music room on the morning of July 21 were tasked with transforming the international security organization proposed by the Allied foreign ministers at the Moscow Conference nine months earlier into a functioning reality. Creating an institution to safeguard world peace was not a new idea. At the end of the Great War the League of Nations had been formed to fulfill just such a role, and every diplomat who gathered at Dumbarton Oaks that morning was old enough to remember what happened to the league. But after a summer of almost unbroken victory and peace on the horizon the delegates were in an optimistic mood. Upon arriving in Washington after a grueling five-day flight from Moscow Andrei Gromyko, who led the Soviet delegation, cabled Stalin: "There are grounds to believe that the USA will be interested in the maintenance of peace. . . . It is only in this light that we can interpret the readiness of the USA to take an active part in the international peace and security." For a Soviet official, Gromyko's words were the equivalent of a high five, and his optimism was shared by Edward R. Stettinius, the under secretary of state who led the American delegation at the conference, and Alexander Cadogan, leader of the British delegation and permanent under secretary for foreign affairs. (A Chinese delegation was also present, but because Japan was not yet at war with the Soviet Union the Chinese would not join the talks until the Soviets had departed.)

During talks in the music room, conference members reached agreement on several key points, including when the UN came into being. The four policemen would become the four permanent members of the eleven-member Security Council. It was also agreed that a military staff committee would be created to oversee the UN's policing activities; the International Court of Justice, to handle legal issues; and the Economic and Social Council to do policy review and dialogue.

However, on two important issues there was persistent and deep disagreement. The Soviets refused to accept the British and American position that a permanent member of the Security Council—in other words, a member of the Big Four—could not be allowed to vote in disputes that it was involved in. The second disagreement arose from Stalin's assertion that, as a polyglot nation of many countries, Russia should receive sixteen seats in the General Assembly. Beneath these differences lay a deeper one: the Americans and British viewed the United Nations as an instrument to promote world peace, and Stalin as a safeguard against a future German attack. In his memoirs George Kennan wrote of Stalin's demand for more seats in the General Assembly: "Insofar as he attaches importance to the concept of a future international organization, he . . . does so in the expectation the organization would serve as an instrument for the maintenance of a Great Power hegemony."

But the harmony would be based on Britain's and the United States' acceptance of Soviet dominance in eastern and central Europe:

We should realize clearly what we are faced with. It is this: That as far as border states are concerned the Soviet government has never ceased to think in terms of spheres of influence. They expect us to support them in whatever action they take in those regions, regardless of whether that action seems to us or to the rest of the world to be right or wrong. We are not expected to inquire as to whether those deeds are good ones or bad ones.

Our people, for reasons we don't need to go into, have not been aware of this quality of Soviet thought, and have been allowed to hope that the Soviet government would be prepared to enter into an international security organization with truly universal power to prevent aggression. We are now faced with the prospect of having our people disabused of this illusion.

And that could "cause violent repercussions in our relations" with the Soviet Union.

Kennan's warning was both prescient and premature. By the summer of 1944 the Soviet Union had become the indispensable ally. On September 11—the day Roosevelt and Churchill arrived in Canada to attend the Second Quebec Conference—one Russian army was menacing Hungary, another East Prussia. And a third was menacing Estonia.

The purpose of the conference was to work out the military endgame. The war was likely to end sometime in the next eight to ten months, but, given the character of the enemy, there would be a lot of hard fighting before it did. On August 31—six days after the German army abandoned Paris—Gerd von Rundstedt, one of Germany's most skilled commanders, produced the "German Miracle": in the final weeks of August 600,000 German soldiers and several crack panzergrenadier units escaped the Allied armies in France and established new defensive positions in Belgium and Holland. Between late July and the early autumn of 1944 the Germans also fielded eighteen new divisions.

On September 1 Hitler, though still recovering from a July 20 attempt on his life, summoned Rundstedt to his headquarters and charged him with defending Belgium, north of the Scheldt and the West Wall, the last formidable German defense line, which ran from Aachen to Metz to the Vosges. Field Marshal Walter Model, who had earned a reputation for extricating troops from hopeless situations in Russia, was given the critical sector to the north of the Ardennes. At first glance the German position looked impossible to defend, but Rundstedt and Model enjoyed one important advantage: so close to home the German defenders would have a significant logistical advantage over the Anglo-Americans, whose supply lines snaked across the United States and Britain to France. The months to come would also reveal whether the gamble that the American planners made in 1942 would pay off: Would a ninety-division army be sufficient if supported by a large navy and air force?

The initial indications were that it would. Since the Cairo meeting in December 1943, victory had followed victory. Rome fell on the eve of D-Day. Operation Dragoon, the invasion of southern Europe that began on August 15, went more smoothly than expected. By summer's end an additional "80,000 to 90,000 Germans were in or on their way to [Allied] POW camps." Inevitably the successes produced speculation about when the war would end. Montgomery believed by Christmas, if his plan was implemented, a large Allied force crossed the Rhine, seized the Ruhr, the industrial heartland of Germany, then moved on Berlin. One of the peripheral advantages of what came to be known as Operation Market Garden is that it would also annoy Montgomery's American rival, General George Patton, whose ego was as big as Monty's and who had his heart set on being the first Allied commander to enter Berlin.

In conception Market Garden, which began on September 17, the day after the Second Quebec Conference ended, was relatively simple. Three airborne divisions, two American and one British, would land at three different points in Holland—Eindhoven, Nijmegen, and Arnhem—and hold the vital sixty-four-mile corridor that ran from the Dutch border to Arnhem open for the tanks of the British XXX Corps. If all went to plan, the tanks would cross the captured bridges, outflank the German units defending the Siegfried Line, and penetrate the Ruhr. But a series of faulty intelligence reports ensured very little would go to plan. Two German panzer divisions were in Arnhem refitting when the operation began. There were also German tanks hidden along the roads up to Arnhem, a possibility that British planners had dismissed a few days earlier, when a young British officer claimed to have seen photos of tanks hidden in the woods along the roads. Most damaging of all, well over half the paratroopers in the British 1st Airborne Division, the unit charged with seizing Arnhem and holding it until XXX Corps arrived, were dropped seven and eight miles from their landing zones.

When the first German units arrived in Arnhem a single British battalion was defending the town. Over the next few days the British public followed the demise of Market Garden in the *Daily Mail* and the other big London papers. On September 23, six days after the start of the operation, the *Mail* reported, BATTLE TO SAVE AIR ARMY, and on the twenty-sixth, with the battle lost, the *Mail* headline read, THE GLORIOUS ACTION IN WHICH THE PARACHUTISTS . . . WENT DOWN FIGHTING UNDER WAVES OF GERMAN ATTACKS. And in its September 28 edition there was an epithet for the men of Market Garden.

SKY MEN TELL GREATEST STORY OF THE WAR
8,000 IN—2,000 OUT

The armed forces edition of the *Daily Mail* was more forthright. The headline above the photos of wounded British paratroopers read:

THE AGONY OF ARNHEM. 230 HOURS OF HELL

The official figures for Market Garden were 1,100 killed and 6,000 captured, but many of the captured only surrendered after being wounded.

Churchill, who was still in Quebec, insisted that Market Garden was "a decided victory," excoriated the naysayers, then left for America, where two important meetings awaited him.

The first was at Hyde Park. It was now clear that an atomic bomb was feasible and would possess unparalleled power. Current estimates had a single bomb producing an explosion three times greater than the firepower of 2,600 planes. During the meeting at Hyde Park Roosevelt and Churchill agreed the bomb would remain an Anglo-American secret, and with the war in Europe in the final innings, Japan was likely to be the target of the first bomb.

However, four days later Roosevelt seemed to have second thoughts. Vannevar Bush and Lord Cherwell both had worked on the bomb in various capacities, and both were critics of the current secrecy policy. After listening to their objections Roosevelt seemed open to employing the bomb as a threat to bring the Japanese to the conference table.

Churchill's second meeting was with Stalin. Initially it was supposed to be a threesome, but citing the upcoming American elections, Roosevelt begged off, leaving Churchill feeling slighted and annoyed. "It was stupid of the President to think he was the only person who could manage Stalin," Churchill told Moran. "The Red Army would not stand still awaiting the results of an election. I am going to Moscow." Then illness intervened. Like his Western colleagues, Stalin was in his sixties and suffering from the infirmities of old age. During a talk with Harriman and Clark Kerr, the British ambassador, he said he never "kept well" anywhere except Moscow, that his trips to the front, which were rare, exhausted him, and that after the Tehran Conference he had needed a fortnight to recover.

Eight days later a half-awake Churchill was lying in the belly of a poorly heated British bomber, examining his foreign secretary's sleeping pills. "What did you take?" he asked.

"I always take a red," a groggy Anthony Eden replied. "I think it's good stuff if you want to sleep on these trips."

"I took two," Churchill said. "I'm a hardened case."

The prime minister arrived in Moscow for the Tolstoy Conference with two goals: 1) to reach an accommodation with Stalin on the Balkans; and 2) to resolve the Polish question, which was now so toxic it was threatening the stability of the alliance. Churchill decided to begin with the easy problem. He told Stalin that Britain had a special interest in two nations in the Balkans: Greece and Romania. About the latter Britain was "not worried," he said. The terms the Soviets were offering on Romania were reasonable and evidenced much statecraft on Moscow's part.

Greece was different. "Britain must be the leading Mediterranean power," Churchill said, and he hoped Marshal Stalin would let him have the first say about Greece. When Stalin offered no objections Churchill went a step further. Because the Americans "might find such an agreement shocking," he said that the term *spheres of influence*—or anything resembling that term—should be avoided. What happened next, reported Martin Gilbert, Churchill's official biographer, "would influence the political balance of power in Eastern Europe and the Balkans for several generations." The prime minister reached into his pocket and produced what he would later call the "naught document": a list of the Balkan states and the amount of influence that Britain and the Soviet Union would exercise in each. "So far as Britain and Russia are concerned," he said, "how would it do for you to have 90 percent predominance in Romania, for us to have 90 percent in Greece, and go fifty about Yugoslavia?" While waiting for the translator to put his proposal into Russian, Churchill picked up a piece of paper, drew a picture of the percentages, then pushed the drawing across the table to Stalin. There was a slight pause, then Stalin scribbled an approving tick on the drawing and pushed it back across the table. Another silence followed, and this one was longer.

Finally Churchill broke the silence with a question. "Might it not be thought rather cynical if it seemed we dispensed with these issues, so fateful to millions of people, in such an offhanded manner? Let us burn the paper."

"No," Stalin said. "You keep it."

The Polish question did not lend itself to such an easy solution. There were two claimants to the Polish state. One was the London Poles, the leaders of the prewar government, who fled to Britain after Poland fell and became the Polish government in exile. The other claimant to the throne were the Lublin Poles. Stalin was intent on extending Russia's postwar border west to provide a buffer against a future German attack and the Lublin Poles were his chosen instrument. They would do Russia's bidding on the border and look after its other interests in Poland. Winston Churchill, the most important Western voice on Poland, arrived at the Tolstoy Conference hoping to square the circle and provide a solution that would satisfy the London Poles, the Lublin Poles, and, most importantly, Stalin. Roosevelt had made it clear that American troops would be brought home as quickly as possible after the war, and with the Americans gone there would be nothing standing between the "white snows of Moscow and the white cliffs of Dover" except a parcel of small, impoverished European nations and France, which had a broken military and a large Communist Party.

Given the circumstances, Churchill concluded, better to befriend the bear than to challenge him. On October 12 Eden informed the Foreign Office that "the Prime Minister and I [have] sought to impress on Marshal Stalin how essential it [is] in the interests of Anglo-Soviet relations that the Polish Question now be settled. . . . The London and Lublin Poles must agree to create a new cross party Polish government. If they refuse or are unable to agree, the British and Soviet Governments, the two Great Allies, must themselves impose a reasonable settlement."

The next day, October 13, Stanisław Mikołajczyk, the leader of the London Poles; his foreign minister, Tadeusz Romer; and Professor Stanisław Grabski, chairman of the National Council of Poland arrived in Moscow for talks. Like Stalin Mikołajczyk was a peasant by birth and a politician by profession. He was also a realist. He arrived at the Kremlin expecting Stalin to demand that he negotiate with the Lublin Poles but hadn't anticipated the Soviet leader's second demand. "If you want to have relations with the Soviet Government," he told Mikołajczyk, "you can only do it by recognizing the Curzon Line." The politics of the line dated back to a failed 1920 attempt by a revolutionary Russia to spread the Marxist doctrine to Poland. With the help of the French, the Poles repulsed the attack, and at a 1921 peace conference they were awarded a large swath of eastern Poland: 52,000 square miles.

The principal contribution of Lord Curzon, the British foreign secretary who gave the line its name, was a 1920 suggestion that the new Soviet-Polish border be called an *armistice line* rather than a border. Upon the fall of Poland in the autumn of 1939 the Curzon Line became a demarcation point between the German-occupied west of the country and the Soviet-occupied east until Barbarossa. When the Tolstoy Conference commenced on October 9, 1944, the Red Army was at high tide and Stalin determined to reclaim the large swath of eastern Poland awarded to the Soviet Union under the 1939 German-Soviet nonaggression pact; on this point he had the support of Churchill, who was haunted by all that empty space between the white cliffs of Dover and the white snows of Moscow.

When the border issue came up during the conference Churchill did not mince words. He told Mikołajczyk, "I do not think it would be in the interest of the Polish government to estrange itself from the British government." The sacrifices Britain has made in "this war have . . . given us the right to ask the Poles for a great gesture in the name of European peace." Perhaps thinking that sounded too harsh, Churchill took a half step back and proposed a compromise. The final status of Poland's borders would be left until the peace conference. At that point the transcript of the meeting notes that Stalin, who was also present, said that the "Soviet Government cannot accept Prime Minister Churchill's formula." Taken aback, the prime minister "made a gesture of disappointment and helplessness."

A little before noon the following day, October 14, Churchill met with Mikołajczyk and his colleagues again. After a brief exchange of pleasantries Churchill told the Poles, "This is crazy that you cannot defeat the Russians. If you reach a formula with me I will [speak] to Stalin at 4 P.M." Mikołajczyk held his ground. "The Polish government will not surrender any Polish territory or agree to join the Lublin Poles. I will not sign a death warrant, against my country." Churchill had had enough. Quarrels between Poles "are not going to wreck the peace of Europe," he told Mikołajczyk, adding that, in his obstinacy, "you do not see what is at stake. It is not in friendship that we shall part. We shall tell the world how unreasonable you are. You will start another war in which 25 million lives will be lost. But you don't care."

ON THE EVENING OF THE fourteenth, discussions of the Polish question were temporarily set aside, and Churchill and Stalin attended a concert at the Bolshoi Theatre. Kathleen Harriman, who was in the audience that night, recalled that "the PM arrived late with UJ [Uncle Joe] coming in later, so the audience did not realize they were there until the lights went up after the first act. A cheer went up . . . and Uncle Joe ducked out so the PM could have all the applause to himself. But then the PM sent [an aide] to get Uncle Joe back and they stood together while the applause went on for many, many minutes. It was most, most impressive; the thunderous clapping sounded like a cloudburst on a tin roof. It came from below and on all sides and the people down in the audience said they were thrilled to see the two men standing together." One of the most surprising things about Stalin was his quick wit. During the intermission, when a guest likened the Big Three to the Holy Trinity, Stalin said, "If that was so, then Churchill must be the Holy Ghost he travels so much."

The next day Churchill fell ill, but by the sixteenth he felt well enough to take another crack at the Poles. This time his persistence appeared to pay off. Mikołajczyk agreed to recognize the Curzon Line, a big concession, but he could not bring himself to agree to Stalin's second demand. He wanted the new Russian-Polish border to be described as a frontier, while Mikołajczyk and his colleagues wanted it to be described as a demarcation line, a phrase that carried less weight. That evening Eden noted, "Stalin not only wants the Curzon line to be the new frontier with Poland, he wants it to be described as such." On the seventeenth, Churchill, who was recovering from a severe case of diarrhea, made a final attempt to persuade Mikołajczyk to accept Stalin's border formulation. This was the sixth discussion between the two men in the past three days, and like the previous five it resolved nothing. In Mikołajczyk's mind border implied statehood; a demarcation line, a soccer game. With

the clock running out, the following day Mikołajczyk made a significant concession. He agreed to discuss the border issue with the Soviet-
controlled Lublin Poles. A few weeks later, after a meeting with Stalin
went surprisingly well, it seemed some form of compromise with the
Lublin Poles was possible, but Mikołajczyk was a moderate, and in the
Poland he would return to after the war there was no place for mod-
erates. The surviving members of the London Poles regarded him as a
turncoat for taking a position in the new Soviet-controlled government,
while the Lublin Poles who controlled the government distrusted him. In
1947 Mikołajczyk fled to the United States, but before his death in 2000
he asked that his and wife's remains be returned to Poland for burial.

The Moscow Conference was about fashioning the future, but on
the sidelines there was a good deal of talk about the present and, in particular, the recent run of Soviet military victories. Between late August
and early September 1944 German Army Group South Ukraine and two
Romanian armies sustained more than four hundred thousand casualties
and were pushed out of Bucharest and Ploesti, whose oil fields had kept
the Luftwaffe in the air for the past four years.

By the end of September Bulgaria, another of Germany's former allies,
had changed sides and the Soviet 57th Army was advancing into western
Bulgaria in preparation for a battle with German Army Groups E and
F in Yugoslavia. Around the same time a Russian cavalry-mechanized
group cleared the passes across the Carpathian Mountains along an
eight-hundred-kilometer corridor. However, the mountainous region—
one of the few major obstacles in the flat north European plain—favored
the defender. The battle at Dukla Pass, which lies between Poland and
Slovenia, was supposed to last six days but continued for a month. The
Red Army prevailed in the end, but the butcher's bill—seventy thousand
casualties on both sides—was higher than anticipated. The Russians also
encountered fierce resistance during the fight for the Hungarian capital
of Budapest.

By late December two Russian armies had the German 9th Mountain Division and two Hungarian divisions encircled inside the capital,
but fierce resistance from several first-class German units would keep
parts of Budapest in German hands until February 1945. Soviet armies
also reclaimed the Baltic states, which Stalin seized in 1940 and which
became a killing ground for Jews during the German occupation. At
the beginning of August detachments of three Soviet Baltic front armies

pushed through to the Gulf of Riga in Latvia and severed communications between German Army Group Center and Army Group North.

A month later the Soviet second Baltic front came close to obliterating Army Group Center. In October another Soviet force overran the 3rd Panzer Army's headquarters and reached the Baltic coast. The German units that escaped to the Courland Peninsula, which borders the Gulf of Riga in the east and the Baltic Sea in the west, survived six Russian attacks in the winter of 1944/45 and did not surrender until the final day of the war, May 8, 1945.

Finland, another small country that had thrown in its lot with Germany, saw the writing on the wall earlier than the Romanians and Bulgarians had; they surrendered to the Red Army in August 1944.

During a discussion of postwar Germany on the final day of the Moscow Conference, Churchill told Stalin that Prussia, which he called "the root of all evil," should be isolated after the war, and the Ruhr and Saarland, Germany's two great industrial centers, returned to farmland. The prime minister said that he was not alone in these views. They were already being discussed in America. Recently "Mr. Morgenthau" had presented President Roosevelt with a similar plan. Mr. Morgenthau was Henry Morgenthau Jr., Roosevelt's secretary of the treasury, and for a moment in late 1944 he was one the most influential voices in shaping the fate of postwar Germany. It was a role that Morgenthau would have found impossible to imagine five years earlier. He was a member of a German Jewish family that had produced cantors and rabbis in the old country and real estate entrepreneurs in the new.

Morgenthau's father was an assertive self-made millionaire and a resolutely secular Jew. As a young man, Morgenthau Jr. seemed intent on becoming everything that his father was not. Recuperating from an illness on a Texas ranch, he developed an affinity for farming, and he followed the inclination to Cornell University, where he studied agriculture. A few years later he purchased a farm in Dutchess County, not far from the Roosevelts', and refashioned himself as a gentleman farmer. Morgenthau seemed to have a complicated relationship with his Jewishness. He did not disown it, but he did downplay it, as did his wife, Elinor. When her five-year-old son asked what religion the family was, Elinor replied, "Just tell them you're an American."

In 1933 Morgenthau was appointed secretary of the treasury, though his principal qualifications for the post were his friendship with Roosevelt and the sudden death of the president's first choice for secretary. When the appointment was announced, *Fortune* magazine dismissed Morgenthau as the "son of a Jewish philanthropist," while Gladys Straus, a wealthy Jewish Republican, wisecracked that Morgenthau was "the only Jew in the world who doesn't know anything about money," while the elder Morgenthau declared his son was "not up to" the new position.

Roosevelt regarded Morgenthau as a friend, though during a talk with Morgenthau and Leo Crowley, a Catholic member of the administration, he indeed said, "You know, this is a Protestant country, and the Catholics and Jews are here under sufferance."

Before the war, says historian Michael Beschloss, whatever guilt Morgenthau may have felt about his reticence to reach out to Jewish refugees was sublimated by his zeal for defense preparedness and aid to Britain. There are a number of theories about who or what transformed Morgenthau from a sympathetic bystander to committed advocate. His son Henry III suggested to Beschloss that the change may have been related to changes in the family circle. The elder Morgenthau was now in his mideighties and no longer the dominant figure he had been, and his wife Elinor was suffering from heart disease. Into the void that their absence created stepped Henrietta Klotz, Morgenthau's longtime aide and a Jewish activist who kept her boss abreast of events in Germany, whether he wanted to hear them or not.

By late 1943 Morgenthau no longer needed prodding from Klotz. There were a number of genteel anti-Semites in the upper reaches of the American government, and that winter Morgenthau called out one of the most prominent, Breckinridge Long, the assistant secretary of state and an elegant aristocrat in the Henry James manner. Long was born into a wealthy family, possessed a Princeton degree, and had a grandfather who had served as James Buchanan's vice president.

Over the years he had also had a number of prestigious postings, including in Italy, where he found Mussolini's Blackshirts "dapper and well dressed . . . and lending an atmosphere of individuality and importance to their surroundings." Long's opinion of Hitler was mixed, although he thought *Mein Kampf* "eloquent in opposition to Jews as exponents of Communism and Chaos." In the winter of 1943, when colleagues at the treasury complained Long was making it difficult for immigrants, and in particular for Jewish immigrants, to enter the United States, Morgenthau confronted him. Long denied the charge vehemently and insisted he was not an anti-Semite. Given the times and Long's upbringing he probably believed he was being truthful. Morgenthau gave the assistant secretary a lecture that afternoon; then, over the holidays, he drew up a report accusing Long in particular and the State Department in general of "willful attempts to prevent action from being taken to rescue Jews from Hitler."

Roosevelt—already under pressure from activists' groups and mindful of the Jewish vote—created the War Refugee Board on January 22, six days after receiving a copy of the Morgenthau report.

In a radio talk in March 1944 Roosevelt addressed the Holocaust directly for the first time. "None who participate in these acts of savagery shall go unpunished," he said. "All who knowingly take part in the deportation of Jews to their death in Poland or Norwegians and French to their death in Germany are equally guilty with the executioner himself. Hitler is committing these crimes in the name of the German people." The speech was not well received at the War Department. It was the opinion of Secretary of War Henry Stimson, of Assistant Secretary of War John McCloy, of Dwight Eisenhower, and of most combat commanders that the most effective way to save lives was to brush aside all other priorities and put every available man and weapon into war until Germany and Japan broke.

When Morgenthau asked McCloy to make sure American commanders received a copy of Roosevelt's refugee order he complied but he was not happy about it. "Getting the army involved in this while the war was still on" was a mistake, he told Morgenthau. Born into a poor Philadelphia family, McCloy was something of a wunderkind. An Amherst and Harvard Law School graduate, like Stimson he served in France during the Great War and in 1940 left a lucrative New York law practice to become Stimson's second at the War Department. Morgenthau and McCloy's disagreement over the value of the War Refugee Board foreshadowed one of the sharpest debates of the war: how a defeated Germany should be treated. McCloy and Stimson favored a soft peace, Morgenthau a hard peace, and he based his case on *Military Government in Germany*, an army handbook he encountered during a visit to Britain and France in the summer of 1944. The handbook noted that on entering Germany "the main and immediate" task of the American soldier would be to ensure the country "worked efficiently." About Germany's war crimes the pamphlet had next to nothing to say. Morgenthau read that to mean that it was not a priority issue. During a talk with Eisenhower later in his visit Morgenthau was relieved to hear the supreme commander, who had German roots, take a hard line on German reconstruction. But when he asked John Winant, the American ambassador to Britain, about Roosevelt's plans for postwar Germany during a visit to London, Winant said he had no idea. Neither did anyone else.

In late August and early September Morgenthau, Hopkins, Hull, and Stimson met on several occasions to discuss the fate of postwar Germany, but opinions rarely changed from meeting to meeting. Morgenthau would describe some version of his vision for postwar Germany, which was draconian. "German schools, radio stations, universities, and periodicals closed. German aircraft, military uniforms, and bands forbidden and war criminals executed expeditiously. German militarism cannot be destroyed by destroying Nazism alone," Morgenthau insisted. Typically Stimson would counter with some version of one of his favorite phrases: "Christianity and Love," though not always. At a meeting on September 9 he became angry at Morgenthau and accused him of attempting to destroy German industry and executing war criminals without a trial. Hopkins, the third member of the German study group, sided with Morgenthau, a turnabout. Previously he and Morgenthau had vied with each other for Roosevelt's attention. Hull, the fourth member of the group, was ailing and had been snubbed so often he refused Roosevelt's invitation to accompany him to the Second Quebec Conference, which began on September 12. Morgenthau did accept Roosevelt's invitation, but a few days before departing for Quebec he told Hull, "The trouble is, Cordell, the president has never really given a directive of how he feels Germany should be treated."

THE EARLY AUTUMN MORNING THAT Roosevelt's train arrived at Wolf Cove Station, Quebec, the sun still had a quantum of summer warmth, and the trees bordering the station were a riot of rich, golden yellows and deep reds. Ten minutes after Roosevelt and his wife, Eleanor, arrived a second train pulled into the station. Clementine and Winston Churchill joined the Roosevelts in their car, and the foursome was whisked away to the Citadelle, where the Second Quebec Conference opened the following day. The war was in an active phase and the first few days were dominated by the military discussions. The American First Army had just crossed the German frontier west of Aachen, and the British were moving three divisions from northern Burma in preparation for Operation Dracula, an amphibious assault on Rangoon. However, on the thirteenth, Churchill and Roosevelt found time to meet with Morgenthau, who had come up to Quebec at Roosevelt's request.

The prime minister's first reaction to the plan Morgenthau described was dismay. "I'm all for disarming Germany," he said, "but we ought not prevent her from living decently," which Churchill defined as allowing the German workman to make a living, albeit a modest one, and sending the hard cases, the Gestapo and Hitler Youth types, to other European countries to rebuild the cities and towns they ravaged during the war. Churchill told Morgenthau his plan went too far. It would partition Germany into several states, internationalize the country's major centers of trade and industry, including Saarland and the Ruhr, and called for the dismantling or outright destruction of German heavy industries. "You cannot indict a whole nation," Churchill said. "The British people would never stand for it." Churchill's umbrage over Morgenthau's harshness was short-lived, however. According to Beschloss, the prime minister feared Roosevelt planned to use Morgenthau's plan as an excuse to reduce lend-lease aide to Britain. After all, if Britain had access to major European markets, including the German markets, why would it need to keep borrowing American money? When news of Morgenthau's visit to Quebec reached the War Department the next day Stimson was beside himself. "Here the President appoints a committee . . . and when he goes off to Quebec, he takes the man who really represents the minority and is so biased by his Semitic grievances that he really is a very dangerous adviser to the President." Fortunately, the next morning, Lord Cherwell, Churchhill's adviser and close friend, found a solution to a problem that was acquiring ugly racial and financial tones. For lack of a better term the solution might be called Morgenthau Lite. An international body would be created to oversee the Ruhr and make decisions about which parts should be transferred to other nations. The Ruhr would lose some of its machinery to other countries, but it would be left to the next two decades how and to what degree the German industry should be rebuilt.

The war was inflicting significant collateral damage on the Churchill-Roosevelt relationship, and by the Second Quebec Conference it was beginning to show. One afternoon, during a talk about lend-lease funding, for whatever reason, Roosevelt chose to humiliate Churchill, changing the subject every time Churchill brought up the subject of lend-lease. Finally, deeply chagrined, the prime minister said, "What do you want me to do? Get on my hind legs like Fala [Roosevelt's dog]?"

ON TUESDAY MORNING, STILL UNABLE to reach the president, Morgenthau asked his sometimes-rival Harry Hopkins to call Roosevelt on his behalf. The president took the call, but he refused Morgenthau's request to issue a statement, saying he would not make a final decision on the plan for postwar Germany until he consulted his secretaries of war, state, and the treasury. During a talk with Roosevelt a few days later, Stimson said the Morgenthau report had been leaked by its author—and, as evidence, he cited a recent Drew Pearson column that praised Morgenthau and excoriated Stimson and Hull.

Eager to bring the messy affair to a close before it became a campaign issue, Roosevelt told the press that his plan for Germany had been misunderstood. He had no intention of returning the entire German nation to a pastoral existence. That was a red herring. His real goal was to aid Britain. Without an influx of new customers, its industrial and financial centers would fall into bankruptcy and take the nation down with them. The closest the debate on the Morgenthau report came to an official end was an exchange between Stimson and Roosevelt on October 3. Stimson complained that a lot of the drama and backbiting of the past few weeks could have been avoided if the treasury secretary had provided him and McCloy with an early copy of *Military Government in Germany*. When Stimson finished, Roosevelt smiled and said, "Henry Morgenthau pulled a boner."

Beschloss, who has written the most definitive account of the debate over postwar Germany, says that it should not have required someone like Morgenthau to blow the whistle on the disgraceful State Department efforts to stop the rescue of Jewish refugees. Had Roosevelt been more on top of the issue and more insistent that his high officials shared his values, many of Hitler's victims might have been saved. But, Beschloss adds, these flaws should not be allowed "to overshadow the greatness in Roosevelt's leadership. . . . The President risked his career," campaigning for military preparedness and Britain in 1939 and 1940. Had he been meeker or more short-sighted Germany might have won World War II.

On September 27—two days after Roosevelt's speech at the Statler—Daisy Suckley wrote in her diary: "It is hard to talk about, and even harder to write about, but I am really frightened at his condition. He seems to me to be slowly failing." Early in the campaign the Republicans made a few attacks on Roosevelt's foreign policy, but foreign policy was a dangerous issue to politicize in the midst of war. The president's health was an easier target. In early October anonymous rumors began circulating about Roosevelt's dramatic loss of weight, his thinning hair, and his heavily furrowed face. The rumors led to speculation that Roosevelt had suffered a paralytic stroke, had cancer of the prostate, or had a mental breakdown and—the theory closest to the truth—that the president was suffering from some form of heart disease. When a nervy reporter asked the president, point-blank, if the rumors were true he snapped, "Don't get me commenting . . . because I might say things I'd be sorry for." As the election neared, Roosevelt's handlers concluded that "Don't get me started!" wouldn't do. To quash the health rumors, Roosevelt would have to demonstrate his vigor in a series of public appearances.

On October 21 a large black Packard was driven out into Ebbets Field in Brooklyn. Despite the steady drizzle, the Packard's canvas top was down, and a wet Roosevelt was sitting in the back seat, waving and smiling at the small crowd of people who had braved the rain to see what the president of the United States looked like in person. The Secret Service detail locked Roosevelt into his braces, then—one ten-pound weight at a time—he swung himself out the car and positioned himself in front of the crowd. As he began to speak, his blue-black navy cape slipped from his shoulders, exposing his head to the rain. Roosevelt confessed to his audience of outer-borough Dodger zealots that he had never seen their team play, but he assured them he had rooted for the Dodgers on a number of occasions.

Next he praised Robert Wagner, the Democratic senator from New York. "We were in the legislature together," he said, then smiled and added, "I would hate to think how long ago that was." By the time Roosevelt finished praising Wagner, who was also up for reelection in 1944, the drizzle had become a hard rain and there were still miles to go and hundreds of hands to shake. Visits to Queens, the Bronx, Harlem, midtown Manhattan, and downtown Broadway were all on the afternoon schedule. But before proceeding any farther the president was taken to a nearby Coast Guard station, where he was given a rubdown and dry clothes. Visiting Philadelphia a week later, Roosevelt mocked the prominent Republican orator who had described his administration as "the most spectacular collection of incompetent people who had ever held public office." Roosevelt said, of that description, "Well, if that's true, it's pretty seditious because the only conclusion to be drawn is that we are losing the war. If that is true it will be news to all of us—and it will certainly be news to the Nazis and the Japs."

The Dewey campaign faced a dilemma. The war years had brought prosperity to millions of people who had subsisted on dog food and stale bread during the Depression. So, after Dewey's few attempts failed to convince voters that the postwar years would bring a return of hard times, he returned, in the final months of the campaign, to the communist threat. He was careful to separate the communism of the Soviet Union, an honored ally, from the communism of Earl Browder, leader of the American Communist Party and draft dodger in World War I. A few days before the election Dewey told a crowd of Boston Republicans that "in this campaign the New Dealers attempt to smother discussion of their Communist Alliance. They smear any discussion of the major question of our day. They insinuate that Americans must like Communism or offend our fighting ally. Not even the gullible believe that. . . . In Russia," said Dewey, "a Communist is a man who supports his government. In America, a Communist is a man who supports a fourth term so our form of Government might be more easily changed."

Dewey had a gift for earnestness; Roosevelt, for sarcasm. During a speech in Boston a week later the president drew attention to the flaw in Dewey's thinking. According to historian James MacGregor Burns, Roosevelt told the audience that in the past few weeks "his opponent had accused New Dealers of fostering Communism and attempting to establish a Monarchy in the United States. 'Now which is it?' Roosevelt asked the laughing audience. 'It can't be both.'" Roosevelt's 1944 victory could not match his prewar victories, but it was still impressive: 432 electoral votes to Dewey's 99.

A December Gallup poll found the election had no effect on attitudes toward the Soviet Union. In July, 47 percent of the Americans who responded to the poll said yes when asked: "Do you think Russia can be trusted to cooperate with us after the war?" In December, when Gallup repeated the question, once again 47 percent of the respondents said yes while the number of Americans who disapproved of Russia dropped slightly. In July, 36 percent of the respondents viewed the Soviet Union

negatively; in December, 35 percent viewed it that way. The takeaway
from the mere one-point drop between the two polls was not that Americans were developing an affinity for the Soviet Union but that, other
than when asked by pollsters, they did not think much about Russia one
way or another.

MEANWHILE THERE WAS THE WAR.

In late August George Patton's Third Army made a five-hundred-mile
thrust across France in twenty-six days, Omar Bradley's Twelfth Army
Group was racing toward the Rhine, and General George Marshall was
surveying his commanders to see how many expected the war to be
over by Christmas. Then came Market Garden and the Scheldt. Harley
Reynolds, a sergeant in the 1st Division, was not surprised by the rapid
German recovery. In Normandy he had several firsthand encounters
with German resiliency. Now, two months later, he was hovering behind
a dragon's teeth tank obstacle on the outskirts of Aachen, an ancient
German city that enjoyed a number of distinctions.

Aachen had been home to Charlemagne a millennium and a half earlier. It was part of the Siegfried Line, the Germans' principal defensive
network in the west. And it was the first German city to face attack by
Allied ground forces. The day Reynolds's unit arrived in the city, buildings were exploding. Bricks were hurled across sidewalks and fifteen-
and sixteen-year-old German soldiers were throwing themselves on
American machine guns. The fighting would last until October 21 and
cost the American victors five thousand dead and wounded. But such
was the intensity of the fighting in the autumn of 1944.

Aachen was immediately overshadowed by the Battle of Hürtgen Forest. The forest was situated about a dozen or so miles to the southeast
of Aachen, and until recently it had been the province of hunters, farmers, and the occasional German soldier seeking solitude after Stalingrad
or Kursk. The decision to target the forest arose from the fear that the
Germans would take advantage of its density to launch flank attacks on
US units moving up to the Ruhr. This was unlikely, given the poor quality of the 275th—the German division guarding the forest—and hard
to justify, given sacrifices the American units would make upon entering the Hürtgen. These sacrifices included loss of reliable air cover in
the winter sky above the forest and vulnerability to hidden booby traps,
minefields, and barbed wire emplacements. After the war the military

historian Russell Weigley would say of the campaign: "The most likely way to make the Hürtgen Forest a menace to the American army was to send American troops charging into its depths." For Ernest Hemingway, who covered the Hürtgen campaign as a war correspondent, the experience was reminiscent of Passchendaele, one of the bloodiest campaigns of the Great War, except that this time, noted Hemingway, the artillery and machine-gun fire was accompanied by air bursts.

Casualty rates soared. By October 16 the US 9th Division had advanced two miles at the cost of 4,500 dead and wounded. The 18th Infantry, which arrived in the Hürtgen on November 8, suffered 500 casualties in five days. As winter drew in and the fighting intensified, life became cheap. "We are taking three trees a day," said one officer, "yet the cost to us was 100 men apiece. The shell bursts overhead, the cries of the wounded, the constant rat-tat-tat of machine gun fire, the frozen bodies, the stain of living with dead day and night: inevitably men began to break."

"Combat fatigue was one of the most important causes of non-effectiveness among combat troops," notes historian Max Hastings. Twenty-six percent of the men who served in combat formations in the European theater of operations between June and November 1944 were reported sick with what would now be called post-traumatic stress disorder. Carlo D'Este, another respected military historian, notes that by the winter of 1944 there were increasing signs of plummeting morale, manifested by the rapidly rising desertion rate, which became so serious, for the first time since the Civil War an American soldier was executed for desertion. The United States Navy and Army Air Corps were among the best units to fight in World War II, says Hastings. But two misjudgments that were made early in the war weakened the effectiveness of the army.

The first was the ninety-division limit, which made a number of battles, including Normandy, closer and costlier than they would have been had a larger ground force been fielded. On paper two million Americans served in combat roles in the European theater. In practice only a fraction of those two million men ever got up close with the enemy. In early 1945, when tens of thousands of Waffen-SS troops and members of the Einsatzgruppen (the Nazi death squads) were blowing up German factories and rail networks, there were only two hundred thousand American combat troops in all of northwest Europe. The army's second error was to make a high IQ score the ticket to a safe desk job. An officer sharp of mind and steady of nerve can often make the difference in combat situations, particularly in close combat, where life-and-death decisions have to be made within minutes and sometimes seconds. But in its wisdom the War Department chose to award high scorers with safe desk jobs. In one test it was found that 89 percent of the soldiers with high IQ scores were dispatched to the army's finance department or a similarly safe position. More often than not, when death was near and honor just a word, it was the low scorers who were called upon to give the last full measure in places like Anzio, Normandy, and the Hürtgen Forest.

21

APOCALYPSE

———

I N EARLY SEPTEMBER 1944 HITLER SUFFERED A RECURRENCE OF
the stomach cramps that had bedeviled him on and off for the past
several years. Whether the cramps were a by-product of the July 20 assassination attempt on his life, the crushing German defeat in Normandy,
or some combination of the two is unclear; but as the autumn days grew
brisker and the Russian juggernaut grew nearer to Germany the Führer's
behavior became a source of concern to his staff at the Wolf's Lair.

The public images of Hitler that adorned buildings and homes across
Germany were now two to three years out of date. The resolute leader
with the penetrating eyes vanished somewhere between Stalingrad and
Kursk, replaced by an ashen-faced recluse who roamed the window-
less walls of a concrete block, sixteen and a half feet thick, a gray flan-
nel dressing gown tucked under his old army shirt. When he tired of
walking, Hitler would lie in a bed set in between the walls. By November his stomach cramps had abated, but he was now having difficulty
swallowing. Hitler's doctors persuaded him to travel to Berlin for an
examination, which revealed a small nonmalignant polyp on his vocal
cords. The polyp was successfully removed, but his underlying condition remained unchanged. All who saw the Führer at the end of 1944

agreed that he had aged prematurely, says historian Alan Bullock. At fifty-five he had become an old man. His voice was hoarse; his complexion, ashen; his hands trembled; and he had difficulty walking. Only his iron will remained intact.

On August 31—in the midst of the German army's flight across France—Hitler summoned his senior commanders to the Wolf's Lair and told them that defeat would not be tolerated—nor, he insisted, was it inevitable. "The time will come when the tensions between the Allies [would grow] so great [that a] break will occur. All coalitions disintegrate sooner or later. The only thing is to wait for the right moment, no matter how hard it is." Then he concluded his talk with a Wagnerian flourish: "I live only for the purpose of leading this fight. Under all circumstances we will continue this battle until, as Frederick the Great said, 'one of our damned enemies gets too tired to fight anymore.'" Watch on the Rhine, the operation that would restore the Reich's fortunes, had echoes of the 1940 Battle of France. A German strike force of more than two hundred thousand men and a thousand tanks would sweep out of the Ardennes on a cold gray morning and, hidden by the snow and fog that kept the Allied air forces grounded, would fall upon an unprepared enemy. However, there were also significant differences between Hitler's 1940 and 1944 plans. The German army that conquered France in 1940 was only beginning to reach its potential. In 1944 a number of German panzer units still had daring young officers like the sleekly handsome twenty-nine-year-old Joachim Peiper, who had won Germany's highest decoration, the Knight's Cross of the Iron Cross. But there were not enough men like Peiper. The German army was overstaffed with sixteen-year-old boys and middle-aged men who lacked the weapons, the training, and the drive that their predecessors had displayed before they were summoned to Valhalla.

The German plan of attack was simple and audacious: an assault force would break out of the Ardennes, drive sixty miles to the northwest, recapture the port of Antwerp, and create such disorder that the war-weary publics in one or both Allied countries would demand a negotiated end to the war. It was a wild riverboat gamble, but Hitler enjoyed one important advantage. Like Stalin he was the state, and as such he could accept large losses with little fear of retribution from the German people.

Churchill and Roosevelt enjoyed no such advantage. If their publics demanded a settlement, they would have to respond in one form or another. The Americans, who were regarded as the weaker of the two Allied forces, would be the main target. On the eve of battle there were eighty-three thousand American troops in the Ardennes. Some, like the 4th and 28th Divisions, were veteran units badly mauled in the Hürtgen Forest and were in the Ardennes to rest and recuperate. Some, like the 106th and the 4th Armored, were new divisions, sent to the Ardennes for training. And some were a mixture of novice and experienced units. Two of the divisions in the latter category—the experienced 2nd and the inexperienced 99th Division—faced north, putting them directly in the path of the German attack.

In early December, with victory now a certainty, the chief priority for most GIs in the Ardennes was keeping warm. Those enterprising enough found shelter in abandoned German pillboxes or barns and outhouses. Others relied on an army greatcoat and a foxhole for warmth. In regions where the ground had frozen over, grenades and explosive charges were used to blast out foxholes. In early December reports began trickling into Allied intelligence about a German buildup in the Ardennes region, but they failed to raise alarms. On the night of December 15, as on the nights of the fourteenth and thirteenth, men played cards, told jokes, drank bootlegged whiskey, and fell asleep in their foxholes, gazing out at the snow-covered trees beneath the brilliant December moon.

December 16, the first day of battle, was a German triumph. Some American units offered fierce resistance, but the swiftness and power of the German assault left many of the weary veterans and nervous replacements dazed. By nightfall the American front had been breached. One entire division was surrounded, and the Germans had seized several key crossroads and bridges. The seventeenth was a day of rumors. One that spread panic had English-speaking Germans in US uniforms infiltrating behind American lines. Another had Belgian towns replacing their British and American flags with the Nazi flags with which they had greeted the Germans in 1940. The most harrowing event of the day was the massacre outside the Belgian town of Malmedy. On the afternoon of the seventeenth a group of American artillerymen and medics—estimated to number between 113 and 120 men—took a series of wrong turns in the Belgian countryside and stumbled into Kampfgruppe Peiper, a battle group of the 1st SS Panzer Division, named after its commander Joachim

Peiper. On another day Peiper, who had a mercurial temperament, might have sent the Americans to a POW camp. But on the seventeenth he was in a hurry. He had been given the honor of leading the attack toward the Meuse River, the first major target on the route to Antwerp, and delays earlier in the day had put Peiper and his 117 tanks, 149 troops, and his 40 antiaircraft guns twelve hours behind schedule.

After the war one of Peiper's subordinates, a former SS lieutenant named Werner Sternebeck, told a visiting American, Michael Reynolds, that shortly before Peiper arrived on scene that morning a group of American soldiers had surrendered after a brief firefight, and he was preparing to hand them over to a POW unit when Peiper arrived. Eager to make up for lost time Peiper ordered the Americans to be executed on the spot.

On the nineteenth, a bleak gray Tuesday, Eisenhower summoned Bradley, Patton, Courtney Hodges, and several other senior commanders to a meeting. The setting was the town of Verdun, its Great War scars protruding above the snow line outside the window. The subject was the stunning swiftness of the German advance, and the mood in the room was bleak. "I want only cheerful faces," Eisenhower told his guests, then briskly moved on to business.

George Patton, commander of the Third Army, had the best idea of the day. In the most elemental sense, he said, the Battle of the Bulge was a battle over fuel. If the fuel-short Germans seized the Belgian crossroads town of Bastogne the huge Allied fuel supplies hidden behind the lines would be at risk. But if the Americans held the town, within a week or two, the German fuel supply would be exhausted and Peiper and his panzer commanders would be walking back to the fatherland in the snow. Patton's idea had the brilliance of simplicity. His Third Army, currently pointing south, would swing north, drive on Bastogne, and reinforce the beleaguered American garrison that was defending the town. Eisenhower ended the meeting, as he began it, with an admonition: "Under no circumstance should the Wehrmacht be allowed past the Meuse River."

The next morning, when Brooke arrived at his office, there was a cable from Montgomery waiting for him. It read: "American front penetrated. . . . Germans driving on Namur [the town that strides the Meuse] with little in front of them. The Northern flank of American First Army in state of flux and disarray." Alarmed, Brooke arranged an afternoon meeting with Churchill, but upon arrival in the PM's office at 3:30 that afternoon he found Churchill "very much the worse for wear, having evidently consumed several glasses of brandy at lunch."

When Brooke got back to his desk he put in a call to Eisenhower. After explaining the gravity of the situation, he requested that Montgomery be given temporary command of the northern wedge of the Allied bulge. It was a big ask, given the current state of Anglo-American relations, but Eisenhower immediately gave his assent.

Further down the chain of command there was less enthusiasm for putting two American armies under British control. Courtney Hodges, commander of the First Army, and William Simpson, commander of the Ninth, made no secret of their displeasure at being put under British command, and General Omar Bradley, Ike's longtime friend, was indignant. The American soldier signed up to fight for the United States, Bradley said, adding that putting him under British officers would affect his morale.

The decision to give Montgomery a large role in what was an American battle could not have been easy for Eisenhower. Monty was difficult to work with and had more than his fair share of amour propre. "Given the circumstances," says British historian Max Hastings, "it would have been understandable if Eisenhower had felt unable to give Montgomery authority over US troops. Yet in this crisis he showed his statesmanship and was rewarded by a highly competent performance." Even senior American commanders—which was not a group with many Monty fans—were impressed by his skillful handling of the battle. Brigadier General William Harrison of the 30th Division came away from a meeting with Montgomery thinking, "Here is a guy who really knows what he is doing." But, as Hastings noted, Montgomery could never quite contain the little engine of his ambition. In the midst of the Ardennes battle he was plotting how to win back the position he had ceded to Eisenhower at the end of the Normandy campaign: commander of Allied ground forces.

Over the next few days there were dozens of small actions in little Belgian towns that no one had heard of before and would never hear of again after the war passed them by. One was the Belgian village of Saint Vith, which sits atop a small hill, had a population of 2,000 in the winter of 1944, and possessed characteristics that made it equally valuable to the Germans attacking the village and the Americans defending it. The most important was the town's proximity to the Belgian plain and the 2.5 million gallons of Allied fuel stored in the region.

The Belgians neutralized that threat by blowing up the fuel dumps, but Saint Vith's access to the Losheim Gap, the axis of the entire German offensive, still made the village an important target for both sides. In late December, in an epic eight-day battle in brutal cold and howling wind, units of the 7th Armored Division under Brigadier General Bruce Clarke held their positions in Saint Vith just long enough to hinder the Germans' access to the two things they needed to reach Antwerp on schedule: time and fuel.

ON THE AFTERNOON OF DECEMBER 19 Brigadier General Anthony McAuliffe was leaning against a staff car in the center of Bastogne, ruminating on the final order that General Troy Middleton, commander of the VIII Corps, had given him that morning: "Hold the Bastogne line at any cost." Sleekly built and strong-jawed, McAuliffe looked like the kind of handsome, upright American hero that John Wayne played in movies. McAuliffe was an artilleryman by training, and he would have remained an artilleryman had not General Matthew Ridgway, commander of the 101st Airborne, been in Washington and his deputy, General Gerald Higgins, in London on the sixteenth, the day the Germans launched Autumn Mist. But they were. And so the weight of holding Bastogne "at all costs," as Middleton put it, fell on the artilleryman. On the seventeenth the men of 101st left a rest camp in Reims and spent the next thirty-six hours driving through the French and Belgian countryside in ten-ton trucks that offered no protection from the cold or from the snow.

A half mile behind McAuliffe, Corporal Bill Bowser was seated in the next-to-last truck in the convoy, a blanket pressed against his body to ward off the cold. If McAuliffe was the idolized version of the American soldier Bowser was its antithesis. He stood five feet two inches in his stocking feet, looked like a bellhop in his dress uniform, and hailed from Punxsutawney, Pennsylvania, home of Punxsutawney Phil, the groundhog who predicted the arrival of spring every February. It was an association that the men in Bowser's company never let him forget, but the ribbing was good-natured. Like most of the men in the division Bowser had seen a good deal of combat in Normandy and again in Market Garden, but, like most of the other men who climbed out of the trucks that December morning, he was about to encounter war at a new level.

Bastogne was still relatively intact the morning the 101st arrived, but the residents were in the midst of an exodus. The snowdrifts were stained with the blood of recently put-down pets, and the roads beyond the town were filled with weeping children and panicked adults, unsure of where to go and what to do upon arriving. Watching the exodus from a half-track Dr. Jack Prior, a member of the 10th Armored Division's medical battalion, wondered how the scene would affect the morale of the troops leaping off the trucks. The 101st was an elite unit, but the men had been on the road for a day and a half in open trucks, and such was the chaos of the Reims departure that some men arrived in Bastogne without weapons, others without winter clothing, and some men without either.

The units falling back on the city from outposts on the perimeter provided a ready source of weapons, but the thousand-yard stare on many of their faces was a reminder to the veterans leaping from the trucks that they were about to dance with the devil again. The first serious fighting began a few hours later—ten miles to the northeast of Bastogne, in the town of Noville. That morning Major William Desobry, of the 10th Armored Division, arrived in Noville with fifteen Sherman tanks and orders to hold the town at all cost. The order was rescinded in late afternoon, and the defenders were ordered to fall back on Bastogne, but by that time most of Desobry's tanks had been reduced to smoking hulks and half of the men in his command were wounded—some lightly; others, including Desobry, seriously.

When Dr. Prior, who had come up to Noville that morning, announced that he planned to stay with the wounded no matter what—and when he asked for volunteers to stay with him—there was silence in the tavern in which the survivors of the morning fighting had congregated. Then Prior's first sergeant leaped to his feet, ran into the street, and ordered what was left of Desobry's tank force to swing by the aid station. The tankers ran into the building, ripped the doors from the walls, strapped the wounded to them, and placed the doors on their tanks. A half hour later Prior was back in the half-track, accompanying the wounded to Bastogne when a squadron of King Tiger tanks emerged out of the late-afternoon fog and incinerated the overmatched Sherman tanks accompanying the wounded and then drove slowly along the road, machine gunning the infantry units that had taken cover in the snow. Prior spent the three hours it took for reinforcements to arrive sitting in a ditch, listening to a dentist-turned-soldier enumerate all the reasons why it was suicidal to wear a helmet with a red cross on it.

Prior refused to be persuaded. Over the next few days the Germans divided their forces. Panzer Lehr Division and other units of General Heinrich von Lüttwitz's XLVII Panzer Corps would keep Bastogne surrounded. The rest of the strike force would continue the drive on the Meuse and Antwerp. On the afternoon of the twenty-second a German major, a German captain, and two German enlisted men arrived in Bastogne carrying a white flag, and rumors quickly began to spread through the town. The one that reached Bill Bowser's ears had the Germans demanding an unconditional American surrender. Bowser was so insulted by the Germans' audacity that he did something he rarely did anymore—he shaved so that he would look properly martial when he encountered the Germans again.

The German major who offered the terms told McAuliffe that he represented General Lüttwitz and that the general had instructed him to offer McAuliffe two options: surrender or obliteration. The major gave McAuliffe two hours to make up his mind. In the American version of the story McAuliffe famously says "Nuts!" to the German major, and he did indeed say it, but that was not what the major heard. Having no idea what "Nuts!" meant, the major's interpreter told him that McAuliffe had told him to "go to hell." A few days later fortune deserted Bill Bowser, and he was badly wounded in a firefight.

While recuperating Bowser encountered a sight that said something about the intensity of the fighting around Bastogne: the padre who visited him had a pistol strapped to his shoulder holster.

On December 23, after a week of snow and clouds, the sky above Bastogne cleared and an armada of C-47s appeared overhead—and hundreds of parachutes fluttered to the ground in an array of different colors, each denoting the cargo the plane was carrying: medical supplies, ammunition, and food.

On December 24—a day of unusually heavy shelling—General McAuliffe sent his men a Christmas message: "What's merry about this Christmas? We are cold and hungry and not at home, but we have stopped four Panzer divisions, two infantry divisions, and one airborne division, and we have given our loved ones at home a merry Christmas—and have [had] the privilege to take part in this gallant feat of arms."

Dr. Prior spent Christmas Eve in his quarters next to the Bastogne hospital, writing too-difficult letters. One was to the wife of a young lieutenant who had left half his chest in a snowbank a few hours earlier and was unlikely to see Christmas morning. The other letter was even harder to write—being more personal:

> I am recommending a commendation for Renée Lemaire. This young woman, a registered nurse in the country of Belgium, volunteered her services at the aid station, the 20th Armored Infantry Battalion in Bastogne Belgium 21 December 1944. At this time the station was holding about 150 patients, since the city was surrounded by enemy forces and evacuation impossible. Many of these patients were seriously injured and in immediate need of nursing attention. This young woman cheerfully accepted the Herculean task and worked without adequate rest or food. . . . She changed dressings, fed patients unable to feed themselves, gave out medications. . . . Her very presence among those wounded men seemed to be an inspiration to those whose morale had declined from prolonged suffering. On the night of December 24 the building in which Renée Lemaire was working scored a direct hit by an enemy bomber. She, along with those she was caring for so diligently, [was] instantly killed. It is on these grounds I recommend the highest award possible to one who, though not a member of the Armed Forces of the United States, was of invaluable assistance to us.

The Luftwaffe had become a rare sight in the European sky by December 1944, but shortly after Prior finished his letter of commendation for Renée Lemaire a German plane dropped a bomb on Prior's quarters and for a moment his dingy, disordered rooms turned a brilliant white. He survived the blast and was on hand two days later when the lead elements of George Patton's Third Army reached Bastogne and broke the siege. It would take until the end of January to reclaim the Allied territory lost during the battle; but the Americans' defense of Bastogne and several other key strongpoints effectively ended any hopes the Germans still harbored of reaching the Meuse.

The American victory also had a subsidiary effect. It ended Montgomery's hopes of reclaiming the mantle of Allied field commander. Eisenhower's promotion to the position at the end of the Normandy campaign had not sat well with the British. Churchill, Brooke, and other leading British politicians and senior officers admired Eisenhower's skills as a diplomat and organizer but found him wanting as a strategic thinker.

His Broad Front plan—the march of the Americans, British, and Canadians across western Europe more or less in step—seemed unimaginative and, to Eisenhower's British critics, likely to prolong the war.

When the Germans came pouring out of the Ardennes in the early morning of December 16 Montgomery got his chance. And, as noted earlier, his performance in the first days of the fighting was admirable. He transferred a British airborne division to Eisenhower, and when the US First Army—which was led by Courtney Hodges, a general not noted for his strategic skill—came under threat Montgomery transferred the First to a British commander. But he did so in a manner one journalist likened to "Christ coming to cleanse the temple." As rumors began to spread that the field marshal had saved the situation, Montgomery ignored the advice of his chief of staff Major General Francis de Guingand and held a press conference in which he was generous in his praise of American arms; but his tone was that of headmaster soothing an earnest but not particularly bright pupil. A few days later an irate Omar Bradley, commander of the Twelfth Army Group, called a press conference of his own. Bradley had a number of things to say, the most notable being that Montgomery's command of First Army was temporary and the unit would soon be returned to American control. The British press countered by suggesting that the American response to Autumn Mist had lacked the Montgomery touch, and Bradley countered by saying he would resign rather than serve under Montgomery.

Patton said he would support Bradley. By this point Churchill was deeply embarrassed, and, in an effort to make amends, he offered a handsome tribute to American arms in a speech to Parliament. However, the source of all the disorder and chaos, Montgomery's wish to be reinstated as Allied ground commander, remained unaddressed for a while. On the next-to-last day of 1944 Bedell Smith, Eisenhower's chief of staff, and Major General J. F. M. Whiteley, the British deputy G-3 at SHAEF, summoned General de Guingand to a meeting and told him there would be no changes in the current command structure. Eisenhower would remain ground commander.

22

HAVE YOURSELF
A MERRY LITTLE CHRISTMAS

———————

IT WOULD BE MONTHS BEFORE THE COUNTRY LEARNED THE COST
of the Ardennes victory: nineteen thousand Americans dead and
twenty-three thousand captured or missing in action. The battle also
took a toll on the commander in chief. By late 1944 Roosevelt had
grown so frail that Dr. Bruenn, his cardiologist, instituted a triage system. Visitors with "essential business," such as Stimson and Marshall,
were usually given immediate access to the Oval Office. Visitors whom
Bruenn deemed "non-essential" had much more restricted access.

Among the people Bruenn put in the latter category was the president's wife, Eleanor. Mrs. Roosevelt was such an ardent advocate of
the causes she championed that, it was reported, "on several occasions
Bruenn had had to ask her not to upset her husband with complaints
about State Department appointments and anti-Communist conser-
vatives." How Roosevelt felt about his condition is impossible to say.
Occasionally he made references that suggested he knew his time was
limited. Yet he continued to carry on as usual. He spent Christmas Eve
of 1944, as he had every wartime Christmas except 1942, at his home
in Hyde Park surrounded by his children and grandchildren. That afternoon a group of soundmen nimbly navigated around the big Christmas

tree in the Roosevelts' living room and set up the feed for the president's Christmas Eve address to the nation.

The speech was somber yet hopeful. Roosevelt spoke of the heroism of the men who were fighting in Bastogne, Saint Vith, the Philippines, Italy, in the skies over Berlin, and in dozens of other battlefields in between on this somber night before Christmas. They are "the pride of our nation," he said. He told his listeners, "Our debt to them is beyond words." After the soundmen left, Elliott Roosevelt, who was on Christmas leave, removed a copy of Charles Dickens's *A Christmas Carol* from a shelf and handed it to his father. Over the years it had become a ritual for the president to gather the family around the Christmas tree and read a passage from *A Christmas Carol*, but on this Christmas Eve the ritual was disrupted by his three-year-old grandson, who, on noticing a gap in one of his grandfather's lower teeth, exclaimed "Grandpa! You've lost a tooth!" The president smiled and continued reading until his grandson asked if he had swallowed the tooth. Roosevelt closed the book and declared that there was too much "competition in this family for reading."

"Next year," said Elliott's wife, Faye Emerson, "it will be a peacetime Christmas."

"Next year," added Eleanor, "we'll all be home again."

However, yet to be decided was the kind of postwar world that America's twelve million soldiers, sailors, and marines would come home to. At the beginning of 1945 Republican and Democratic leaders were at odds on the question, and America's military leaders had their own ideas about how to fashion the country's postwar future. Traditionally Roosevelt's way of dealing with discussions of the future was to avoid them—and, if that proved impossible, to make the new world aborning sound like a Disney movie. Perhaps because he sensed a growing public interest in the country now that the war was coming to an end, he was unusually candid in the State of the Union message he sent to Congress on January 6. He began with the usual bromides about love and laughter and peace ever after, then he became relatively forthright. He spoke of the "complexities of international relations," of the dangers that would accrue should one nation "assume it had a monopoly on wisdom or virtue." He warned that the current disorder in Greece, which was in the midst of a civil war, and in Poland, which was being swallowed up by

Russia, did not lend themselves to easy solutions. "The Atlantic Charter must be our lodestar," he said. "But it cannot resolve all the problems in our war-torn" world now or for a good many years to come. "Nonetheless," he said in conclusion, new international organizations such as the United Nations must be seeded and allowed to grow because "only through institutions capable of life and growth can we move forward into a better world."

One of Roosevelt's sometime allies, Arthur Vandenberg, the Republican senator from Michigan, was unhappy with the president's vision of a postwar world. One of the most influential figures in Congress, Vandenberg, the ranking member on the Senate Foreign Relations Committee, entered Congress an isolationist but, as the war progressed, so had Vandenberg's views.

Now, more often than not, he voted with the internationalist wing of the Republican Party. The distinguishing feature of the internationalists was the belief that a lasting peace could only be created in a world based on American values and American virtues. Americans who were old enough to remember the Great War had heard that argument before. In 1919 President Woodrow Wilson had proposed just such a program at the Paris Peace Conference. The ridicule and abuse that Henry Cabot Lodge, the most powerful Republican of the era, and his isolationists heaped upon Wilson upon Wilson's return to Washington was so punishing that it may have played a role in the stroke the president suffered while traveling the country to promote America's entry into the League of Nations. Vandenberg's response to Roosevelt's State of the Union address on January 10, 1945, would have warmed Wilson's heart. "I know of no reason why we should not stand by our ideals, our dedication, our commitments," he said in a speech. "The first thing we must do is to reassert, in high places, our American faith in these . . . objectives of the Atlantic Charter." The speech was praised by several right-leaning press barons, including Colonel Robert McCormick of the *Chicago Tribune*, who had spent most of the interwar years promoting isolationism.

Another bellwether of changing times was the February 5, 1945, edition of *Time* magazine. Two years earlier the magazine had done a flattering cover story on "Uncle Joe." Now it was warning its readers that if Roosevelt and Churchill failed to persuade Stalin to accept a united peace the Allies' united victory would dissolve into a defeat.

Another sign that a new world was aborning was the new interest American liberals were taking in realpolitik. Vera Micheles Dean, director of research at the Foreign Policy Association, one of the most influential think tanks of the 1940s, was a leading spokesperson for this new brand of two-fisted liberalism. In an article in the *New Republic* she urged her fellow liberals to put away their childish ideas about a world government:

> Our tendency to admonish Britain and, to a lesser degree, Russia in lofty tones is due to the belief that the United States alone is guided by idealistic considerations, as contrast with the sordid motives of other countries. . . . This aspiration toward an ideal settlement of international problems is responsible for the current [concern] over the prospect that the Atlantic Charter may not be applied in Poland and Greece. But our tendency to demand perfect solutions of international problems constitutes a real threat to postwar stability. What troubles our conscience is that Britain and Russia are resorting to what we call. . . . power politics, but, as an English paper put it; do we want powerless politics? Any nation or institution which seeks to achieve political ends is always using some form of political power. . . . We can question the ends Britain or Russia are seeking . . . but we would find it much easier to deal with other nations if we stopped taking a holier-than-thou attitude.

Most American military and civilian leaders believed that Russia would emerge from the war as a superpower—the master of a domain that stretched from the forests of the Polish border to the beaches of Vladivostok on the Pacific coast. But the American military and diplomatic communities were at odds about how to respond to Russia's rise as a hegemon. One school of thought, led by Averell Harriman, the American ambassador, and General John Deane, the head of the American military mission to the Soviet Union, viewed the United States' present relationship with the Soviet Union as too one-sided. "We give and they take," Deane complained to Washington. "We must be tougher if we are to gain their respect and be able to work with them in the future." At the same time, Deane made clear the tough-love policy he and Harriman favored was not intended to challenge Russia's rise as hegemon but, rather, to make the Soviet-American relationship more equitable and more two-sided. "We have few conflicting issues with Russia," Deane noted, "so there is little reason why we should not be friendly now and in the foreseeable future."

James Forrestal, who became secretary of the navy in May 1944, had a more hawkish view of Russia. The offspring of an immigrant Irish Catholic family, Forrestal was Horatio Alger come to life. He grew up poor in upstate New York, attended Princeton University, where he was voted Most Likely to Succeed, served in World War I as a navy pilot, made a fortune on Wall Street, dabbled in Democratic politics, and had a chameleonlike personality. Colleagues and friends described him as alternately pugnacious, shy, compulsive, and as a workaholic. Introspective and solitary, Forrestal was also reflexively anti-communist, and that impulse of his would one day make him a founding father of the national security state.

Unlike Harriman and Deane, Forrestal viewed Russia as a hegemonic power by nature. After Stalin retrieved the territory lost to Germany, Forrestal expected Stalin to seek new conquests, most likely in Asia but also perhaps in South America as well. In early September 1944 Forrestal wondered out loud why it was that "whenever an American suggests we act in accordance with the needs of our own security, he is apt to be labeled a God-damned fascist or imperialist, while if Uncle Joe suggests that he needs the Baltic provinces, half of Poland, Bessarabia, and access to the Mediterranean, all hands agree that he is a fine, frank, candid, and thoroughly delightful fellow because he is explicit in what he wants."

By the end of September Forrestal had traded his sarcasm for a bullhorn. Russia, he warned, was "the emerging enemy toward which not only naval planning but, indeed, the whole of postwar US foreign and national security policy should be directed." If, as some of his colleagues suspected, Forrestal was exaggerating the Russian threat to extend his power and also the Pentagon's postwar military budget—then, to a degree, the plan worked. On December 26 the postwar naval planning section presented Forrestal with a late Christmas present, an assessment of America's postwar future. The focus of the paper was the importance of naval power in the postwar world, but the planners began by describing what they thought that world would look like.

Their conclusions read like a first draft of George Orwell's *1984*. They envisioned a breakdown of the world order in the years after the war, and the creation of a new revolutionary era. Fascism would not disappear entirely, but the most prominent feature of the new order would be the clash between capitalism and socialism, and that clash would be accompanied by social unrest, revolution, civil wars, trade wars, and clashes over markets; and over natural resources and radical shifts in the balance of world power. It would be a world of cartels, monopolies, subsidies, quotas, and state control of international trade and finance.

Though the United States would emerge from the war as the wealthiest and most powerful nation on earth, its wealth and capitalist economy were likely to incite what one observer called "envy, animosity and fear" and leave America politically and economically isolated.

The planners also warned that a war with Russia, the paladin of the new socialist world order, could not be ruled out. The Soviet Union would emerge from the war as the second-most powerful nation in the world—and given the size of its population and the strength of its military, it also possessed the potential to challenge the Unites States for the top spot. A member of the army's Strategy & Policy Group suggested that Stalin's ultimate goal was to create a Monroe Doctrine for Eurasia, and he warned that allowing Stalin to do so would challenge the most fundamental Anglo-American goal: to prevent the Soviet Union from dominating the resources and manpower of Europe and Asia.

The famous "Long Telegram" that George Kennan, the American chargé d'affaires in Moscow, sent Washington in February 1946 would echo some of the planners' concerns. But at the beginning of 1945, with the Battle of the Bulge still raging and Stalin promising an offensive to relieve pressure on the American forces in the Ardennes, the Joint Chiefs of Staff were eager to avoid a clash with their Russian counterparts. In December, when rumors circulated that the staff school at Fort Leavenworth had become a hotbed of anti-Soviet feeling, Stimson sent an aide to Fort Leavenworth with orders to instruct the school's commandant to "investigate the report and take steps to halt these activities." Two months later, and still concerned about alienating the Soviets, Stimson considered creating a screening program to ensure anti-Soviet officers were kept out of joint US-Soviet military programs.

ON CHRISTMAS EVE 1944 A German staff car arrived at a bunker in Adlerhorst, a bunker complex hidden in deep forests to the north of Frankfurt. During the Battle of France Hitler had used the complex as a command post, but until the beginning of Autumn Mist he rarely paid a visit to it. The Führer regarded himself as a man of the people, and the imposing halls and lush drawing rooms that were left behind by its previous owner, Emma von Scheitlin, a glamorous Austrian aristocrat, were not in keeping with his view of himself. The staff car stopped in front of cabin number one, Hitler's residence, and Heinz Guderian, the acting German chief of staff, stepped out into the snow. The *acting* in his title said a great deal about Guderian's relationship with the Führer. Other German commanders would disagree with Hitler, but, on being overruled, they would accede to his wishes.

Guderian, who had the rough-hewn face of a fighting soldier and a sharp temper, did dare to press—and he paid the price for it on several occasions. Hitler sacked him in 1941 after a disagreement over Operation Barbarossa. Hitler recalled him in 1943 and sacked him *again* when Guderian expressed doubts about Operation Citadel, the Kursk offensive. There was another falling out in October 1944, when Guderian objected to the Führer's plan to move the 2nd Panzer from Poland, which was under Russian assault, to Hungary to capture the Hungarian oil fields.

On his Christmas Eve visit Guderian reached a new level of frankness. He told Hitler flatly that Autumn Mist should be shut down immediately and all available troops should be moved to the eastern front. Predictably Hitler lost his temper. "Who's responsible for producing this rubbish?" he shouted. "It's the greatest imposter since Genghis Khan!" In point of fact, "greatest *failure*" would have been closer to the truth, because Autumn Mist cost Germany 600 tanks, 1,600 aircraft, and 100,000 dead and wounded.

On January 8 Army Group Center warned Berlin that the Red Army was now strong enough to cover the 155-mile distance between the Vistula River in Poland and the German province of Silesia—in six days. That may have been an understatement.

On January 12, more than two million Russian troops, roughly a dozen times the size of the Allied force that landed in Normandy on D-Day, swept across a four-hundred-mile front supported by thousands of heavy artillery pieces and assault guns, IS (Iosef Stalin) heavy tanks, T-34 medium tanks, aircraft, and Katyusha rockets. In the north, the 3rd White Russian Front (a Russian front was the equivalent of American army group) drove toward East Prussia, the spiritual home of the German military class since the Middle Ages.

To the left of the 3rd, the 2nd White Russian Front was driving on the Polish city of Danzig, where the war began in September 1939. Farther to the left was the 1st Belorussian Front, led by Marshal Georgy Zhukov, Russia's most renowned commander, and to Zhukov's left, at the far end of the flank, was Marshal Ivan Konev's 1st Ukrainian Front.

In early January Propaganda Minister Goebbels assured the German people that the army had checked the Soviet advance in its tracks. In East Prussia the announcement was greeted with bitter sarcasm. Between January 12 and mid-February 8.5 million people—most of them women, children, or the elderly—fled west across the deep winter snows in uncovered wagons and carts in temperatures that fell to minus-twenty degrees Celsius at night. Horses collapsed and were shot for their meat. Women and children fell through cracks in the ice and drowned. Russian fighters dropped out of the sky at first light and swept across the refugee encampments, leaving behind upturned carts, broken toys, abandoned luggage, and frozen bodies, which the living laid out neatly in open wagons under a dirty blanket or a thin layer of frozen straw.

In mid-January, when the Red Army arrived in force and the mass rapes began, the Russian novelist Aleksandr Solzhenitsyn, who was a captain in the Red Army, described the scenes he had witnessed in a poem called "Prussian Nights":

> *The little daughters on the mattress*
> *Dead, how many have been on it.*
> *A Platoon, a Company perhaps*
> *A girl's been turned into a woman.*
> *A woman turned into a corpse*
> *It's all come down to simple phrases*
> *Do not forget, Do not forgive!*
> *Blood for Blood, a Tooth for a Tooth!*

"There is no doubt," says historian Catherine Merridale, that the actions of the Red Army soldiers

> were encouraged, if not orchestrated by Moscow. Propaganda played an active part in shaping the perceptions of the enemy and justifying vengeance. The Soviet Information Bureau stoked the collective rage of the soldiers with manufactured images that [cut so deeply] into a man's mind [that] he could think of them as part of his own experience. . . . The universality of the men's own tales is evidence of this. . . . Again and again in German recollections of what the Russian occupiers told them, the vengeful memory summoned was not a parallel violation of a German raping a Russian woman, but horror of a different order. . . . The image of a German soldier swinging a baby torn from its mother's arms against a wall—the mother screams, the baby's brain splatters on the wall, and the soldier laughs.

Life in Berlin also became unbearable during that final winter of the war. The favorite joke of the 1944/45 holiday season was: "Be practical, give a coffin." And the Berlin Zoo bunker—a vast, concrete forest that served as both an embodiment of the totalitarian state and as an air-raid shelter—became a meeting place for sexual encounters. During Allied bombing raids random strangers would gather under the spiral staircases of the bunker and fornicate. It was rumored that some of the visitors were fourteen- and fifteen-year-old girls eager to lose their virginity before the Red Army arrived.

Like its counterparts in other parts of the capital the zoo bunker was perpetually overcrowded in the winter of 1945. People pushed into the bunker bundled in their warmest clothes and carrying small cardboard suitcases filled with sandwiches and thermoses. The luminous paint on the bunker ceilings provided light when an Allied air raid knocked out the electrical system, but as yet no one had discovered a quick way to repair a bomb-damaged water system. As a result, when a shell exploded, toilets flooded over and the stench of human waste and human remains seeped into every ventricle of the bunker.

"*Bleib Übrig!*"—meaning: "Survive!"—Berliners told each other. In the main Berliners had a lower opinion of Hitler than their countrymen in other parts of the country did. When Lothar Loewe, a Hitler Youth member, returned to Berlin in December 1944 after a several-month absence he was surprised at how many unfriendly stares he received when he gave the Nazi salute upon entering a department store. In parts of the country where national socialism remained popular, people continued to believe in miracles. Just before Christmas 1944 a German woman wrote to her husband, a prisoner in a French POW camp: "I have such faith in our destiny! Nothing can shake a confidence which is born from our long history, from our glorious past, as Dr. Goebbels said. We have reached a very low point at this moment, but we have men who are decisive. The whole country is ready to march, weapons at hand." It was to Germans like that woman that Hitler devoted his 1945 New Year's Day speech:

> German *Volk*! National Socialists! My Comrades! . . . I want to assure you again just as during our struggle for power, [that] my belief in the future of our Volk is unshaken. One has received the highest calling when Providence lays before one such difficult trials. Therefore, I alone must make every effort to lead the German *Volk* through these hard times and open the door to the future for which we all work and fight. I cannot finish this appeal without thanking almighty God for all the help he has given to the *Volk*. . . . I thank God for my own salvation only because I am able to offer up my life for the service of my *Volk*.

23

YALTA: THE GRAND
ALLIANCE AT HIGH TIDE

A LITTLE AFTER 9:00 A.M. ON THE MORNING OF FEBRUARY 2 THE
cruiser *Quincy* sailed past a half-sunken merchantman and
entered Malta's harbor. It was a raw, windy morning, but the president
had ordered an aide to wrap him in a heavy blanket and wheel him
out on to the deck. Malta was no longer on the front line, but its pockmarked little squares were a reminder of the "locust years"—1941 and
1942—when the Luftwaffe and the Regia Aeronautica paid daily visits
and when the British Eighth Army seemed one defeat away from oblivion. At around 9:30, the HMS *Orion* emerged out of a fog, and as that
big ship passed the *Quincy* Churchill appeared on its deck and waved to
the president, who waved back.

With the German war drawing to a close Allied civilian and military
leaders had assembled in Malta to discuss the endgame and to prepare
for the conference with Stalin, which would follow the Malta meeting.
Later that afternoon Churchill cabled his wife, Clementine: "My friend
has arrived in the best of health and spirits." That was a white lie; a few
days later the prime minister was full of trepidation when a frail-looking
Roosevelt, bundled in a blanket, was lowered on to the ground from his
plane at the Sochi airport in the Crimea. For the past year the president

had looked unwell. Now he looked like a man approaching the final stage of life. "He is frail and ill," Churchill cautioned the two young men who were charged with the president's safety. Several members of the British delegation were also struck by Roosevelt's appearance. Anthony Eden thought Roosevelt had aged years in the six months since their meeting at the Second Quebec Conference. Marian Holmes, Churchill's secretary, was also shocked. "What a change in the President, since we saw him in Hyde Park last October," she said. "He seems to have lost so much weight; [he] has dark circles under his eyes, and looks altogether as if he is hardly in this world at all."

Averell Harriman, who visited Roosevelt in Washington after the 1944 election and saw him again at Yalta, was "terribly shocked" at how much Roosevelt had deteriorated in the two and a half months in between. "I fear his last election campaign took a lot out of him," Harriman said later. "He didn't get up as much in the morning. He seemed to tire when a conversation went on too long. I used to say Roosevelt had a Dutch Jaw, and when that Dutch Jaw was set you couldn't move him. At Yalta I believe he didn't have the strength to be quite as stubborn as he liked to be."

A little after noon on February 3 the president's plane, the Sacred Cow, swept out of the winter sky, bumped across a short concrete runway, and landed at the Sochi airport. Overhead the president's escort, a flight of P-38s, dipped their wings in a salute and vanished back into the sky. Upon Churchill's arrival twenty minutes later the two leaders inspected the Soviet honor guard—the president from the back seat of a lend-lease jeep, and Churchill on foot, panting to keep up. The honor guard was replaced by a gaggle of smiling Soviet dignitaries who had come to the airport to greet their Western guests. Then a Red Army band closed the proceedings with renditions of "The Star-Spangled Banner," "God Save the Queen," and "The Internationale." On the drive down to Yalta later in the day the members of the Roosevelt party were surprised to see Soviet soldiers—many, stocky young women—positioned at intervals along the roads.

For a moment the pomp and circumstance made it almost possible to imagine oneself back in czarist Russia. The visitors smiled and waved as they passed the young guards in their handsome bemedaled uniforms, but deeper into the journey the landscape changed and the visitors found themselves surrounded by the fierce energy of death. There was no animal or human life visible—just naked trees, wet from the light rain, and mile upon mile of pockmarked terrain and ruins. The only reminders of the region's previous existence as a human habitat were the upturned tanks and staff cars, body parts, and the occasional letter trapped in a tree branch or under a rock—but the letters were so wrinkled and disordered by the elements, it was impossible to identify the sender.

THE LIVADIA PALACE, THE SITE of the Yalta meeting, began its life as a wedding present. In 1861 Czar Alexander gifted the palace to his new wife Alexandra Feodorovna. Two czars later, Alexander's grandson Nicholas, the last Romanoff czar, had the palace redone in white Inkerman granite at a cost of four million golden rubles, a fortune at the time. Livadia's other advantage as a meeting place included its size (it had fifty rooms) and beauty—the palace stood 150 feet above sea level and offered commanding views of the sea and mountains to the north and east—and it was surrounded by lush parks and gardens.

Concerned about Roosevelt's physical fragility Stalin, whose admiration for Roosevelt was genuine, made sure he received the best of everything, including a spacious three-room suite and access to the only private bathroom in the palace. However, even the leader of the Union of Soviet Socialist Republics was powerless to do anything about the bedbugs, which prowled the palace in the thousands, oblivious to their victims' rank and station—generals were bitten as frequently as housemaids.

The Yalta Conference was a number of things, but first and foremost, it was a test. Despite frequent disagreements over lend-lease aid, over the fate of Poland, and over the second front, the necessities of war had kept America, Britain, and the Soviet Union bound to one another through four years of war. Now, with the end in sight, the great question was: Would the bonds grow and strengthen in the postwar years? Or would they break—and usher in a new era of power politics?

The long-standing hostility between Russia and the West that existed before the war—and the long-standing expressions of anti-communism in Britain and in America—would make progress difficult. In 1945, as in 1935, Stalin and his foreign minister, Molotov, were convinced that, at heart, the British and Americans were anti-Soviet imperialists intent on defeating communism; the presence of Edward Stettinius, who had recently replaced Cordell Hull as secretary of state, could only have fed Soviet suspicions.

Stettinius's gleaming teeth were as eye-popping as his predecessor Joe Davies's; he had held senior positions at General Motors and US Steel, and he was the living embodiment of capitalism, decked out in his smartly tailored $500 suits. During a talk with Milovan Djilas, the leader of the Yugoslav Communist Party, in the summer of 1944 Stalin said, "Perhaps you think that just because we are allies of the English we have forgotten who they are and who Churchill is. They find nothing sweeter than to trick their allies." Alex Cadogan, the permanent under secretary at the Foreign Office and an anti-Semite, also harbored a deep distrust of the Russians, who he seemed to believe were all Jewish. "They are the most stinking creepy set of Jews I've ever come across," he wrote in his diary. However, with a few exceptions, the conference delegates kept their ugly thoughts to themselves.

At Stalin's request, Roosevelt agreed to chair the first plenary sessions of the conference, and, perhaps because it was just more convenient, on the day of the first session—February 4—the president slipped into the palace ballroom, where the talks would be held early, so the transfer from wheelchair to conference chair could be conducted in private. When the other delegates arrived, Roosevelt offered a few words of welcome, then seemed to slip into himself. One guest described him as sitting in his chair, his mouth open and looking "woolier than ever."

The plenary sessions had different themes. On the first evening the subject was the war. General Aleksei Antonov, deputy chief of the Soviet General Staff, opened the proceedings with a detailed description of the four-pronged assault the Red Army launched in early January. Antonov noted that the assault had been a great success—some advance Red Army units were now within fifty miles of Berlin. Antonov also noted that the Red Army began the offensive earlier than planned and in terrible weather, to relieve pressure on the American units caught fighting in the Ardennes.

After Antonov finished, the principals began to talk among themselves. Stalin opened the conversation by noting that the Red Army had attained a two-to-one superiority in the field: 180 Russian divisions to the Germans' 80 divisions. Then he asked Churchill about the situation in the west. The prime minister said that in neither Italy nor France did the Anglo-American force enjoy a large advantage.

At this point Marshall interrupted with some numbers. Currently, he said, Germany had 79 divisions in the west; the Anglo-Americans, one division fewer: 78. Churchill noted that the Western allies enjoyed an overwhelming superiority in tanks, in planes, in oil, in spare parts, and in other sinews of war. Four years into the war, the effects of the 90-division decision were still being felt. Stalin asked Churchill what he and Roosevelt wished him to do. "Put very shortly," Churchill replied, "we would like a continuance of the Russian offensive." Stalin said he considered it his "moral duty" to honor the request. Barring weather difficulties the Russian drive would continue through March. At a dinner party later that evening Stalin was less accommodating. He refused to toast the British king's health and he took exception when Roosevelt called him Uncle Joe. The storm passed quickly, however. The Red Army might have more divisions than their Western allies, but the Red Army rode in American cars and trucks, and they relied on British merchantmen for a host of goods. As the night passed and the alcohol flowed, the genial Uncle Joe reappeared, who toasted "Churchill's courage . . . and his willingness to stand by Russia's side in the dark early days of Operation Barbarossa." Next the conversation turned to the smaller nations and their place in the new world that the Big Three were creating. Roosevelt agreed with Stalin that nations like Norway and Holland lacked the standing to pass judgment on the policies of the great powers.

Churchill had a more nuanced view. "The eagle should allow the small birds to sing," he said, "and care not wherefore they sing."

The next day, February 5, Roosevelt, Stalin, and Churchill spent a drizzly Crimean afternoon discussing the fate of Germany. The questions addressed included: Should Germany be dismembered? And if so, in how many parts? Should the Allies publicize their postwar plans for Germany now—or wait until the surrender? There was also the vexing question of from whom the Allies should accept the German surrender. Obviously parlaying with Hitler, Himmler, or Goebbels was out of the question, and finding a suitable substitute would be challenging. In one form or another many senior Germans officers had been complicit in war crimes, especially the officers who served on the eastern front. There was also the ongoing question of France's status. Should it be allowed to regain its great power or left to sink into that of a second-tier nation?

After a few welcoming remarks by Roosevelt, Stalin took command of the meeting. It was time to make a final decision on the dismemberment issue, he said. At Tehran Roosevelt had spoken of dividing Germany into five parts, and Churchill had proposed a two-part partition at the Moscow Conference. Did they still hold those views? "In principle," Churchill said, he did, then he immediately added a *but*. An eight-day conference was not the place to make final decisions on an issue as complex as dismembering a nation and dividing its parts. First there had to be "a very searching examination of the historical, ethnographical, and economic facts, and then a prolonged examination by a special committee."

Stalin, who was eager to act on dismemberment, posed a hypothetical. "Suppose," he asked Churchill, a German group claimed they had overthrown Hitler "and were prepared to accept unconditional surrender. How would you respond?" In such a case, Churchill said, "the three great powers must immediately consult and decide whether such people were worth dealing with. If it was decided they were, the terms of surrender would immediately be laid before them; if not, the war would continue."

After Churchill finished, Stalin brought up the plan that Roosevelt had suggested earlier: agree in principle to the dismemberment of Germany and task three foreign ministers—Stettinius, Eden, and Molotov—with coming up with a workable plan, and include a clause in the surrender agreement stating that Germany would be dismembered. Churchill thought the statement too bold and that it could end up having the opposite effect: making the Germans fight harder. To assuage the prime minister's concern Stalin and Roosevelt said that the Allied terms would be kept a secret until the German surrender.

It was nearly 5:00 P.M. by the time the Big Three turned to the second issue on the agenda. Should France be given a zone of occupation? Stalin objected on two grounds. France's relatively minor role in the war did not entitle it to a zone, and if it was given one Norway, Denmark, and Holland and other countries that had played minor roles in the war would demand zones. Churchill, who advocated for France at several points in the conference, assured Stalin that would not be the case nor would Soviet interests be affected. Britain and the United States had agreed to cede a portion of their zones to the French. Stalin remained skeptical. If France was given a zone, he said, three-power control of Germany would become four-power control, and that would complicate the Allies' postwar plans for Germany. Churchill conceded that that was so but added the Americans planned to leave Europe within two years and Britain did not want to be left alone in western Europe with the

German wolf. Even wounded he was a dangerous beast; France, he said, had a large navy and could help Britain police Germany in the years to come. When Stalin asked Roosevelt his opinion the president said he agreed with Churchill that France should have a zone of occupation and with Stalin that postwar oversight of Germany should remain in the hands of the Big Three.

The final issue on the agenda that afternoon was reparations. Britain and the United States had agreed to forgo them, but the Soviet Union—with its ruined towns and villages and its twenty million dead—did want them and made Russia's case to the Western allies. Stalin chose Ivan Maisky, the quick-witted former Soviet ambassador to Britain, to do so. Maisky began by noting that the Soviet Union wanted two types of reparations. The first one was goods in kind—plant machinery, rolling stock, and similar items. "Germany should only be allowed to keep 20 percent of the current heavy industry," Maisky said. That would be sufficient to meet its real economic needs. Then turning to payments in kind, which was the second form of reparation, Maisky said that Russia wanted $10 billion paid out over a ten-year period.

Churchill gasped at the sum. If there was any way in which the British economy could be substantially benefited by reparations Britain would get in the line behind Russia, he said. But after World War I America and Britain lent large sums of money to Germany, and the debt was never repaid. "Once bitten, twice shy," Churchill said. Then he presented Maisky with a hypothetical: "What if Germany is reduced to a state of starvation? Do we intend to stand by and say it serves her right? Or do we intend to provide enough food to keep people alive?"

"Moscow has already addressed that problem," Maisky replied. After the war the German people would be allowed a "Middle European standard of living," which he described as modest but "decent." That evening Churchill stood at a window in his villa, looking up into the black sky. Then he turned to his daughter Sarah and said, "I do not suppose at any moment in history has the agony of the world been so great or widespread. Tonight the sun goes down on more suffering than ever before in the world."

THE FOLLOWING DAY—FEBRUARY 6—ROOSEVELT LUNCHED with Churchill and Alex Cadogan. In a letter to his wife that evening Cadogan said the luncheon had been amusing but that he was surprised at how much Roosevelt had aged. During the meeting that followed lunch the Big Three discussed a wide range of issues: the United Nations, the rights of small nations, a new model of the German U-boat—and France, again. But Poland dominated the conversation. Concerned about public opinion in Polish America, Roosevelt suggested tweaking the Curzon Line slightly to give the Poles more breathing space in the southern part of the country.

He also suggested that the Poles be allowed to keep some of the oil-bearing regions of the country as compensation for the loss of Königsberg, the large East Prussian port, which had been under Polish control during the interwar years and which was now about to fall under Russian control. Churchill seconded Roosevelt's proposal. "If Russia were to make the territorial concessions the president has suggested, we should both admire and acclaim the Soviet action," he said. Unhappy with the direction the conversation was taking, Stalin called for a time-out; after a ten-minute break to collect his thoughts, he reappeared, cold-eyed, crisp, and vaguely menacing. The Curzon Line, he reminded his visitors, was not created by a Russian but by an Englishman, Lord Curzon, and a Frenchman, Georges Clemenceau. How could he return to Moscow with an "open face" if Russia's claims were denied? People would say Curzon and Clemenceau were better stewards of Russia than Stalin and Molotov.

As to the creation of a Polish government, Stalin said, that would be decided by the Lublin Poles—or as they should be rightfully called, the Warsaw government. Then he turned on the London Poles, accusing them of a wide range of misdeeds, including killing 212 Russian soldiers and raiding Soviet supply dumps for weapons. Sensing an explosion Roosevelt suggested an adjournment, but Churchill was not ready to leave. According to the information at Britain's disposal, he said, "the Lublin government could not be regarded as representing more than one third of the Polish people if they were free to express their opinion"—and, thus, had no right to present themselves as guardians of the Polish nation. According to Churchill biographer Martin Gilbert, at this point Roosevelt intervened again and said "somewhat testily, [that] Poland has been a source of trouble for over 500 years." Churchill got the last word of the afternoon. "We must do what we can to put an end to their troubles," he said. And with that the meeting drew to a close.

Over the next few days Roosevelt and Churchill grew increasingly uneasy. The international press was promoting Yalta as the birthplace of a new, more equitable world. Failure to deliver on that promise would arouse public opinion in Britain and the United States, and might fatally undermine the alliance. The Big Three solved the dilemma with a Declaration of Liberated Europe, a pledge to support free and fair elections in nations formerly under German rule. They further agreed that Poland would be the first liberated nation to hold elections. Predictably, the declaration received a great deal of attention, but it was the literary equivalent of a Potemkin village: all show and no substance.

After reading the declaration, Roosevelt's chief of staff Admiral William Leahy told him that the agreement was so elastic the Russians could stretch it all the way from Yalta to Washington without even technically breaking it. "I know, Bill, I know," Roosevelt replied. "But it was the best I could do for Poland at this time." The president's reluctance to press Stalin on Poland had its roots in the Pacific war. Stalin and Roosevelt had discussed a possible Russian role in the Pacific previously, but in an offhanded way. At a meeting on February 8 the two men were more specific. Roosevelt said that while an American victory in the Pacific was now assured, Japan had a four-million-man army, and the closer American forces got to the homeland, the more furious the Japanese defenses had become. The upcoming invasion of Iwo Jima on February 19—and of Okinawa on April 1—added urgency to Roosevelt's desire to share the burdens of the Pacific war with an ally. Stalin was open to a Soviet role in the region but at a price: the southern half of the island of Sakhalin, the Manchurian railway lines, as well as the Kurils for Soviet air bases and the port of Darien for shipping. Chiang Kai-shek would have to establish a commission to approve Soviet use of Chinese railways and ports, but Roosevelt considered Chiang such a cipher that, for the time being, he planned to keep the agreement with Stalin a secret. If he told Chiang then, historian Robert Dallek said, "the whole world would know about it within 24 hours."

On February 12 Roosevelt flew from Yalta to Saudi Arabia to meet with the Saudi king, Ibn Saud. This would be his last appearance on the international stage.

24

NEVER FORGIVE,
NEVER FORGET

The honor of defending Berlin from the "Jewish-Bolshevik" hordes massing to the east of the city fell to Colonel General Gotthard Heinrici, a minister's son with a half-Jewish wife. "I don't want him," Hitler said in March, when Guderian proposed Heinrici for command of Army Group Vistula, the force being assembled to meet the Soviet assault. The command already had a leader: Reichsführer Heinrich Himmler had been given command of the force in January, but it proved to be a bad fit. Himmler had never experienced, let alone led, men in battle, and after a few weeks of constant shelling the Reichs-Führer checked himself into a sanatorium in Hohenlychen, a town well out of harm's way. Guderian suggested Heinrici again, and Himmler pledged to support the appointment, provided that Guderian, not he, inform Hitler of the change in command.

The new leader of Army Group Vistula bore little resemblance to the glamorous Aryan warriors who adorned the posters outside the zoo complex. Short and slim with narrow shoulders, Heinrici suggested a clerk in a provincial counting office, but what he lacked in physical glamour he made up for in experience, skill, and steadfastness. He was particularly skilled in the defensive battle. In France, Russia, Italy, and half a dozen places in between he saved battles that other commanders thought lost. "Heinrici only retreats when the air is full of lead and even then only after careful consideration," an admiring staff officer observed.

But that officer made the observation in 1944, when there were still places to retreat to. In April 1945 there was a 2.5-million-man Soviet force assembling in the deep forest to the east of Berlin, and the only thing between the Russians and the capital of the Reich was an ad hoc force of 500,000 men created from the odds and ends of two German army groups badly mauled during the winter fighting in East Prussia and given the name Army Group Vistula.

In early April the roads to the south of Berlin began to fill with "Golden Pheasants," high-level Nazi officials who sat in the backs of their chauffeured Mercedes-Benzes, staring out the windows at the spring fields, ruminating on the shape of things to come. On April 12, four days before the main Soviet assault, Albert Speer, the armaments minister, arrived at Heinrici's headquarters in Prenzlau, a town sixty-two miles north of Berlin. Heinrici was relieved to see him. A few days earlier Speer's office had issued two conflicting orders on how to respond to the Red Army's arrival, and, like most of his colleagues, Heinrici was confused. Speer apologized for the confusion but said it was deliberate. He wanted to give his field commanders an excuse for ignoring Hitler's scorched-earth policy. When Lieutenant General Hellmuth Reymann, commander of the Berlin sector, arrived at Heinrici's headquarters later that evening, the conversation grew heated. Reymann said that all he had to defend the capital were ninety-two battalions of old men with old weapons—poorly trained Volkssturm men with a mean age of fifty to sixty and a few weeks of training; plus several battalions of Alarm troops, units made of cooks and clerks; and "a handful of tanks." The only weapon he had ample supply of were flak guns. When Reymann finished speaking Speer asked how he planned to defend the city. "Blow up Berlin's bridges before the Russians arrive," Reymann said.

Speer frowned. "You realize if you do, you'll disrupt the entire public utilities service for over two million Berliners."

"That's unfortunate," Reymann said, "but what else can I do? It's that or my head." Outside the window exploding shell bursts were hanging in the April sky like young moons.

"You realize the bridges carry water pipes, gas mains, and electric cables," Speer replied. If they were destroyed doctors could not perform surgeries, life would come to a standstill, and there would not even be any drinking water.

Reymann refused to budge, saying, "I've sworn an oath. I'm obliged to carry out this order."

Heinrici abruptly ended the argument. "I forbid you to blow up a single bridge," he told Reymann. "If there is an emergency, you must contact me and request my permission." A few days later, Hitler ended the talk of a national redoubt with the announcement that he would remain in Berlin. "If in the coming days and weeks every soldier on the eastern front does his duty," he said in address to the nation, "Asia's last assault will fail. Berlin [will] remain German, Vienna will once more be German, and Europe shall never be Russian. At this hour the entire German population looks to you, my fighters of the east, and hopes that . . . through your leadership, the Bolshevik attack will drown in a bath of blood. At the very moment fate removed the greatest war criminal of all times [Roosevelt] . . . the turning point of this world will be determined."

Hitler was talking nonsense of course, and many of his listeners probably knew it, but with the sky full of Allied bombers and the Red Army assembling in the east—and the need to believe—all of it overwhelmed rational thought. There was a need for reassurance, even if it came in the form of fairy tales.

BY EARLY APRIL BERLIN WAS more a ruin than a city. The Brandenburg Gate, the triumphant arch that had symbolized German greatness for centuries, now shared a pockmarked field with overturned Mercedes staff cars and packs of feral dogs. In other parts of the city roofless homes hovered above cratered streets and canyons of smashed brick, and in every quarter of the city the air smelled of soot, ash, and decomposing bodies. Berliners with no powerful friends to turn to had little hope of escaping Berlin. Fearful that the Anglo-Americans would attempt to seize the capital, Stalin ordered Berlin cordoned off.

In between hunting for food and seeking shelter from the American and British bombers, Berliners considered the future. What men feared most was being pulled off a street in Berlin or Hamburg and sent to a Soviet gulag. For German women the great fear was rape, and the closer the Red Army got to Germany the more harrowing the rape stories became. On a late winter day, in the town of Neisse on the Polish-German border, Soviets troops raped 182 nuns. In the diocese of Katowice in Poland another Red Army unit left behind 66 pregnant nuns. In the German hospital of Hausa Deshler a group of Soviet soldiers burst into the maternity ward and raped a woman who had just given birth and another about to give birth. Such stories, carried west by retreating German soldiers, were a reminder of the reckoning to come.

Roosevelt's death, on April 12, of a hemorrhagic stroke, provided Hitler with a brief respite from reality, but it was short-lived. When news reached Berlin on April 14 that the 20th Panzer Division had been badly mauled in an encounter with the Soviet 8th Guards Army, Hitler was said to have been so angered he ordered all ranks stripped of their medals until the lost ground was retaken. The influx of poorly trained seventeen- and eighteen-year-olds and the loss of experienced sergeants and officers created a morale crisis in the final weeks of the war. An officer in the Infantry Regiment Grossdeutschland noted that what most of the young soldiers in his command wished for was a wound that would take them to the rear, out of harm's way.

In some units the morale crisis was so acute offenders were shot after a summary court-martial or sent into no-man's-land to dig trenches in sight of the Russian guns. Desperate to restore morale German officers cited the example of Frederick the Great, who had snatched victory from defeat at the eleventh hour. Roosevelt's death produced the most bizarre rumor: American, British, and German forces would link up, and together the three great nations of the West would throw back the Russian hordes. Most units also had a handful of diehards, men committed to Hitler and national socialism. "You can't imagine what a terrible hatred is aroused here," a senior lieutenant wrote his wife. "I can promise you we will sort them out one day. . . . We have sworn an oath that each man will kill ten Bolsheviks. God will help us achieve this."

East of Berlin preparations were being made for the last battle. The Red Army would deploy three fronts: Marshal Zhukov's 1st Belorussian Front and Marshal Ivan Konev's 1st Ukrainian Front would lead the attack on April 16; Marshal Konstantin Rokossovsky, commander of the 2nd Belorussian Front, would follow up shortly thereafter. The target for the sixteenth was the Seelow Heights, a horseshoe-shaped plateau with rises that reached a hundred feet at some points.

On the fifteenth sporadic Russian artillery fire muffled the sound made by men and equipment moving into position. The final hours before an assault were always tense. But on this cool April evening fear mingled with excitement. In the coming days comrades gone to an early grave at Smolensk, at the gates of Moscow, at Stalingrad, and at Kursk would all be avenged. The attack would go in at 3:00 A.M. German time. In the final minutes before the battle some men slipped photos of wives and children into their kits; others reread tattered copies of the poem "Wait for Me":

> Wait for me and I will return, only wait very hard. Wait for me when the sky is black and the sun has gone. Wait when you are filled with sorrow as you watch the yellow rain, wait when the wind sweeps the snow drifts, wait in the sweltering heat. Wait when others have stopped waiting, forgetting their yesterdays. Wait even when from far no letters come to you. . . .
>
> Wait for me when others are tired of waiting, wait for me and I'll return defining every death. Those who do not wait will say I was lucky. They will never understand that in the midst of death you with your waiting saved me, only you and I will know how I survived. It was because you waited as no one else did.

Shortly before zero hour on April 16 Marshal Zhukov and his entourage arrived at the headquarters of Colonel General Chuikov, who was the hero of the Stalingrad campaign and currently commander of the 8th Guards Army. Chuikov was not particularly happy about Zhukov's visit. He felt the marshal had bigfooted him at Stalingrad, taking most of the credit for a victory that Chuikov felt rightly belonged to him and his men. But tonight he had little time to brood about battles past. At 3:00 A.M. the sky lit up from horizon to horizon; flocks of frightened birds took flight, and the air rumbled with sounds of war: the *whoosh* of Katyusha rockets, the roar of thousands of heavy guns, the steady *rat-a-tat* of machine-gun fire, the thump of exploding mortar shells.

Overhead 143 floodlights switched on, and the night sky turned a brilliant white. The men in the assault units plugged their ears, took a final sip of vodka, and rose to their feet. Within seconds, men began complaining about the intensity of the light, which affected Russian eyes the same way it did the Germans'. At the request of the frontline commanders the lights were turned off; then almost immediately the order was rescinded and the sky became a brilliant white again. Despite the complaints the opening hours of the Soviet assault went well. The Soviet

Air Forces controlled the sky; the Russian tank and infantry units, the ground. That afternoon, Peter Sebelev, a Soviet engineer, wrote to his wife: "There has not been a day at the front like today." Shouts of "To Berlin!" echoed up and down the line as the troops marched toward the German positions.

Under cover of darkness on the evening of the fifteenth, Heinrici pulled his main attack force back to secondary positions. The withdrawal was part of a rope-a-dope strategy he had developed in Italy and Russia: meet the enemy with a scratch force; then, two or three days later, when his guard is down, counterattack with the main force. Gerhard Codder, the eighteen-year-old son of a school principal, was assigned to the scratch force. On the morning of the sixteenth, he awoke to shouts of "The Russians are coming!" from the foxhole in front of his. A moment later Russians, Estonians, Turkmen, and Ukrainians were rushing across a muddy field toward Codder. The German airmen who occupied the bunker complex in front of Codder were able to drive the attackers back, but the day was still young. Around noon he was sitting under a tree, trying to get some rest, when a Russian tank peeked out from a bend in the road. The commander standing in the hatch was not much older than Codder, maybe twenty-two or twenty-three. A German antitank gun on the heights above Codder opened fire, and the commander slumped forward in the hatch, dead. The rest of the crew leaped from the tank and fled down the slope to the Soviet positions. As the afternoon progressed, Marshal Zhukov's mood darkened. Chuikov's 8th Guards Army was bogged down, and the marshal's rival, General Konev, was driving toward Berlin from the south. "So you've underestimated the enemy," Stalin said when Zhukov called with a situation report around 3:00 P.M. that afternoon. "I was thinking you were already on the approaches to Berlin."

A few hours later the Soviet tanks reappeared, and this time they arrived in force. Codder counted forty tanks on his side of the road and twenty on the other side. The airmen in the foxhole in front of him took aim but held their fire. "Don't worry," an older soldier shouted to Codder. "Unless they get up to us, you, have nothing to fear."

"I want those bastards in front of my gun before I fire!" another veteran shouted. The Russian infantry were halfway up the rise when the German 88 guns on the heights opened fire. Men fell in the dozens, then in the hundreds, but the attackers kept coming, shouting Russian battle songs as they rushed the German positions.

Codder and the men around him opened fire. Shell fragments hurtled across the late-afternoon sky, the wounded screamed, but the attackers kept moving forward, heedless of death. Toward midnight Zhukov spoke to Stalin again. Earlier in the day he had seemed unperturbed by Zhukov's lack of progress; now he sounded annoyed. "Are you sure you can capture Seelow tomorrow?" he asked.

"Yes," Zhukov said.

Unsatisfied by the reply, Stalin brought up the marshal's chief rival in the race to get to Berlin first. "We are thinking of ordering Konev to send tank armies toward Berlin," he said. Over the next few days the German grip on Seelow Heights broke under the weight of the Russian advantage in men and matériel and the weight of Zhukov's furious desire to reach Berlin before his rival. By April 19 the heights were in Soviet hands, and Generals Heinrici and Theodor Busse were arguing about who would arrive in Berlin first, the Russians or the British and Americans.

25

BIRTHDAY AND DEATH

O N April 20 the Red Army celebrated Hitler's birthday with a furious artillery barrage. Later in the morning British and American bombers appeared over Berlin, but the city had been bombed so often there were almost no worthwhile targets left. The morning did bring one piece of good news. To honor the Führer's fifty-sixth birthday Berliners would receive an eight-day ration allowance, plus a small can of vegetables and a half ounce of real coffee.

A little before noon Hitler slipped out of the bunker complex and escaped upstairs to a small garden, where a group of Hitler Youth were waiting for him under the gray morning sky. A few days earlier the boys, who ranged in age from fourteen to sixteen, had checked a Russian tank attack and were in the garden this morning to be decorated for their valor. The ceremony produced one of the most iconic photos of World War II: an avuncular Hitler, his face half-hidden, in a greatcoat, pinching the cheek of one of the smaller boys, who beams with martial pride. But for every fifteen-year-old national socialist hero, there were hundreds of boys like the one Dorothea von Schwanenfluegel encountered on a Berlin street that morning. The boy was sitting in a shallow dugout across the street from the queue that Frau Schwanenfluegel was standing in. He looked so sad and forlorn in his oversize helmet and boots that she surrendered her place in the line and walked across the street. According to a historian, "there were tears in the boy's eyes and an anti-tank grenade on the ground next to him. When she asked what he was doing there, he said he had been ordered to lie in wait until a Soviet tank appeared, then slip under it and explode the grenade. Then he began to cry again. His words were garbled, but he seemed to be calling out for his mother. At that point, Frau Schwanenfluegel realized she would have to make a terrible decision: If she encouraged the boy to run away, the SS would execute him if they caught him. If she gave him refuge, she and her family would be at risk. She sat with the boy for a few minutes, then got up and walked back to the queue."

HERMANN GÖRING SPENT THE MORNING of April 20 at Carinhall, his home to the north of Berlin. Within the hour, the estate he had spent half a lifetime building—where he had interred the remains of his beloved first wife, Carin (for whom, of course, the hall was named) and entertained Charles Lindbergh, the Duke and Duchess of Windsor, and former president Herbert Hoover—would be a smoldering ruin. Göring returned to his dressing room and put on a suit.

Today was Hitler's birthday, and although the two men rarely spoke anymore, Göring would be expected to make an appearance. After he finished dressing, an engineer officer escorted Göring to a demolition site near the front of the house; he pressed his 250 pounds against a plunger, and Carinhall disappeared into a swirling cloud of fire and dust. (If he hadn't done this, the Russians would have.) Then he climbed into the back seat of the car that would carry him to Berlin.

The Führer's birthday guests included Grand Admiral Karl Dönitz, who was whispered to be Hitler's successor; Speer, the crafty armaments minister who had a Houdini-like ability to get out of tough spots; Marshal Wilhelm Keitel, chief of the armed forces high command; Keitel's number two, General Alfred Jodl; General Hans Krebs, chief of staff at OKH; Himmler, who was in secret talks with Norbert Masur, a representative of the World Jewish Congress; Ribbentrop, the foreign secretary; and Göring, who was coldly received by the Führer. Following some awkward small talk with the other guests, Göring left Burker and traveled south to Obersalzberg, a mountain retreat near Berchtesgaden.

After Hitler retired to his bedroom, his mistress, Eva Braun, appeared in the little sitting room where Hitler's typists often gathered. Traudl Junge, one of the youngest members of the typing staff (she was in her early twenties), noticed Braun was wearing a silvery-blue brocade dress that seemed more appropriate for a party than a requiem and that "a restless fire burned her eyes." It was if she wanted to "numb the fear that awakened in her," Junge later said. "She wanted to celebrate, even when there was nothing left to celebrate. She wanted to dance, drink, forget. And I was only too willing to be infected by her . . . lust for life, to get out of the bunker where the heavy ceiling suddenly weighed down so palpably on our spirits, and the walls were white and cold."

As the last desperate days of the Third Reich played themselves out Eva Braun became a kind of pied piper. Evenings she would bring everyone who still remained in the bunker up to her living room on the first floor; a table would be set out with fine wines and foods unavailable elsewhere. Someone would produce a gramophone, someone else a record, often "Bloodred Roses Speak Happiness to You," and play it until the morning barrage began. At dawn, Junge recalled, "Eva Braun would still be whirling around in a desperate frenzy like a woman who has already felt the faint breath of death. No one said anything about the war. No one mentioned victory, no one spoke of death. This was a party given for ghosts."

THE NEXT MORNING, WHEN Marshal Zhukov's 1st Belorussian Front reached the approaches to the German capital, the city was on fire. Flames danced from rooftop to rooftop; buildings collapsed, shells flashed across the Tiergarten; feral dogs rushed through the broken streets, barking wildly. At the zoo bunker, the most heavily protected of the city's bunkers, people fought one another for entrance into its thick-walled interior. For a moment on the previous day it seemed that Zhukov's rival, General Konev, who was driving on Berlin from the south, would reach the capital first. But Zhukov was quick to counter the threat. He marshaled the best units from two of his best armies, the 1st and 2nd Guards, and ordered them to arrive on the outskirts of Berlin by 4:00 A.M. on the twenty-first. The troops missed the deadline by ten hours but avoided Zhukov's ire because Konev's 1st Ukrainian Front had fallen even further behind schedule.

The most that can be said about the contest to reach Berlin first, says historian Catherine Merridale, "is that it secured Soviet primacy over the Anglo-Americans in the battle [for] Berlin but in strategic and human terms the contest was a disaster. Laborers with no military experience . . . were threatened with a bullet in the head or the *shtrafbat*, the penal battalion, if they lost their nerve and refused to march into the inferno. Even veterans who fought at Stalingrad and Kursk had difficulty holding their nerve. The RAF and the American Eighth Army Air Force had reduced the streets of Berlin to ruins and every ruin could harbor a sniper or a member of the Hitler Youth eager to sacrifice himself in a blaze of glory."

On the afternoon of the twenty-first Hans Wulle-Wahlberg, a Swiss journalist, was making his way across Potsdamer Platz when a Soviet artillery shell exploded and wounded several onlookers. A few weeks earlier a crowd would have rushed to the scene to help. Now just Wulle-Wahlberg and two other Good Samaritans stopped to help the wounded. "People are too busy trying to save themselves to worry about anyone else," Wulle-Wahlberg concluded. Later that afternoon the Red Army put on an impressive display of shock and awe in hopes of cowering the Germans into surrender and avoiding a nasty street fight. The city was surrounded by five Soviet rifle and four Soviet tank armies. The 3rd Shock Army and the 2nd Guards Tank Army attacked Berlin from the north; the 8th Guards and the 1st Guards Tank Army struck from the east; the 5th Shock Army and the 47th Army swept north, looped around, and struck Berlin from the west, while Konev's tanks and rifle divisions pushed into Berlin from the south. But there were still tens of thousands of German soldiers prepared to sacrifice themselves for the fatherland, and among them were the foreign fighters of the Waffen-SS—the Swedes, Norwegians, Belgians, Danes, and Dutchmen who had fought under the swastika and, having no home to return to, were now prepared to die under it. There also were men who fought because they could not imagine a world without Hitler.

Katyusha rockets announced the beginning of the street fighting. Red Army tanks rumbled onto the streets. Rows of buildings exploded. (Experience had shown that destroying buildings one at a time was inefficient.) After a street was cleared, the Red Army soldiers would tunnel down into the cellars and blow up walls, doors, and other obstacles with tank rifles, then squirrel past leaking pipes and dead rats into the next basement. The German civilians who sheltered in the basements were at great risk. The ferocious underground firefights put the civilians caught in them in great danger, but fleeing to the streets risked arousing the sporting instincts of the Red Army fliers, who periodically swooped down and raked the streets. In war, however, everything is relative, and, compared with what was to follow, the first wave of Soviet troops was well behaved, notes historian John Erickson. Most of the troops were veterans and, in the main, led by officers who knew how to inspire men and how to discipline them.

ON THE MORNING OF APRIL 21 Hitler exercised the mantle of command for the final time. That morning he ordered the sleekly handsome SS general Felix Steiner to attack south from his position in Eberswalde, a town thirty miles north of Berlin, and check the Soviet drive on the city. The plan was grandiose to begin with, and the more Hitler spoke, the more grandiose it became. Every available man between Berlin and the Baltic Sea up to Stettin and Hamburg, including the private army Göring had kept locked away at Carinhall, was to be assembled for a strike that would deter the Red Army's advance.

When Steiner told Hitler that Germany no longer possessed the resources to launch an attack on such a large scale, the Führer hung up on him. Uncertain what to do next Steiner consulted Krebs, who had replaced Guderian as the OKH's German army high command chief of staff. While the two men were discussing Hitler's order the Führer came back on the line and gave Steiner a blistering dressing-down. Then, just before hanging up, he said, "You will see, Steiner. You will see. The Russians will suffer their greatest defeat before the gates of Berlin."

The order Steiner received failed to explain how this miracle would come to pass, though Hitler was clear about the consequences if his order were to be ignored. He told Steiner, "You are liable with your head for the execution of this order. The fate of the Reich capital depends on the success of your mission." General Karl Koller, the Luftwaffe chief of staff, received a similar warning. He was instructed to see to it that all air force personnel in the northern zone were made available to Steiner. Officers who failed to comply by holding back troops or in some other manner would be executed within five hours of receiving a guilty verdict. That afternoon, when Hitler called a meeting to discuss the assault, everything was in place—except Steiner, who had disappeared. Agitated, Hitler ordered Koller to send up a search plane. When the pilot returned empty-handed a now very agitated Hitler called Himmler. The Reichsführer also had no information on Steiner's whereabouts. A few hours later the mystery resolved itself. Steiner couldn't be found anywhere because he hadn't gone anywhere. He was still at his headquarters. Hitler was so distraught he collapsed in his chair and began to rant. The army had betrayed him; the SS had betrayed him; his generals were incompetent and untrustworthy. Goebbels, the Hitler whisperer, was summoned to the Reich Chancellery. It is unclear what the propaganda minister, who also was beginning to contemplate suicide, said, but it was effective. Hitler emerged from their talk becalmed and resolved. He announced he would remain in Berlin until the fighting ended, then commit suicide. He would have preferred a soldier's death, he said, but was now "too weak to fight in battle." Anyone who wished to leave the bunker complex was free to do so. Before he left, Goebbels told several members of the Führer's staff that Hitler had invited him to move his wife and six children into the chancellery and that he intended to accept the invitation. It was an odd request, and its consequences would be so terrible that men and women who thought they no longer had the capacity to feel would be shocked and sickened.

It was now late afternoon and hundreds of roofless schools, shops, and office buildings were bathing in the late April sun. Traudl Junge surveyed the scene from a small alcove inside the bunker complex. "The Wilhelmplatz looked bleak, the Kaiserhof had collapsed like a house of cards," she noted, "and its ruins ran almost all the way down to the Reich Chancellery. All that was left of the Propaganda Ministry was the white façade, which stood in an empty square. But the sky above the ruins, usually full of American and British bombers this time of day, was empty." That gave Traudl Junge something to be grateful for. Until recently most German civilians had experienced the war in the east through the death notices that arrived in the mail. The war in the west was more personal. German civilians had been living under British and American bombs since early 1943. Lancasters and Flying Fortresses had destroyed thousands of homes and killed an untold number of men, women, and children and given rise to hundreds of black jokes. A favorite joke of one Frau W., who shared a cellar near the chancellery with several other women, was: "Better a Ruski on top than a Yank on top."

Another woman in the cellar who kept her wedding ring in her panties said, "If they get that far the ring won't matter anyway."

Later that night Eva Braun drew up her will and gave it and her jewels to one of the officers flying south. In an accompanying letter Braun asked the old friend who had agreed to oversee her estate and distribute her jewels to friends and family to help them during the "difficult times to come." "Forgive me if this sounds a bit confused," she told her friend, "but I am surrounded by the six Gs [Goebbels] children and they are not being quiet." Then Braun seemed to lose control. In the final page of the letter to her friend she wrote, "What should I say to you. I cannot understand how it should all have come to this, but it is impossible to believe anymore in God."

On the morning of April 22 the Red Army announced its arrival in the center of Berlin with a tremendous artillery barrage that frightened Traudl Junge out of a deep sleep. "You could hardly put your head out of doors," she recalled later. There were also a few tattered posters blowing in the morning air. One said, "Every German will defend the capital. We shall stop the Red Hordes at the walls of our Berlin." That afternoon, when a group of senior officers arrived at the Führerbunker to confer with Hitler, Junge asked if the artillery fire, which was still intense, came from German or Russian batteries. The officers feigned ignorance and disappeared behind the heavy iron doors that guarded the Führer's conference room.

For the next few hours voices could be heard rising and falling, but it was impossible to understand what they were saying. At one point an agitated Martin Bormann appeared, gave one of the typists a document to type, and then disappeared back into the conference room. At around three the door opened again and the guests filed out. Hitler was standing motionless in a little anteroom behind them. There would come reports that he had burst into tears during the meeting, but when Junge saw him later in the day his eyes were dry, although she thought "he looked like his own Ghost Mask." Eva Braun's response was more visceral. She leaped from her chair, rushed across the room, and threw her arms around Hitler the way a mother might comfort a frightened child. "You know I shall stay with you," she said. "I'm not letting you send me away. I don't want to die, but I can't help it. I'm staying with you." That evening Hitler sat in silence in a corridor near his office, stroking the puppy on his lap.

THE NEXT DAY, APRIL 23, the Soviet 1st Belorussian Front advanced toward the east and northeast of Berlin while the 1st Ukrainian Front pulverized the northern wing of Army Group Center and passed Jüterbog, a small town sixty miles north of Berlin. The 1st Ukrainian was now more than halfway to the Elbe River town of Magdeburg, where it would link up with American troops, in effect cutting Germany in half. On the twenty-fourth, as the 5th Shock Army and the 1st Guards Army fought their way into Berlin, the German high command put out a call for reinforcements. The only unit to answer the call was a group of French SS men who had nothing left to lose. On the twenty-sixth, Chuikov's 8th Guards and the 1st Guards Tank Army reached the southern suburbs of Berlin and seized Tempelhof, the city's main airport. Marching just behind the Red Army was a group of German communists led by Walter Ulbricht, who had begun life as a cabinet-maker, deserted the German army twice in World War I, became a leading figure in the German Communist Party in the 1930s, and fled to France, then Germany, after Hitler came to power.

Officially Ulbricht and his colleagues would serve as administrators in the postwar zone assigned to the Soviet Union. Unofficially they were placeholders. Stalin's ultimate goal was control of Germany, and to that end he employed a number of stratagems, some contradictory. He supported the creation of a new German newspaper, *Deutsche Volkszeitung*, to impress upon the German people their implicit guilt in Hitler's crimes while simultaneously allowing the mass-circulation *Pravda* to criticize the Russian propagandist Ilya Ehrenburg for taking a hard line against the German people. Stalin also lied to his allies about his intentions. On April 15 he told Harriman that the Soviet Union would attack Dresden next. It wasn't even a good lie. There was nothing left to destroy in the city. A few days later he instructed General Antonov, his deputy chief of staff, to inform Eisenhower that the Red Army would occupy the entire eastern bank of the Elbe River and the Vltava valley in Bohemia. When Stalin was asked why so many German troops were fleeing west to surrender he blamed Goebbels's propaganda for dividing the German people.

By April 23 the half-trained, ill-disciplined second wave of Russian soldiers began arriving in Berlin, and almost immediately the incidence of rape shot up. It is estimated that 2 million German women were raped in 1945. In Berlin alone up to 130,000 women were assaulted, some quite young. A drunken Russian soldier shot a fourteen-year-old girl when she tried to resist his advances. In another sector of the city a group of drunken Soviet soldiers broke into an apartment where three young women had taken refuge, and they took turns raping them.

ONE OF THE VIVIDEST ACCOUNTS of the final days of the war was written by a Berlin woman in her early thirties who had been an editor at one of the city's publishing houses until it was shut down. After the war she published an account of her experiences in a book called *A Woman in Berlin*; she, the author, was simply: Anonymous. Of her first encounter with rape, an experience thousands of German women endured that final spring of the war, she wrote:

> One of them grabs my wrist and jerks me along the corridor. Then the other is pulling as well, his hand on my throat so I can no longer scream. I no longer want to scream for fear of being strangled. They're both tearing away at me; instantly I'm on the floor. Something comes clinking out of my jacket pocket, must be my key ring. . . . I end up with my head on the bottom step of the basement stairs. I can feel the damp coolness of the floor tiles. The door above me is ajar and lets in a little light. One man stands there keeping watch, while the other tears my underclothes, forcing his way. . . .
>
> When I struggle to come up the second one throws himself on me, forcing me back on to the ground with his fists and knees. Now the other keeps look out, whispering, "Hurry up, hurry up." . . . The door opens. Two, three Russians come in; the last is a woman in uniform. And they laugh. The second man jumps up, having been disrupted in the act. The two men go out with the other three leaving me lying there.
>
> I pull myself up on the steps, gather my things, drag myself along the wall to the basement door. . . . "Open up," I shout. "I'm all alone."
>
> Finally the two iron levers open. Everyone stares at me. Only then do I realize how awful I look. My stockings are down to my shoes, my hair is disheveled and I'm still hanging on to what is left of my garter.

Looking into her shattered mirror later that day, the diarist shouted, "Damn this to hell! . . . I have to find a single wolf to keep away the pack. An officer, as high-ranking as possible, a commandant, a general, whatever I can manage." A few days later, the woman felt well enough to begin her search. "I wander up and down, peering into courtyards, keeping my eyes open, then go back into our stairwell, very cautiously. I practice the sentences I would use to address an officer . . . determined to be more than mere booty, a spoil of war." After more days passed the woman got her wish. "I'm just about to give up for the day . . . when I see a man with stars coming out of an apartment across the street. . . . He sees me with the bucket, laughs and says in broken German 'Du, Frau.' I laugh back and shower him with my best Russian . . . [and] we chatter away . . . and I learn that he's a first lieutenant. Finally we arrange to meet again that night at 7:00. . . . He's busy until then. His name is Anton So-and-So—a Ukrainian."

She asks: "Will you definitely come?'"

"Of course," he says reproachfully.

A few days later the woman was sitting in the pitch-dark corridor of the Rathaus (town hall), exchanging rape stories with several other women. The darkness, the result of a recent visit by the RAF, seemed to enhance candor. "They say every second woman is pregnant," a voice says in the darkness. "To which another voice, a shrill one, replies. 'Even if it's true, surely you could go to anyone and have it taken care of.' . . . 'Absolutely not,'" the diarist said. "I'd sooner do something to myself." Then abruptly she said, "I don't want to think about that" and changed the subject.

AT 1:00 A.M. ON APRIL 23 a large Mercedes-Benz staff car arrived at the headquarters of the German 12th Army, and Field Marshal Keitel emerged from the back seat and—baton under arm, medals gleaming in the first shafts of morning light—marched into the headquarters of the 12th. An aide was on one side of him, an adjutant on the other. He asked to speak to the 12th's commander, General Walther Wenck.

When Wenck arrived Keitel's adjutant laid out a set of maps on a table. Then the marshal turned to Wenck, whose honors included being the youngest general in the German army, and said, "The battle for Germany has begun. No less than the fate of Germany and Hitler are at stake." Next he told Wenck, "It is your duty to attack and save the Führer.

You must attack Berlin from the sector Belzig-Treuenbrietzen [two small villages to north of the 12th's lines]. We must save the Führer." As he listened to the increasingly hysterical Keitel it occurred to Wenck that this was probably the first time in his life the marshal had been anywhere near a real battlefield.

But Wenck was wrong. In the Great War Keitel had fought at the first battle of the Marne and was badly wounded in Flanders, but that version of Keitel began to disappear in the interwar years—and it vanished completely when Hitler established himself as national leader. After Keitel and his aides left, Wenck summoned his staff and said, "Here is how we will actually do it. We will drive as close to Berlin as we can but we will not give up our position on the Elbe. With our flanks on the river we can keep open a channel of escape to the west. It would be nonsense to drive toward Berlin only to be encircled by the Russians. . . . Let's get every soldier and civilian who can make it to the west."

Wenck was more informal in talk later that day. "Boys, you've got to go in once more," he said. "It's not about the Russians anymore, it's not about the Reich anymore. It's about the duty to save people from the fighting and the Russians."

General Helmuth Weidling, commander of the LVI Panzer Corps, also had an eventful April 23. When he called the Führerbunker that morning General Krebs informed him the Führer had ordered him executed for retreating in the face of the enemy. Weidling was stunned by the accusation. The only crime he was guilty of was losing his temper when Artur Axmann, the leader of the Hitler Youth, offered him a group of fourteen- and fifteen-year-olds to defend the city. "You cannot sacrifice these children for a case that is already lost," Weidling snapped. "I will not use them, I will demand the order to send these children into battle be rescinded." A few hours later Weidling arrived at the Führerbunker to defend himself and did it so skillfully he left the bunker commander of Berlin. However, the circumstances made the appointment a mixed blessing. Weidling would meet a Red Army of 1.5 million men with 45,000 Wehrmacht and SS troops; 40,000 Volkssturm, many in their fifties or older, and 60 tanks. That evening, at a depot in the government district, the strike force was reinforced by a handful of King Tiger tanks and Nebelwerfer rocket launchers. Then, knowing that fate and 1.5 million Russians awaited them, it swung southeastward into the cold spring night.

That evening Hitler had another unexpected guest: Albert Speer. The bond between the two men had fragmented long ago, but recent events had combined to create a new commonality. They were both facing death: Hitler almost embracing it, Speer still looking for an exit, though he made no mention of it. When the succession question came up Hitler mostly dodged it. But from the little he did say Speer sensed he was leaning toward Grand Admiral Dönitz, whose U-boats had enjoyed great success in the early years of the war. Later that evening the Führerbunker was disrupted by a cable from Göring. It began: "My Führer, is it your wish, in view of your decision to remain in Berlin, that I take over complete control of the Reich in accordance with the decree of June 21 1941 with full powers in domestic and foreign affairs . . . if no answer has been received by 10 P.M., I shall have to assume you have been deprived of your freedom of action and I will consider the terms of your decree as being in force and act for the good of our people and the Reich."

Hitler replied to Göring three times that night. In the first cable he was threatening: "Your actions represent high treason against the Führer and National Socialism. The penalty for treason is death. But in view of your earlier services to the Party, the Führer will not inflict this supreme penalty on you if you resign all your offices. Answer Yes of No." Hitler's second reply was curt and businesslike. He informed Göring that he had rescinded the 1941 order that made the Reichsführer his successor. Hitler's third reply was defensive and had an element of pathos: "Your assumption that I am prevented from carrying out my own wishes is an absolutely erroneous idea, whose ridiculous origins I do not know. I request that this be strongly countered immediately, and I shall, by the way, only hand over my powers to whom and when I consider it to be right. Until then I shall be in command myself."

If Hitler could not bring himself to punish Göring, Bormann could. That evening he ordered the SS commander in Obersalzberg to arrest Göring and charge him with treason.

April 23 was less than two weeks into the Truman presidency, but it was already apparent to Washington insiders that the new president was the antithesis of his predecessor. Modest and straightforward, Truman had slipped into the vice president's role effortlessly. He gave speeches, appeared at charity events and Boy Scout conventions, represented the president at funerals, and left the war to Roosevelt, who showed no interest in enlightening his vice president on military matters. As a result, the day the president died, Truman had yet to be briefed on the atomic bomb project or on the recent decline in Soviet-American relations.

The main point of contention between the two sides, as it had been throughout the war, was Poland's status. Roosevelt had been prepared to give Stalin some leeway in the country, provided he did not overstep. Truman was not so inclined. On the afternoon of the twenty-third he summoned Stimson, Marshall, Admirals King and Leahy, Secretary of the Navy Forrestal, Secretary of State Stettinius, Harriman, and General John Deane, who had flown in from Moscow a few days earlier for a conference at the White House. Truman's opening remarks foreshadowed the Cold War to come. "Our agreements with the Soviet Union have so far been a one-way street, and this cannot continue," he said.

He went on in this vein for several minutes, then asked his guests for their opinions. Forrestal favored a hard line. Stalin had his eye on Hungary, Bulgaria, and Greece, he said, "and I think we might as well meet the issue now rather than later." Harriman was slightly more optimistic: "The real issue is whether we are to be party to a program of Soviet domination of Poland. Obviously we are faced with the possibility of a break with the Russians but I feel if properly handled it might be avoided."

Stimson, who spoke next, warned that if the United States took a hard line on Poland it could disrupt relations with Russia—and that was too high a price to pay. "I think that perhaps the Russians are being more realistic than we are in regard to their own security," he said. Admiral Leahy agreed: "I left Yalta with the impression the Soviet government had no intention of permitting a free government to operate in Poland. I'd have been surprised had Stalin behaved any differently." General Marshall, the most powerful military voice in the room, sided with Leahy and Stimson, saying, "I hope for Soviet participation in the war against Japan," and "the Russians have it within their power to delay their entry into the Far Eastern war until we have done all the dirty work . . . the possibility of a break with Russia is very serious." On that solemn note, Truman's first meeting of the day concluded.

At 5:30 Truman received a second set of visitors. Molotov and Andrei Gromyko, the Soviet ambassador to the United States, arrived at the White House, and, lacking Roosevelt's gift for small talk, Truman immediately got to the point: unless a decision on Poland acceptable to all parties was found he doubted postwar collaboration between the United

State and the Soviet Union would be possible. Then he handed Molotov a letter to pass on to Stalin. It read, "In the opinion of the United States the Crimean [i.e., Yalta] decision on Poland can only be carried out if a group of genuinely representative democratic Polish leaders are invited to Moscow for consultation. The United States and British Governments have gone as far as they can to meet the situation and carry out the intent of the Crimea decision in their joint message delivered to Marshal Stalin on April 18. The Soviet Government must realize that the failure to go forward at this time with the implementation of the Crimea decision on Poland would seriously shake confidence in the unity of the three governments to continue collaboration in the future as they have in the past." Truman and an increasingly frustrated Molotov went back and forth about Poland and the Yalta accords for several minutes, then Molotov lost his temper and shouted, "I have never been talked to like that in my life!"

"Carry out your agreements and you won't get talked to like that," Truman replied.

In early April, when *Völkischer Beobachter*, the last Nazi broadsheet, shut down, Goebbels created *Der Panzerbär*, the Armed Bear, a four-page paper that disappeared six days after its creation. Berlin was dying now; garbage and human waste piled up in the streets. Food and water were scarce and transportation almost nonexistent. The Berlin telegraph office shut down for the first time in its hundred-year history. The city's train network, which had carried the Reich's soldiers into two world wars, was reduced to a heaping wreck, and hunger and fear had turned the German people, famous for their good order and discipline, into desperadoes. A woman who visited the Karstadt department store was shocked by the chaos. "Everyone was pushing and kicking to get through the doors. There were no longer queues . . . people just grabbed everything. In the food department there was a several-inch long carpet of sticky mud on the floor made up of condensed milk, marmalade, noodles and honey. When a clerk shouted, 'Get out! Get out!' the crowd ignored him and continued to grab coats, dresses, shoes off the shelves. When another clerk grabbed a box of chocolates from a boy, the boy cried for a moment, then pulled himself together and said, 'I'm going to get another,' and he did."

As the Red Army tightened the noose around Berlin, life in the city's bunkers took on eighteenth-century character. At the Anhalter bunker near Berlin's main train station the lavatory system collapsed and the only source of drinking water for the bunker's twelve thousand inhabitants was a pump at the train station, which was just far enough away from the bunker to give a sniper time to get off a good shot. The task of providing the bunker with water fell to its youngest inhabitants, who were mostly young women in their teens and early twenties. Many would be killed running back and forth between the station and the bunker. But those who survived earned the gratitude of the men and women who had been too weak or frightened to fetch for themselves. In the main the German officer corps remained faithful to Hitler, but with the Red Army in the streets of the capital, officers and enlisted men alike were looking for ways to square their desire to surrender with their duty to the fatherland.

On the morning of April 24 as the Red Army's grip on Berlin was tightening, Traudl Junge wrote in her diary, "Hitler has withdrawn to his room and won't see anyone." Meanwhile, in a conference room in another part of the bunker senior officers were studying a street map of Berlin and discussing salvage operations. "The Führer takes no further interest in that," Junge noted, "but the General Staff isn't giving up yet. Some kind of army under General Wenck is supposed be on its way to the West. . . . So if Wenck is told to come back and storm Berlin we could be saved."

Early the next morning Bernhard Happici, a Catholic priest, was awakened by thunderous artillery fire. The sky overhead was bloodred and people were shouting in the street below, but the cacophony made it impossible to understand what they were saying. When Father Happici arrived at the maternity home next to his church later that evening the nuns who ran the home were sitting in a circle, quietly saying their prayers, oblivious to the booms of the Czech antiaircraft gun across the street. As the nurses and other members of the staff arrived Father Happici's unease intensified. The message he would deliver to these women, who had devoted their lived to others, was terrible. He whispered a prayer and began:

> Within the near future, we expect Soviet occupation. Very bad rumors had been spread about the Russians. In part, they have been proven to be true. But one should not generalize. If any of you present should experience something bad, remember the story of little Saint Agnes. She

was twelve when she was ordered to worship false Gods. She raised her hand to Christ and made the sign of the Cross and for this her clothes were ripped off and she was tortured before a pagan God. Yet this did not daunt her, though the heathens were moved to tears. Her public exposure brought flattery from some and even offers of marriage. But she answered, Christ is my spouse. So the sentence of death was passed. For a moment she stood in prayer, then was beheaded, and the angels bore her swiftly to paradise. You must remember, if like Saint Agnes, your body is touched and you do not want it, then your eternal reward in Heaven will be doubled for you have worn the crown of martyrs. . . . Do not feel guilty. You are not guilty.

It is unclear if Happici believed every word of what he saying. In an earlier life he had been a man of science, but his words becalmed his listeners. As he was preparing to leave, the nuns and nurses rose from their chairs and began to sing "Abide with Me."

Hermann Göring had had a tumultuous four days since leaving the Führerbunker for Obersalzberg. Upon his arrival on the twenty-first, he and his family were put under house arrest. The previous night an SS officer had appeared and put a pistol with a single bullet in it on his night table. The next evening Hitler stripped him of all his offices. On April 25 the SS men changed strategies. They ordered Göring to sign a document stating that his failing health required that he surrender his offices of state effective immediately. When Göring balked at the terms, the SS men drew their pistols; the Reichsführer picked up his pen and signed the document while his wife and gardener looked on.

Later that morning Allied bombers made two visits to the Obersalzberg region. The first wave of planes dropped their bombs on the edge of what was called the Führer Area. The second wave, which arrived a half hour later, destroyed the Berghof, Hitler's home in Obersalzberg, badly damaged the homes of Göring and Martin Bormann, and blew up the local SS barracks and a wing of the Platterhof Hotel, where Hitler began writing what became *Mein Kampf*.

IN THE EARLY-MORNING HOURS of April 26 Keitel sent a cable to his naval opposite number, Grand Admiral Karl Dönitz, commander of the German forces in the northern sector of the country. Keitel had a predilection for histrionics, but in this instance he was not exaggerating when he told Dönitz: "The battle for Berlin is to be a fight for Germany's destiny."

The German sky was now a wholly owned subsidiary of the Allied bomber force, and it would fall to Dönitz to support Berlin by moving air transports into the city by land and water routes. General Weidling began the day on a positive note. "Day of Hope," he wrote in his diary that morning. Then Soviet T-34 tanks began emerging from alleys, Katyusha rockets flashed across the sky, and the day took on a familiar hue. That evening a German officer in the Panzer Division Müncheberg wrote, "Scarlet night, heavy artillery fire. Uncanny silence. We get shot at from many houses. Foreign workers no doubt."

During a visit to the Führerbunker later on the twenty-sixth, Weidling tried to persuade Hitler to break out of Berlin. "What is the point?" the Führer replied. "Your proposal is perfectly all right, but I have no interest in wandering around the woods. I am staying here, and I will fall at the head of my troops. You, for your part, will continue to do your duties." Early the next morning, the twenty-seventh, Hitler ordered Berlin's subway system flooded to slow the Soviet advance into the city, but having failed to issue some kind of warning, the principal victims of the flooding were Berliners.

A soldier on guard at the Anhalter station that morning gave a vivid account of the day. "Suddenly water starts to pour into the station. There are screams, sobs, curses. People fight around the ladders that run through the airshaft up to the streets. Masses of gurgling water rush over the stairs. Children and the wounded are abandoned and trampled to death. The water covers them, rises three feet or more, then slowly goes down. The panic lasts for hours. Many are drowned. On somebody's orders," the soldier wrote, "the engineers have blasted the locks of the canal between Schöneberg and Mockern bridges to flood the tunnels against the Russian advance." The someone was Hitler—and his decisions to forgo any form of warning cost thousands of men, women, and children their lives. The twenty-seventh was also notable for another reason: by the end of the day, Weidling and his command were completely cut off from the rest of Germany.

APRIL 27 WAS ALSO A somber day in London. That morning the good and great of Europe—King George of Britain, King Olaf of Norway, King Peter of Yugoslavia, King George of Greece, Queen Wilhelmina of the Netherlands, and Winston Churchill—all gathered at Saint Paul's Cathedral to pay homage to President Roosevelt. After the service two of the mourners, MP Henry Channon and his son, were walking toward their car when they turned around to take a final look at the cathedral and saw Winston Churchill "standing bare-headed, framed between two columns of the portico sobbing." Later that day Churchill lunched alone in the Downing Street annex, then paid homage to Roosevelt in a House of Commons speech. "I conceived an admiration for him as a statesman, a man of affairs and a war leader," he told the crowded house. "I felt the utmost confidence in his upright, inspiring character and outlook, and a personal regard—an affection, I must say—for him beyond my powers to express today. His love of his own country, his respect for its constitution, his power of gauging the tides and currents of its mobile public opinion, were always evident. But added to these were the beating of that generous heart, which was always stirred to anger and to action by spectacles of aggression and oppression by the strong against the weak. . . . When death came suddenly upon him, he had finished his mail. That portion of his day's work was done. As the saying goes, he died in harness and we may well say in battle harness, like his soldiers, sailors, and airmen who, side by side with ours, are carrying on their task to the end all over the world. What an enviable death was his! He had brought his country through the worst of the perils and the heaviest of its toils. Victory had cast its sure beam upon him." Churchill's ending was particularly powerful: "There died the greatest American friend we have ever known and the greatest champion of freedom who has ever brought help and comfort from the New World to the Old."

Two days before Churchill's homage to Roosevelt, 850 delegates representing 46 nations gathered in San Francisco to establish a new world order, based on the principles of justice for all and the sanctity of human rights; but the sharp exchanges between two of the leading delegates, Anthony Eden and Molotov, highlighted how difficult it would be to bring the new world order that Roosevelt envisioned to life.

In his presentation Eden championed the rights of small countries, including the principle of consent and the need for standards to prevent the smaller powers from being bigfooted by their larger neighbors, while Molotov argued that the United Nations concept could only succeed in a world policed by a core group of large nations powerful enough to enforce the peace militarily if necessary.

In early April, as the Red Army began advancing on Berlin, the Cold War was beginning to take shape. In a recent paper officials at the Research and Analysis Branch of the Office of Strategic Services had noted that the Soviet Union would emerge from the war as the dominant power in Europe and Asia and urged that the United States take a two-tier approach to the new hegemony: continue to seek common ground with the Soviet Union while simultaneously creating an American-led defense force composed of European and perhaps South American nations to ensure that democratic values prevailed in the postwar world.

By April 28 it had become possible to walk from Germany's eastern front to its western front in fifteen minutes, provided the Soviet shelling was not too heavy. The day began badly and only got worse. In an early-morning call to Marshal Keitel, General Krebs, who was now Hitler's principal conduit to the outside world, said that unless General Wenck's 12th Army and General Busse's 9th Army relieved Berlin within the next forty-eight hours, all would be lost.

The morning also brought reports in the foreign press of Reichsführer Heinrich Himmler's betrayal. "Faithful Heinrich," as Hitler affectionately called the Reichsführer, was secretly exploring surrender terms with Western allies through a Swedish emissary, Count Folke Bernadotte. The revelation had personal as well as political implications: unable to punish Himmler, who had placed himself out of reach, Hitler ordered the execution of his emissary, Hermann Fegelein, the husband of Eva Braun's sister. Braun pleaded with Hitler to spare Fegelein. "He was just trying to find a better life for his wife and child," she said.

Hitler was unmoved. An SS escort took Fegelein out to a park next to the German Foreign Office and executed him under a "blossoming spring tree." Later in the day more news about Himmler emerged. This time the dateline was San Francisco. During an off-the-record talk with members of the British delegation Anthony Eden casually mentioned that Himmler had made an offer of unconditional surrender through Count Bernadotte. The story seemed so big to Jack Winocour, the head of the British Information Service, that he left Eden's hotel room expecting the story to break on the wires within minutes. Two hours later he went to bed, wondering why a story so palpably important was being ignored. For a moment Winocour considered releasing the story himself, but that was the kind of initiative his superiors in London frowned upon; then, an hour after the clock in his hotel room rang in the new day, Winocour received a call from Paul Rankine, a Reuters correspondent on deadline and in need of a story. "Anything going on?" Rankine asked. Winocour hesitated for a moment and then told Rankine he'd give him the story, provided he was not mentioned as a source. When the story broke, initially it more than lived up to Winocour's expectations. It was front-page news in Britain and the United States. But within a few days Truman became suspicious. The only person claiming Heinrich Himmler had the authority to surrender the German state to the Western allies was Heinrich Himmler. Truman asked Admiral Leahy to look into the Reichsführer's offer, Leahy conferred with Bedell Smith and Eisenhower—and a few days later Truman was told the only person Himmler was speaking for was himself.

TRAUDL JUNGE SPENT THE AFTERNOON of the twenty-eighth with the six Goebbels children, who, thanks to their father's public relations skills, had become the most famous children in Germany. In 1942 the children appeared thirty-four times in the weekly newspapers, and in 1943 the Goebbels' two oldest children, Helga and Hilde, were sitting in the front row of the Berlin Sportpalast when their father gave his famous Total War speech.

On April 22 the children took up residence in the Von bunker, adjacent to the lower Führerbunker, and by most accounts acclimated well to their new surroundings. They played in the corridors of the bunker, read fairy tales on a landing, and drank chocolate with "Uncle Führer." Junge was another frequent visitor to the children's quarters. On the afternoon of the twenty-eighth she was present for a charming display of sibling rivalry. After Helmut, the only Goebbels boy, finished reading a composition he wrote for Hitler's birthday, his sister Helga said, "You stole that from Daddy." When Helmut replied, "Or Daddy stole it from me," Junge and the other adults laughed. As the banter continued Junge glanced over at Magda Goebbels. Inside her handbag was "the poison [that] would save her children from exposure to a world where National Socialism was viewed not as the path to righteousness but as a corrupting pestilence." Later in the day news arrived that Benito Mussolini and his mistress, Clara Petacci, had been captured by communist partisans while attempting to flee to Spain; the couple would be executed on the twenty-ninth, and on the thirtieth their bodies would be displayed hanging upside down in a Milan square. The day's final piece of bad news came from General Wenck, who reported that his 12th Army was being been pushed back along the entire front and he would be unable to relieve the capital. Keitel did not challenge the decision.

The next day SS troops swept through the ruined streets of the capital, searching for deserters. There was no longer any point to the searches. Within seventy-two hours the city would be in Soviet hands, but for some of the veteran SS men the hunt had taken on the character of a sport. The first time that Aribert Schulz, a member of the Hitler Youth, encountered a red-haired SS man, he was executing a German sergeant for abandoning his uniform and switching into civilian clothes.

The following evening Schulz encountered the SS man again—this time he was interrogating a Russian tanker, and his manner was notably warmer than it had been the previous evening. At the end of the interrogation he patted the tanker on the back and made a gesture as if to say, "You're free to leave." The Russian tank man smiled and thanked his host; then, as he turned to leave, the SS man shot him in the back.

By April 29 random sex had become as common as random death. (An erotic fever was sweeping through the remaining German sections of Berlin.) "Everywhere," Traudl Junge recalled later, "even on the dentist's chair I saw bodies linked in lascivious embrace. The women had discarded all modesty. They were freely exposing their body parts. SS officers who had been out searching cellars and streets for deserters to hang had also been tempting hungry and impressionable young women back to the Reich Chancellery with promises of parties and endless supplies of food and champagne."

It's impossible to say when Hitler began considering suicide, but it's likely that Himmler's betrayal and Mussolini's capture made him conclude that suicide was the only remaining option. In his final days, as the mantle of command slipped away, Hitler often marched through the Führerbunker raging at Göring, Himmler, and his other betrayers. Yet at other times Hitler seemed remarkably composed for a man facing imminent death. He dined with the Goebbels family, made small talk with the cooks, engineers, and young women in the typing pool. As Cornelius Ryan, a Hitler biographer, noted, it was as if "Hitler could not bear to be alone; he kept walking up and down, through the small dark bunker rooms talking with everyone who remained."

He also made practical preparations. He had his dog, Blondi, put down to test the strength of the poison he and Eva Braun would take the next day. A few hours later Braun appeared at her wedding, wearing a long black taffeta dress and black suede Ferragamo shoes. After the ceremony the newlyweds spent an hour making small talk with their guests: Martin Bormann and General Krebs, Goebbels, Traudl Junge, and her friend Frau Christian. Later in the day Hitler summoned Traudl Junge to his rooms to record his last will and testament. Junge had been looking forward to this moment for days. But the deep thoughts she'd been expecting to hear never emerged. Hitler offered no insights or explanations for Germany's catastrophic downfall, just the old bromides: it was the Jews' fault; it was his generals' fault; it was everyone's fault but his.

That evening Hitler had a final talk with General Weidling, who arrived at the bunker with a three-day beard and the expression of one about to deliver bad news. The German forces defending Berlin "were down to a two-day supply of ammunition," he said, and he urged Hitler to order a breakout. Goebbels, who was also present, objected. But Hitler seemed to just want to bring things to an end. He said, "We would merely flee from one Kessel to another. Am I, the Führer, supposed to sleep in an open field or in a farmhouse . . . and just wait for the end? It would be far better for me to remain in the Chancellery."

Shortly after the newlyweds retired to Hitler's quarters, a frenzied Magda Goebbels appeared in the doorway to his quarters and demanded to see him. Hitler told the officer guarding his quarters to send her away. The incident had its antecedents in Hitler's decision to commit suicide and Goebbels's anger when the Führer informed him it was his duty to remain alive and continue the struggle. The argument would have been bizarre under any set of circumstances. What made it tragic is that Magda and Joseph Goebbels planned to kill their six children before killing themselves. "My children are too young to speak for themselves," the new Reichschancellor wrote in a defense of his decision, "but [they] would . . . unreservedly agree with this decision if they were old enough."

That night the crowds in the zoo bunker were so large it became impossible to take an accurate head count. The stairways and landing smelled of baby diapers, vomit, and decaying corpses. People went mad and committed suicide. Others found a place to sit and waited patiently for death to find them. Two elderly women poisoned themselves the day they arrived in the zoo bunker, and, hidden by the swirling crowds, their decaying bodies went unnoticed for several days. At the final conference on the twenty-ninth General Weidling pointed to the positive stories the army field paper was writing about—Berlin's imminent relief—and said to his colleagues, "The men knew better."

APRIL 30 BEGAN LIKE EVERY other day since the Red Army's arrival in Berlin except now the Soviet cannons were only a few streets away from the Führerbunker and Joseph and Magda Goebbels were finding it harder to hide the truth from their six children, who had been told Germany was winning the war when the Goebbels family took up residence in the Führerbunker on April 22. Eva Braun spent the morning with Traudl Junge. The first few minutes of the conversation were awkward. Braun was now Frau Hitler, and Junge, like the other members of the Bunker staff, was unsure how to address Hitler's wife. "You may safely call me Frau Hitler," Braun said with a smile. Then she opened her wardrobe closet, took out a silver fox fur, and handed it to Junge. "I'd like to give you this coat as a goodbye present," she said. "I always like to have well-dressed women around me."

Hitler was also composed that morning. A creature of habit, he went through his usual morning routine, then lunched with Traudl Junge and two other young women from the typing pool. "It was the same conversation as yesterday, the day before yesterday, and for many days past," Junge recalled later. "A bouquet of death under a mask of cheerful calm." On the evening of the twenty-ninth, Hitler had bid goodbye to group officers and female secretaries in the main dining room in the upper level of the bunker. On the morning of the thirtieth he repeated the exercise with a second group of staff members. Back bent, he moved slowly down a reception line, offering each somber face a weak smile and a trembling hand. Then at around 3:30 that afternoon Bormann, who was standing deathwatch with two aides, heard shots. When they arrived in Hitler's quarters he was sprawled facedown across a table in the anteroom. His wife of four hours was lying next to him.

When Heinz Linge, Hitler's personal servant, arrived he called for gasoline. There are several versions of what happened next. In one, Bormann, his aides Otto Günsche and Erich Kempka, and a Dr. Ludwig Stumpfegger carried the bodies up to the bunker entrance, waited for a pause in the Russian artillery fire, then immersed the bodies in gasoline.

But it was a damp afternoon, and the bodies had to be doused several times before they finally caught fire. In another version the bunker's air intake picked up the rancid smell of the decaying bodies and spread them back down to the rooms in the lower bunker.

A few hours after Hitler's death Goebbels made his first foray into diplomacy. That evening the Russians received a message from the Führerbunker on a Soviet frequency. The gist of it was that the German delegation wished permission to cross the lines to discuss surrender terms. The Russians signaled their consent, and a little before midnight General Krebs and Colonel Theodor von Dufving, accompanied by two German soldiers and a translator, arrived in the Soviet zone and were taken to an apartment house in Tempelhof for talks with senior Soviet officers. Unbeknownst to the German visitors one of the Russians they were speaking to was General Vasily Chuikov, who, two and a half years earlier, had checked the German advance on Stalingrad. The surrender talks continued deep into the night but failed to produce agreement. The German position remained: Germany was worthy of the rights attendant on an honorable defeat.

The next morning, May 1, Magda Goebbels poisoned her six children. Then, later that afternoon, husband and wife walked up to the chancellery garden. Goebbels took out a pistol and shot his trembling wife in the forehead, then turned the pistol on himself. A few days later a Russian forensics team found the bodies of the Goebbels family in a small room in the bunker complex. Both husband and wife had been scorched almost beyond recognition. "To see the children was horrible," said Major Boris Polevoi, one of the investigators. "The only one who seemed disturbed was the oldest Helga. . . . The rest were lying in peace."

IN A MAY 9 VICTORY speech, Joseph Stalin made it clear that Russia's day had arrived. He intoned:

> The great day of victory over Germany has come. Fascist Germany
> has acknowledged herself defeated and declared unconditional sur-
> render on 8 May. Being aware of the wolfish habits of the German
> ringleaders who regard treaties as empty scraps of paper, we have no
> reason to trust their words. However, this morning, in pursuance of
> the act of surrender, German troops began to lay down their arms

and surrender to our troops in mass. This is no longer an empty piece of paper. This is the actual surrender of Germany's armed forces.

Now we state with full justification that the historic day of the final defeat of Germany—the day of our peoples' victory over German imperialism—are over.

On a wet spring morning a few weeks after Stalin's speech, the anonymous female German diarist encountered a married couple at a Berlin train station. They'd been traveling for nineteen days from Czech territory and had bad things to report. The man told how the Czech at the border was stripping Germans of their shirts and beating them with dog whips. "We can't complain," his wife said wearily. "We brought it on ourselves."

The diarist continued:

Apparently all the roads from the east are swarming with refugees. On the way home, I saw people coming out of the cinema. I immediately got off the train and went into the half-empty auditorium for the next showing. A Russian film entitled *At Six P.M. after the War*. A strange feeling, after all the pulp novels I've been living, to sit in the audience again and watch a film.

There were soldiers in the audience, alongside several dozen Germans, mostly children. Hardly any women, though—they're still reluctant to venture into dark places with all the uniforms. But none of the men paid any attention to us civilians; they were all watching the screen and laughing diligently. I devoured the film, which was full of salt of the earth characters, sturdy women, healthy men. It was a talking movie in Russian. I understood quite a bit, since it takes place among simple people. The film had a happy end—victory, fireworks over the turrets of Moscow. . . . Our leaders never risked anything like that for all their promises of future triumphs.

Once again I feel oppressed by our German disaster. I came out of the cinema deeply saddened but I help myself by summoning the things that dull my emotions. Like that bit of Shakespeare I jotted in my notebook back then in Paris when I discovered Spengler and felt so dejected by his *Decline of the West*. A tale told by an idiot, full of sound and fury and signifying nothing.

ACKNOWLEDGMENTS

FOR THEIR ASSISTANCE AND INSIGHT, I would like to thank these historians: Richard Overy, University of Exeter; Mark Stoler, University of Vermont; Ralph B. Levering, Davidson College; Geoffrey Roberts, University College Cork; and Susan Butler, author of *Roosevelt and Stalin: Portrait of a Partnership*.

I am very grateful to my editor, Bob Pigeon, for his support, his patience, and his vast knowledge of military history; and to my agent, Ellen Levine, for her years of encouragement and advocacy. And my gratitude to the enthusiastic team at Hachette Books: editorial assistant Alison Dalafave, publicity associate Anne Hall, and marketing manager Quinn Fariel.

Thanks to Jane Cavolina for her wonderful work on the manuscript—and her friendship; and to Ben Rosenstock, an outstanding editorial assistant and fact-checker. And to the excellent editorial production team at Hachette, headed up by Cisca Schreefel.

Finally, my wife Sheila's help and support were absolutely incalculable.

JOHN KELLY,
February 18, 2020

NOTES

CHAPTER 1:
THE DAY BEFORE THE DAY OF DEAD

2   "We shall populate the Russian desert!": Alan Bullock, *Hitler and Stalin: Parallel Lives* (New York: Vintage, 1991), 724.

2   "What is our life": Ibid.

2   "German forces attacking": Rodric Braithwaite, *Moscow 1941: A City and Its People at War* (New York: Vintage, 2007), 61.

3   "Are those ours?": Catherine Merridale, *Ivan's War* (New York: Picador, 2006), 83.

3   "The rumors can't be true": Ibid.

3   "You will hear it often": Bullock, *Hitler and Stalin*, 734.

4   It is impossible to know: Antony Beevor, *Stalingrad: The Fateful Siege* (New York: Penguin, 1999), 3.

4   "Why does Germany seem": Simon Sebag Montefiore, *Stalin: The Court of the Red Tsar* (London: Weidenfeld & Nicolson, 2003), 357.

5   Stalin, who looked "plainly worried": John Erickson, *The Road to Stalingrad* (New York: HarperCollins, 1975), 109.

5   "What are we to do?": Braithwaite, *Moscow 1941*, 63.

5   German special forces units: Erickson, *The Road to Stalingrad*, 109.

5   "Try to worry less": Merridale, *Ivan's War*, 85.

6   Timoshenko called again: Alexander Werth, *Russia at War: 1941–1945: A History* (New York: Dutton, 1964), 151.

6   "a surprise attack is possible": Merridale, *Ivan's War*, 85.

6   a deep sigh of relief: Ibid.

6   "Even the wives": Werth, *Russia at War*, 147.

7   "Who's calling?" the duty officer: Braithwaite, *Moscow 1941*, 65.

7   Stalin was sitting at a table: Constantine Pleshakov, *Stalin's Folly: The Tragic First Ten Days of World War II on the Eastern Front* (New York: Houghton Mifflin, 2005), 6.

7   "Hitler simply does not know": Montefiore, *Stalin*, 323.

7   the count bursts into "angry tears": Beevor, *Stalingrad*, 9.

7   "a breach of faith": Bullock, *Hitler and Stalin*, 736

7   Schulenburg presents Molotov: Montefiore, *Stalin*, 324–25.

8   "Today at four o'clock": Braithwaite, *Moscow 1941*, 69.

CHAPTER 2: STALIN REGAINS HIS NERVE

9   Stalin tried to buy time: RT Russiapedia.

9   "It was the most horrible sight": John Kelly, *Never Surrender* (New York: Scribner, 2015), 70.

10   In the two scenarios tested: John Erickson, *The Road to Stalingrad* (New York: HarperCollins, 1975), 51.

10   "thinks he's outsmarted me": Simon Sebag Montefiore, *Stalin: The Court of the Red Tsar* (London: Weidenfeld & Nicolson, 2003), 276.

10   And it might have, had Stalin used: Ibid., 304; Alan Bullock, *Hitler and Stalin: Parallel Lives* (New York: Vintage, 1991), 705.

10   In the spring of 1941: Erickson, *The Road to Stalingrad*, 62.

11   calling him a "little shit": John Lukacs, *June 1941: Hitler and Stalin* (New Haven, CT: Yale University Press, 2007), 74.

11   all documents claiming war: Bullock, *Hitler and Stalin*, 717–18.

11   Tass news service article: Alexander Werth, *Russia at War: 1941–1945: A History* (New York: Dutton, 1964), 147.

12   "We were expecting a war": Catherine Merridale, *Ivan's War* (New York: Picador, 2006), 88.

12   "Weighed down by heavy cares": Martin Gilbert, *The Second World War: A Complete History* (New York: Henry Holt, 2009).

13   Just outside Bialystok: Werth, *Russia at War*, 152.

13   "The men are fighting": Ibid., 155.

13   then repeated the order: "Attack!": Edwin P. Hoyt, *Stalin's War: Tragedy and Triumph, 1941–45* (New York: Rowman and Littlefield, 2003), 46.

15   "It is your duty": Montefiore, *Stalin*, 330.

15   "Everything is lost": Ibid., 330–32.

15   "Comrade Stalin is not here": Richard Overy, *Russia's War: A History of the Soviet Effort* (New York: Penguin, 1998), 78.

16   "I have no doubt": Montefiore, *Stalin*, 334.

16   Stalin began to take command: Ibid.

16   *By the graves:* Konstantin Simonov, "Smolensk Roads," All Poetry, https://allpoetry
      .com/Smolensk-Roads.

17   "Comrades, citizens, brothers": Werth, *Russia at War*, 165–66.

18   "Some of the troops": Merridale, *Ivan's War*, 188–89.

18   "twenty minutes to finish": Ibid., 212.

18   it was "no exaggeration": Overy, *Russia's War*, 94.

18   "In order to defeat [him]": Beevor, *Stalingrad*, 26.

19   "There is only one duty": Bullock, *Hitler and Stalin*, 731.

20   "The Russian colossus": Earl F. Ziemke, *The Red Army, 1918–1941: From Van-
      guard of World Revolution to America's Ally* (London: Taylor & Francis, 2004).

CHAPTER 3: SAVING STALIN

22   "I don't think the president": David Roll, *The Hopkins Touch: Harry Hopkins
      and the Forging of the Alliance to Defeat Hitler* (New York: Oxford University
      Press, 2013), 87.

22   six months later Hopkins was: Ibid., 115.

23   "some lonely bay or other": Ibid., 117.

23   Hopkins gave a provocative speech: Robert Sherwood, *Roosevelt and Hopkins:
      An Intimate History* (New York: Harper and Brothers, 1948), 315.

24   Hopkins drove out to Chequers: I. M. Maisky, *The Maisky Diaries*, ed. Gabriel
      Gorodetsky (New Haven, CT: Yale University Press, 2015), 372.

25   "There is no place I'd rather be": *All Things Considered*, National Public Radio,
      February 3, 2010.

25   what could be done: Maisky, *The Maisky Diaries*, 375.

25   The day of his departure: Sherwood, *Roosevelt and Hopkins*, 317.

25   Hopkins lunched with the novelist: *Time*, June 12, 1939.

26   "Tell him, tell him, tell him": Roll, *The Hopkins Touch*, 122.

26   "Fighting in the Smolensk": Alexander Werth, *Russia at War: 1941–1945: A His-
      tory* (New York: Dutton, 1964), 180–81.

27   "built like a football coach's dream": Roll, *The Hopkins Touch*, 126–27.

28   "I don't care to discuss": Ibid., 130.

28   "No man could forget": Sherwood, *Roosevelt and Hopkins*, 344.

28   "Stalin brought a powerful will": Richard Overy, *Why the Allies Won* (New York:
      W. W. Norton, 1997), 259.

29   "As I crawled": Roll, *The Hopkins Touch*, 133.

29   he was now "lively again": Martin Gilbert, *Winston S. Churchill: Finest Hour*
      (London: William Heinemann, 1966), 1155.

29   "mighty swelling sea": Alexander Cadogan, *The Cadogan Diaries*, ed. David
      Dilks (New York: G. P. Putnam's Sons, 1972), 396.

29   "Awful bunk, but the PM loves it": Ibid.

30   "Even at my ripe old age": James MacGregor Burns, *Roosevelt: The Soldier of Freedom* (New York: Harcourt Brace Jovanovich, 1970).

30   a barge ferried Churchill: Elliott Roosevelt, *As He Saw It* (New York: Duell, Sloan, and Pearce, 1946), 25.

31   "Watch. See if the PM": Ibid., 23.

31   "Churchill reared back": Ibid., 28–29.

31   "Father . . . usually dominated": Ibid.

32   "You would have to be": Martin Gilbert, *Churchill and America* (New York: Simon & Schuster, 2005), 231.

32   On December 10: Robert Dallek, *Franklin D. Roosevelt: A Political Life* (New York: Penguin, 2017), Roll, *The Hopkins Touch*, 141.

32   to give immediate aid: Winston S. Churchill, *The Second World War, vol. 2, Their Finest Hour* (Boston: Houghton Mifflin, 1949), 1160.

32   When the subject of Russia: Roosevelt, *As He Saw It*, 30.

33   Churchill and Roosevelt also disagreed: Burns, *Roosevelt*, 127.

33   "drag things out, parlay, stall": Roosevelt, *As He Saw It*, 54.

33   "the American army sees": Gilbert, *Winston S. Churchill: Finest Hour*, 1161.

35   Placentia Bay affected Roosevelt: Dallek, *Franklin D. Roosevelt*, 422–23.

CHAPTER 4: WAR WITHOUT END

36   "If a second front is not established": I. M. Maisky, *The Maisky Diaries*, ed. Gabriel Gorodetsky (New Haven, CT: Yale University Press, 2015), 347.

36   "Bearing good news?": Ibid., 385.

37   "So now, Mr. Churchill": Ibid.

37   "only four months ago": Andrew Nagorski, *1941: The Year Germany Lost the War* (New York: Simon & Schuster, 2019), 205.

37   "Whatever happens and whatever you do": Maisky, *The Maisky Diaries*, 347fn.

38   "I don't want to mislead you": Ibid., 386–87.

38   "It seems to me that Britain": Alexander Werth, *Russia at War: 1941–1945: A History* (New York: Dutton, 1964), 287.

38   "All about us the corn": Waldo Heinrichs, *Threshold of War* (New York: Oxford University Press, 1988), 100.

38   "The behavior of the Russians": Richard J. Evans, *The Third Reich in History and Memory* (New York: Oxford University Press, 2015), 334.

39   665,000 Soviet prisoners: Alan Clark, *Barbarossa: The Russian-German Conflict, 1941–45* (New York: William Morrow, 1985).

39   his "firm decision": Ibid., 120.

40   On September 4: Ibid., 105.

40   "The courage, endurance, and tenacity": Richard Overy, *Russia's War: A History of the Soviet Effort* (New York: Penguin, 1998), 105.

41   "I feel very keenly": Lynne Olson, *Those Angry Days: Roosevelt, Lindbergh, and America's Fight Over World War II, 1939–1941* (New York: Random House, 1941), 290.

41   "Mr. President, I am sure": Robert Dallek, *Franklin D. Roosevelt: A Political Life* (New York: Penguin, 2017), 417.

42   In a fireside talk on May 27: Warren Kimball, *The Juggler: Franklin Roosevelt as Wartime Statesman* (Princeton, NJ: Princeton University Press, 1994), 7.

42   "world war for world domination": Fireside Chat 17: "On An Unlimited National Emergency," May 27, 1941, University of Virginia Miller Center, Presidential Speeches, Franklin D. Roosevelt Presidential Speeches.

42   "You know I am a juggler": Kimball, *The Juggler*, 7.

43   "The enemy is growing stronger": James MacGregor Burns, *Roosevelt: The Soldier of Freedom* (New York: Harcourt Brace Jovanovich, 1970), 135.

43   "its minimum demands": Ibid., 138.

44   "and in his high-pitched voice": Ibid., 138–39.

44   *All of the seas*: Ibid., 139.

44   "all present were struck": Ibid.

45   "Only ossified brains": *The Battle of Russia*, directed by Dave Flitton (Arlington, VA: PBS, 1994).

45   "I will raze the damn city": Alan Bullock, *Hitler and Stalin: Parallel Lives* (New York: Vintage, 1991), 734.

45   panzers had reached Oryol: Antony Beevor, *Stalingrad: The Fateful Siege* (New York: Penguin, 1999), 34.

46   I thought I'd seen . . . retreats: Rodric Braithwaite, *Moscow 1941: A City and Its People at War* (New York: Vintage, 2007), 212.

47   "Your function will be": W. Averell Harriman, *Special Envoy to Churchill and Stalin, 1941–1946* (New York: Random House, 1975), 81–82.

47   The reception at the Moscow airport: Herbert Feis, *Churchill, Roosevelt, Stalin: The War They Waged and the Peace They Sought* (Princeton, NJ: Princeton University Press, 1966), 16.

47   The short, powerfully built figure: Harriman, *Special Envoy*, 84.

48   On the drive back: Ibid.

48   "The paucity of your efforts": Ibid., 89.

48   In his report on the Moscow Conference: Ibid., 93.

49   shot "for panic mongering": Beevor, *Stalingrad*, 34–35.

49   "Mobilize everything you have": Overy, *Russia's War*, 93.

49   "There is a mood": Braithwaite, *Moscow 1941*, 224.

51   Intoxicated by the shouts: Overy, *Russia's War*, 94–95.

51   "For all military purposes": Ibid., 95.

51   The Luftwaffe had reduced: Braithwaite, *Moscow 1941*, 212–13.

52   1,523 industrial plants were relocated: Werth, *Russia at War*, 214.

52   "Nor are you going to shoot": Laurence Rees, *The Nazis: A Warning from History* (New York: Random House, 2012).

53   "You are convinced": Bullock, *Hitler and Stalin*, 734.

53   "Have you gone off your head?": Braithwaite, *Moscow 1941*, 237.

53   "We knew that we would die": Clark, *Barbarossa*, 162.

54   "I can still see von Kluge": Ibid., 165.

54   "the whole world is looking": Walter S. Zapotoczny Jr., *Beyond Duty: The Reason Some Soldiers Commit Atrocities* (Stroud, UK: Fonthill Media, 2017).

CHAPTER 5: ONE DAY IN DECEMBER

57   "as literally drunk": John Kelly, *Never Surrender* (New York: Scribner, 2015), 49.

58   Roosevelt's popularity soared: Burton W. Folsom and Anita Folsom, *FDR Goes to War* (New York: Threshold, 2013), 69.

58   OHIO: Over the Hill in October: Dean Acheson, *Present at the Creation: My Years in the State Department* (New York: W. W. Norton, 1970), 21.

59   "This was piracy": James MacGregor Burns, *Roosevelt: The Soldier of Freedom* (New York: Harcourt Brace Jovanovich, 1970), 140–41.

59   "Then the people shrank": Ibid., 142.

59   "We have wished to avoid": Robert Dallek, *Franklin D. Roosevelt: A Political Life* (New York: Penguin, 2017), 437.

59   "Even the President": Robert Sherwood, *Roosevelt and Hopkins: An Intimate History* (New York: Harper and Brothers, 1948), 386.

60   "Good morning, Commander!": Mitsuo Fuchida, *From Pearl Harbor to Calvary* (1961; repr., n.p.: Echristian, 2011).

61   "This means war": Dallek, *Franklin D. Roosevelt*, 439.

61   "My God, this can't be true!": Nigel Hamilton, *The Mantle of Command: FDR at War, 1941–1942* (New York: Houghton Mifflin, 2014), 64.

61   "My God! There's another wave": Ibid.

62   "in all my fifty years": Nicholas Best, *Seven Days of Infamy* (New York: Macmillan, 2016), 132–33.

62   "Japanese aircraft have raided": W. Averell Harriman, *Special Envoy to Churchill and Stalin, 1941–1946* (New York: Random House, 1975), 111.

63   "Against the advice": Hamilton, *The Mantle of Command*, 62.

63   "a dreadful time": John F. Wukovits, *The Bombing of Pearl Harbor* (New York: Greenhaven Publishing, 2011), 91.

64   Cables flew back and forth: Alexander Cadogan, *The Cadogan Diaries*, ed. David Dilks (New York: G. P. Putnam's Sons, 1972), 416–24.

65   'pleasing and warm': Elisabeth Barker, *Churchill and Eden at War* (New York: St. Martin's, 1979).

65   "surprised and amazed": United States Department of State, Foreign Relations of the United States: Diplomatic Papers (Washington, DC: US Government Printing Office, 1961), 502.

65   "If our people were to learn": Ernest Llewellyn Woodward, *British Foreign Policy in the Second World War*, vol. 2 (London: HM Stationery Office, 1970), 230.

66   "I have to report to you": Winston S. Churchill, *The Second World War* (London: Bloomsbury, 2013), 496.

66   "slapped his thighs": Hamilton, *The Mantle of Command*, 88–89.

67   a sense of security: Lord Moran, *Churchill at War, 1940–45* (New York: Carroll & Graf, 2002), 10.

67   "slept the sleep of the saved": Martin Gilbert, *Churchill and America* (New York: Simon & Schuster, 2005), 245.

69   "If only by the law of averages": Burns, *Roosevelt*, 177.

69   "Our strongest weapon": Franklin D. Roosevelt, "Christmas Address to the American People," in *The War Messages of Franklin D. Roosevelt, December 8, 1941 to April 13, 1945* (Washington, DC: United States of America, 1945), 24.

69   "I spent this anniversary and festival": Dallek, *Franklin D. Roosevelt*, 447.

70   the Americans "have not": Alan Schom, *Eagle and the Rising Sun: The Japanese-American War, 1941–1943* (New York: W. W. Norton, 2004), 259.

71   "there must be one man": Burns, *Roosevelt*, 181.

CHAPTER 6: THE WORST OF TIMES

73   "Any attempt to withdraw": Alan Clark, *Barbarossa: The Russian-German Conflict, 1941–45* (New York: William Morrow, 1985), 181–82.

73   "The Germans are in disarray": Rodric Braithwaite, *Moscow 1941: A City and Its People at War* (New York: Vintage, 2007), 292–93.

73   both men overrated their military skills: Ibid., 292–94.

74   "whoever survived the winter": Catherine Merridale, *Ivan's War* (New York: Picador, 2006), 147–48.

75   winter of 1942 and the spring of 1943: Richard Overy, *Russia's War: A History of the Soviet Effort* (New York: Penguin, 1998), 122.

75   At the Tolstoy estate: Ibid., 124.

75   "village after village": Ibid., 122–23.

75   "suicide in field conditions": Antony Beevor, *Stalingrad: The Fateful Siege* (New York: Penguin, 1999), 46.

75   "You must remember": Ibid.

76   "I thought perhaps that I had done": Winston S. Churchill, *The Second World War* (London: Bloomsbury, 2013), 513.

77   Plymouth "was wasting away": Crispin Gill, *Plymouth: A New History: 1603 to the Present Day* (London: David and Charles, 1979), 195.

77   journey up to London: Maureen Waller, *London 1945: Life in the Debris of War* (New York: St. Martin's Press, 2013), 1.

77   the tunes of glory had faded: Angus Calder, *The People's War: Britain, 1939–1945* (New York: Random House, 1969), 241.

77   "embarrassed, unhappy, and increasingly baffled": W. Averell Harriman, *Special Envoy to Churchill and Stalin, 1941–1946* (New York: Random House, 1975), 124.

78   "I look to you": John Toland, *The Rising Sun: The Decline and Fall of the Japanese Empire, 1936–1945* (New York: Random House, 1970), 206.

79   "God knows we did our best": W. David McIntyre, *The Rise and Fall of the Singapore Naval Base, 1919–1942* (Hamden, CT: Archon Books, 1979), 202–9.

79   "our men fought on": Ibid.

79   "the lack of real fighting spirit": Martin Gilbert, *Winston S. Churchill: Road to Victory, 1941–1945* (New York: Houghton Mifflin, 1986), 62.

79   On January 31 Churchill won: Ibid., 55–56.

80   Cripps was a throwback: Calder, *The People's War*, 270.

80   Stalin again pressed Britain: Mark A. Stoler, *The Politics of the Second Front: American Military Planning and Diplomacy, 1941–1944* (Madison: University of Wisconsin, 1971), 36.

81   "The increasing gravity": Gilbert, *Winston S. Churchill: Road to Victory*, 73.

81   "coup in relations with Russia": Gabriel Gorodetsky, *Stafford Cripps' Mission to Moscow, 1940–42* (Cambridge, UK: Cambridge University Press, 2002), 135–36.

81   "difficult to do business": I. M. Maisky, *The Maisky Diaries*, ed. Gabriel Gorodetsky (New Haven, CT: Yale University Press, 2015), 414–15.

81   "I know you won't mind": Susan Butler, ed., *My Dear Mr. Stalin: The Complete Correspondence of Franklin D. Roosevelt and Joseph V. Stalin* (New Haven, CT: Yale University Press, 2005), 63.

81   Later that spring, with European capitals abuzz: Maisky, *The Maisky Diaries*, 414–15.

83   "He's always angry": John Ray Skates, *The Invasion of Japan: Alternative to the Bomb* (Columbia: University of South Carolina Press, 1994), 18.

83   "white man's countries": Jeremy Black, *War and the World: Military Power and the Fate of Continents, 1450–2000* (New Haven, CT: Yale University Press, 1998), 258.

83   "go to Europe and fight": Mark A. Stoler, *Allies and Adversaries* (Chapel Hill: University of North Carolina Press, 2003), 71.

83   a "new front": David Roll, *The Hopkins Touch: Harry Hopkins and the Forging of the Alliance to Defeat Hitler* (New York: Oxford University Press, 2013), 186.

84   "Do you see any reason": Ibid.

84   on April 8, General Alan Brooke: Arthur Bryant, *The Turn of the Tide: A History of the War Years Based on the Diaries of Field-Marshal Lord Alanbrooke, Chief of the Imperial General Staff* (Garden City, NY: Doubleday, 1957), 282.

85   "The hurricane-like eminence": Lord Alanbrooke, *War Diaries, 1939–1945* (Berkeley: University of California Press, 2003), 19.

85   "from a bombed out 'insane asylum'": Bryant, *The Turn of the Tide*, 98.

85   "one's senses become numb": John Kelly, *Never Surrender* (New York: Scribner, 2015), 190.

85   "Lost another part of the Empire": Bryant, *The Turn of the Tide*, 282–83.

85   Brigadier Vivian Dykes: Roll, *The Hopkins Touch*, 187.

86   "landed to relieve the Russians": Gilbert, *Winston S. Churchill: Road to Victory*, 87.

86   "to maintain the invasion force": Ibid.

86   the "serious weight": Andrew Roberts, *Masters and Commanders* (London: Penguin, 2009), 146.

86   "Our military leaders": Robert A. Nisbet, *Roosevelt and Stalin: The Failed Courtship* (New York: Regnery Gateway, 1988), 34.

86   "Please put Hopkins to bed": Roll, *The Hopkins Touch*, 189.

86   "It is only when you see": George N. Crocker, *Roosevelt's Road to Russia* (n.p.: Pickle Partners Publishing, 2018).

87   had become "quite gray": Alan Bullock, *Hitler and Stalin: Parallel Lives* (New York: Vintage, 1991), 778.

87   "We were in a good state": Beevor, *Stalingrad*, 62.

88   During the 1930s Molotov approved: Simon Sebag Montefiore, *Stalin: The Court of the Red Tsar* (London: Weidenfeld & Nicolson, 2003), 225.

88   in the late 1940s: Ibid., 521.

88   "has all the grace": Stoler, *The Politics of the Second Front*, 93.

88   "It is unlikely": Ibid., 44.

89   "Congress," Elsey began, "has generally": Nigel Hamilton, *The Mantle of Command: FDR at War, 1941–1942* (New York: Houghton Mifflin, 2014), 276.

90   "had dealings with all kinds": Oleg Rzeshevsky, *War and Diplomacy* (Abingdon, UK: Routledge, 2013), 180.

90   The Soviets "hoped to hold on": Mark Stoler and Molly Michelmore, *The United States in World War II: A Documentary History* (Indianapolis, IN: Hackett Publishing, 2018), 69.

91   Molotov presented Churchill and Eden: Stoler, *The Politics of the Second Front*, 50.

91   "The air raid scares": James MacGregor Burns, *Roosevelt: The Soldier of Freedom* (New York: Harcourt Brace Jovanovich, 1970), 210.

91   "With broken heart": Toland, *The Rising Sun*, 313.

CHAPTER 7: THE LONGEST SUMMER

93   "the situation in Alaska": Robert Sherwood, *Roosevelt and Hopkins: An Intimate History* (New York: Harper and Brothers, 1948), 158.

93   Libyan port city of Tobruk: Martin Kitchen, *Rommel's Desert War: Waging World War II in North Africa, 1941–1943* (New York: Cambridge University Press, 2009), 216–17.

94   "Naturally serious attention was given": Alexander Werth, *Russia at War: 1941–1945: A History* (New York: Dutton, 1964), 384.

94   Brooke pushed back the curtain: Arthur Bryant, *The Turn of the Tide: A History of the War Years Based on the Diaries of Field-Marshal Lord Alanbrooke, Chief of the Imperial General Staff* (Garden City, NY: Doubleday, 1957), 324.

95   secretary of war, Henry Stimson: Forrest C. Pogue, *George C. Marshall: Ordeal and Hope* (New York: Viking, 1968), 328.

95   "it gave me some thoughtful": Martin Gilbert, *Winston S. Churchill: Road to Victory, 1941–1945* (New York: Houghton Mifflin, 1986), 67.

95   During a talk with Roosevelt: Sherwood, *Roosevelt and Hopkins*, 589.

96   "Have the American planners": Ibid., 587.

96   "a pink piece of paper": Gilbert, *Winston S. Churchill: Road to Victory*, 128.

96   "If the success of an operation": Pogue, *George C. Marshall*, 334.

97   Fort Jackson, South Carolina: Ibid., 335.

97   "Here at least": Angus Calder, *The People's War: Britain, 1939–1945* (London: Panther, 1969), 345.

97   TOBRUK FALL MAY BRING: R. W. Thompson, *Winston Churchill: The Yankee Marlborough* (Garden City, NY: Doubleday, 1963), 294.

97   "No responsible General": Calder, *The People's War*, 299.

97–98 "I am sure myself that Gymnast": Nigel Hamilton, *The Mantle of Command: FDR at War, 1941–1942* (New York: Houghton Mifflin, 2014), 330–31.

98   "If the British position": Richard Steele, *The First Offensive: 1942* (Bloomington: Indiana University Press, 1973), 160.

99   Upon receipt of Marshall's draft: Pogue, *George C. Marshall*, 341.

100   "Well, what are you doing": Douglas Fairbanks Jr., *A Hell of a War* (New York: St. Martin's Press, 1993).

101   "Most Immediate and Secret": Nigel West, *Historical Dictionary of Naval Intelligence* (Lanham, MD: Scarecrow Press, 2010), 255.

101   "On fire in the ice": David Irving, *The Destruction of Convoy PQ-17* (London: Cassell, 1968), 17.

103   In theory Operation Blue: James A. Huston, *Out of the Blue: US Army Airborne Operations in World War II* (West Lafayette, IN: Purdue University Press, 1972).

103   A Russian soldier discovered a copy: Antony Beevor, *Stalingrad: The Fateful Siege* (New York: Penguin, 1999), 73.

104   "Black figures jump down": Ibid., 77.

105   "The majority of our commanders": Catherine Merridale, *Ivan's War* (New York: Picador, 2006), 151.

105   "They've forgotten my Stavka order": Beevor, *Stalingrad*, 84.

106   "each meter of Soviet territory": Richard Overy, *Russia's War: A History of the Soviet Effort* (New York: Penguin, 1998), 158.

106   *Remember the Rain*: Konstantin Simonov, "Smolensk Roads," All Poetry, https://allpoetry.com/Smolensk-Roads.

106   *We know what today lies*: Werth, *Russia at War*, 410.

107   Stalin had ordered the director: Ronald Bergan, *Sergei Eisenstein: A Life in Conflict* (New York: Arcade Books, 2016).

107   "The Germans are not human": Werth, *Russia at War*, 414.

107   "If you don't want to": Ibid., 417.

108   *I do not like the job I have to do*: Archibald Wavell, *Life*, October 30, 1950, 90.

108   bathed in "totalitarian lavishness": Gilbert, *Winston S. Churchill: Road to Victory*, 173.

109   "The Germans seem to have drained": Ibid., 174.

109   "There are twenty-five": Gilbert, *Winston S. Churchill: Road to Victory*, 176.

110   Stalin switched to personal attacks: Ibid., 177.

110   "hoped to shatter twenty German cities": Ibid., 179.

111   "is the first time in history": Ibid., 185.

112   "We had barely sat down": Ibid., 191.

112   "realized what I had to say": Ibid., 196.

112   "The fact that we have met": Ibid., 197.

113   a British-Canadian force assaulted Dieppe: Sherwood, *Roosevelt and Hopkins*, 626.

CHAPTER 8: WE'VE GOT TO FEEL
WE HAVE VICTORIES IN US

116   In July Eugene "Bull" Connor: Glenn Feldman, *The Irony of the Solid South: Democrats, Republicans, and Race, 1865–1944* (Tuscaloosa: University of Alabama Press, 2013), 193.

117   "The Negro," he wrote: James MacGregor Burns, *Roosevelt: The Soldier of Freedom* (New York: Harcourt Brace Jovanovich, 1970), 265–66.

117   "the sad departures": Ibid., 267.

118   "an impassioned effort": Robert Dallek, *Franklin D. Roosevelt: A Political Life* (New York: Penguin, 2017), 477.

118   "I'm not supposed to be here": Ibid., 479.

119   On September 18: Herbert Feis, *Churchill, Roosevelt, Stalin: The War They Waged and the Peace They Sought* (Princeton, NJ: Princeton University Press, 1966), 84–85; Winston S. Churchill, *The Second World War*, vol. 4, *The Hinge of Fate* (Boston: Houghton Mifflin, 1950).

119   "Its survival became": Richard Overy, *Russia's War: A History of the Soviet Effort* (New York: Penguin, 1998), 164.

120   "a barren, naked, lifeless steppe": Ibid., 165–73.

121   "Keep after the enemy": Antony Beevor, *Stalingrad: The Fateful Siege* (New York: Penguin, 1999), 108–9.

121   "It seemed as though the houses": Overy, *Russia's War*, 172.

121   "Make every German feel": Beevor, *Stalingrad*, 130.

121   *Everything has perished*: Overy, *Russia's War*, 172.

122   "They leapt from their boats": Beevor, *Stalingrad*, 135.

122   "behind the Volga!": Alexander Werth, *Russia at War: 1941–1945: A History* (New York: Dutton, 1964), 467.

124   "Men arrived shocked and fearful": Overy, *Russia's War*, 43.

124   "the dour determination": Konstantin Simonov, quoted in Overy, *Russia's War*, 43.

CHAPTER 9: GENERAL DETERMINATION
AND GENERAL "THEY WILL BEAT US!"

126   "I received your message": *Stalin's Correspondence with Roosevelt and Truman: 1941–1945* (Halifax, Nova Scotia: Capricorn, 1965), 72.

126   it would be a great mistake: Herbert Feis, *Churchill, Roosevelt, Stalin: The War They Waged and the Peace They Sought* (Princeton, NJ: Princeton University Press, 1966), 86.

127   "The situation is critical": Mark A. Stoler, *Allies and Adversaries* (Chapel Hill: University of North Carolina Press, 2003).

127   "desire to kill Germans": Jonathan Dimbleby, *Destiny in the Desert: The Road to El Alamein* (London: Profile Books, 2002).

129   "I ought to let you know": Winston S. Churchill, *The Second World War*, vol. 4, *The Hinge of Fate* (Boston: Houghton Mifflin, 1950), 568–69.

129   "We shall do no good": Alexander Cadogan, *The Cadogan Diaries*, ed. David Dilks (New York: G. P. Putnam's Sons, 1972), 493.

130   "Dear generals and soldiers": Laurence Rees, *The Nazis: A Warning from History* (New York: Random House, 2012).

131   "I won't leave the Volga": Richard Overy, *Russia's War: A History of the Soviet Effort* (New York: Penguin, 1998), 178.

132   "tired, listless, prone to bouts": Ibid., 182.

132   "Well, that finishes it!": Ibid., 184.

CHAPTER 10: TURN OF THE TIDE

135   "You have grown fat": Rick Atkinson, *An Army at Dawn: The War in North Africa, 1942–1943* (New York: Henry Holt, 2007), 287.

135   "When he gets away": Lord Moran, *Churchill at War, 1940–45* (New York: Carroll & Graf, 2002), 96.

137   "has his eye on the Pacific": Atkinson, *An Army at Dawn*, 284.

137   "Eisenhower as a general": Ibid., 282.

138   "We came, we saw": Ibid., 289.

138–39   "It is," Hopkins wrote: Charles L. Robertson, *When Roosevelt Planned to Govern France* (Amherst: University of Massachusetts Press, 2011), 72.

139   ran afoul of General Henri Giraud: Atkinson, *An Army at Dawn*, 292.

CHAPTER 11: DEATH STANDS AT ATTENTION

141   "The history of mankind": H. G. Wells, *The World Set Free* (1914; repr., n.p.: Jungle Land Publishing, 2015), 7.

143   "The bomb flashed": Ibid., 54.

143   "In the last few months": Adrian Berry, *The Book of Scientific Anecdotes* (Amherst, NY: Prometheus Books, 2013), 173–74.

144   "inarticulate unpleasant little man": Kenneth S. Davis, *FDR: The War President, 1940–1943* (New York: Random House, 2000), 307.

144   "every effort on creating the bomb": Richard Rhodes, *The Making of the Atomic Bomb* (New York: Simon & Schuster, 2012), 373.

145   "I think the whole thing": Joseph Persico, *Roosevelt's Centurions: FDR and the Commanders He Led to Victory in World War II* (New York: Random House, 2013), 254.

145   "Demanding, critical, abrasive": Oliver Stone and Peter Kuznick, *The Untold History of the United States* (New York: Simon & Schuster, 2013), 137.

146   When Groves proposed Oppenheimer: Rhodes, *The Making of the Atomic Bomb*, 449.

147   the Nobel laureate Heisenberg: Jeremy Bernstein, *Hitler's Uranium Club: The Secret Recordings at Farm Hall* (New York: Springer, 2013), 37.

147   with "particular urgency": Rhodes, *The Making of the Atomic Bomb*, 403.

148   "The 'seal of silence'": David Holloway, *Stalin and the Bomb: The Soviet Union and Atomic Energy, 1939–1956* (New Haven, CT: Yale University Press, 2008), 78.

148   On September 25, 1941, Gorsky: Ibid., 82.

149   "We not only need Russia": Mark A. Stoler, *Allies and Adversaries* (Chapel Hill: University of North Carolina Press, 2003), 125.

CHAPTER 12: THE END OF THE BEGINNING

151   "wild torrential African rain": Alan Moorehead, *African Trilogy* (London: Hamish Hamilton, 1945), 461.

151   "It is still bitterly cold": Rick Atkinson, *An Army at Dawn: The War in North Africa, 1942–1943* (New York: Henry Holt, 2007), 277.

151   "No more goddamn drugstore cowboys": Carlo D'Este, *Bitter Victory: The Battle for Sicily: 1943* (New York: Harper Perennial, 2008), 55.

151   "Not until there is some reason": Forrest C. Pogue, *George C. Marshall: Organizer of Victory, 1943–1945* (New York: Viking Press, 1973), 180.

151   Rommel arrived in Tunisia: Alan Moorehead, *The End in Africa* (London: Chivers, 1973), 122–23.

152   "I bless the day you urged Fredendall": Atkinson, *An Army at Dawn*, 272.

152   "Lloyd's very last resort": Ibid., 274.

152   "likened it to the sound": Ibid., 340.

153   "passionate will to command": Ibid., 386.

153   "The party is all yours": Stephen E. Ambrose, *The Supreme Commander: The War Years of General Dwight D. Eisenhower* (New York: Random House, 1969), 174.

154   Williamsburg, Virginia, has been invaded: Pogue, *George C. Marshall: Organizer of Victory*, 202.

155   "Now what was the name": Ibid.

156   "Since yesterday, we have been surrounded": Martin Gilbert, *Winston S. Churchill: Road to Victory, 1941–1945* (New York: Houghton Mifflin, 1986), 401.

156   May 11, Harry Hopkins traveled: Ibid., 401.

157   "mark the beginning of the doom": Maurice Matloff, *United States Army in World War II: Strategic Planning for Coalition Warfare* (Washington, DC: Department of the Army, 1947), 128.

157   fixation with the Middle East: Mark A. Stoler, *Allies and Adversaries* (Chapel Hill: University of North Carolina Press, 2003), 112–13.

158   "The British did so many stupid things": Ibid., 121.

158   study of the Trident Conference: Arthur Bryant, *The Turn of the Tide: A History of the War Years Based on the Diaries of Field-Marshal Lord Alanbrooke, Chief of the Imperial General Staff* (Garden City, NY: Doubleday, 1957), 501–4.

159   "We must . . . face the fact": Gilbert, *Winston S. Churchill: Road to Victory*, 415–16.

159   "over the greater part": Ibid., 416.

159   "I am much concerned": Ibid., 417.

160   two different visions of America's place: Ibid., 415–19.

CHAPTER 13: THE POLISH AGONY

161   mass execution of Polish soldiers: Benjamin B. Fischer, "The Katyn Controversy: Stalin's Killing Field," CIA Center for the Study of Intelligence, April 14, 2007.

162   "We are now using the discovery": *Hoover Digest* (Stanford, CA: Hoover Institution on War, Revolution, and Peace, 2000), 178.

162   twenty-two thousand Polish generals: Geoffrey Roberts, *Stalin's Wars* (New Haven, CT: Yale University Press, 2006), 170–71.

163   the 1940 killings went on: US Foreign Policy Research, Records Relating to the Katyn Forest Massacre, National Archives, Washington, DC, https://www.archives.gov/research/foreign-policy/katyn-massacre; Fischer, "The Katyn Controversy."

163   "How many people": Stephen Fritz, *The First Soldier: Hitler as Military Leader* (New Haven, CT: Yale University Press, 2018), 290.

164   nature compensated by endowing Manstein: Richard Overy, *Russia's War: A History of the Soviet Effort* (New York: Penguin, 1998), 197–99.

165   SOLDIERS OF THE REICH: Alan Clark, *Barbarossa: The Russian-German Conflict, 1941–45* (New York: William Morrow, 1985), 328.

166   Hoth's advance began well: Overy, *Russia's War*, 206; David M. Glantz and Jonathan M. House, *The Battle of Kursk* (Lawrence: University Press of Kansas, 1999).

167   "On no account": Overy, *Russia's War*, 337.

167   German units began withdrawing: Clark, *Barbarossa*, 337–38.

168   Stalingrad and Kursk transformed: Robert Dallek, *Franklin D. Roosevelt: A Political Life* (New York: Penguin, 2017), 523–24.

168   "In all fairness": Ibid., 525.

169   "we'll find out about it later": Robert Sherwood, *Roosevelt and Hopkins: An Intimate History* (New York: Harper and Brothers, 1948), 741–45.

169   "a strange looking little man": Geoffrey C. Ward, *Closest Companion* (New York: Simon & Schuster, 1995), 229.

169   Max Hastings has suggested: Max Hastings, *Winston's War: Churchill, 1940–1945* (New York: Vintage Books, 2011), 458.

170   "We ought to make": Dallek, *Franklin D. Roosevelt*, 526.

170   "Stalin is an unnatural man": Ibid., 527.

171   "swamped by a dark cloud": Arthur Bryant, *The Turn of the Tide: A History of the War Years Based on the Diaries of Field-Marshal Lord Alanbrooke, Chief of the Imperial General Staff* (Garden City, NY: Doubleday, 1957), 578–79.

172   "The conclusions from the foregoing": Mark A. Stoler, *Allies and Adversaries* (Chapel Hill: University of North Carolina Press, 2003), 125.

CHAPTER 14:
MR. CHURCHILL AT HARVARD

173   "Nothing, Clemmie! Charles got nothing!": Lord Moran, *Churchill at War, 1940–45* (New York: Carroll & Graf, 2002), 138.

173   "giving the V for victory": Ibid., 139.

174   "Eden urged him to extend": Martin Gilbert, *Winston S. Churchill: Road to Victory, 1941–1945* (New York: Houghton Mifflin, 1986), 483.

174   Churchill boarded the train: Ibid., 492.

175   "a genial Henry VIII": Moran, *Churchill at War*, 140.

175   "Twice in my lifetime": Ibid., 140–41.

175   at a "less propitious" moment: Robert Sherwood, *Roosevelt and Hopkins: An Intimate History* (New York: Harper and Brothers, 1948), 750.

176   the president had second thoughts: Forrest C. Pogue, *George C. Marshall: Organizer of Victory, 1943–1945* (New York: Viking Press, 1973), 284–85.

176   The invasion, code-named Avalanche: Winston S. Churchill, *The Second World War*, vol. 5, *Closing the Ring* (Boston: Houghton Mifflin, 1951), 120–21.

177   "dancing, kissing, and backslapping": Rick Atkinson, *The Day of Battle: The War in Sicily and Italy, 1943–1944* (New York: Henry Holt, 2008), 200.

177   "All out of my hands": Ibid., 201.

177   "Come on in and give up!": Robert W. Black, *The Ranger Force: Darby's Rangers in World War II* (Mechanicsburg, PA: Stackpole Books, 2009), 180.

177   "spring rain on a taxi window": Atkinson, *The Day of Battle*, 204.

178   "On what beach": Atkinson, *The Day of Battle*, 207.

178   "I am not satisfied": Jon B. Mikolashek, *General Mark Clark: Commander of US Fifth Army and Liberator of Rome* (Haverton, PA: Casemate, 2013), 59–60.

178   In the three-day battle: C. J. C. Molony, *The History of the Second World War: The Mediterranean and the Middle East*, vol. 5 (Uckfield, UK: Naval and Military Press, 2016), 328.

179   "a sort of slum": W. Averell Harriman, *Special Envoy to Churchill and Stalin, 1941–1946* (New York: Random House, 1975), 235.

180   Molotov approved almost every major request: Mark A. Stoler, *Allies and Adversaries* (Chapel Hill: University of North Carolina Press, 2003), 127.

181   "was not concerned with beating Hitler": David Roll, *The Hopkins Touch: Harry Hopkins and the Forging of the Alliance to Defeat Hitler* (New York: Oxford University Press, 2013), 300.

181   "Not one American soldier": Ibid., 301–2.

181   "the chief task": Ibid., 302.

181–182 confer with Chiang Kai-shek: Ibid.

182   "There is still a very distinct": Pogue, *George C. Marshall: Organizer of Victory*, 300.

CHAPTER 15: COMMANDER IN CHIEF

183   Armistice Day 1943: Susan Butler, *Roosevelt and Stalin: Portrait of a Partnership* (New York: Knopf, 2015), 3.

184   shouted, "It's the real thing!": David Roll, *The Hopkins Touch: Harry Hopkins and the Forging of the Alliance to Defeat Hitler* (New York: Oxford University Press, 2013), 305.

185   "Ike," he said, "you and I know": Robert Sherwood, *Roosevelt and Hopkins: An Intimate History* (New York: Harper and Brothers, 1948), 770.

186   "gravely weakening our ability": Martin Gilbert, *Winston S. Churchill: Road to Victory, 1941–1945* (New York: Houghton Mifflin, 1986), 561.

186   Chiang's most influential American supporter: Lord Moran, *Churchill at War, 1940–45* (New York: Carroll & Graf, 2002), 157–58.

187   "weak, grasping, and indecisive": Joan Hoff, *A Faustian Foreign Policy from Woodrow Wilson to George W. Bush* (New York: Cambridge University Press, 2007), 89.

187   Roosevelt offered Chiang: David Roll, *The Hopkins Touch: Harry Hopkins and the Forging of the Alliance to Defeat Hitler* (New York: Oxford University Press, 2013), 310–11.

187   Roosevelt, Churchill, and the Combined Chiefs: Mark A. Stoler, *Allies and Adversaries* (Chapel Hill: University of North Carolina Press, 2003), 156–57.

187   Overlord, he said: Stoler, *Allies and Adversaries*, 166–67.

187   "never stopped talking": Moran, *Churchill at War*, 159.

187   "There is an ominous sharpness": Ibid., 159.

187   "Brooke got nasty": Ibid.

CHAPTER 16:
THE CITY OF A HUNDRED PROMISES

188   The Tehran Conference: W. Averell Harriman, *Special Envoy to Churchill and Stalin, 1941–1946* (New York: Random House, 1975), 241.

189   "Don't take it badly": Simon Sebag Montefiore, *Stalin: The Court of the Red Tsar* (London: Weidenfeld & Nicolson, 2003), 411.

190   "Bloody bad landing!": Martin Gilbert, *Winston S. Churchill: Road to Victory, 1941–1945* (New York: Houghton Mifflin, 1986), 568.

190   The Roosevelt party arrived: Harriman, *Special Envoy*, 263–67.

191   "walked toward the boss": Susan Butler, *Roosevelt and Stalin: Portrait of a Partnership* (New York: Knopf, 2015), 69–70.

191   "It would be of great value": Harriman, *Special Envoy*, 266.

192   "The trouble with de Gaulle": Ibid.

192   "Paris has been": Ibid.

192   "Reform from the bottom": Ibid.

192   the Big Three was becoming: Ibid., 263–64.

192   whether anything had gone wrong: Lord Moran, *Churchill at War, 1940–45* (New York: Carroll & Graf, 2002), 165.

193   "To the steel-hearted citizens": Antony Beevor, *Stalingrad: The Fateful Siege* (New York: Penguin, 1999), 418.

194   doodling was a legacy: Ibid., 80–81.

194   "dwelt at length": Ibid., 82–93.

195   "get in a dig": Ibid., 105.

195   "to the swiftest possible justice": Ibid.

195   the British Parliament: Ibid., 107.

196   "was counting on an Allied invasion": Gilbert, *Winston S. Churchill: Road to Victory*, 584.

197   "What can be done for Russia": Butler, *Roosevelt and Stalin*, 113.

198   "who, by his courage and foresight": Butler, *Roosevelt and Stalin*, **Page TK**.

CHAPTER 17: A WALK IN THE SUN

200   "Whole armies slithered": David M. Glantz and Jonathan M. House, *When Titans Clashed: How the Red Army Stopped Hitler* (Lawrence: University Press of Kansas, 2015), 174–75.

200   "Sometimes there are moments": Catherine Merridale, *Ivan's War* (New York: Picador, 2006), 232–33.

201   "If the German people fail": Alan Bullock, *Hitler and Stalin: Parallel Lives* (New York: Vintage, 1991), 176.

201   "In front of you here": Alan Clark, *Barbarossa: The Russian-German Conflict, 1941–45* (New York: William Morrow, 1985), 363.

201   Two months before the SS speech: Ibid., 364.

202   "secluded, velvet room": Ibid., 363.

202   "I and my Hitler Youth": Ibid., 364.

202   "To speak to Hitler alone!": Ibid.

204   Beria wrote Stalin, "If you agree": Simon Sebag Montefiore, *Stalin: The Court of the Red Tsar* (London: Weidenfeld & Nicolson, 2003), 417–18.

204   "Hullo. Hullo. Hullo.": Rick Atkinson, *The Day of Battle: The War in Sicily and Italy, 1943–1944* (New York: Henry Holt, 2008), 308.

206   "keep on giving it all you have": Jon B. Mikolashek, *General Mark Clark: Commander of US Fifth Army and Liberator of Rome* (Haverton, PA: Casemate, 2013), 76.

207   a cruel piece of luck: Atkinson, *The Day of Battle*, 254.

207   Kesselring or Rommel: Ibid.

210   Operation Instructions Number 34: Martin Blumenson, *General Lucas at Anzio* (Washington, DC: Center of Military History, United States Army, 1990), 330.

210   General Lucian Truscott: Atkinson, *The Day of Battle*, 330.

210   "I don't see how we": Ibid., 331.

210   Alexander's Fifteenth Army Group: Blumenson, *General Lucas at Anzio*, 329–30.

210   However, G2, military intelligence: Ibid., 328.

211   "It is essential": Mikolashek, *General Mark Clark*, 86.

211 "We look forward": Atkinson, *The Day of Battle*, 348.

212 "Don't stick your neck out": Blumenson, *General Lucas at Anzio*, 340.

212 "They will end up putting me ashore": Ibid., 335.

213 "This is the most important thing": Ibid., 341.

213 "Had I been able to seize": Ibid., 343.

213 "We thought we had thrown": Winston S. Churchill, *The Second World War*, vol. 5, *Closing the Ring* (London: Bloomsbury, 2013), 432.

213 "My head will probably fall": Blumenson, *General Lucas at Anzio*, 345.

214 "a piece of gross stupidity": Robert M. Edsel, *The Monuments Men: Allied Heroes, Nazi Thieves, and the Greatest Treasure Hunt in History* (New York: Center Street, 2009), 47.

CHAPTER 18: "NICE CHAP, BUT NO GENERAL"

218 "limitations imposed on us": *Stalin's Correspondence with Attlee, Roosevelt and Truman, 1941–1945* (London: Lawrence & Wishart, 1958).

218 "Everything is as ready": Martin Gilbert, *Churchill: A Life* (New York: Henry Holt, 1991), 268.

219 "I am," he told McCloy: Ibid., 773.

219 "If I had written down": Mark A. Stoler, *Allies and Adversaries* (Chapel Hill: University of North Carolina Press, 2003), 103.

219 "coordinate and drive forward": Stephen Ambrose, *D-Day: June 6, 1944: The Climactic Battle of World War II* (New York: Simon & Schuster, 2013), 71.

219 "full-scale assault on the Continent": Ibid.

219 "Well, there it is": David Eisenhower, *Eisenhower at War: 1943–1945* (New York: Random House, 1986), 100.

219 Morgan named his new organization COSSAC: Ambrose, *D-Day*, 75.

221 "no victors and vanquished": Eisenhower, *Eisenhower at War*, 56.

221 "Nice chap, but no": Antony Beevor, *D-Day: The Decision to Launch* (New York: Viking, 2009), 6.

221 "We [are] pushing Eisenhower": Stephen Ambrose, *Eisenhower: Soldier and President* (New York: Simon & Schuster, 1990) 90.

222 "ruthless, ambitious officer": Carlo D'Este, *Eisenhower: A Soldier's Life* (New York: Henry Holt, 2015), 5.

222 The commander who led: Eisenhower, *Eisenhower at War*.

223 "While still indefinite": David Stafford, *Ten Days to D-Day: Citizens and Soldiers on the Eve of the Invasion* (Waterville, ME: Thorndike Press, 2004), 279.

223 "Gentlemen," Stagg said: Russell Miller, *Nothing Less Than Victory* (New York: Harper Perennial, 1998).

223 The Associated Press was already reporting: Beevor, *D-Day*, 12.

224 "I feel so much for you": Ibid., 14.

224 "The landings in the Cherbourg-Havre area": Ibid., 8.

225 "observe the orders given": Eisenhower, *Eisenhower at War*, 247–48.

226   Eisenhower paced back and forth: Gordon A. Harrison, *Cross-Channel Attack: United States Army in WW II: The European Theater of Operations* (Washington, DC: Center of Military History, United States Army, 2004).

226   "Okay! Let's go!": Ambrose, *D-Day*, 187–89.

226   "What cruel luck": Ibid., 185.

227   as historian Stephen Ambrose has noted: Ibid., 198.

227   the pilots had been instructed: Beevor, *D-Day*, 62–63.

228   armed with a dime-store clicker: Ibid., 64.

228   "All preliminary reports": Andrew Rawson, *Eyes Only: The Secret Correspondence Between Eisenhower and Marshall* (Cheltenham, UK: History Press, 2011).

228   speech in the House of Commons: Winston S. Churchill, *The Dawn of Liberation: 1945* (Boston: Little, Brown, 1945).

229   "I have received your communication": Winston S. Churchill, *The Second World War*, vol. 6, *Triumph and Tragedy* (Boston: Houghton Mifflin, 1953), 59.

229   British 3rd Division stormed Sword Beach: Eisenhower, *Eisenhower at War*, 267.

230   "were deemed untrustworthy": Beevor, *D-Day*, 119.

231   Omaha would be the toughest beach: Ibid., 88–89.

232   "Are they going to swim ashore": Ambrose, *D-Day*, 323.

232   "Target Dora! All guns": Ibid., 322.

232   "functioning at all mentally": Beevor, *D-Day*, 97–98.

234   Rundstedt's initial instinct: Eisenhower, *Eisenhower at War*, 263–64.

234   "We can't go in!": Ambrose, *D-Day*, 337.

235   "I guess that makes me company commander": Eric Larrabee, *Commander in Chief: Franklin Delano Roosevelt, His Lieutenants, and Their War* (New York: Simon & Schuster, 1988), 459.

236   "Back to the château!": S. L. A. Marshall, "First Wave at Omaha Beach," *Atlantic*, November 1960.

236   "My fellow Americans": Franklin D. Roosevelt, "D-Day Prayer," June 6, 1944, HistoryPlace.com, https://www.historyplace.com/speeches/fdr-prayer.htm.

CHAPTER 19: THE TWO FACES OF WAR

237   "Tell me, General, in Warsaw": Norman Davies, *Rising '44: The Battle for Warsaw* (New York: Viking, 2002), 22.

237   what Churchill called "giant countries": Joseph E. Davies, *Mission to Moscow* (New York: Pocket Books, 1943), 22.

238   America's entry changed the emotional climate: Davies, *Rising '44*, 47.

239   "I am sick and tired": Susan Butler, *Roosevelt and Stalin: Portrait of a Partnership* (New York: Knopf, 2015), 124.

239   "Call it what you will": Herbert Feis, *Churchill, Roosevelt, Stalin: The War They Waged and the Peace They Sought* (Princeton, NJ: Princeton University Press, 1966), 286.

240 Harriman, who acted as Roosevelt's second: W. Averell Harriman, *Special Envoy to Churchill and Stalin, 1941–1946* (New York: Random House, 1975), 256–83.

240 Roosevelt seemed prepared: Butler, *Roosevelt and Stalin*, 124.

241 Stalin ratcheted up the pressure: Alan Bullock, *Hitler and Stalin: Parallel Lives* (New York: Vintage, 1991), 850–51.

241 The breakthrough confronted: Martin Gilbert, *Winston S. Churchill: Road to Victory, 1941–1945* (New York: Houghton Mifflin, 1986), 871.

241 The Poles chose the second option: Davies, *Rising '44*, 260.

242 a column of Tiger tanks: Gilbert, *Winston S. Churchill: Road to Victory*, 872–73.

242 "I think the information": Winston S. Churchill, *The Second World War*, vol. 6, *Triumph and Tragedy* (Boston: Houghton Mifflin, 1953), 131.

242 "Hatred of these villains": Jan Rosinski, *The Warsaw Underground: A Memoir of Resistance, 1939–1945* (Jefferson, NC: McFarland, 2013), 120.

243 "never convince his soldiers": Wacek [Jan Rossman], "In the Warsaw Sewers," *Zeszyty Historyczne*, no. 109 (Paris: Instytut Literacki, 1994).

243 "We will try to do everything": Bullock, *Hitler and Stalin*, 852.

243 "We are thinking of world opinion": Ibid., 852–53.

243 "I do not consider it would prove": Davies, *Rising '44*, 302.

243 "at variance with the spirit": Churchill, *The Second World War*, vol. 6, *Triumph and Tragedy*, 143.

243 Roosevelt too was appalled: Ibid., 144.

244 Joint Chiefs of Staff's concern: Robert Dallek, *Franklin D. Roosevelt: A Political Life* (New York: Penguin, 2017), 572.

244 "At 4 P.M. the Pres. telephoned": Geoffrey C. Ward, *Closest Companion* (New York: Simon & Schuster, 1995), 325.

245 "We all agreed": Ibid.

246 "a 62-year-old man": Dallek, *Franklin D. Roosevelt*, 550.

246 "You did many fine and wonderful": James MacGregor Burns, *Roosevelt: The Soldier of Freedom* (New York: Harcourt Brace Jovanovich, 1970), 498.

247 "worried and tired": Dallek, *Franklin D. Roosevelt*, 551.

247 "I'll beat that son of bitch": William Manchester, *American Caesar: Douglas MacArthur, 1880–1964* (New York: Little, Brown, 2008), 366.

248 "I don't know if I can take it": Dallek, *Franklin D. Roosevelt*, 570.

CHAPTER 20:
THE GRAND ALLIANCE AT HIGH TIDE

250 "There are grounds to believe": Susan Butler, *Roosevelt and Stalin: Portrait of a Partnership* (New York: Knopf, 2015), 295.

250 "Insofar as he attaches importance": George F. Kennan, *Memoirs, 1925–1950* (New York: Pantheon Books, 1967), 220.

250 We should realize clearly: Ibid., 219, 222.

253   THE GLORIOUS ACTION: Peter Clarke, *The Last Thousand Days of the British Empire: Churchill, Roosevelt, and the Birth of the Pax Americana* (New York: Bloomsbury, 2010), 73–75.

253   "It was stupid of the President": Jon Meacham, *Franklin and Winston: An Intimate Portrait of an Epic Friendship* (New York: Random House, 2004), 304.

254   "What did you take?": Lord Moran, *Churchill at War, 1940–45* (New York: Carroll & Graf, 2002), 207.

254   The prime minister arrived in Moscow: Martin Gilbert, *Winston S. Churchill: Road to Victory, 1941–1945* (New York: Houghton Mifflin, 1986), 991–93.

254   "Britain must be the leading": Ibid., 991.

254   "would influence the political balance of power": Ibid., 992.

254   "So far as Britain and Russia": Ibid.

255   "Might it not be thought rather cynical": Ibid.

255   "white snows of Moscow": Kevin Ruane, *Churchill and the Bomb in War and Cold War* (New York: Bloomsbury, 2016), 104.

255   "the Prime Minister and I": Gilbert, *Winston S. Churchill: Road to Victory*, 1002.

256   "If you want to have relations": Ibid., 1007.

256   "I do not think": Ibid., 1008.

256   "Soviet Government cannot accept": Ibid.

256   "This is crazy": Ibid., 1012.

257   "the PM arrived late": Ibid., 1017.

259   Morgenthau's father was: Michael R. Beschloss, *The Conquerors: Roosevelt, Truman, and the Destruction of Hitler's Germany, 1941–1945* (New York: Simon & Schuster, 2002), 44–46.

259   "Just tell them": Ibid., 46.

260   "son of a Jewish philanthropist": Ibid., 49.

260   "this is a Protestant country": Ibid., 51.

260   "dapper and well dressed": Ibid., 56.

260   "eloquent in opposition to Jews": Roger Daniels, *Guarding the Golden Door: American Immigration Policy and Immigrants Since 1992* (New York: Farrar, Straus & Giroux, 2005), 76.

261   "willful attempts to prevent action": Beschloss, *The Conquerors*, 56.

261   created the War Refugee Board: Ibid., 58.

261   "Getting the army involved": Ibid.

261   "the main and immediate" task: Ibid., 71.

262   "German schools, radio stations": Ibid., 116.

262   "The trouble is, Cordell": Ibid., 114.

263   "I'm all for disarming Germany": Ibid., 125.

263   "You cannot indict": Ibid.

263   "Here the President appoints": Ibid., 126.

264   "What do you want": Ibid., 130.

264   "Henry Morgenthau pulled a boner": Herbert Levy, *Henry Morgenthau, Jr.: The Remarkable Life of FDR's Secretary of the Treasury* (New York: Skyhorse Publishing, 2015), 1024.

264   "to overshadow the greatness": Beschloss, *The Conquerors*, 286.

264   "It is hard to talk about": Geoffrey C. Ward, *Closest Companion* (New York: Simon & Schuster, 1995), 329.

265   "Don't get me commenting": Robert Dallek, *Franklin D. Roosevelt: A Political Life* (New York: Penguin, 2017), 582.

265   "We were in the legislature together": David Reid, *The Brazen Age: New York City and the American Empire* (New York: Random House, 2016), 10.

266   "Well, if that's true": James MacGregor Burns, *Roosevelt: The Soldier of Freedom* (New York: Harcourt Brace Jovanovich, 1970), 527.

266   "in this campaign the New Dealers": Ralph B. Levering, *American Opinion and the Russian Alliance, 1939–1945* (Chapel Hill: University of North Carolina, 2017), 173.

266   "his opponent had accused": Burns, *Roosevelt*.

266   "Do you think Russia": Adam J. Berinsky, *In Time of War: Understanding American Public Opinion from World War II to Iraq* (Chicago: University of Chicago Press, 2009), 140.

268   Russell Weigley would say: Rick Atkinson, *The Guns at Last Light* (New York: Henry Holt, 2013), 314.

268   "We are taking three trees a day": Max Hastings, *Armageddon: The Battle for Germany, 1944–45* (New York: Alfred A. Knopf, 2004), 179.

268   "Combat fatigue was one": Citing a postwar U.S. Army report, ibid., 184.

268   Carlo D'Este, another respected: Ibid., 185.

268   two misjudgments that were made: Ibid., 185–86.

CHAPTER 21: APOCALYPSE

271   "The time will come": John Lukacs, *The Hitler of History* (New York: Vintage Books, 1998), 165.

271   "I live only for the purpose": William L. Shirer, *The Rise and Fall of the Third Reich* (New York: Simon & Schuster, 1959–60).

271   Watch on the Rhine: Max Hastings, *Armageddon: The Battle for Germany, 1944–45* (New York: Alfred A. Knopf, 2004), 204–5, 213–27.

273   "I want only cheerful faces": Dwight D. Eisenhower, *Crusade in Europe* (Garden City, NY: Doubleday & Co., 1948), 350.

273   "American front penetrated": Peter Clarke, *The Last Thousand Days of the British Empire: Churchill, Roosevelt, and the Birth of the Pax Americana* (New York: Bloomsbury, 2019), 130.

274   "Given the circumstances": Hastings, *Armageddon*, 253–54.

274   "Here is a guy": Ibid., 254.

274   Montgomery could never quite contain: Ibid.

277   McAuliffe famously says "Nuts!": "Surrender? 'Nuts!' Gen. Anthony McAuliffe's 1944 Christmas Message to His Troops," National Archives Foundation, https://

www.archivesfoundation.org/documents/surrender-nuts-gen-anthony-mcauliffes
-1944-christmas-message-troops/.

277   "What's merry about this": Ibid.

278   I am recommending: Don Addor, *Noville Outpost of Bastogne* (Cheshire, UK: Trafford Publishing, 2004), 186–87.

279   "Christ coming to cleanse": Russell F. Weigley, *Eisenhower's Lieutenants: The Campaigns of France and Germany, 1944–1945*, Book 2 (Bloomington, IN: Plunkett Lake Press and Indiana University Press, 1981).

CHAPTER 22: HAVE YOURSELF
A MERRY LITTLE CHRISTMAS

280   "not to upset her husband": Robert Dallek, *Franklin D. Roosevelt: A Political Life* (New York: Penguin, 2017), 598.

281   "Grandpa! You've lost a tooth!": James MacGregor Burns, *Roosevelt: The Soldier of Freedom* (New York: Harcourt Brace Jovanovich, 1970), 554.

281   "Next year," said Elliott's wife: Ibid., 554.

281   "assume it had a monopoly": Franklin Delano Roosevelt, "State of the Union 1945," American History, http://www.let.rug.nl/usa/presidents/franklin-delano -roosevelt/state-of-the-union-1945.php.

282   "only through institutions capable": Ibid.

282   "I know of no reason": Ralph B. Levering, *American Opinion and the Russian Alliance, 1939–1945* (Chapel Hill: University of North Carolina, 2017), 181–82.

282   "The first thing": Ibid., 182.

283   Our tendency to admonish: Ibid., 183–84.

284   "whenever an American suggests": Ibid., 215.

284   "the emerging enemy": Ibid.

285   "envy, animosity and fear": Ibid., 217.

285   The planners also warned: Ibid., 219.

286   "Who's responsible for": Richard Hargreaves, *Hitler's Final Fortress: Breslau 1945* (Mechanicsburg, PA: Stackpole Books, 2011), 47.

286   more than two million: John Toland, *The Last 100 Days* (New York: Random House, 1965), 4.

287   *The little daughters*: Walter S. Zapotoczny Jr., *Beyond Duty: The Reason Some Soldiers Commit Atrocities* (Stroud, UK: Fonthill Media, 2017).

288   "There is no doubt": Catherine Merridale, *Ivan's War* (New York: Picador, 2006), 312–13.

288   "Be practical, give a coffin": Antony Beevor, *The Fall of Berlin 1945* (New York: Penguin, 2003), 1.

288   *Bleib Übrig!*"—meaning: "Survive!": Ibid., 2.

289   "I have such faith": Ibid., 4–5.

289   German *Volk*! National Socialists!: Adolf Hitler's speech on New Year's Day, 1945.

CHAPTER 23: YALTA:
THE GRAND ALLIANCE AT HIGH TIDE

290   "My friend has arrived": Martin Gilbert, *Winston S. Churchill: Road to Victory, 1941–1945* (New York: Houghton Mifflin, 1986), 1167.

290   when a frail-looking Roosevelt: Ibid.

291   "What a change": Ibid.

291   was "terribly shocked": W. Averell Harriman, *Special Envoy to Churchill and Stalin, 1941–1946* (New York: Random House, 1975), 388.

293   "Perhaps you think": Mary Ann Glendon, *A World Made New: Eleanor Roosevelt and the Universal Declaration of Human Rights* (New York: Random House, 2001), 5.

293   "They are the most stinking": Michael J. Cohen, *Britain's Moment in Palestine: Retrospect and Perspectives, 1917–1948* (Abingdon, UK: Routledge, 2014), 352.

293   the four-pronged assault: Susan Butler, *Roosevelt and Stalin: Portrait of a Partnership* (New York: Knopf, 2015), 359.

294   "Put very shortly": Gilbert, *Winston S. Churchill: Road to Victory*, 1174.

294   "The eagle should allow": Jonathan Fenby, *Alliance: The Inside Story of How Roosevelt, Stalin and Churchill Won One War and Began Another* (New York: Simon & Schuster, 2015), 358.

295   "In principle," Churchill said: Gilbert, *Winston S. Churchill: Road to Victory*, 1178.

295   "a very searching examination": Henry Morgenthau, *Morgenthau Diary (Germany)* (Washington, DC: US Government Printing Office, 1967), 56.

295   "Suppose," he asked Churchill: Butler, *Roosevelt and Stalin*, 363.

295   "the three great powers": Winston S. Churchill, *The Second World War*, vol. 6, *Triumph and Tragedy* (Boston: Houghton Mifflin, 1953), 352.

295   dismemberment of Germany: Butler, *Roosevelt and Stalin*, 364–65.

296   "Germany should only be allowed": Gilbert, *Winston S. Churchill: Road to Victory*, 1181.

296   could be substantially benefited: Ibid.

296   "Tonight the sun goes down": Ibid.

296   In a letter to his wife: Ibid., 1183.

297   "If Russia were to make": Ibid., 1184.

297   According to the information: Ibid., 1185.

297   "Poland has been a source": Ibid., 1186.

297   "We must do what we can": Ibid.

298   "I know, Bill": John Toland, *The Last Days* (New York: Random House, 1965), 108.

298   "the whole world would know": Robert Dallek, *Franklin D. Roosevelt: A Political Life* (New York: Penguin, 2017), 612.

CHAPTER 24:
NEVER FORGIVE, NEVER FORGET

299   "I don't want him": John Toland, *The Last 100 Days* (New York: Random House, 1965), 257.

300   "Heinrici only retreats": Ibid.

301   "I've sworn an oath": Ibid.

301   "If in the coming days": Ibid., 405.

301   Berlin was more a ruin: Mark Caruthers, "The Streets of Berlin, April 1945," Owlcation.com, https://owlcation.com/humanities/Berlin-April-1945-The-Cauldron.

302   "You can't imagine": Antony Beevor, *The Fall of Berlin 1945* (New York: Penguin, 2003), 208–9.

303   Wait for me and I will return: James Riordan, ed., *The Young Oxford Book of War Stories* (Oxford, UK: Oxford University Press, 2001), 36.

304   "There has not been a day": Catherine Merridale, *Ivan's War* (New York: Picador, 2006), 327.

304   "So you've underestimated the enemy": Beevor, *The Fall of Berlin 1945*, 222.

305   "We are thinking of ordering Konev": Ibid., 229.

CHAPTER 25: BIRTHDAY AND DEATH

308   "a restless fire burned": Traudl Junge, *Until the Final Hour: Hitler's Last Secretary* (New York: Arcade Publishing, 2004), 159–60.

308   "Eva Braun would still be whirling": Ibid., 160.

309   "secured Soviet primacy": Catherine Merridale, *Ivan's War* (New York: Picador, 2006), 328.

309   "People are too busy": Cornelius Ryan, *The Last Battle* (New York: Simon & Schuster, 1995), 420.

310   In war, however, everything is relative: John Erickson, *The Road to Berlin* (New York: HarperCollins, 1985), 582–83.

310   "You will see, Steiner": Ibid.

310   "You are liable with your head": Ibid.

311   "The Wilhelmplatz looked bleak": Junge, *Until the Final Hour*, 161.

311   "Better a Ruski": Anonymous, *A Woman in Berlin: Eight Weeks in the Conquered City: A Diary*, trans. Philip Boehm (New York: Picador, 2006), 20.

312   "Forgive me if this": Antony Beevor, *The Fall of Berlin 1945* (New York: Penguin, 2003), 278–79.

312   "You could hardly put": Junge, *Until the Final Hour*, 161.

312   "Every German will defend": Henry Steele Commager, *The Story of the Second World War* (Lincoln: University of Nebraska Press, 2004), 424.

312   "You know I shall stay": Junge, *Until the Final Hour*, 162.

314   One of them grabs: Anonymous, *A Woman in Berlin*, 53–54.

315   "Damn this to hell!": Ibid., 64–65.

315   "They say every second woman": Ibid., 195.

315   "The battle for Germany": Ryan, *The Last Battle*, 444–45.

317   "Your actions represent": John Toland, *The Last 100 Days* (New York: Random House, 1965), 493.

318   Forrestal favored a hard line: Ibid., 455–56.

319   "In the opinion of": Ibid.

319   woman who visited the Karstadt: Ryan, *The Last Battle*, 451.

320   "The Führer takes no further interest": Junge, *Until the Final Hour*, 172.

320   Within the near future: Ryan, *The Last Battle*, 456.

322   "What is the point?": David H. Lippmann, "Battle of Berlin: Third Reich Death Knell," Warfare History Network, December 5, 2016.

323   "standing bare-headed, framed between": Martin Gilbert, *Winston S. Churchill: Road to Victory, 1941–1945* (New York: Houghton Mifflin, 1986), 1301.

324   the Soviet Union would emerge: Mark A. Stoler, *Allies and Adversaries* (Chapel Hill: University of North Carolina Press, 2003), 233–34.

325   Inside her handbag: Junge, *Until the Final Hour*, 170–71.

326   "Everywhere," Traudl Junge recalled: Beevor, *The Fall of Berlin 1945*, 360.

326   "SS officers who had been": Ibid.

326   "Hitler could not bear": Ryan, *The Last Battle*, 494.

327   "The German forces defending Berlin": Toland, *The Last 100 Days*, 520.

327   "My children are too young": Roger Manvell and Heinrich Fraenkel, *Doctor Goebbels: His Life and Death* (New York: Simon & Schuster, 2010), 291.

328   "You may safely call me": Junge, *Until the Final Hour*, 186.

328   "the same conversation": Ibid.

329   "To see the children": Ryan, *The Last Battle*, 504.

330   "We can't complain": Anonymous, *A Woman in Berlin*, 254–55.

INDEX